Women's Voices

Projection of Women in Literature

Women's Voices

Projection of Women in Literature

Editors

Arvind Nawale
Kamlakar Gavane
Eunice Fonyuy Fondze-Fombele

AUTHORSPRESS

Worldwide Circulation through Authorspress Global Network

First Published in 2022

by

Authorspress

Q-2A Hauz Khas Enclave, New Delhi-110 016 (India)

Phone: (0) 9818049852

E-mail: authorspressgroup@gmail.com

Website: www.authorspressbooks.com

Women's Voices: Projection of Women in Literature

ISBN 978-93-5529-238-4

Printed in India at Thomson Press (India) Limited

Foreword

It is a truth that requires universal acknowledgement that only when women's rights and human rights are recognized as synonymous, it is then and only then that women's voices can be heard loud and clear, locally and globally. Women can break the silence and become vocal about their dreams and desires, fears and doubts in absolute freedom when the phallocratic system and patriarchy are forced to recognize the rights of women as human rights, implying the need for gender equality in all spaces of the operational state apparatus.

Literary writing representing women underpin the indisputable fact that gender equality will not be possible till the mind is liberated from patriarchal, sexist value systems and till that happens women will be in chains. It is the invisible chains that have silenced women through centuries and the silent suffering woman has been emblematic of romanticized notions of motherhood and nationhood. Women have been located as the preservers of tradition and culture and their passivity has been valorised as a cultural necessity. As a result, any resistance to this systematic eliding of the identity of the adult and mature woman is regarded as transgression of the patriarchal norms.

The Foucauldian defining paradigm of repressive silence in *The History of Sexuality*, Vol-1 and the discursive counter-balance of the voices of silence however need to recognize concrete realities that contribute to epistemic understanding of women's position both as it is situated historically and anthropologically. This may be considered to be a pre-condition for a holistic understanding of representations of woman in literary and cultural narratives, wherein though language is in play, recognition of historical data problematize performance and play. In other words, it is the compulsions to adhere to the socially constructed image that gains recognition, whereas demand for recognition of social and personal identity may be often considered as subversive. Therefore, de-colonizing the mind of both men and women in the social structure by demolishing stereotypes of the Western iconic figure of the Angel in the house and the Indian (Hindu) counterpart of the domestic goddess Lakshmi, may lead to the possibility of an alternate process, though in practice such alternatives are still exceptional. Literary and cultural texts however have created the fissures within the patriarchal space by interrogating and refracting the stereotypes.

Though the nature of oppression may vary, the constant is the marginalization of women in most human societies. Literary writing is able to represent the nuanced invisible structures that operate in familial and inter-personal relationships, thereby revealing the fault-lines and the fragile overtures towards gender sensitization and gender mainstreaming.

Literary texts have tracked the journey of women from victimhood to subject status with sense and sensibility. The mapping of a woman's journey highlights her experiences as she traverses a rough terrain of hostile borders, barbed lines of control and the inexorable cultural and social conditioning of compulsory feminization and domestication. Male authored texts, both printed and visual, have systematically consolidated the stereotypes, so that any behavioural tangent has been identified as subversive and transgression from the established norms of the patriarchal state have been punished with relentless emotional or physical torture and violence in all sections of society.

Does that mean that women as subjects are all enchained by tradition and social practices, and that there can be no question of claiming a level playing field for women and men? Michel Foucault makes a succinct observation about such power relations –

> "There cannot be relations of power unless the subjects are free. If one or the other were completely at the disposition of the other and became his thing, an object on which he can exercise an infinite and unlimited violence, there would not be relations of power... Even though the relations of power may be completely unbalanced or when one can truly say that he has "all power" over the other, a power can only be exercised over another to the extent that the latter still has the possibility of committing suicide, of jumping out of the window or killing the other. That means that in the relations of power, there is necessarily the possibility of resistance" (McNay, Lois, *Foucault and Feminism: Power, Gender, and the Self.* USA: North Eastern University Press, 1992. Page 173)

Literatures of the world have reiterated the inexorable marginalization of the second sex, addressing the abjectness of women of all classes, their lack of identity and independence and the systematic exploitation and oppression of women in a patriarchal social system. Women writers and male writers have sensitively represented the nuanced inter-personal relationships that interrogate the binaries of power and disempowerment that are inherent in the masculine and feminine cultural constructions.

In *Women's Voices: Projection of Women in Literature* the dedicated endeavour of the three editors is worthy of unstinted praise. Two of the editors are Indian male academicians Dr Arvind Nawale and DrKamalkar Gavane, and the third editor, Dr Eunice Fonyuy Fondze-Fombele, is a female editor from Cameroon. In fact, the editorial team is in itself, a striking evidence of gender balance, diversity and recognition of inclusivity and intersectionality. The 35 research papers included in this carefully curated volume spans a very wide trajectory, from the global north to the global south.

The critically informed essays address representations of women in such dominant literary genres such as novel, drama, poetry, short stories, oral literature and myth. Contextual parameters demand attention as gender representations vary according to specific geographical locations, such as Africa, India, the USA and the Caribbean. It should be noted that the papers focus mostly on literatures written in English or in English translation. Intersectionality becomes the predominant critical tool as gendered literary texts are prioritized and problematized and the importance of context for a holistic reading of a text, emerges as a crucial necessity.

In this important volume, literary texts as diverse as plays by Tennessee Williams, Vijay Tendulkar, Mahesh Dattani, Poile Sengupta and fiction by Alice Walker, Jhumpa Lahiri, Shashi Deshpande, Manju Kapur, Arundhati Roy, Mahasweta Devi and Taslima Nasrin and so on are skillfully analyzed through close readings. Women-centric texts such as *Goblin Market, Bridget Jones' Diary, Pride and Prejudice, Lihaf, Wide Sargasso Sea* and *Sultry Days* are read from the feminist standpoint of transitioning from objectification of women to women as active agents of social change.

I am confident that the edited book, *Women's Voices: Projection of Women in Literature* will be a worthy addition to gender-specific world literature studies. This much-needed volume will undoubtedly enable comparing and contrasting the variabilities in the representations of imagined women in both male-authored and female-authored literary writing.

Dr. Sanjukta Dasgupta

(Convenor, English Advisory Board, Sahitya Akademi, New Delhi, President, Executive Committee, Intercultural Poetry and Performance Library at ICCR, Kolkata, Former Professor & Head Dept of English and Dean Faculty of Arts, Calcutta University, Kolkata, Visiting Professor, Jagiellonian University, Krakow, Poland. Recipient of Charles Wallace Scholarship, Fulbright Postdoctoral Research Fellowship and Associate Fellowship at IIAS)

Preface

In March 2021, the World Economic Forum (WEF) released an insight report on the global gender gap with statistics revealing that the closing of the global gender gap has been extended by an extra 35 years. This delay in the process of achieving gender parity was heightened by the Covid-19 pandemic throughout 2020 and 2021 with the emerging variants. The impact intensified pre-existing gender inequalities that may continue to be detrimental to women's empowerment and self-actualization. The WEF called for the world to immediately implement gender-sensitive strategies that can help in the long run to moderate damaging consequences on gender equity and reduce inequalities.

It is from the backdrop of this report, we, the editors launched a call for papers on 'Projection of Women in Literature' in order to reflect on women's existential and experiential conditions as reflected in the literatures. This has enabled contributors to write and discuss projections of women in literature from their lived experiences in the patriarchal culture that propagates man's superiority over woman considering her as inferior, the culture of feminism that projects a culture of gender equity, gender complementarity and women's empowerment and issues of self-identity construction, self-realization, self-actualization and so on. The book scrutinizes the voices of women as depicted by both men and women in literature in a bit to project constructive gender myths that can in the short and long run mitigate gender inequalities. This social justice can only be achieved if the world succeeds to cultivate a culture of inclusivity and gender equity.

Human existence and experience are shaped and influenced by culture. Rethinking women's images, roles, responsibilities, attitudes and perceptions in literature is an important process in the search for a culture of inclusivity and reduced inequalities. This book is designed to help its readers reflect on the roots of socio-cultural beliefs that have shaped and still shape the mindset of people about women. This intervention is aimed to cause people to rise above socio-cultural hindrances and meanings and values that work at the expense of women with the focus to recognize the inequalities caused by the culture of gender discrimination and in turn cultivate a culture of meanings and values that work at no one's expense.

The major motivation of the book is also to exploit the cumulative effect of gender dialogue in literature within the creative space as writers, within the created space as characters and the intervention of feminism and empowerment theories in literary criticisms. Contributors of the work find meaning in the gender dialogic course of action between characters as speaking subjects, between literary texts and cultural texts, between readers and texts in relation to change of attitude and a more radical over-hauling of gendered attitudes. On the one hand, the literary gender dialogue as revealed in this edited volume demonstrates writers who view genders from the optics of patriarchy and socio-cultural myths that hinder change of attitude. Alternatively, the literary gender dialogue projects women's voices revealed through the optics of feminism and empowerment theories. In this respect, the gender dialogue reveals a configuration of genders differently within articulatory space.

This book of scholarly papers cover important writers like Ismat Chughtai, Shashi Deshpande, Jane Austen, Paule Marshall, Khushwant Singh, Bernard Malamud, Sarah Joseph, Parveen Shakir, Alice Walker, Jhumpa Lahiri, Taslima Nasreen, Manju Kapur, Amish Tripathi, Vikram Chandra, Abimbola Adunni Adelakun, Arundhati Roy, Christina Georgina Rossetti, Tennessee Williams, Mahesh Dattani, Shobha De, Vijay Tendulkar, Poile Sengupta, Mahasweta Devi, Kavita Kane, Jean Rhys, creative artists like women in oral literature and so on and themes/topics as wide as different women's issues, feminism, liberal feminism, contradictions in gender myths, womanhood, gender and intersectionality, third world feminism, hegemonic females, women's marginalization in Afro-American writings, emancipation of women, gender aesthetics, transgression of masculinity and regeneration of idyllic female space, patriarchal domination, positions of women, social stigmatization and victimization of women, matrimony and expatriate sensibilities, women's identity crises, post-colonial feminist approach and so on.

The topics/themes addressed by contributors in this edited compilation attempt to serve as the foundation as well as a good resource for all things relating to women's study and the multidisciplinary subjects associated with it for subsequent study, providing numerous opportunities for the students, teachers, and researchers of women's study in India and aboard to pick one that meets their interest for further study. We are honored and privileged in editing papers of such scholarly contributors and presenting this book to the vast global readership.

The gender dialogue that either asphyxiates or liberates women as revealed in this intervention has the ultimate intention to correct the culture of inequalities while negotiating and renegotiating the culture of inclusivity that consciously and continuously considers gender equity and work to reduce inequalities and meet the aspirations of goals 3, 5, and 10 of The Sustainable Development Goals (SDGs), which are also known as the Global Goals, adopted by the United Nations as a universal call to protect the planet and ensure that by 2030 all people enjoy peace and prosperity.

Women's voices have been audible in oral as well as written creative spaces as they decry inequalities and or project their strengths and audibility as women. The criticism in this edited book projects the voices of women that speak of the collective and individual destiny of women; women vocalizing societal mores and values that project gender equity, even as they create autonomous identities for individual women; women vocalizing their personal glitches, dilemmas and complexities they confront in society as they search for self-actualization and self-identity construction and women articulating the interconnectedness and the interdependency of humans and other species that calls for complementarity in existence.

This book *Women's Voices: Projection of Women in Literature* comprises thirty-five scholarly papers which attempt to portray a realistic picture of today's world, in which innocence is suffocating in the 'blood-dimmed tide' of corruption, where women are expected to be nothing more than a doll in the hands of men, where there is an ubiquitous sense of gender discrimination in the average household worldwide, and where helpless women are forced to bear the brunt of patriarchal dominance. It offers a critical appraisal of some of the outstanding writers and their writings, both male and female and Indian and overseas and gives the varied and analytic interpretation of their projection of women's multi-façade voices providing critical and historical perspectives with commendable scholarly engagement, finding a way to women's voices... women's emancipation! This was our attempt and we hope this volume would turn out to be as such!

We are indebted to many people for their direct and indirect contributions to this project of ours projecting women's voices and experiences. Our sincere thanks go to those who accepted to review the papers we sent for reviewing for making suggestions and sharing with us in critical arguments. We are thankful to Mr. Sudarshan Kcherry, Managing of Authorspress Publication, New Delhi for bringing out the present volume flawless and in time and Prof. Dr. Sanjukta Dasgupta, a critic, author, translator, poet and Convenor of English Advisory Board, Sahitya Akademi, New Delhi, President of Executive Committee, Intercultural Poetry and Performance Library at ICCR, Kolkata and Former Professor & Head Dept of English and Dean Faculty of Arts, Calcutta University, Kolkata, Visiting Professor, Jagiellonian University, Krakow, Poland. Recipient of Charles Wallace Scholarship, Fulbright Postdoctoral Research Fellowship, Associate Fellowship at IIAS and so on for writing the Foreword to the book. Thanks are also due to our Universities, Management and institutional authorities for their inspiration and to our family members for their constant support. We also thank our esteemed contributors from different states of the India's as well as some from Cameroon, Scotland United Kingdom, Bangladesh, Lagos Nigeria for contributing their scholarly papers and helping us accomplish this project successfully.

Thanks.

Dr. Arvind Nawale
Dr. Kamlakar Gavane
Dr. Eunice Fonyuy Fondze-Fombele

Contents

CHAPTER 1

Women Issues in Ismat Chughtai's "The Quilt" ("Lihaaf")

Arvind M. Nawale

Abstract

Ismat Chughtai began her literary career at a period when women's attempts to produce poetry or fiction were considered counter-cultural. Her most contentious Urdu short tale, "Lihaaf," which was translated into English as "The Quilt," depicts the sensory complexities of a Muslim family life. It tells the narrative of Begum Jan, an unhappy housewife whose Nawab husband has little time for her, forcing her to seek sexual and emotional consolation in the companionship of a female servant. In the story, Chugthai has instilled the notion of female sexuality and criticised the way women are subjugated. This paper attempts to investigate how Ismat Chughtai has successfully addressed a critical societal topic about sex and lesbianism within our society's closest circle, succinctly describing the conditions that force the women to make such a risky decision and sending a message to such women to fight against the senseless and unreasonable limitations imposed on their lives.

Keywords: Homosexuality, Lesbian identity, Quilt or Lihaaf, Women Subjugation.

Introduction

In the pre-partition era of India, discussing female sexuality was deemed to be unthinkable due to prevailing cultural mores. Even though, following the footsteps of some Western fiction writers and motivated by India's Progressive Writers Movement which questioned these accepted ideals on culture and religion that defined boundaries for issues pertaining female sexuality, some writers came forward and started writing boldly on such uncovered issues. Ismat Chughtai is a well-known amongst them. She followed in the footsteps of western academics in exploring topics of female sexuality so openly in her literary works, even defending herself in a court of law in Lahore for her liberal approach to such issues. She is, "the foremost feminist litterateur who, along with Rashid Jahan, Wajeda Tabassum and Qurratulain Hyder, gave birth to a revolutionary feminist movement in Urdu Literature" (Kusari par 1). Her works "have been acknowledged mostly as iconoclastic, audacious and a challenge to patriarchy and Muslim familial structures" (Ullah et al. 103). Ismat's most renowned and argued short story is "Quilt." For the literary world, it was a literary landmark, establishing Chughtai's particular literary style with its emphasis on the sensory intricacies of everyday women's lives.

"The Quilt" ("Lihaaf") and Women Issues:

Ismat Chughtai began her writing career at a time when women's attempts to write poetry or fiction were regarded as against contemporary cultural norms. Her short story "Lihaaf," first written and published in an Urdu Journal *Adab-i-Latif* in 1942, and then translated into English by M. Asaduddin under the title "The Quilt," caused such a stir among the public that it was not only banned, but she also had to face a legal trial on charges of obscenity in Lahore High Court in 1944, which she eventually won. In her autobiography, *Kaghzi Hai Pairahan*, which has been translated into English as *A Life in Words: Memoirs* by M. Asaduddin, Ismat expresses:

> When I wrote "Lihaf", there was a veritable explosion. I was torn to shreds in the literary arena. Some people also wielded their pens in my support. Since then I have been branded an obscene writer. No one bothered about the things. I had written before or after "Lihaaf". I was put down as a purveyor of sex. It is only in the last couple of years that the younger generation has recognized that I am a realist and not an obscene writer. . . I am still labeled as the writer of Lihaaf. The story had brought me so much notoriety that I got sick of life. It had become the proverbial stick to beat me with and whatever I wrote afterwards got crushed under its weight. . . "Lihaaf" had made my life miserable. (Chugtai 35)

The "Quilt" (Lihaaf), Ismat's most controversial short story, shocked the literary world and became one of Chughtai's major works, heralding the birth of her particular literary style with its attention to the sensory intricacies of ordinary life. At its publication, the Muslims were outraged thinking "how *sharif* Muslim women could write so brazenly and that too on taboo subjects exposing the myth of middleclass respectability and civility?" (Kaukab 58). She received a harsh criticism from both public and civil and religious authorities after publishing it because that was a critical time of pre-partition period for Muslims to maintain a collective identity based on strong ideological foundations that could provide a basis for their identification with common moral and social values. However, this story not only altered the course of Urdu literature, but also laid the groundwork for a shift away from the traditional romantic form of literature toward an objective portrayal of social realities of the time, calling into question some of the people's deeply held religious and social beliefs.

It is a story of a dissatisfied housewife named Begum Jan whose Nawab husband has little time for her, compels her to seek sexual and emotional comfort in the company of a female servant. Chughtai shows the difficulties of women in a framework in which they are treated as duty fulfillers rather than as individuals through the figure of Begum Jan, a recently wedded woman. Begum Jan, as a simple lady, was completely unaware of such a thing. She was a very beautiful, young and well figured women with typical female impulses and aspirations. However, she was taken aback by life after marriage. She, a prisoner in her own home, condemned to the restrictions of purdah and deprived of companionship, seeks sexual fulfilment first via her female servant and then through the child narrator in her absence.

We have a glimpse of the same pain projected in one of the most celebrated Hindi film *Devdas*, in which Paro, a young teen girl has to marry a wealthy, fatherly-aged Thakur. The Thakur marries Paro only for ceremonial purposes; to fulfil his socio-religious formalities; to provide a Thakurani to his Royal Thakur family; and to provide a motherly present to his mature, even married children. This unequal marriage is a social evil that contributes to a plethora of issues in both individuals' lives and in society too. Here, in "The Quilt" ("Lihaaf"), such marriage had made Begum Jan's life miserable. However, unlike Paro in *Devdas*, here, she forges her own path. This narrative sheds light on such a way of living among the affluent class of Muslim households in India.

In the beginning, the story commences with the retention of a woman about an incident she had experienced several years ago when she was a girl of only nine years.

> In winter when I put a quilt over myself its shadows on the wall seem to sway like an elephant... Sorry. I'm not going to regale you with any romantic tale about my own quilt. It's hardly a subject for romance. It

> seems to me that the blanket, though less comfortable, does not cast shadows as terrifying as the quilt, dancing on the wall (Chughtai 36).

The incident was what the narrator teenage girl experienced when her mother kept her with her aunt Began Jaan "When Amma decided to go to Agra, she left me with Begum Jaan for a week" (38) and what she experienced regarding quilt while staying there.

> I woke up at night and was scared. It was pitch dark and Begum Jaan's quilt was shaking vigorously as though an elephant was struggling inside. Then I heard two people whispering. Oh God, who was this other person?. .. but I heard Rabbu crying. Then came the slurping sound of a cat licking a plate... I was scared and got back to sleep (38).

The memory of the quilt had such a strong impact on the small girl that even as an adult in later time, she still could not erase it from her memory.

Begum Jan, the women protagonist of "The Quilt," is impoverished, therefore she gets married to the wealthy Nawab. Her family does not have much money, therefore they believe their daughter would benefit economically by marrying the prominent Nawab. "Her poor parents agreed to marry her off to the Nawab who was of 'ripe years' because he was very virtuous" (36). However, after marriage, he placed her in the home with all of his other belongings, and then he quickly lost interest in her. As the Begum, who was full of her youth, started to grow older and to wither due to her husband's complete negligence to her. This illustrates how marriage turns women into commodities and lowers them to only basic transactions. For the most part, the Nawab spends his time with the attractive young men he maintains at his home, he even pays for their stay. The Begum spends her restless nights, looking miserable and distressed. She pines for her husband's affection and company, but the Nawab is unable to spend even a single minute for her. He "didn't have a moment to spare … nor did he allow her to go out" and she "remained a prisoner in the house" (37). Her youth dwindles and she loses all interest to live.

The Nawab shows no interest in his wife's life, wishes, desires, or issues, and in fact entirely disregards and neglects her presence in his life. The Nawab is unaware that she married with certain aspirations and wants, but he is completely unaware of, or rather, oblivious to, his new bride's physical and emotional demands. He never acknowledges her sexual urges, who lies alone, imprisoned and ignored. However, it was Rabbu who filled this gap in her life!

> It was Rabbu who rescued her from the fall. Soon her thin body began to fill out. Her cheeks began to glow and she blossomed in beauty. It was a special oil massage that brought life back to the half-dead Begum Jaan… Rabbu used to massage her back for hours together. It was as though getting the message was one of the basic necessities of life. Rather – more important than life's necessities… Rabbu was the only person allowed to remain inside on such occasions (37).

Begam Jaan uses her sexuality to empower herself. The 'Quilt' is the place to empower it as well as to hide its sexual urges. She has to "fulfil her wishes by channelizing her sexual energy in the new homosexual relationship with Rabbu" (Manuja 166).

The interaction that takes place between the narrator and Begum Jan while Rabbu was absent for some period also plays a crucial role in the plot of the story. When Rabbu leaves the house, Begum Jan becomes extremely lonely and pines for Rabbu's presence. The narrator, a nine-year-old girl set to serve Begum Jan in Rabbu's absentia. As ordered by, the girl started massaging her back in a pleasant manner. Begum Jan exhaled deeply, as if relieved, and feels as if a new life is entering her. Begum Jan instructs the kid to scratch and massage her other body parts too.

> I was embarrassed… She made me lie down with my head on her arm….I tried to protest… I felt very uncomfortable…. I wanted to run away, but she held me tightly. I tried to wriggle out… She was pressing me as though I were a clay doll (39) …I could neither scream nor cry… (40).

The little narrator girl was afraid of and longed to get rid of that as she was unable to understand Begum Jan's purpose, so terrified and flees from Begum Jan's chamber. She is relaxed when "Rabbu returned that night" and considering Begum Jaan as "more terrifying than all the loafers of the world" she "ran out" (40). The narrator girl even wished for her mother to return and pick her up, "My heart yearned in anguish for Amma" (40).

After Rabbu's return, theie lesbian sessions resumed. The narrator girl recounts it, "There was sound of someone smacking her lips, as though savouring a tasty pickle"… and … "There was only the smell of attar, sandalwood and henna, nothing else" (40). Since that day of her experience with Begum Jan, the narrator girl has attempted to avoid entering Begum Jan's chamber and instead spends time with domestic staff. It is strange to see that the story portrays operation of women not only by men but also by other women as the Begum who herself was oppressed by her husband, in turn she tries to oppress the narrator girl. The nine year old girl recounts things in the story as she remembers them without self-consciousness or any inhibiting sense of social taboos as "The quilt crept into my brain and began to grow larger" (40).

Even in the character of Nawab Saheb, there are numerous indications pointing toward his gay relationships. At the beginning of the narrative, it was said that "No one had ever seen a nautch girl or prostitute in his House" (36). He retained students who were exclusively young, fair and with a slim waist "He kept an open house for students – young, fair and slender-waisted boys whose expenses were borne by him (36). The potential of a homosexual connection with the boys went overlooked since the public was more focused on Nawab's qualities for performing Hajj and assisting numerous others in undertaking the holy pilgrimage. However, the notion of Nawab's homosexual or gay relationship with other boys becomes dubious owing to his paying their whole expenditures and his lack of sexual interactions with Begum Jaan.

Begam Jaan attempts to gain her husband's affection by doing superstitious rites and reading talismans and scriptures all night, but she fails every time. She also attempts to escape her troubled head by reading romance books, but nothing consoles her.

> She gave up on amulets, talismans, black magic and other ways of retaining the love of her straying husband? She arranged for night long reading of the scripture but in vain. One cannot draw blood from a stone. The Nawab didn't budge an inch. Begum Jaan was heartbroken and turned to books. But she didn't get relief. Romantic novels and sentimental verse depressed her even more. She began to pass sleepless nights yearning for a love that had never been (36-37).

She subsequently has to quench her thirst in company with Rabbu. She accomplishes her desires by focusing her sexual energies on her new lesbian connection with Rabbu. One had no idea when Begum Jan's life began to deteriorate? Was it when she made the error of being born female or when she arrived at the Nawab's residence as his bride?

Nawab never acknowledged his wife's sexual expectation while she lay imprisoned and mistreated. He "tucked her away in the house with his other possessions and promptly forgot her... The frail, beautiful Begum wasted away in anguished loneliness" (36). The fact that he purposefully imprisoned a young girl in order to satisfy the societal requirement of marriage, oblivious to the reality that he would never be able to satisfy her sexual demands. While the Nawab resumed his gay adventures, Begum Jan was sentenced to a life of seclusion and servitude. Another critical element is how such injustice and oppression may drive a woman into a state of total loneliness, alienation, and melancholy must have to be pondered and seriously taken. Finally, for her sexual fulfilment, she opposes norms, traditions, and other male-framed restrictions in her private space and asserts her sexual rights in an unnatural (lesbian) manner.

Begum Jaan's life is a microcosm of pain, sadness, exploitation, and servitude. Is she a mistaken creation of the Almighty? Or is she a subject whose sole purpose is to provide for the royal requirements of the Nawab family? Or is she supposed to suffer the destiny of being burned alive on a bed of hot coals? The author has highlighted these issues wisely in front of the so-called contemporary intellectual society. However, it seems that the question remains unanswered till in its entirety and spirit. The lady has yet to achieve an accurate, real, dignified, honorable, and acceptable social standing.

Chughtai portrays Begum Jaan's suffering realistically and interprets homosexuality (lesbian relationship) as her means of escape from loneliness. Thus, she infused her works with the concept of female sexuality and self-actualization, reintroduced a female perspective by decentralizing this male-centered perspective and critiqued the way women are marginalized. As pointed by Shikha Thakur,

> the feminist stance of the story brings in fine nuances in the interrogation of the patriarchy and fortifies the feminist reconstruction of the self, in which gender identity markers are diminished, the authoritative approach of male-centeredness is annihilated and gender extremism is eviscerated, thereby unveiling and voicing the feminine sexuality in terms of sexual desires and dreams" (582) and in it, she "deconstructs the patriarchal metanarrative and builds the architecture of her narratives to give female agency a clear and valid voice. The narratology develops the central character as gradually energized to challenge the imposed inequalities and to subvert the same (581).

Chughtai, with the zeal and vitality of a crusader, utilizes her own lived experience, her own language, and characters from her own community to courageously unveil a world beyond the veil, a world that has been completely quiet and absent in Urdu literature, being dominated as it was by male writers. Regarding this short story, Rinku Debnath rightly observes:

> It is about that loneliness and seclusion, the marginalization that one faces. Chughtai forces us to inspect into the attitude of the society and

more precisely it raises questions like is it changing towards an open and embracing egalitarianism or are we just reproaching into a cocoon? She breaks the narrow domestic shackles and transcend from local to global through her stories, the appeal takes a universal voice which reverberates across the oceans (Debnath 272).

Conclusion

Chughtai's this short story speaks for itself as completely liberal representations of those delicate themes that are rarely discussed even in contemporary Muslim writings. Tahira Naqvi has rightly stated, "no other Urdu fiction writer has approached women's issues with the same degree of sensitivity and concern (42). When it was taboo to discuss about sexuality amongst women, she "had the courage to portray a lesbian relationship" (Katoria 2). Her vivid representation serves as an act of anti-colonial resistance, attempting to alter the subcontinent's heteronormative sexual mentality. As a self-assured and unafraid women and writer, she stood up to society's pervasive masculine chauvinistic traits. Hers was an outspoken voice that jarred the Urdu reader. Her subject matter and character development show both her feminine sensitivity and feminist conscience. Ismat Chughtai has successfully addressed a critical societal topic about sex and lesbianism within our society's closest circle. She has succinctly described the conditions that force the women to take such a risky decision. Above all, she has sent a message to such women to fight against the senseless and unreasonable limits imposed on their lives.

Works Cited

Chughtai, Ismat. "Short Story Lihaaf" [The Quilt] Translated from Urdu by M. Asaduddin. *MANUSHI*, pp. 36-40, www.manushi-india.org/pdfs_issues/PDF%20file%20110/9.%20Short%20Story%20-%20Lihaaf%20%5BThe%20Quilt%5D.pdf. Accessed 7 July 2021.

.... *Kaghazi Hai Pairahan. Trans. M. Asaduddin. Autobiographical Fragments.* MANUSHI, 1999.

Debnath, Rinku. "Chughtai's The Quilt: A Mirror of Troubled Sexuality." *South-Asian Journal of Multidisciplinary Studies (SAJMS)*, vol. 4, no. 5, pp. 262-274.

Katoria, Megha. "Woman and Sexuality: Gender-Class Interface in Selected Short Stories of Ismat Chughtai." *The Criterion: An International Journal in English*, vol. 2, no. 4, Dec. 2011, pp. 1-9.

Kaukab, Farzana. *Ismat Chughtai Shakhsyat aur Fun. (Ismat Chughtai Personality and Art).* 2005. Bahauddin Zakariya University Multan, PhD dissertation. eprints,hec.gov.pk/1427/1/1 126.html.htm accessed on 26.10.2012.

Kusari, Saswata. "Lifting 'the Quilt': Ismat Chughtai's A Life in Words and the Subversion of the Normative | Taylor & Francis Group." *Taylor & Francis*, 2020, www.taylorfrancis.com/chapters/edit/10.4324/9781003081968-13/lifting-quilt-ismat-chughtai-life-words-subversion-normative-saswata-kusari.

Manuja, Ankita. "Reclaiming New Spaces Of Identity: A Study into the Suffocated Psyche in Ismat Chughtai's Lihaaf." *Research Journal of English Language and Literature (RJELAL)*, vol. 5, no. 1, Jan.-Feb. 2017, pp. 165-166.

Naqvi, Tahira. "Ismat Chughtai: A Tribute." *The Annual of Urdu Studies*, vol. 8, 1993, pp. 40-45.

Thakur, Shikha. "Re-defining Sexuality: From Object to Subject in Ismat Chughtai's Lihaaf." *Language in India*, vol. 18, no. 1, Jan. 2018, pp. 577-583.

Ullah, Inayat, et al. "Mimicry, Colonialism and Sexuality: Analysis of Ismat Chughtai's 'The Mole' Through Fanonian Lens." *Gomal Journal of Social Sciences & Humanities*, vol. 1, no. 1, Mar. 2017, pp. 102-112.

CHAPTER 2

Patterns of Liberal Feminist Womanhood in Shashi Deshpande's *A Matter of Time*

Kamlakar Gavane

Abstract

Nature has created men and women as equal and unique human beings. You need not be a feminist to know that women are not subordinate human beings. Man is a thinking animal and any thinking being can understand this fact. Shashi Deshpande is always against using art as a tool to propagate any specific ideology. Novel as a work of art is about the lives and actions of the people. It is not the duty of the writer of the novel to preach a particular ideology. Urmi, Mira and Vanaa, in their different ways, come to an idea of women and their lives through their own lives, through the lives of other women around them. Feminism always seems to me a word which has as many meanings as there are people. It can have no one meaning. Some of these traditional women characters are authoritarian to exercise power over other female characters. For example, Jaya's mother (*That Long Silence*) Indu's (*Roots and Shadows*) and Saru's mother (*The Dark Holds No Terror*) belong to this type. The second type of suffering women is the converse of the traditional type. Here, the woman is bolder, more self-reliant and rebellious. She cannot conform to Sita's version of womanhood and is consciously inclined towards what could be designated as radical feminist ideology. Such Ibsenian Nora kind of women characters are very rare in Shashi Deshpande's novels. They are mostly the heroine's friends and classmates. Saru's friends Nalu (*The Dark Holds No Terror*) holds a feminist ideology to life for the sake of which she chooses to lead an independent life as spinster. The third type of women characterizes the women in between. Most of Deshpande's heroines belong to this category. This woman is neither traditional nor radical in her ideas and practice. She might walk out of her home in protest against her suffering, but gradually realizes that walking out does not solve her problems.

Keywords: Liberal Feminism, patriarchy, expression, Ibsenian.

The traditional women characters in Shashi Deshpande's novels are the victims of patriarchy. Some of these traditional women characters are authoritarian to exercise power over other female characters. For example, Jaya's mother (That *Long Silence*) Indu's (*Roots and Shadows*) and Saru's mother (*The Dark Holds No Terror*) belong to this type. The second type of suffering women is the converse of the traditional type. Here, the woman is bolder, more self-reliant and rebellious. She cannot conform to Sita's version of womanhood and is consciously inclined towards what could be designated as radical feminist ideology. Such Ibsenian Nora kinds of women characters are very rare in Shashi Deshpande's novels. They are mostly the heroine's friends and classmates. Saru's friends Nalu (*The Dark Holds No Terror*) holds a feminist ideology to life for the sake of which she chooses to lead an independent life as spinster.

The third type of women characterizes the women in between. Most of Deshpande's heroines belong to this category. This woman is neither traditional nor radical in her ideas and practice. She might walk out of her home in protest against her suffering, but gradually realizes that walking out does not solve her problems. Saru in *The Dark Holds No Terrors* broods over her agonies even after she escapes her marital home. Indu in Roots and Shadow leaves her husband to seek refuge in her ancestral home, but she is unable to accept her fate as any ordinary woman might do. These heroines suffer more because they are a aware of the escape routes of two other types of women – the traditional and the radical – but hesitate to choose those options. Their initial position is one of remaining at the crossroads. It is towards the end of the novels, that Shashi Deshpande's female protagonist realizes herself and learns to live up to the challenge. Saru decides to face her husband and not run away. Indu and Jaya decide to confront their husbands and talk the matter out in order to arrive at a solution. Shashi Deshpande's women characters have a strength of their own, and in spite of challenges and hostilities, remain uncrushed. Urmila in *The Binding Vine*, for example, declares: "I am not going to break." Deshpande has created authentic female characters-flesh-and blood characters with recognizable credentials. She has successfully delineated their problems and plights, yearnings and aspirations, failures and foibles in the Indian context. R. S. Pathak rightfully remarks –

> "Deshpande's novels have, like those of Jane Austen, a narrow range, they are more or less a fictionalization of personal experiences. Most of the

> novels present a middle-class housewife's life, Deshpande's main concern in the urge to find oneself, to create space for oneself to grow on one's own." (Pathak 194)

Here, Freud's terminology of the situation as "motor force of life" could help to understand the situation better. Since their sexual hunger is frustrated and repressed, the Deshpande women strive for expression through sexual relationship or affair with men other than their husbands. Saru's affairs with Boozie (her boss) and Padmakar Rao (her college mate) seem to be temporary substitutes for her unfulfilled marital life.

Gopal's walking out on his family initiates the narrative of the novel and a major part of it deals with the attempts of the other characters to find out the cause of his desertion. His desertion of his family for no obvious reason expresses his mental conflicts and his fragmented personality. His desertion becomes the immediate cause of the mental turmoil which his wife, his mother-in-law and his eldest daughter, Aru, experience. In a way this act of desertion stands for his sincere effort to discover meaning in life and integrate his fragmented self. The novelist's concern with the human predicament becomes more pronounced as Gopal, the protagonist, touches the philosophical dimensions of life and death in his yearnings. The most striking example of silence is Kalyani who spends nearly forty years in total silence with her husband, Shripati. Human relationship is the main theme of this outstanding novel.

A Matter of Time deals with the dilemma of wife-desertion. The liberated feminist approach of Deshpande, even as it tries to subvert and undermine mechanisms of patriarchy, explores the issue of consolidation of the female identity in the larger context of modern society and ponders over the realities of common human existence. Female bonding, resistance and quest for female identity are the central issues in this novel.

But at that same time, the novel goes a step further to create a metaphysical perspective without playing down gender issues and thus it extends the horizon of the narrative structure. The novel underlines wife-desertion as yet another dimension of betrayal and cruelty to women. Gopal's desertion of Sumi and their three daughters, Aru, Charu, and Seema, suddenly results in a 'swift dismemberment' of the family leaving despair-filled hearts behind. It is like a death in the family, "a death without a body". In Sumi, she is like the cry of despair.

The irony is that disgrace not so much to the man who walks out on his family but to the wife who is deserted. The impact of the shock of this event is traced mainly in two characters, who assume the central position in the novel: Sumi and her eighteen-year daughter, Aru, "charting their inner space". Their reactions are different as one is mature and the other stands at the beginning of the journey of her life.

In "*A Matter of Time*", for the first time, there is an attempt to understand the male psychology and Gopal who deserts his wife and children is not condemned without a hearing. Although Sumi reasons out that the metaphysical question of the ultimate truth of human life and the persistent human search for meaning in existence is Gopal's reason, yet she question, "...what about this fit in?" (AMT 27) But she will not coerce him into coming back to her and here she exhibits her dignity.

On the contrary, she explores ways of coming to terms with the painful reality and going on with life. She tries to get a job and learns to ride a scooter and above all, discovers the writing talent within her and produces a play for her school children On the other hand, Aru is filled with anger and resentment against her father and thinks that he should not be allowed to go scot-free, and explores possibilities of bringing legal action against him.

Shashi Deshpande insists upon a 'space' for women. If the 'self' of woman is disregarded, through the 'unwritten story', women will record her protest and create characters in real life like Kalyani, Sumi and Aru to challenge the stereotyped images of women. This novel weaves an intricate pattern of relationships within an extended family spanning across generations. Manorama, Kalyani, Sumi and Aru belong to four generations of the same family, each representing a specific mode of experience. Manorama is the typical product of patriarchal value system, for she resented the birth of Kalyani, her daughter, as she wanted a son. She forces a marriage between two unwilling partners, her daughter Kalyani and her younger brother Shripati and she even holds Kalyani responsible for all her sorrows and calls her an enemy. But it is Kalyani who represents the survival power of women which tides her across her mother's ill treatment and her husband's rejection. The narrator observes:

> "......the real miracle is Kalyani herself, who has survived intact, in spite of what Shripati did to her, Kalyani who has survived Manorama's myriad acts of cruelty" (AMT 151)

That there is a transition from Manorama to Kalyani is evident when Kalyani says to Aru:

> "My mother didn't care for my children either. Daughters again, she said......I'm luckier than my mother. She is the one unlucky who didn't know how to enjoy her children and grandchildren" (AMT 226).

When Gopal walks out on Sumi, it appears to Kalyani like a reenactment of her own life, but unlike her mother, she gives emotional support to her daughter. But it is in Sumi that we see the struggles to learn to live alone and assert oneself against the tide of tragedy. If Sumi is trying to work out a strategy to withstand the shock and the emptiness left behind by Gopal, and creates a life for herself and her daughters, Aru is full of the sense of injustice and protest against her father. If Sumi is trying to retain self-identity, Aru fights for the rights of women.

There are three kinds of suffering women characters in the novels of Shashi Deshpande. The first type of women characters are typically traditional women. They think that it is their duty – religious and ethical – to be with the husband and family at any cost. The second type of suffering women is the converse of the traditional type. Here, the woman is bolder, more self-reliant and rebellious. She cannot conform to Sita's version of womanhood and is consciously inclined towards what could be designated as radical feminist ideology. The third type of women characterizes the women in between. Most of Deshpande's heroines belong to this category. This woman is neither traditional nor radical in her ideas and practice.

The Ibsenian Nora kind of women characters are very rare in Shashi Deshpande's novels. They are mostly the heroine's friends and classmates. Saru's friends Nalu (*The Dark Holds No Terror*) holds a feminist ideology to life for the sake of which she chooses to lead an independent life as spinster. Saru in the novel *The Dark Holds No Terrors,* continuously goes against the stream and behaves against the will of her mother. Hence, her mother is always angry upon her. This leads to physical and mental exhaustion of Saru. Manu is an interesting character. In the beginning of the novel he is a student and he becomes a lecturer of English literature afterwards in the novel.

Unlike Charles Dickens, Shashi Deshpande does not introduce the characters to the reader. The central character goes on narrating incidents and when the point of another character comes she only gives a hint instead of giving a full introduction. Though it appears

Dickensian, it is quite different from that. The Dickensian plots show that the narrator goes back to the beginning – 'To begin the life with the beginning of my life' – *David Copperfield.* But Jaya does not begin her life with the beginning. She only catches those incidents that throw light on her character and personality and the personality of those who are in contact with her. In *A Matter of Time,* for the first time, there is an attempt to understand the male psychology and Gopal who deserts his wife and children is not condemned without a hearing. Although Sumi reasons out that the metaphysical question of the ultimate truth of human life and the persistent human search for meaning in existence is Gopal's reason.

Works Cited

Bhatnagar, Parvati, "Search of Identity: A Study of Shashi Deshpande's The Dark Holds No Terrors," in *The Quest: A Literary Journal*, Ravi Nandan Sinha (ed.) vol. 15, num.1, June 2001. p. 56.

Nityanandam, Indira, *Three Great Indian Women Novelists.* Creative Books: New Delhi. 2000. p. 34.

Pathak, R.S. *Modern Indian Novel in English.* Creative New Literature Series-28. Creative Books: New Delhi. 1999. p. 194.

Ramamoorthi, P. "My Life is my own: A Study of Shashi Deshpande's Women" in Dhawan, R.K.(ed) *Indian Women Novelists.* Prestige Books, New Delhi. 1991. p 12.

Reddy, Y.S. Sunita. *A Feminist Perspective on the Novels of Shashi Deshpande.* Prestige: New Delhi. 2001. p. 104.

Sandhu, Sarbajit. "The Image of Woman in That Long Silence" in Dhawan, R.K. (ed) *Indian Women Novelists.* Prestige Books, New Delhi. 1991. p 138.

Sathupati, Prasanna Shree, "Conflict and Identity in Shashi Deshpande's Novels," in *Indian Women Novelists*, R. K. Dhawan (ed.), Prestige Books, New Delhi. 1995. p. 39.

Sharma, Anjana, "In Exile / At Home: The Urban Middle Class in Shashi Deshpande," in *Desert in Bloom: Contemporary Indian Women's Fiction in English.* Pencraft International: New Delhi. 2004. p. 108.

CHAPTER 3

Women in African Oral Literature: Static, Shifting and Contradictory Gender Myths Conceptualisations

Eunice Fonyuy Fondze-Fombele

Abstract

African oral artists have conceptualised women in diverse and ambivalent imaginings. Using gender relations and feminism as categories of analysis, the aim of this paper is to delineate differing ways women have been conceptualised in selected oral African literary representations and the possible narratives such images create. The result is that the research demonstrates how varied conceptualisations of women in African oral literature convey reasons behind women's positioning and conditioning in the society and takes into account the need for continued, conscious and deliberate interrogation of the systems and values of male domination. While destructive gender myths conceptualisations portray reasons behind women's disempowerment and marginal positioning, constructive gender myths conceptualisations with feminist content present pictures of women's strengths and agency, with a right to exist in freedom and dignity and to achieve their strategic gender interests and needs. The contention is that oral artists, writers, critics and activists of all genders should recognize the inalienable and profound role of culture in shaping women's self-actualization and self-awareness and shift from cultural/literary conceptualisations that alienate and contravene progressive self-identity constructions.

Keywords: African women, Oral Literature, Gender myths, male domination, Feminist Literature

Introduction

Discussions on women's depiction, gender and feminisms in literature have evolved rapidly in the last three decades and have earned their own place in literary criticism. This study takes the view of studying African oral literary texts with gender and feminism on the agenda as Lizbeth Goodman rightly stated that, "reading with gender on the agenda is a vital part of the reading and studying of literature and cultural representations" (Goodman viii). The depiction of women in African oral literature presents static, shifting and contradictory conceptualizations that invite consistent exploration. These differing female conceptualizations in African oral literature are deciphered in the manner women's images, attitudes, responsibilities and roles are captured and how these reflect marginal spaces or freedoms and agency for women in the society. Conceptualizations that are void of feminist content tend to produce static gender myths and socio-cultural attitudes that oppress and marginalize women in society and should be deconstructed in discourse. This is because when women and men get used to these negative myths, they become deeply entrenched in their imagination and thought systems, causing them to accommodate and internalize negative categories of gender relations and so resist change. Meanwhile conceptualizations that are pro feminism, those that prop into women's experience while reconstructing gender positive myths are encouraged. These positive conceptualizations showcase women's dynamic involvement as active movers of destinies with their men in gender relations as they confront patriarchy and promote dialogue on gender identity in their creative spaces. This essay aims to demonstrate through selected African oral literary pieces from various African backgrounds how women's conceptualization is static in some cases and is shifting though contradictory in order cases, reflecting society's shifting attitude towards women's identity. Hence, it establishes oral literature and culture as media through which women and men in their gender relations can negotiate and renegotiate their strategic gender interests and needs in ways that portray transformative potentials.

Conceptual Explications

Working definitions of key terms as they are used and understood in this study are necessary – "gender', "myth", "gender relations", "strategic gender interests and needs", "gender in oral literature", "feminism", "feminist literature", "gender myths," and "male domination". The term gender in the context of this paper describes "all the socially given attributes, roles, activities, and responsibilities connected to being a male or a female in a given society. Our gender identity determines how we are perceived, and how we are expected to think and act as women and men, because of the way society is organized" (March 18). Gender therefore is a constitutive element in socio-cultural relationships based on supposed differences between the sexes. In literature the study of gender "refers to ways of seeing and representing people based on sex difference" (Goodman vii). Literary texts represent gender as "a social or cultural category, influenced by stereotypes about female and male behaviour that exist in our attitudes and beliefs. Such beliefs are often said to be culturally produced or constructed" (Goodman vii). Gender consequently becomes a principal method of interrogating and problematizing relationships of power for a reconstruction of positive gender relations.

Gender relations are:

> the social relationships between men as a sex and women as a sex. Gender relations are simultaneously relations of cooperation, connection, and mutual support, and of conflict, separation, and competition, of difference and inequality. Gender relations are concerned with how power is distributed between the sexes. They create and reproduce systemic difference in men's and women's positions in a given society. They define the way in which responsibilities and claims are allocated and the way in which each is given a value. (March 18)

Gender relations therefore help in the analysis of inter and intra-gender relationships in order to see where gender myths conceptualisation position women and men in relation to progressive social change.

Gender and feminist analysis as used in this study describes the analytic process employed that "explores and highlights the relationships, by asking: who does what? Who has what? Who decides? How? Who gains? Who loses?" (March 18). In the process the analysis is able to decipher men and women's strategic gender interest and needs as depicted in the literatures. Strategic gender interests and needs are those that, "if met, the existing relationship of unequal power between men and women would be transformed" (March 18). To analyze literature with gender on the agenda is therefore to have a concern for gender issues that affect the production and consumption process of texts.

Feminism is understood in this study as a politics that recognizes "the historical and cultural subordination of women (the only world-wide majority to be treated as minority), and a resolve to do something about it" (Goodman viii). Feminism has always incorporated a concern for ideas and consciousness raising, while also acting in the public sphere to improve the situation of women's lives. In the field of literature, feminist thought has been and is very influential; it has pointed and continue to point out "the historical silences of women authors not included in the canon; it has fired the canon in order to shake up static views about women's creative work and domestic roles, enabling women's literature" and enabling shifting though contradictory wide-ranging depictions of women (Goodman viii). In *Radical Feminism Today*, feminism as understood in this study is aptly articulated:

> From the outset, it should be obvious that feminism is a social enterprise, a moral and political framework concerned with redressing social wrongs. It is an ethical stance in that it starts and continually returns to questions of value, of good and evil, right and wrong, of what is worthwhile and significant and what is not. Feminism is centrally concerned with judgments of what ought and what ought not to be the case, with what constitutes right action and the good life and with what operates to prevent that, with human conditions within which we want to live and those which must be resisted because they are morally wrong. (Thompson 7).

Therefore feminist literature is understood here as "forms of [oral literature and]writings which deliberately and creatively experiment with language in order to suggest images and ideas which engage the reader's imagination" (Goodman vii), particularly, when these ideas and images carry feminist content that either debunk negative static myths or reconstruct constructive and transformative gender myths for socio-cultural innovation.

Gender myths are understood in this study as a body of philosophies which society constructs in the cultural psyche to legitimise and regulate the location of gender, men and women, within power structures and these principles. Myths, especially gender myths work in a way that they are said to have:

> actually been naturalized by the dominant culture or class [or gender] to justify its hegemony. In other words, while myths are instituted to express a certain ideology and to protect a particular political and economic interest, they are, nevertheless, represented as a natural and universal phenomenon to coerce the dominated into an acceptance of their domination. Through myth and rituals the activities of the ruling class [or gender] are recycled as the will of the gods. (Gigandi 150)

This study looks at gender myths as unfixed categories that should be consciously and purposefully relayed towards women's self-actualisation, mobilization and self-retrieval and towards complementarity in gender relations.

Male domination is the relations of power that feminist politics identifies and resists, "while struggling for a world where women are recognized as human beings in their own right" (Thompson 8). According to feminist politics, male domination "constitutes the conditions under which we live, but that it ought not to be so". These living conditions do not signify the fact that "all men are invariably oppressive to all women all the time, nor that women are invariably the passive, peaceable victims of male will power. It is a social system, a matter of meanings and values, practices and institutions" (Thompson 8) that the feminist stand point should identify, challenge and resist consciously, deliberately and continuously.

Interrogating Static Conceptualizations of Women

The representation of women in some major oral genres of literature like proverbs and folktales, from basically patriarchal cultures like those of most African societies, is predominated by static dehumanized, caricatured and stereotypical conceptualisations of women. To demonstrate how damaging and derogatory gender myths are conceived epistemologically, articulated ideologically in discourse and used to other women practically, some proverbs are selected for use in this study. A proverb is a terse statement containing folk wisdom, its verbal economy, invariability, daily conversational use and the fact that proverbs are borrowed constantly by other oral genres to enrich their performances make them to be easily entrenched in a peoples' collective memory and so can have greater effects in gender socialization. Some proverbs from the Nso and Beti cultures of Cameroon, the Yoruba and Igbo cultures of Nigeria and the Gikuyu culture of Kenya are selected and used to exemplify how socio-cultural attitudes shape women's personality and collective communal attitude towards women's self-actualisation and self-realisation.

A proverb from the Nso culture designates the woman as an inherent witch, "If you are sent on an errand to catch and bring a witch, the first woman you meet on your way, catch her". This proverb conceptualizes the woman as an inherently evil being with depraved powers that can attack the community in several ways. This view is reinforced by three Gikuyu proverbs, "A warrior's downfall is caused by a woman", "An assembly can be spoilt by one small woman" and "two wives/women are two pots of poison" (Ndungo 87, 97,98). These proverbs express the fact that women are cunning, dangerous, and can create chaos and upheavals that could lead to disintegration of a healthy ordered society. That is why Sadiyya Shaikh notes about women in Muslim Kenya that:

> Women are viewed as possessing a fatal attraction which men are incapable of resisting. Women's innate capacity for sexual allurement is considered to be incredibly dangerous, particularly because it distracts and beguiles men away from their religious devotion. … Accordingly women's power is viewed as twofold; first due to their power of sexuality and second due to their innate capacity to deceive and defeat men not by force, but by cunning and intrigue. (Shaikh 89)

This type of personality conceptualization can only but give women a depraved position in the society and this demonstrates that practices that oppress and subjugate women have roots in gender myths. It shows how women's subordinate status is conceived epistemologically, articulated ideologically in discourse before it is othered ontologically in practice.

That women are physically and mentally weak and therefore inferior to men is conceived in proverbs like this Gikuyu proverb, "A woman and an invalid are the same" (Ndungo 98) and this Yoruba proverb, "A woman chief will never aspire to a king's throne" (Kolawole 21). The conceptualisation of women in these proverbs demonstrates how women's marginal positions and conditions are institutionalised through gender myths in folk culture. A feminist theorist has rightly noted that social conditions of male domination, "function most efficiently to the extent that women (and men) accept the reality of their position, embrace it as natural and unalterable, desire its continuation and fear its destruction, and believe it is their own meaningful existence" (Thompson 22). Proverbs as presented here carry that ideology that functions to legitimise relations of ruling with ideology denoting, "systematic meanings which excuse, permit, legitimise and provide justifications for relations of ruling" (Thompson 22).

Some other proverbs reveal society's attitude to women and family matters like child sex preferences and barrenness. A Yoruba proverb says that, "instead of improving her reputation, the witch continues to give birth to baby girls" (Kolawole 20). The lexical items "the witch" in the proverb show that, like the Nso proverb, this Yoruba proverb also conceives of the woman as a natural witch whose reputation in the society is already bad and can only be improved upon if she bears a male child. This proverb also determines the community's attitude to childbearing, demonstrating the importance and preference given to the male child. Some Igbo proverbs exhibit the image of a barren woman as a failure and unhealthy being, "If a woman does not conceive pregnancy, she does conceive lies, both are forms of conception", If a woman is barren, she should at least be healthy" (Chukwuma 22). These proverbs show that society identifies problems of barrenness and lack of the male sex in the family to women's unhealthy nature and men are ideologically exonerated from the blame.

Proverbs also demonstrate how violence in marriage, marital norms and women's responsibilities and roles are institutionalized in folk culture, revealing women as oppressed and subsumed beings. The Yoruba proverb which says, "A wife has a negative personality but complaints of ill luck and her husband's shabby treatment" (Kolawole 19), demonstrates society's complacent attitude towards violence on women. Her abuse in marriage is blamed neither on the social circumstance surrounding the marriage nor on the husband's personality. It is blamed on her inherently negative personality. Conceptualising the woman with an inherent negative nature goes to justify her marginal positioning and conditioning in patriarchal cultural societies of Africa. Women themselves sometimes quote these kinds of proverbs and folktales that work against woman's agency as reasons enough to maintain the patriarchal status quo. Men and women are therefore being ruled by these damaging myths without them realising it.

The muting of women in the literatures and the society is also validated by myths about women's attitude conveyed through proverbs. A Beti proverb states that, "women have no mouth" (Schipper 88) and two Yoruba proverbs reiterate this image of the woman as a silenced being, "A weeping wife who also complains will destroy the family", "Any family that allows the woman to be vocal will see the abnormal growth of the wild Arere tree inside the house" (Kolawole 19). The Beti proverb dispossesses the women of their articulatory organ and conceptualises the myth of silence as an identity marker for the female gender. In the first Yoruba proverb, the wife is intimidated to suffer and weep in silence in order to prevent family disintegration. To achieve this role of guardian of family integration, she is socialised into silence as the norm. In the second proverb the wife is forewarned about abnormal circumstances that will ensure in her home if she is vocal in decision making. These proverbs institutionalise and seal the culture of the muting of women in patriarchal African cultures. They configure speech as male prerogative and silence as women's virtue. The paradox in this muting conceptualisation of women is that they are usually stigmatised in the society for being garrulous and flippant and men are assumed to be reserved, taciturn and terse in their speech. That's why an African female literary critic maintains that speech/vocality "signifies more than voicing and means attention – compelling, 'weighty' speech (connoting power). And silence signifies more than voicelessness and means frivolous speech (connoting powerlessness)" (Okereke 136). Although silence is sometimes loaded with meaning and considered powerful than speech, where silence is imposed as destiny of the female gender, it becomes oppressive, and dispossesses them of talent and potential.

In talking about the general female cast in some oral tales and proverbs, Helen Chukwuma confirms negative gender myths propagated in folk culture when she states that, "The commoner character types include the old woman, the barren woman, the cantankerous wife and the step-mother, all of whom have uncomplimentary exposure as objects of caustic satire" (Chukwuma 22). Also, Douglass Killiam corroborates this view point when he describes the scenario that surrounds female casting in some oral forms:

> Essentially, however, the female presence in traditional literature is dominated by characters who are either dehumanized, for example the old woman in folktales and proverbs, or presented as caricatures, like the wives and co-wives in folktales whose survival is dependent on the whims and caprices of men. Where a woman is given some positive image, as in the folktale of the beautiful girl who rebels against her parents in order to choose her own suitor, the plot is so structured that the girl is the ultimate loser for daring to assert an identity in a basically patriarchal culture. (Killiam 305)

The above conceptualizations point to the need to revisit gender myths that undermine women's self-actualization. They demonstrate that myths provide the raison d'être for gender inequality, oppression and diverse harmful practices against or involving women. If myths are deployed to validate the oppression of women and to validate or institutionalise privileged spaces for men to the extent that they significantly control a peoples' mind-set and become obstacles to change, they could also be employed to validate social change. This means that as society is progressing and women's empowerment and gender equity awareness have gained grounds, damaging gender myths have certainly outlived their usefulness as they were meant to promote patriarchal ideals, mores and ideologies and should shift to constructive myths of gender complementarity.

Shifting and Contradictory Gender Myth Conceptualisations of Women

In a bit to shift from damaging gender myth conceptualisations, women oral performers are now consciously and purposefully using the space of folk songs during nuptial, nativity and work song performances to revitalise the woman's image in African literature and call for the need for a transformed gender awareness. Folk songs play a great role in identity construction given the performance contexts that comprise performers and the active audience that directly participate in the performance, listen to the song-poem messages and enjoy the aesthetic value of the performance. Folk songs performances create sites of self-expression, positive bonding, communal entertainment, therapeutic humour, satirising of patriarchy and sites where they pour out their emotional conflicts, desires, lessen stress and touch on the consciences of the audience members. Through folk song-poems in their various performance spaces, African women are changing their vision and language in order to change society. Strong feminist content that demonstrates women's strengths and transforming, but nonetheless contradictory images, roles and responsibilities, talents and potentials, is captured in women's folk songs as illustrated in selected songs from Cameroon, Senegal and Nigeria.

The songs "Father of this compound", "Teeth" and "We are Proud" from Ngar-Buh in Cameroon conceptualise the bold steps taken by women oral performers in their work song space to prop into women's experience, to challenge male domination's myopic monologist perception and depiction of women.

Father of this Compound

Soloist: Who is the father of this compound?
Chorus: The father of this compound is the hoe,
but we still sit in the marriage,
we sit and make our way to heaven (Fondze-Fombele 309)

Teeth

Soloist: Teeth in the fowl's mouth
Chorus: Are growing in the jaw, instead of in the mouth
(Fondze-Fombele 318)

We are Proud

Soloist: Oh marriage!
Chorus: We are proud of our marriages, what about you?
Are you proud of your marriage?
Soloist: Oh hoe
Chorus: We are proud of our hoe, what about you?
Are you proud of your hoe?
Soloist: Oh beans from Ngar-buh
Chorus: We are proud of our beans, what about you?
Are you proud of your beans?
Soloist: Oh maize from Ngar-buh
Chorus: We are proud of our maize, what about you?
Are you proud of your maize? (Fondze-Fombele 312)

In these songs, women are dramatising their distinctive relationship with social change. Work songs performance space of creativity is an avenue for women to assert their liberated selfhoods and it affords them opportunity to bring forth an inner essence to bear on social realities. The women employ the theme of social change to assert a distinctive female voice and identity that is firmly on the side of social change, progress and potentialities. Social change emerges in the songs as a redraft of consciousness in which the women present an alternative point of view on realities. That is why the thematic focus of the song "Teeth" is change of attitude which makes room for something unusual to start happening. The dynamism exercised by the women as captured through the metaphor of the fowl's teeth which are, ironically on the jaw, instead of the usual position in the mouth, signals a call for change of attitude as societal ideals are changing. The social experience of women has changed with the gender equity and empowerment awareness spirit and they capture these changes through the songs. They are all the more aware of their predicaments as women as they are aware of the necessity to change the patriarchal status quo that marginalises and oppresses them epistemologically and ideologically. It is in this sense that work (empowerment) songs feature women's assertion, their ability to bend status quo, shut off the social system of male domination, while boasting about the joys of subtle but sure intervention on social transformation. The metaphor of change of positioning of teeth in the mouth depicts how women oral performers have a profound influence over their society, with a vision of life that allows them to communicate truth through performance and song-poems, and it is this vision that defines their indigenous feminism. The songsters exercise freedom and fluidity in the choice of aesthetic features as they use the symbol of teeth and change of positioning. Aesthetics becomes style in practice and a mode of appreciation that embraces change and which constantly resists and explodes established forms and concepts and revalues women's traditional activities that were devalued by the ideology of male domination.

In "Father of this Compound" the women use the hoe as metaphor to demonstrate that social change must come with change of attitude. The social background that informs the song is changes in prices of cash crops in the world market that affected the indigenous population in Ngar-Buh adversely, especially men's position as bread winners and heads of the family. The income from the sales of coffee used to give men power as control over women who had access to tend and ready the crop for the market but did not have access and control over the income from the sales of the cash crop, men's crop. With the fall of the price of the coffee in the world market, women have saved the social situation by taking over the children's education and family up keep as they use the hoe to work, tend and nurture women's crops like beans, maize, peanuts, etc. in large quantities for sale. The women have gained a modicum of power-as-capacity and are proud of it, as in "We are Proud" wherein the women indicate what gives them pride as they revalue marriage, the hoe, crops and ethical values like love, solidarity, unity and cooperation. The hoe in the songs apart from being the literal farm tool that they use in tilling the soil for planting, it symbolises any occupation that the women do to guarantee livelihood. This is indicative of the fact that married women in Ngar-Buh do not rely very much on their husbands for the up-keep of the home. They rely on the hoe, which epitomizes the "father" or bread winner of this compound. It is the hoe that helps them provide food, clothing and shelter, medical expenses, school fees for the family. They are making a point that social change should come with change of attitude towards women. However, it is interesting to note the contradiction in their life experiences, revealed during the interview sessions with the women. They did not claim the right to family head status given the roles they play as major family bread winners. Women clearly stated that the head of the family is the man, the husband, but in their oral literature, they express, albeit in metaphorical terms, that the head of the house is the hoe, the symbol of the empowerment tool in their largely agrarian community. The songs are crafted to articulate the view that the community can function more forcefully if everyone, whatever the status, sex or gender is given the opportunity to contribute to its growth and development. That is why in "Stop it", the women reiterate that young girls and boys should grab the metaphoric hoe and be strong instead of wasting time and energy in unnecessary visiting and backbiting.

Stop it

Soloist: Stop saying he/she said this
Chorus: Grab your hoe and be strong
Soloist: Stop slandering
Chorus: Hold your hoe and be tough
Soloist: Discontinue back biting
Chorus: Take hold of your hoe and be resilient.

(Fondze-Fombele 315-316)

The Eton women of Cameroon's struggle against the system of male domination as they fight for a world where women should have a fully human status is captured in the excerpts of the Bikutsi songs represented below.

The Female Person

The female person
Eeeeeeee the women population eeee
Thw women are a race
The most unfortunate of humans
The doings of men are never disclosed like those of women
The man's theft is not known like that of a woman
The man's wickedness is never denounced vigorously as that of the women
The man's sterility is hidden, that of the woman is exposed.

(Fondze-Fombele 334)

Hei Women

Hei women
Hei women
O oooh ooh eeh
Have you ever seen an ugly man?
No we only know ugly women o
Come then the first Friday of the month,
I will show you an ugly man o (2x) (Fondze-Fombele 345)

Man, an Adulterer

Chorus: Man is just flattery words
My friend, when he attracts you
You never imagine that he has ever wooed another woman!
This flatterer

My friend, when praises you
You cannot know that he already sang praises to another
This flatterer
My friend, his voice is smooth today
Can you imagine that yesterday it was smooth for another woman?
My friend, when he woos a young girl
The game rarefies in the forest
This flatterer
My friend, but the day he repels you,
you cannot imagine that you were his little dear.
This flatterer (Fondze-Fombele 342)

The Eton women are particularly satirical of men's poor comportment that aids in the dehumanisation of women. These Bikutsi songs by women during the nuptial rite feature strong feminist content, substantial articulations against male domination and women's intense displeasure for ideologies that represent the male as the human norm, at the expense of a human status for women. They resist that system of domination that regards the female as subsidiary, subsumed, ancillary or even an absence from the human norm and their needs, values, interests, rights and responsibilities trivialised and or ignored.

The homage, Lullabic song, nuptial and birth songs from Yoruba, Nigeria and Senegal capture the various strategies women oral artists use to resist domination as they deconstruct gender myths that patriarchy had built. The Yoruba homage song pays respect to women. In Yoruba cosmology it is believed that women are in a vantage position, (based on their privileged knowledge about life), to control the world, especially at the cultic and mysterious levels, much more than men are privileged to do. This is a dialogic perspective that helps to bring out women's important role that patriarchy has warped into defining a woman as witch, thereby monologically exposing but the negative qualities of this knowledge conveyed by women's work song. The Senegalese nuptial song "Carry the Canary on your Head" unveils male domination by castigating men who practice teenage marriages. The Nigerian birth song "I will not Pound" features the female character who demonstrates resistance from male excesses by withdrawing from traditional women's roles and responsibilities in order to make her point. At this point crying is a show of weakness and not resistance and so she will not cry but rather take action by refraining from assuming the roles assigned to her by male supremacist tendencies.

Homage (Nigeria)

I pay homage to you, our mothers
You who hold the reins of the world
Let life be positive for us. (Illesanmi 31)

Carry the canary on your head (Senegal)

Pick up your hoe
And take the path to your field.
Lonely man why are you so sad?
You who have sold your daughter! (Lo 33)

I'll not pound (Nigeria)

I'll not grind
A bride has taken over from me
I'll not cook
I'll not cry
A bride has taken over from me
I'll not talk
I'll not farm
A bride has taken over from me (Iwoketok 152)

The nativity performance in Nigeria offer the performance space where women express their feminist standpoints about their individual worth and personalities. Helen Chukuma reiterates that "birth songs offer a refreshing diversion from the canon. First birth songs are gender restrictive being exclusively an all-female affair. Secondly, they are songs of celebration and cheer rehearsing female fulfilment in procreation, further they afford the women free expression and psychic release from inhibitions of socio-cultural norms and expectations" (Chukwuma 23). The following Igbo birth songs exemplify women's perspectives about who they are as human beings in their own right. The first song urges the men to see women's individual worth as they resist the fact that bareness should be identified with women only. The song calls for men to appreciate the merits, qualities, and abilities of women and not only value them as procreators. The second song demonstrates women in solidarity, through the mother and daughter-in-law, who seize the cultural asset, children, to fight men who think they can use and dump women at will.

My husband I am a beauty
My husband I am a beauty
I am not a creator of children (Chukwuma 34)

My husband asked us to leave
My husband asked us to leave
My husband asked us to leave
My mother-in-law asked us to be bearing children (Chukwuma 26)

Patriarchal culture through its optics, view and define women differently while these women in their songs see themselves and redefine themselves through the optics of strong contents of African feminism and so configure women differently and positively within the work songs, nuptial and nativity performance articulatory spaces. Critics like Lloyd Brown and Ode S. Ogede have rightly maintained that the female voice in oral tradition was and is audible, albeit the token recognition accorded it in criticism. Despite this paucity in the criticism of the female voice in the oral tradition, women have had and are having a collective mouth that speaks to their collective destiny as daughters, sisters, wives, mothers, and aunts; nurturers of people, upholders and preservers of the moral ethics of the community, socio-cultural and political transformers and economic developers. Thus their creativity in the oral literary tradition which has only been defined by the collective need of the people is now also being redirected to their personal aspirations, individual lives and experiences. On the one hand, they are by this act unveiling the cloud of silence that was enveloping their individual lives, condemning them to absence as autonomous identities, hence deconstructing derogatory gender myths. On the other hand, they are by this act, reconstructing constructive gender myths for socio-cultural and politico-economic transformation and development, demonstrating the interconnectedness and interdependency of genders who should work to complement each other.

Conclusion

This study set out to discuss conceptualisations of women in oral African literature using the gender and feminist critical categories. It has revealed that the system of male domination composed myopic monologic perceptions and depictions of women in literature, burying them under static and destructive gender myths from which they need to exhume. Women's oral literary voices aim at upsetting male dominant views on women through a re-utterance of female realities and female lived experiences. Patriarchy and male dominated literary creativity orchestrates prejudiced images, roles, and responsibilities of women as they speak a monologue of culture that derogates women's images and value men's personalities as movers and moulders of politics, with issues like war and nationalism being valid subjects for literature. But African women oral performers have joined women writers, critics and activists to create gender myths that initiate a dialogue on inter-personal relationships, domestic life, private spaces and the politics of intimacy, interconnectedness and interdependency as worthy of literary rigour while they are constructing positive gender myths for socio-cultural and politico-economic transformation. The women have achieved the most difficult part of learning, which is to unlearn derogatory gender myths, a necessity for relearning constructive gender myths. Their songs are pedagogy for unlearning and relearning for women have been identified in African history as effective myth makers (Lauter 1984). A feminist critic has noted that, "Myths are protean and should be deliberately re-directed towards the enhancement of women's role" (Kolawole 26) and a feminist historian has also reiterated that, "mythic thinking is a continuous process and not a stage that human beings passed through thousands of years ago" (Lauter 1). The study has noted that myths are creations of culture and not essential aspects of nature. They are created not only to explain reality but also cultural practices of power relations in order to justify and legitimise them. As the society continues to be enlightened on issues of female equity, emancipation and empowerment, African oral performers are enhancing on their role as myth makers, as they are perceived deploying shifting, though sometimes contradictory but constructive gender myths that recreate positive attributes, images, gender relations for socio-cultural and politico-economic development.

Works Cited

Brown, Lloyd W. *Women Writers in Black Africa.* Wesport Conn: Greenwood Press, 1981. Print.

Chukwuma, Helen. "Feminism and Fecundity in Igbo Birth Songs." Chukwuma, Helen. *Feminism in African Literature: Essays on Criticism.* Enugu: New Generation Books, 1994. 22-37. Print.

Fondze-Fombele, Eunice Fonyuy. "The Idea of Feminism: A Cross-Cultural Gender Analysis of Selcted Oral and Written Literature by Cameroonian Women." Yaounde: Ph.D. Thesis, Faculty of ALSS, The University of Yaounde, June 2012. Print.

Gigandi, Simon. *Reading the African Novel.* London: James Curry Limited, 1987. Print.

Goodman, Lizbeth. *Approaching Literature: Literature and Gender.* New York: Routledge, 1996. Print.

Illesanmi, T. M. "The Significance of the Myths of Women in Socio-political Role Sharing among Yuroba People." Kolawole, Mary E. Modupe. *Gender Perceptions and Development in Africa: A Socio-Cultural Approach.* Lagos: Arrabon Academic Publishers, 1998. 29-44. Print.

Iwoketok, Uwemedimo Enobong. "Analysis of Lullabic Songs in Traditional African Communities: Some Nigeria Examples." *African Research Review: International Multi-Disciplinary Journal, Ethiopia* (2009): 147-157. Web.

Killiam, Douglas and Ruth Rowe. *The Companion to African Literature.* Oxford: James Curry, 2000. Print.

Kolawole, Mary E. Modupe. "Women's Oral Literature as Site for Dynamic Self-Expression." Kolawole, Mary E. Modupe. *Gender Perceptions and Development in Africa: A Socio-Cultural Approach.* Lagos: Arrabon Academic Publishers, 1998. 15-28. Print.

Lauter, Estella. "Introduction: Steps Towards a Feminist Archetypal Theory of Mythmaking." Lauter, Estella. *Women as Mythmakers.* Bloomington: Indiana University press, 1984. 1-6. Print.

Lo, Cheikh Tidiane. "Traditional Poetry in Contemporary Senegal: A case Study of Wolof Kasak Songs." *Oral Tradition* (2016): 27-52. web.

March, Candida, Ines Smyth, and Maitrayee Mukhopadhyaya. *A Guide to Gender-Analysis Frameworks.* London: Oxfam, 19999. Print.

Ndungo, Catherine Nwihaki. "Images of Women in African Literature: A case of Gikuyu and Swahili Proverbs." *Images of Women in African Literature: A case of Gikuyu and Swahili Proverbs.* Nairobi: Kenyan University Library, 1998. Print.

Ogede, Ode S. "Counter to Male Domination: Images of Pain in Igede Women's Songs." *Research in African Literatures:Special Issue: Women as Oral Artists* (1994): 105-120. Print.

Okereke, Grace Eche. "African Gender Myths of Vocality and Gender Dialogue in African Literature." Kolawole, Mary E. Modupe. *Gender Perceptions and Development in Africa: A Socio-Cultural Approach.* Lagos: Arrabon Academic Publishers, 1998. 133-158. Print.

Schipper, Mineke. *Source of all Evil: African Proverbs and Sayings on Women.* Chicago: Ivan R. Dee. Inc., 1991. Print.

Shaikh, Sadiyya. ""The Veil: A Feminist Theological Analysis"." Musimbi, R. A. Kanyoro and Njoroge J.N. (Ed.). *Groaning in Faith: African Women in the Household of God.* Nairobi: Acton Publishers, 1996. 82-90. print.

Thompson, Denise. *Radical Feminism Today.* London: Sage Publications, 2001. Print.

CHAPTER 4

From Proto – to Post-Feminism: Writing and Re-Writing Womanhood from *Pride and Prejudice* to *Bridget Jones' Diary*

May Toudic

Abstract

In the eye of many modern feminist critics, the domestic, marriage-focused plots of Jane Austen are far from promoting female empowerment. An author whose characters always end up married, never outwardly rebelling against the status quo, is thus dismissed as anti-feminist, or at the very least excluded from the feminist tradition. It is then unsurprising that *Bridget Jones' Diary*, Helen Fielding's 1999 modernisation of *Pride and Prejudice*, is treated in the same way. Written during the rise of popular 'chick lit', it is usually considered as an example of 1990s post-feminism. With its commercial success and focus on 'frivolous' topics such as romance, physical appearance and navigating modern life, *Bridget Jones' Diary* is regularly dismissed by literary and feminist theorists alike, relegated to a lower class of literature. But while the outward plot and themes of both *Pride and Prejudice* and *Bridget Jones' Diary* seem to promote traditional, patriarchal and/or postfeminist views on femininity, a closer look reveals them to be a critique of these modes of thinking. From Elizabeth's defiance of Regency expectations to Bridget's failure to conform to the modern ideas of feminine perfection, these two versions of the same story both represent complex and shifting ideas of feminism and femininity.

Keywords: Feminism, re-writing, modernisation, womanhood, post-feminism

In the eye of many modern feminist critics, the domestic, marriage-focused plots of Jane Austen are far from promoting female empowerment. Edna Steeves, for instance, writes that 'Jane Austen was not a bold woman, that she never closely examined the social situation', and believed that Austen's time had not been 'ripe for rational and meaningful discussion of women's rights', while Marilyn Butler describes her heroines as 'meek, self-disciplined, and selfeffacing' (ctd. in Marshall 39-40). As Ray remarks, 'there is an implicit pride and prejudice inherent in feminist theory that elevates certain expressions of feminism – particularly depictions of rage, rebellion, or repression – and disparages portrayals of marriage or family life, especially portrayals of rewarding or fulfilling domesticity' (3). An author whose characters always end up married, never outwardly rebelling against the status quo, is thus dismissed as anti-feminist, or at the very least excluded from the feminist tradition. It is then unsurprising that *Bridget Jones' Diary*, Helen Fielding's 1999 modernisation of *Pride and Prejudice*, is treated in the same way. Written during the rise of popular 'chick lit', it is usually considered as an example of 1990s post-feminism, a movement which 'draws on and invokes feminism as that which can be taken into account, to suggest that equality is achieved, in order to install a whole repertoire of new meanings which emphasise that it is no longer needed' (McRobbie, 'Post-feminism and Popular Culture' 255). With its commercial success and focus on 'frivolous' topics such as romance, physical appearance and navigating modern life, *Bridget Jones' Diary* is regularly dismissed by literary and feminist theorists alike, relegated to a lower class of literature.

The dismissal of popular female fiction has indeed been rooted in literary tradition since Austen's time. The Romantics and their contemporary critics, with their belief in the concepts of authorial genius and sublime inspiration, despised utilitarian writing and popular fiction. As Franklin observes, 'it is no coincidence that this occurred just as women had begun to dominate the market as readers and authors, commanding the new genre of children's literature and inflecting the novel and poetry with women's experience and concerns' (118). Despite being outnumbered two to one, female authors outperformed their male counterparts by the 1790s and began to pose a threat to the patriarchal status quo. At the same time, female intellectuals had begun to question the exclusion of women from the civic humanist discourse (Franklin 122). These proto-feminist writers found themselves caught in what Frost refers to as 'a sociological and literary double bind', stuck between 'the constraints of a society that demanded female passivity and that viewed their writings as violations of its codes of propriety' and 'self-imposed constraints generated by their participation in and conditioning by the patriarchal regime into which they were born' (253).

By the 1990s, feminism has become more widely accepted, and was even considered by some to have reached its goals. Many authors and film directors were instead preoccupied with femininity, a concept referred to by Hanson as 'the dark "Other" of feminism'(16). Female authors were free to write with seemingly no societal constraints, but were still often relegated to the 'chick lit' category, struggling to be taken seriously 'among a rash of pink-jacketed books dealing with "girlie" subjects in a comic fashion' (Hanson 16).

Both Austen and Fielding, however, draw directly from the works of other female and feminist writers, thus contributing to the creation of an intertextual network of women writing through the ages. *Pride and Prejudice* is full of reflections, conversations and characters referencing the ideas brought forth in Mary Wollstonecraft's *A Vindication of The Rights of Woman.* The character of Elizabeth, for instance, personifies Wollstonecraft's ideal of the 'rational, independent thinking woman', and is set against characters such as Lydia, who portray 'the sentimental, pleasure-seeking, and emotionally-governed female that Wollstonecraft insists is the product of an unjust and unreasonable educational system' (Ray 32). Austen, too, takes a critical view towards the education system of her time, opposing in conversation Mr. Darcy and Caroline Bingley, who believe a woman must be taught a number of skills from music, to reading, drawing and speaking modern languages in order to be accomplished, with Elizabeth, who points out the impossibility of those expectations (25). As Hui-Chun remarks, Elizabeth's response reflects the idea that a woman's sense of accomplishment should not rest on pre-determined standards, that education for her female contemporaries was 'dependent upon social class and wealth, and thus an unfair standard by which to judge all women' (79).

With *Bridget Jones' Diary*, Helen Fielding goes a step further by making the intertextuality a feature of the novel, presenting it as a modern retelling of *Pride and Prejudice.* To White, this transposition presents a set of contrasts between 18th and 20th century dilemmas, opening up 'a variety of implications about why Austen seems so very useful for contemporary readers and viewers, not just in these narratives of Fielding's but also in the flush of Austen films of the 1990s' (256). Instead of simply pasting the text into a modern setting,

Fielding plays at bending the rules, selecting what to take and what to leave from the original text, and directly referencing it and its other adaptations. The narrative itself follows the romance plot of the original text:

> Bridget first meets Mark Darcy at a party where he appears arrogant and rude, then is distracted by a Willoughby-figure (Daniel). When catastrophe strikes in Bridget's family, the wealthy Mark first blames himself (just as Darcy does in Pride and Prejudice), then travels off in secret to sort matters out, returning to claim Bridget and take her away from the awkwardnesses and embarrassments of her middle-class relations (Hanson 18). From this plot structure, Fielding deviates when needed in order to provide more accurate insights into modern life and romance. As Hanson remarks, her Darcy is a much more ambivalent figure, reflecting Giddens' idea that 'confluent love', an 'active, contingent love, [which] therefore jars with the 'forever', 'one-and-only' qualities of the romantic love complex' is beginning to replace the traditional idea of romantic love (ctd. in Hanson 19).

This idea is underscored by Bridget's reflections on the BBC adaptation of Pride and Prejudice and its actors' real-life relationships, much less romantic in her opinion. To her, the difference lies in the absence of 'any actual goals'; as much as she wishes 'for Darcy to get off with Elizabeth', she affirms that she 'would hate to see Darcy and Elizabeth in bed, smoking a cigarette afterwards. That would be unnatural and wrong and I would quickly lose interest' (Fielding 215). Fielding then pushes the meta quality of this commentary further by having Bridget and her friend hold 'a long discussion about the comparative merits of Mr. Darcy and Mark Darcy, both agreeing that Mr. Darcy was more attractive because he was ruder but that being imaginary was a disadvantage that could not be overlooked' (215). Fielding's references to *Pride and Prejudice* are never meant to be subtle; when Bridget first meets Mark Darcy, she remarks:

> It struck me as pretty ridiculous to be called Mr Darcy and to stand on your own looking snooty at a party. It's like being called Heathcliff and insisting on spending the entire evening in the garden, shouting 'Cathy' and banging your head against a tree. (Fielding 12)

Thus, the original text not only exists in the adaptation, but acts as a sort of prophecy, dictating the plot and the characters' actions.

In addition to directly referencing the original text, the meta commentary in Bridget Jones' Diary serves to discuss the practice and reception of modern adaptations. At the work party Bridget attends, she finds herself caught in a conversation about the very TV adaptation she is so enthusiastic about, with people whose opinions far differ from hers. Natasha believes it to be 'disgraceful' that 'a whole generation of people only get to know the great works of literature […] through the television', and that people should have to prove they have read the original text before watching the adaptation (Fielding 86), going on to complain about the 'arrogant individualism which imagines each new generation can somehow create the world afresh' (Fielding 88). Through her own modernisation, Fielding defends others by poking fun at the elitism of those who believe adaptations are necessarily lesser than the original text. The characters we as readers are supposed to empathise with, Bridget and Mark, are amused by this defensive stance; Mark argues that creating the world afresh is 'exactly what they do, do', to which Natasha responds by turning bright red and rambling on aggressively, incapable of remaining calm when her thesis is challenged (Fielding 88). This behaviour adds to the character's already ridiculous elitism, thus exposing Fielding's opinion on literary purists in a way reminiscent of Elizabeth's stance on female accomplishment.

Beyond the reproduction of plot and selected themes, *Bridget Jones' Diary* imitates *Pride and Prejudice* in the way it uses narrative style to carry through its feminist message. Both works begin with a grand, confident proclamation; Austen with the iconic 'it is a truth universally acknowledged, that a single man in possession of a good fortune, must be in want of a wife' (2); Fielding with Bridget's statement that she 'WILL NOT Drink more than fourteen alcohol units a week. Smoke. Waste money', etc… (2). Both of these statements originate from outside the main character; the first is a belief held by Elizabeth's mother, while the second is a list of things modern society has imposed on Bridget, habits and values she feels forced to adopt in order to fit in. These first sentences represent the pressure put on women in their respective times and provide an opportunity for the characters to grow and break free from these expectations.

While *Pride and Prejudice* is written in third person and *Bridget Jones' Diary* in first, both employ focalisation, a narrative practice which 'entails having access to a character's thoughts and observations' (Jonsson 2). This is evident in *Bridget Jones' Diary* through Bridget's first person, stream of consciousness narration and, though it is more subtle in *Pride and Prejudice*, is found in the way Austen provides the reader with Elizabeth's thoughts and perspective on the novel's events. Austen's third person focalisation is made possible by free indirect discourse, 'which entails a third-person narration where the narrator is more or less invisible, and rather imitates the inner thought processes in the character (Bodenheimer, ctd. in Jonsson 2). Wang and Yan argue that Austen's feminist strategies are reflected through this narration; not only does she 'neglect the narrative modes used by male writers of her time who concern much about important historical events', but 'effectively gets rid of the control of masculine discourse and establishes feminist narrative authority' by making female characters the main figures of her novels (1828-29). Wang and Yan also remark that unlike most of her contemporaries, 'Austen does not passionately identify herself with any of her characters and none of her books are written in the first person. She gives her heroines an impersonal freedom' (1829). By using Elizabeth's point of view as narrative focus, Austen thus turns her into an active observer, setting an intelligent eye on the world and the people around her.

In addition to giving a voice to women through their narration, Austen and Fielding both address the struggles and concerns faced by the women of their respective times. Among these concerns is the pressure of ever-changing beauty standards on women. In *Pride and Prejudice*, beauty is seen as something one is or isn't born with; Jane is constantly described as naturally beautiful, and Charlotte Lucas as unattractive. Other attractive traits must be given by nature to a woman, such as 'a certain something in her air and manner of walking, the tone of her voice, her address and expressions' (Austen 25). Besides this vague and natural beauty, attractiveness in women can be improved, according to characters such as Darcy and Caroline Bingley, through education, application and practice of the arts. Attempts to modify one's physical appearance through clothing is considered frivolous and materialistic, as demonstrated by Elizabeth's opinion of Lydia, who is obsessed with buying bonnets and dresses with no concern for modesty of economy.

In *Bridget Jones' Diary*, the natural beauty of the 18th century has been replaced by 1990s concepts of diet culture and ultimate control over physical appearance (Nilsson 8). From the very beginning, Bridget is concerned with her weight, resolved to 'reduce [the] circumference of [her] thighs by 3 inches (i.e. 1½ inches each), using [an] anti-cellulite diet' (Fielding 3). She obsessively records every calorie, cigarette and alcohol unit consumed in a day, assesses the numbers as 'good' or 'bad' and makes excuses for consuming things she believes are bad. This prominence of diet culture isn't simply treated as normal behaviour; from a quirky and slightly relatable concern, Bridget's obsession with her weight is slowly revealed to the reader as problematic, possibly turning into an eating disorder. In a conversation with her friend Tom, for instance, she proves to know exactly the number of calories present in a given food item and reveals she aims to eat a thousand calories a day, to which he replies: 'But I thought you needed two thousand just to survive' (Fielding 224). In this moment, the reader's eyes are opened at the same time as Bridget's, who realizes:

> I have spent so many years being on a diet that the idea that you might actually need calories to survive has been completely wiped out of my consciousness. Have reached point where believe nutritional ideal is to eat nothing at all and that the only reason people eat is because they are so greedy they cannot stop themselves from breaking out and ruining their diets. (Fielding 224-25)

The shape and size of one's body, however, is not the only thing which can and must be controlled in order to fit modern beauty standards. Every aspect of a woman's appearance is subject to the same treatment. Again, Fielding shows her awareness of this issue through Bridget's half-aware point of view. Bridget spends an entire day getting ready for her date with Daniel; waxing, shaving, cleansing, exfoliating, dyeing, massaging and exercising as she reflects: 'being a woman is worse than being a farmer there is so much harvesting and crop spraying to be done […]. The whole performance is so highly tuned you only need to neglect it for a few days for the whole thing to go to seed' (Fielding 27). The body's natural state is a source of disgust and is objectified to the point of being compared to a field. As McRobbie explains, it has become 'increasingly difficult to function as a female subject without subjecting oneself to those technologies of self that are constitutive of the spectacularly feminine' ('TOP GIRLS? Young Women and the New Sexual Contract' 60). Norms of appearance and presentation are placed on women everywhere, from their home to their workplace, until they are so deeply ingrained they are perceived to come from their own minds. The patriarchal authority is then 'subsumed within a regime of self-policing whose strict criteria form the benchmark against which women must endlessly and repeatedly measure themselves' (McRobbie, 'TOP GIRLS? Young Women and the New Sexual Contract' 63). To McRobbie, this self-policing system of expectations on women's appearance is born of their increasing presence in the work force. Women have to do what they can to avoid being perceived as a threat; they thus get themselves 'endlessly and repetitively done up, so as to mask [their] rivalry with men in the world of work (i.e. [their] wish for masculinity)' (McRobbie, 'TOP GIRLS? Young Women and the New Sexual Contract' 67).

While the modern woman is expected to control and care about her appearance, she must not show herself to be too concerned with it, at the risk of seeming frivolous and/or materialistic. This double standard is present in *Bridget Jones' Diary*, through Bridget's ambivalence towards her own spending habits. After a shopping trip, she comes home with items she knows she will never wear and laments over the wasted money, believing it is all a punishment 'for being obsessed by shopping in a shallow, materialistic way' (Fielding 105). As Nillson remarks, there is an irony in Bridget's claim that 'our culture is too obsessed with outward appearance, age and status' (Fielding 82), in between breakdowns of her food consumption and description of her getting ready for dates (9). Unlike Lydia, Bridget is aware of the limit imposed on women in caring about their appearance. She knows she must be well-dressed but not materialistic, made-up but not shallow, skinny but healthy-looking, and loses herself in trying to keep up with both sides of the double standard.

While the depictions of beauty standards in *Pride and Prejudice* and *Bridget Jones' Diary* are not always perceived as a feminist critique, the independence of their respective protagonists contributes to an interpretation of the two novels as feminist texts. Wollstonecraft praises independence as 'the grand blessing of life, the basis of every virtue', to be secured by pursuing one's desires above even material security (1). *Pride and Prejudice's* Elizabeth embodies this idea of female independence throughout her story. She is aware from the start that her wild spirit contrasts with the expectations of 'proper' society; when she arrives at Pemberley to see Jane, is it said 'that she should have walked three miles so early in the day, in such dirty weather, and by herself, was almost incredible to Mrs. Hurst and Miss Bingley; and Elizabeth was convinced that they held her in contempt for it (Austen 21). She displays intelligence while rejecting higher class ideas of education, praising her family's free approach to education by explaining to Lady Catherine: 'such of us as wished to learn never wanted the means. We were always encouraged to read, and had all the masters that were necessary. Those who chose to be idle, certainly might' (Austen 98). Though knowledge is important to her, Elizabeth believes in the right of women to decide whether or not it is important to them, and whether learning is a worthy use of their time. Another demonstration of her independence and agency is in her refusal of two financially viable marriage proposals, putting into practice Wollstonecraft's idea of personal wants before material security. When rejecting Collins, she struggles to make herself heard and asks him not to consider her 'as an elegant female, intending to plague [him], but as a rational creature, speaking the truth from her heart' (Austen 67). With these rejections, Austen is thus endorsing a woman's right to govern herself and determine her own future' (Ray 38). Elizabeth cares about her future and her family but refuses to make these obligations the sole reason for her marriage. She exercises her agency by choosing her own husband and is empowered by this choice, even when the pressure shifts from her family wanting her to marry to the powerful Lady Catherine wanting her not to. To the woman's plea to refuse Darcy's upcoming proposal, Elizabeth refutes that she is 'not to be intimidated into anything so wholly unreasonable', as 'that the arguments with which [Lady Catherine has] supported this extraordinary application have been as frivolous as the application was illjudged' (Austen 207). While she respects reason, she cannot be convinced by empty arguments and refuses to be swayed by power. Ultimately, Elizabeth chooses Wollstonecraft's idea of a perfect marriage, one where the woman, strong of body and mind, becomes 'the friend, and not the humble dependent of her husband' (30). Darcy and Elizabeth have a deep respect of each other's opinions, one that changes each of them for the better, and Darcy's respect for Elizabeth in particular ensures she can preserve a sense of agency even as a married woman.

In *Bridget Jones' Diary*, independence is more external. She is 'a free agent, single and childless and able to enjoy herself in pubs, bars and restaurants' (McRobbie, 'Post-feminism and Popular Culture' 261). Unlike Elizabeth, Bridget has the opportunity to live on her own, pursue a career and handle her own finances (Lindgren 10–11). In her reflections on the new year, she states her intentions to 'improve career and find new job with potential. Save up money in form of savings. Poss start pension-also' (Fielding 3). She is aware of her potential to move up in society, not through marriage but through her own work and self-improvement. To McRobbie, the need to self-monitor as Bridget does through her diary comes from the separation of young women from communities with fixed gender roles; without this traditional model, 'individuals are increasingly called upon to invent their own structures', and maintaining a diary or planner provide a more tangible illusion of structure and stability (McRobbie, 'Post-feminism and Popular Culture' 260). In the face of increased agency, the pressure is on women to make the right decisions and constantly strive towards success. Although Bridget is more focused on romance than Elizabeth is, she also exercises her right to choose a partner and asserts her standards, refusing Daniel's original offer of a no-strings-attached relationship. As Jonsson remarks, 'Bridget does not accept the terms that Daniel is presupposing she will agree to and dismisses him, despite admitting experiencing hopelessness due to her singlehood.

> There's more than one bloody way to live: one in four households are single, most of the royal family are single, the nation's young men have been proved by surveys to be completely unmarriageable, and as a result there's a whole generation of single girls like me with their own incomes and homes who have lots of fun and don't need to wash anyone else's socks. (Fielding 37)

While traditional expectations on women to marry and have children are still prominent in 1990s society, the women of Bridget's generation are beginning to break free and envisage the possibility of life without this traditional family model. More even than Elizabeth, Bridget shows power and agency in her choice of a man, because she has the option to not marry at all.

In conclusion, while the outward plot and themes of both *Pride and Prejudice* and *Bridget Jones' Diary* seem to promote traditional, patriarchal and/or postfeminist views on femininity, a closer look reveals them to be a critique of these modes of thinking. Austen's focus on Elizabeth, with her 'defiant nature in opposition to the expectations of proper feminine behaviour', provides her with 'an outlet for critical energies that she could not otherwise share with the world' (Hui-Chun 77). Fielding's commentary on modern femininity is just as powerful; as Jonsson argues, 'Bridget's behaviour of setting goals of self-perfection, which she can only fail, does not indicate that she is a powerless character [...] Instead, Bridget sees through the ideals imposed on her by society, such as losing weight, by failing to achieve her goal but still liking herself in the end' (Jonsson 10). Every one of her failure challenges the modern ideas of feminine perfection and conditional feeling of self-worth.

Works Cited

Austen, Jane. *Pride and Prejudice*. Edited by R. W. (Robert William) Chapman, Project Gutenberg, 1813. *Project Gutenberg*, https://www.gutenberg.org/ebooks/42671.

Fielding, Helen. *Bridget Jones's Diary*. Penguin Books, 1999. *Internet Archive*, http://archive.org/details/bridgetjonessdia00fiel_1.

Franklin, Caroline. 'Enlightenment Feminism and the Bluestocking Legacy'. *The Cambridge Companion to Women's Writing in the Romantic Period*, edited by Devoney Looser, Cambridge University Press, 2015, pp. 115–28. Cambridge Core, *Cambridge University Press*, doi:10.1017/CCO9781139061315.011.

Frost, Cy. 'Autocracy and the Matrix of Power: Issues of Propriety and Economics in the Work of Mary Wollstonecraft, Jane Austen, and Harriet Martineau'. *Tulsa Studies in Women's Literature*, vol. 10, no. 2, 1991, pp. 253–71, doi:10.2307/464017. JSTOR.

Hanson, Clare. 'Fiction, Feminism and Femininity: From the Eighties to the Noughties'. *Contemporary British Women Writers*, edited by Emma Parker, vol. 57, Boydell and Brewer, 2004, pp. 16-27.

Hui-Chun, CHANG. 'The Impact of the Feminist Heroine: Elizabeth in Pride and Prejudice'. *International Journal of Applied Linguistics & English Literature*, vol. 3, no. 3, 2014, pp. 76-82. *ProQuest*, doi:http://dx.doi.org.ezproxy.is.ed.ac.uk/10.7575/aiac.ijalel.v.3n.3p.76.

Jonsson, Ida. *Petticoats or Miniskirts: A Comparative Analysis of Feminine Narration in Pride and Prejudice and Bridget Jones's Diary*. 2018. Stockholm University, Independent thesis. *DiVA*, http://www.diva-portal.org/smash/record.jsf?pid=diva2%3A1280194&dswid=2666

Lindgren, Johanna. *Women of Substance: The Aspect of Education, Career and Female Identity in Pride and Prejudice and Bridget Jones's Diary*. 2009. Växjö University, Independent thesis. *DiVA*, http://www.diva-portal.org/smash/record.jsf?pid=diva2%3A206Women%20of%20Substance:%20The%20Aspect%20of%20Education,%20Career%20and%20Female%20Identity%20in%20Pride%20and%20Prejudice%20and%20Bridget%20Jones%27s%20Diary518&dswid=2666

Marshall, Christine. '"Dull Elves" and Feminists: A Summary of Feminist Criticism of Jane Austen'. *Journal of the Jane Austen Society of North America*, 1992, pp. 39–45.

McRobbie, Angela. 'Post-feminism and Popular Culture'. *Feminist Media Studies*, vol. 4, no. 3, Nov. 2004, pp. 255-64. *DOI.org (Crossref)*, doi:10.1080/1468077042000309937.

.... 'TOP GIRLS? Young Women and the New Sexual Contract'. *Cultural Studies*, vol. 21, no. 4-5, July 2007, pp. 718-37, doi:10.1080/09502380701279044.

Nilsson, Kristina. *The Accomplished Woman – No Changes Accomplished?: A Comparison of the Portrayal of Women in Jane Austen's Pride &*. 2009. Växjö University, Independent thesis. *DiVA*, http://www.diva-portal.org/smash/record.jsf?pid=diva2%3A206518&dswid=2666

Ray, Melissa A. *A vindication of Jane Austen: Mary Wollstonecraft's feminist ideology embodied in 'Pride and Prejudice'*. 2013. Ann Arbor, M.A. dissertation. *ProQuest*, https://search.proquest.com/docview/1418802657/abstract/AC24ABFA7D8B4631PQ/1.

Wang, Xueqing, and Liu Yan. 'Analysis of the Feminism in Pride and Prejudice.' *Theory & Practice in Language Studies*, vol. 1, no. 12, Dec. 2011, pp. 1827-30. eue.

White, Laura Mooneyham. 'Jane Austen's World as Postmodern Simulacrum in Fielding's Narratives of Bridget Jones.' *Persuasions*, vol. 24, 2002, pp. 256-69. Wollstonecraft, Mary. *A Vindication Of The Rights Of Woman*. A.D. Matsell, 1792. Internet Archive, http://archive.org/details/AVindicationOfTheRightsOfWoman

CHAPTER 5

Community, Gender and Intersectionality: A Re-reading of Third World Feminism from the Perspective of the Subcontinent

Elham Hossain

Abstract

Gender cannot be a primary factor for determining a woman's fate. Community and its power-structure, ideology, class, socio-economic realities, religion, location, psychological framework, belief-system, sexual orientation and assumptions form the heterogeneous discourse of feminism. Like different forms of postcolonialism, there exists feminisms in connection with differences of experiences, ideological productions and cultural relativism. First World feminist discourse puts emphasis on the homogeneity of the category of women. But the framework of the intersectionality adopted by the Third World feminist discourse as a theoretical framework challenges the categorization of the Western feminism. Besides, Third World feminism proves its potential against transnational or global feminism by putting importance on the relevance of the concept of nation-state that can be attributed to the formation of identity of women from spatial perspective. In the postcolonial fictions, specifically, of the subcontinent, feminism analogously walks side by side with the postcolonial discourse as patriarchy and imperialism exert hegemony upon the subordinates who can be analogous with women and who raise question of representation, voice, racial minority and marginalization and seek to reinstate themselves in the power-structure. This paper, in conjunction with the framework of intersectionality, seeks to show how the women of the subcontinent respond to the First World feminist discourse in the era of globalization and develop their own kind of feminism. In support of the deliberation, some literary texts and literary theories will be explored intensively. This paper will also draw insights from bell hooks' notions of 'Homeplace' and 'Radical openness'.

Keywords: Third World feminism, homeplace, intersectionality, patriarchy, gender

The term 'Third World' is deliberately imposed upon the countries which were once ruled and exploited by the colonial nations. Ghanaian author Ama Ata Aidoo "proposes the terms "bourgeois nations" for the first world countries, and "proletarian nations" for third world ones" (Katrak xii). Aidoo smells a deliberate politics of the self-declared First World nations to ahistoricise the economically growing nations which are still wrestling restlessly to override the aggression of neo-colonial enterprises. For many reasons women are not given sufficient space in economic activities and education. They are rather treated as subservient to men. But due to the development of global communication, industrialization and corporatization of the nation-state, women show a desire to share the space and encounter antagonistic forces. They are not free subject of thought and action. This condition of women varies from country to country as the nature of post-colonialism varies from country to country. Hence, there exist post-colonialisms and feminisms. Feminism in proletarian nations is different from that of bourgeois nations regarding the diversity of political, social, cultural and economic realities.

During the COVID-19 pandemic the phenomenon of sexual violence or the obnoxious incident of rape in Bangladesh and some other parts of the subcontinent makes women raise a question regarding their right to share a space in the society side by side with men. However, this space or homeplace, as defined by bell hooks in her book *Yearning: Race, Gender, and Cultural Politics* (1990) refers to a place of safety and security and that is not a home which says, "You do not belong here…" (hooks 41). So, the home is the place "where all that truly mattered in life took place – the warmth and comfort of shelter…" (41). A homeplace teaches dignity, too and enables women to confront the issues of humanization. Bell hooks has said in the Chapter "Homeplace" of her aforesaid book that a black woman, unlike an American white woman does not primarily wrestles for political equality with men. She rather struggles for safety, security and dignity. She stands against sexism and racism. Homeplace generates community resistance shared by all the women of the Third World where domestic and social security is more an important issue than political equality. Thus, feminism in the Third World has taken a new and distinctive dimension posing itself against patriarchy which is analogous with colonial and imperial hegemony. It provides an impetus of resistance against the fetishistic worship of commodities, cultural aggression and imperial hegemony promulgated by globalization or re-colonialism under the subterfuge of liberalism and neo-liberalism.

But in the Third World women are to fight against domestic, normative, cultural and ideological repression more than political exploitation as it is usually found in the First World countries. Namibian author Milly Jafta depicts this stern reality in her short story 'Home Coming'. In this story, a woman in her fifties is returning to her native village which she left nearly forty years ago. By this time, she has had several daughters whom she could not provide enough time for their proper nursing and care. Now at the ebb of her life she apprehends that they may not take much interest in her return to them after forty years. Her daughter who has come to receive her at the bus stop seems to her to be a 'stranger' (Jafta 864). The breach between mother and her daughter has been caused by her inability to attend them with sufficient time and this inability has made her children grow up in a different framework of mind and it has the chances to generate resistance against the oppressive system of patriarchal domination and hegemony. The woman can't believe her ears when her daughter repeatedly asks her whether she is walking too fast for her because in forty years of her career as a housemaid nobody lends his/her ear to her to know whether she has her personal life or not. So she woefully asserts, "Someone was actually asking me whether I could keep up. Not telling me to walk faster, to have no males in my room, to get up earlier, to pay more attention, to wash the dog…." (Jafta 864). These are the words that depict the predicament and location of a Third World woman and at the same time the woman's ability to define herself makes the readers think of her homeplace. Actually, homeplace turns into a community where people can return easily and pose resistance against the system that occupies, assaults, challenges and subjugates womanhood.

In the same vein, a child of a housemaid or a female garment factory worker who, due to her hectic workload does not find enough time to take care of her child, may turn into a voice against the cruelty of the repressive socio-economic system. Usually the impetus behind this resistance emanates from a sense of value provided by its mother's struggle. Metaphorically interpreted, rebellion and revolution against the colonizers or even against the domestic antagonism that oppresses the (mother) country emerge out of some significant discourses of which feminist discourse is one. Even the response of the postcolonial generations towards the ex-colonizers and the present day imperialists is shaped by the mother country which plays the role of the homeplace whose dehumanized and marginalized condition stimulates this impetus of resistance. Thus, mother and homeplace become synonymous and they serve as a site of resistance, and according to bell hooks, this site serves a 'meaningful community of resistance' (47). This location constructs a discursive narrative and challenges the deliberate system of Otherization and dehumanization practiced by both the patriarchy and the colonial discourse. As patriarchy categorizes girls as good and bad, colonial discourse also categorizes the natives as good subjects and bad subjects on the basis of their adherence to and resistance against its hegemonic authority. From the patriarchal perspective, if a woman adheres to traditional gender roles, she is considered good, but if she opposes the patriarchal attempt of the politics of objectification, she is considered bad. Both patriarchy and colonial discourse objectify women. In this connection, Simone de Beauvoir sounds very relevant when she enunciates, "One is not born a woman, but becomes one" (1). So, the project of construction and destruction or making and unmaking is run by both patriarchy and colonialism. Hence, the study of feminism of the Third World countries which go through the experiences of colonialism, imperialism and neo-colonialism will, of course, be different from that of the First World countries. Borrowing the framework of the First World feminism while exploring the feminist narrative of the Third World countries may be misleading. Homeplace, in this connection, attributes immensely to the study of the feminism of the Third World countries.

Bell Hooks believes, when homeplace will be reconceptualized as a site for subversion and resistance, political issues can be addressed effectively. Here lies a delicate difference between the First World feminism and Third World feminism. In the First World countries, feminism primarily encounters political injustice and it is usually enunciated by the women from the educated women of the privileged stratum of the society. But the Third World feminism is to fight at first against sexism, dehumanization and marginalization. Besides, the intersectionality between the Western and the local cultural values works as a major obstruction that Third World feminism has to overcome. Here feminist daughters find their motherlands as "spaces where fathers still have most of the privileges and power, and that mothers and mother cultures relate differently to their daughters than they do to their sons imposing different demands and expecting different forms of conformity" (Narayan 9). Yet in a Third World country like Bangladesh, homeplace articulates a site of self-recovery where the postcolonial generations can heal their wounds and become whole.

Historically true, in this subcontinent feminist movement was initiated by men and subsequently women joined it. During the colonial era the colonial masters at first talked against Sati and in course of time, Ram Mohan Ray and Ishwar Chandra Bidyasagar raised revolutionary voice against social and cultural injustices against women and demanded reformation of the status of women in the patriarchal social framework. During the formation period of nationhood and nationalism during the first decades of 20th century under the leadership of MK Gandhi, Nehru, Rabindranath Tagore women were allowed significantly an access into local political affairs. After liberation in 1947 women started their struggle for equal opportunities and wages in income generating activities side by side with their male counterparts. Thus, feminist movement in this subcontinent went through various phases of history which experienced varieties of political, social, economic, cultural and ideological realities. These long and varied experiences have brought about distinct characteristics of the study of feminist discourse in this Subcontinent. Though many attempt "to dismiss Third World feminist politics as symptoms of "Westernization", it has achieved its distinct position as women here confront problems "within a variety of Third World national contexts…" (Narayan ix). These attempts of dismissal emerges out of the peculiarities of location and the assumption that Third World feminism takes resort to Western vocabulary. But the intentions, accent and appropriations that Third World feminism has populated prove that it exclusively belongs to the perspective of the women of the Third World countries. It emerges out of the failure of Western feminism which carries the load of Eurocentric biases. In this space Third World feminism develops its own language, own voice and own discursive narrative. In this connection, Mikhail Bakhtin sounds relevant when he asserts, "Language becomes "one's own" only when the speaker populates it with her own intention, her own accent, when appropriates the world, adapting it to her own semantic and expressive intention" (Bakhtin 119). This transformation of language into a voice gives rise to a new tenet and Third World feminism is that very tenet which attains formation through accumulation and articulation of the experiences of the people in different phases of their history. In this connection, bell hooks sounds very relevant while enunciating:

> I have been working to change the way I speak and write, to incorporate in the manner of telling a sense of place, of not just who I am in the present but where I am coming from, the multiple voices within me. I have confronted silence, inarticulateness. When I say, then, that these words emerge from suffering, I refer to that personal struggle to name that location from which I come to voice-that space of my theorizing. (146)

The multiple voices which are a distinct feature of Third World feminism emanate from the experiences exuded from its encounter with the colonial enterprises in different phases of their history. Even in post-colonial situation while struggling restlessly for the formation of nationality and nationhood Third World feminism gets rolling through the paradigm shifts and attributes to the definition of women from the context of the socio-economic realities.

In this subcontinent, development process affects both men and women in different ways. After the colonial era is over, transitional nature of the economy of the Third World countries, penetration of capitalism and the sweep of urbanization have generated some sectors of employment which take over many of the economic activities, such as garments industry, food processing industry, small entrepreneurship supported by microcredit projects run by a good number of NGO's and many more like these. Millions of women are supporting themselves and their families by working in these sectors and earning money. But after doing their time-consuming daily work how much time is left for them to invest for the care of their family? Modernization, which is not gender neutral, in agriculture sector, has ensured male mobility and women have been left alone to do household chores. Corporate world tends to objectify them. But the condition of women varies from country to country, culture to culture. Even today "In some countries, especially in the Middle East, South Asia and Latin America, women cannot do paid-work or travel without their husband's or father's written permission" (Momsen 2). In Martinique most clerks are women. A vast majority of domestic servants in Lima are women. But the picture is not the same in Lagos. 90% of the sales persons in Accra are women. In Algeria this job is mostly done by men. As gender is a socially constructed discourse imposed upon women, its conceptualization is crosscut by the conceptions of class, race, religion and ethnicity. For this reason, feminism is not a homogeneous discourse; it is rather marked for its heterogeneity. In other words, it can be affirmed that feminism is not singular; it is rather plural. Feminism of the West must not be the same as that of the East or Global South or the Orient as the realities and experiences vary. In the Third World countries like Bangladesh feminism runs in flux and intersectionality. It is not here an elitist or educated upper middle class movement for political equality or equal share of the ownership of the power-structure of the society; rather it is here a movement for empowerment of a woman as a partner, not as an owner; it is for being integrated into the totality of human reality. It is not an anti-uterus movement in the subcontinent; it is rather a movement for ensuring a partnership of women with men in home and outside. It is also for a voice of women in public and private against violence to them with a view to raising public awareness about rape, dowry, dowry related harassment, issues relating to women's poverty, employment, health, issues of ecology, communalism, early marriage, parochialism of attitude towards women, bigotry, sexual violence, gendered capitalism, sexism, patriarchy, disempowered passivity and racialized gender identity. Here women have to fight against local myths, folk tales, old *Shastras* and even religious ideologies for constructing their own self.

First World feminism finds society in binaries, that is, as centre and margin. Centre is discursively an agentive authority while the margin serves as a space of disempowered passivity. But the subtle difference between the First World feminism and the Third World feminism is that the margin in the third world turns into a space of radical openness or resistance. Afro-American feminist bell hooks in her insightful book *Yearning* has found the homeplace or margin as a location of radical openness and voices.

Voices emerge out of the place where they confront silence and inarticulateness. Voices are broken because they come out of sufferings, pangs and agonies. Voices are a resistance, too. The location of these voices can be termed as home whose very meaning "changes with experience of decolonization, of radicalization" (hooks 148). Home to a decolonized is not similar to the colonizers. It is constructed in alienation and estrangement and formed through shifting and dynamics. Those who were once colonized while unwilling to lose identity and challenging the colonial process of Otherization, seek for radical openness to voice their new knowledge and experience. But according to bell hooks, this space of radical openness "is a margin – a profound edge" (149). This margin is an integral part of the whole power-structure. It tends to go to the centre realizing that it is an inevitable part of the whole. According to bell hooks,

> This sense of wholeness, impressed upon our consciousness by the structure of our daily lives, provided us with an oppositional world view – a mode of seeing unknown to most of our oppressors, that sustained us, aided us in our struggle to transcend poverty and despair, strengthened our sense of self and our solidarity. (149)

Hence, this marginality generates a counter hegemonic discourse which challenges the Western feminism which eroticized and exoticized the women of the former colonies, now Third World countries. This disposition can make the Third World feminists enunciate the voice of resistance by challenging the Western feminism which does not develop any form of negotiation or dialogues with the women of the Third World countries but only speak about them and which is mostly stereotyped by an elitist disposition. So, when the women talk about their own pain in their own voice from the former colonies, it can be termed as 'Third World feminism'. The term 'Third World' is deliberately imposed upon the countries which were once colonies by the former colonizers. This branding or labelling can be interpreted as a politics of marginalizing even in the postcolonial situations and this margin is the location or site of resistance. Bell hooks thinks that "To be in the margin is to be part of the whole but outside the main body" (149). Center is not willing to let the margin takes up the center and at the same time it depends on the margin for recognition as center. Margin, living on the edge develops a particular way of seeing realities. For example, to defend her dialectics bell hooks has referred to Frederick Douglas who wrote his famous 1845 slave narrative. Bell hooks, after the story of deprivation of motherly care and affection, concludes that the location of deprivation helped Frederick write this revolutionary narrative. In this connection, it can be asserted that the feminist movement emerging in the Third World is not a mindless mimicking of the agenda of Western feminism. It is rather a response to the post-colonial realities which carry on the legacy of the former colonizers to subjugate women in the Third world countries. True, corporatization of economy has created income generating jobs for women. But how much time do the corporates allow the workers, particularly the female workers to spend for the nurture and care of their children? Here again the story of Frederick Douglas seems to be magnetically relevant. Frederick could meet his mother only four or five times in his whole life. She used to work as a slave in a white man's farm twelve miles away from her house. She came to meet her children at night only on a sojourn because she had to return to her work before the sun rose. Otherwise, she would have been whipped mercilessly. The present day corporates do not use whips, but they use strict laws as an apparatus to ensure the subjugation of their subordinates. The threat of firing from the job at any moment without ensuring any financial security is one of the most potent strategies to control these working women. Hence, Third World feminism is not the voice of the haves; it is the voice of the have-nots.

Varieties of issues related to the women of the subcontinent are not usually covered by the First World feminist discourse which sweepingly categorizes women inclusively with a single term 'women'. But women from the upper class or upper middle class background do not have the same experiences as those of the women of the lower middle class or lower class. Regarding the social, political, economic and moral support in this subcontinent, the term 'women' is crosscut with indigeneity, ethnicity, class, sex and gender. They have to fight against not only patriarchy but also local myths constructed with a view to stereotyping them. In the past they had to fight against colonial discourse which boasted for its masculinity and thus left no stone unturned to misrepresent and malrepresent women. Women as colonized subjects all over the world have the same experiences of being misrepresented and malrepresented. In colonial literature local women are depicted with all their passivity, fragility and uncouthness. For example, Shakespeare's *The Tempest* depicts Caliban's mother not as a woman, but as a notorious witch. Prospero has imprisoned her into a tree. Othello is doomed for his adherence to the ideology of his mother, symbolized by the handkerchief. In *Heart of Darkness* Kurtz's mistress is depicted with all her primitive posture and cruelty and she is devoid of any voice. Readers never see her speak. In E. M. Forster's *A Passage to India* Indian women do not have any role as well as voice. They are passive and they have no participation in economic activities. These are a few of the examples which exhibit the deliberate role of stereotyping women of the Third World countries.

In response to such deliberate attempt of distortion of women by colonial literature, postcolonial nations are developing a new form of feminism or counter-feminism. Literature of the postcolonial nations is now depicting women with all their strength of fighting against patriarchy, myths, ethnicity, indigeneity, class, sexism and gender repression. Syed Waliullah has portrayed the character of Jamila in his novel *Tree without Roots.* Jamila, though silenced by patriarchal hegemony, ultimately sounds her protest against the authority of her husband. In Amitav Ghosh's *The Shadow Line*, the female protagonist Thamma responds to the violence of riot and gives out an air that she is growing historically conscious and developing an ability to question the history. Nigerian author Chimamanda Ngogi Adichie is depicting women with all their realities and the power to struggle against the patriarchal attempt of transforming her into "the absolute other, the absolute stranger" (Cixous 232). Chinua Achebe in *Things Fall Apart* shows how his protagonist meets his ultimate tragedy for showing negligence and belligerence to women. Ekwefi challenges patriarchy; deserts her first husband and comes back to Okonkwo, and lives with him as his wife. In *God of Small Things* Arundhati Roy has depicted the strength of breaking a powerful taboo of casteism by a woman, Ammu who secretly makes love with Velutha, an untouchable, though her relationship ultimately comes to a horrible end. Through Mammachi's attempt of becoming self-reliant by running a business of pickle, Roy shows how Indian women embraced by the sense of self-dignity and self-respect are attempting to break through the social and cultural taboo. Abul Bashar, a prominent novelist of West Bengal depicts the evil of early marriage and complicated relation among father, son and step mother. Apart from Freudian psycho-analysis, the problem of early marriage, suppression of the liking and disliking of women by various social and religious stereotypes that, in the term of Louis Althusser, work as ideological state apparatuses. Niser Hossain in Abul Bashar's novel *FUL BOU (Beloved Wife),* is a prosperous, influential and socially dignified man. He is an old man. His daughter is married off and his son Millat is a young and educated bachelor. The old man married the girl Razia who was to marry Millat. So, the anxiety grows up in the triangular relationship driven by Oedipal complex. Abul Bashar portrays that the women of the subcontinent are to fight with multifarious realities. Suppose, Razia and Millat wrestle helplessly against the system crosscut by religion, custom, belief-system and tradition. It is not for political equalities, but for existence. It is the existential reality which is threatened by the violence against women and girls. It covers a trajectory that claims subjugation, exploitation, disempowerment and deprivation. Thus, the Third World literature or postcolonial literature is addressing women with all the realities against which they are wrestling to have a room of their own on the basis of gender equality.

Actually, gender equality can ensure an atmosphere where a woman feels secured in respect of her needs. Janet Henshall Momsen asserts that gender equality:

> ...necessarily mean equal numbers of men and women or girls and boys in all activities, nor does it mean treating them in the same way. It means equality of opportunity and a society in which women and men are able to lead equally fulfilling lives. The aim of gender equality recognizes that men and women often have different constraints and have different aspirations. Above all, the absence of gender equality means a huge loss of human potential and has costs for both men and women and also for development. (8)

So, gender equality obviously ensures the liberty of women from passivity, servility, structural hierarchy and domesticity. The true nature of feminist discourse is echoed in the voice of Sarojini Naidu in *All India Women's Conference* in Bombay in 1930 and of Indira Gandhi in 1980. According to Naidu, women have the potential and creative energy to legislate the moral of the world. Indira Gandhi put emphasis on women's being more alive and more interested because, she thinks that they comprise half of the human race. In fact, consciousness of women in the partnership with men, not in subordination to men, constitutes the feminist discourse of Third World feminism. This consciousness emerges out of the location or homeplace or, clearly speaking, the sense of belonging. This homeplace stimulates resistance, too when it turns antagonistic to women.

In mythology and literature of this subcontinent there are lots of analogies which metaphorically depict women's response to and resistance against patriarchy. Sita in Valmiki's *Ramayana* obviously appears to be an appropriate example of resistance against patriarchy. Her power of resistance comes from the place of her belonging. Out of resentment emanated from Rama's persistent suspicion about her chastity, Sita went back into the womb of the mother Earth. Again, in *Manusamhita* and *Mahabharata* the responsibility of maintaining the purity of caste has been imposed upon women. Hence, husbands are asked to keep watchful eyes upon their wives so that they could not go, in secret, in contact with other men and contaminate the caste and blood (Mukhapaddhayay 7). In the *Shastra* of this subcontinent marriages for women were declared compulsory and so if a woman died unmarried she would not get proper funeral and she would be denied heaven. In connection with this ancient belief-system, even today it is believed by many that a woman's life is not safe unless and until she is married to a man. That is, a man is her protector and provider. After marriage a woman is stereotyped by the term wife, mother, and motherhood. It is even said that a woman is complete only in motherhood. Again, a barren woman or if a woman cannot give birth to a child she is stigmatized in the society and the blame falls solely upon her. On the other hand, a man, in accordance with the popular patriarchal belief, is complete by birth. He holds the centre and a woman is the *Other*, led to the margin of the society. Therefore, when a woman of the Third World country like Bangladesh or India determines to be self-reliant, she has to wrestle with not only economic constraints but also the existing belief-system fortified by religious and cultural values and ideologies.

In fact, the realities that the women of the Third World countries encounter are not same as those of the First world countries and hence, the theoretical instruments and the framework of thoughts of the First World cannot encapsulate the Third World feminist discourse. Authentic representation of the women of this subcontinent is possible only when they are seen through the lens of its own. It is really remarkable that the writers of this subcontinent have already started this project of voicing the women here in their own language. The presence of a good number of female authors in the field of South Asian literature has added a new dimension to the development process of the feminist narratives which are striving successfully to locate a specific and individual space for women in the society with a consistent challenge to the political, aesthetical, ethical and ethnographical apparatuses that tend to silence them. Besides, a feminist theory formulated with the epistemological elements of this subcontinent is the demand of the day because, according to Pramod K. Nayar, it

> ...argues that the representation of women as weak, docile, innocent, seductive or irrational – sentimental is rooted in and influences actual social conditions, where she does not have power, is treated as a sex-object or a procreating machine, has fewer political and financial rights and is abused. (83)

It is true that the formation-process of this theory is remarkably going on through the feminist narratives produced by the feminist writers of this subcontinent like Mahasweta Devi, Anita Desai, Arundhati Roy, Tahmima Anam, Amrita Pritam, Ismat Chugtai, Jhumpa Lahiri and many more.

Works Cited

Bakhtin, Mikhail M. *The Dialogic Imagination: Four Essays*, ed. Michael Holoquist. University of Minnesota Press, 1994.

Beauvoir, Simone De. *The Second Sex*. Vintage Classics, 2015.

Cixous, Helene. "Conversations", in *Twentieth Century Literary Theory: A Reader*, ed. K. M. Newton. Macmillan Press Ltd, 1997. pp. 225-233.

hooks, bell. *Yearning: Race, Gender, and Cultural Politics*. Boston: South End Press, 1990.

Jafta, Milly. *The Home-Coming*, in *Anthology of African Literature,* ed. Anthonia C. Kalu. Viva Books, 2008, pps 863-864.

Katrak, Ketu H. *Politics of the Female Body: Postcolonial Women Writers of the Third World.* Rutgers University Press, 2006.

Momsen, Janet Henshall. *Gender and Development.* London and New York: Routledge, 2004.

Mukhapaddhayay, Jivan. *Prachin Bharat e Bibah*. Chandrabindu, 2013.

Narayan, Uma. *Dislocating Cultures: Identities, Traditions, and Third World Feminism.* New York and London: Routledge, 1997.

Nayar, Pramod K. *Contemporary Literary and Cultural Theory: From Structuralism to Ecocriticism*. Pearson, 2010.

CHAPTER 6

Contested Femininities: Hegemonic Females in Paule Marshall's *Brown Girl, Brownstones* and George Lamming's *Season of Adventure*

Clara Ijeoma Osuji

Abstract

Paule Marshall and George Lamming's main wife/mother characters in *Brown Girl, Brownstones* and *Season of Adventure* are, perceptively, cloaked in the trappings of male personalities in manners that appear to question their femaleness. While a considerable number of critical volumes have been written on the two narratives, literary research that interrogates discursive connections between femininities and female-hegemony in the two texts, still remains uncommon. Thus, this chapter examines the intersection of femaleness and hegemony in *Brown Girl, Brownstones* and *Season of Adventure.* It interrogates the idea of hegemonic femininities that appears to at once validate and threaten conventional feminine ideals erected around the concept of emphasised-femininity. The two main wife/mother characters are portrayed as not quite females and definitely, not males at all. Consequently, viewed as an aberration, their femininities as wives, mothers and women in their communities appear to be on trial throughout the series of events in the two narratives. The paper argues that the characterisation of these females are couched in tones that resist the readers attempt to frame them within conventional feminine gender personality traits such as gentleness, longsuffering and ineffectuality. It concludes that the domain of hegemony is not necessarily gender-specific since Marshall and Lamming's main husband/father characters – Mr. Piggott and Deighton Boyce, ultimately, become the tragic victims of female hegemony as reflected within the worlds of the two novels.

Keywords: Contested-Femininities, Hegemony, Expectations, Emphasised-Femininity

Introduction

The trope of the strong female character that comes to ruin as a result of daring to step out of her community's conventional demands and expectations of the conducts and attitudes of femaleness is a familiar trope. There seems to be some sort of protection around the idea that women oppress men, especially, in marital relationships. As a result, there are silences around male oppression by hegemonic females. When some situations become too obvious to be ignored such as the cases of Silla and Agnes in *Brown Girl, Brownstones* and *Season of Adventure*, the femininities of such women are often contested. This is because of the commonly internalised and, often, intractable notion that males are naturally superior to females. The British-American anthropologist, Ashley Montagu, asserts that "[m]ale superiority has been dependent upon female inferiority, and as long as everyone believed that the male was naturally superior to the female, neither men nor women were disposed to see the facts for what they were" (238). The implication of Montagu's assertion is that males are superior to females as long as females accept their supposed inferiority. Remarkably, the two main wife/mother characters in *Brown Girl, Brownstones* and *Season of Adventure* (Silla and Agnes) do not, consciously or otherwise, align their personalities, attitudes and conducts to fit into the socio-familial ideals of emphasised femaleness of their individual communities. James W Messerschmidt explains that a significant aspect of the concept of emphasised femininity is compliance to masculinity (51). Since the two female characters resist this widely-acceptable form of femininity, their femaleness is often put on trial in a manner that make them come across as hybrid gender-individuals that is reminiscent of Joana Russ's notion of the female man.

Russ's notable work, *The Female Man,* is a feminist utopian writing where she explores the relationship between gender and sex. Her remarkable lines: "Men succeed. Women get married. Men fail. Women get married [...] men start wars. Women get married" (63), articulately, summarises her core perspective of gender-role differences in this novel. It points to the age-old conviction in many societies that women are more relevant in marriage as wives and mothers. On the other hand, men have an array of attractive and respectable occupation, interests and callings which makes marriage to be a remote engagement for them. Interestingly, Russ's idea of male gender roles resonates strongly with the characters of Silla and

Agnes and might lend itself as an appropriate gender categorisation for the two women in both narratives. Indeed, Marshall and Lamming's characterisation of the mother/wife-characters of Silla and Agnes demands a new definition that will address the trait of hegemonic femininities. In the two novels, there are hints that these wives and mothers are troubled-women, or at best, masculinised-females who have insisted on crossing the female gender role/conduct-boundary, thus, their cloak of hegemony remains at their own peril.

Femaleness and hegemony are contraries. Marxist theorist, Antonio Gramsci, defines hegemony as a form of control by a dominant class which is based on consent and coercion (57). R.W Connell appears to have adapted this idea in the definition of hegemonic masculinity as the legitimatisation of the subordination of women by men (77). Although hegemonic masculinity subordinates other masculinities and femininities, the implication is that men may generally have authority because of their gender, but access to that authority may differ due to issues such as social class, ethnicity, age, religion, physical strength and even personality traits, as exemplified by the shortcomings of the husband/father characters in *Brown Girl, Brownstones* (Deighton Boyce) and *Season of Adventure* (Mr. Piggott). Chinweizu makes reference to the power of the womb, the cradle, the kitchen that drives the most consequential coup in human history (21). The power attached to these female roles constitutes a coup against men that paved way for their marginalisation and, most times, their total control by women. He recognises that often, the female power is "hard to see, hard to challenge and even harder to overthrow" (23). This is one of the remarkable aspects of the characters of Silla and Agnes that their husbands find at once exasperating and intriguing in both narratives.

The theoretical framework which guides this paper is drawn upon from concept of the psychoanalytic theory of the Swiss psychologist and psychiatrist, Carl Gustav Jung, which is grounded on the idea of the Archetypes and the Unconscious. There are many notions that articulate the occurrences of Jung's concept of the archetypes, but one of the most powerful ones that is relevant to the analysis of contested femininities is "Anima/Animus." Jung explains anima/animus as the feminine designation in men, and the masculine in women, which is an indication that the psyche has both male and female characteristics (*Secret of the Golden Flower* 60). Precisely, anima represents the female element that is found in all males while animus represents the male element that is found in all females. Jung's notion of anima/animus hints at the notion of gender fluidity. This postulation is based on Jung's recognition that human beings are fundamentally bisexual. Thus, Jungian concept of anima/animus is helpful in the analysis of contested female characters in the two novels. Silla and Agnes are examined as strong female characters whose enhanced or well-developed contra-sexual nature (animus) often gains ascendency over their femininity, thus activating their masculine sides as fierce, strict and aggressive women. Manhood is associated with power and revolves around the idea of being successful, capable, reliable, and in control (Cheng 300). Silla and Agnes are all these – successful, capable, reliable, and in control. Therefore, as a result of the convergence of socio-familial forces and systems that shape femaleness in their individual communities, their femininities are questioned.

Contested Femininities in Marshall's *Brown Girl, Brownstones* and Lamming's *Season of Adventure*

> "Of all things upon the earth that bleed and grow, a herb most bruised is woman."
>
> Miss Thompson, Brown *Girl, Brownstones*

Marshall and Lamming share a common ancestry. Both novelists are from Barbados in the West Indies and seem to have interest in the stereotypical portrayal of female characters who are strong, risk-takers, financially independent and hegemonic – often to their own detriments. In *Brown Girl, Brownstones* and *Season of Adventure,* the characters of Silla Boyce and Agnes Piggott represent typical dominating females as wives and mothers whose conducts towards their husbands and children appear illegitimate, based strictly on socio-familial gender order of femaleness. Jane Pilcher and Imelda Whelehan explain that "gender order is a patterned system of ideological and material practices, performed by individuals in a society, through which power relations between men and women are made, and remade, as meaningful. It is through the gender order of a society that forms or codes of masculinities and femininities are created and recreated, and relations between them are organized" (61). However, the character trait of Silla and Agnes which orders their brand of femininity is more consistent with typical male character qualities and/or socialisation. Thus, in much of their socio-familial interactions, both female characters exhibit overtly controlling conducts and their husbands bear the brunt of much of their hegemonic dispositions at home. A brief familiarisation with both novels will help grasp the contexts within which the two characters are assessed. Firstly, a casual look at Marshall's first novel, *Brown Girl, Brownstones.*

Marshall's *Brown Girl, Brownstones* is essentially the account of ten year-old Selina Boyce. The text is a bildungsroman, therefore, details the coming-of-age experiences of Selina, whose parents, Deighton and Silla Boyce migrate to the United States of America from Barbados. They settle in Brooklyn, New York City – on Chauncey Street, where Selina and her elder sister, Ina, are born. Set during the Depression and World War II in Brooklyn, New York City, the immigrant Barbadian families are portrayed as highly motivated people that desire material success and comfortable life in America. Although the narrative revolves around the protagonist, Selina, but in this chapter, her mother – Silla, is the focus of analysis. Silla is ambitious and desperately desires the better life associated with the American dream. As a result, she channels all her energy towards actualising this desire. *Brown Girl, Brownstones* provides realistic representation of a typical black family struggle for survival within a new cultural environment. Although Silla succeeds in buying the brown stones apartment, she is deserted and lonely after her husband's deportation and death.

Similar to some other notable strong female characters such as Merle Kinbona in Marshall's *The Chosen Place, The Timeless People*, Silla is a very strong female character – an enigma of sorts. The hegemonic female embodiment of Silla Boyce is manifested in her unyielding and assiduous nature. She is a woman that is feared by her children and spited by her husband, but remains unbroken. Her husband's attitude to her dream of buying one of the brown stone apartment irks her in no small measure, thus, she dismisses him as a man who "don know his own mind. He [Deighton] is always looking for something big and praying hard not to find it" (21). Silla insists that Deighton, her husband, is not a "real-real Bajan [Barbados] man," because he refuses to live by the materialistic standard of the Barbadian-American community. Despite all her pressures, Deighton refuses to share her interest in struggling to fit into their new environment as an American by trying to forge a better life, stamped by the status-symbol of owning a brownstone property in Brooklyn.

He rejects all her entreaties to adopt American values in order for their family to succeed economically. Rather, he plans to eventually return to his native Barbados with his family in pursuit of his own dream for a carefree life. Silla sees this plan as the height of irresponsibility and works harder in order to own a brown stone apartment.

A price Silla has to pay for her strong character trait as a female is being categorised under the cultural stereotype of a fluke gender – the image of a female man. Projecting a strong male body encased in a female individual, Silla is portrayed outside the common idea of women's gendered vulnerabilities as wives and mothers. Nancy Julia Chodorow, the feminist sociologist and psychoanalyst, explains that males identify with the masculine role in society a lot more than they identify with fatherhood while by contrast, "feminine identification is predominantly parental" (176). Perhaps, this explains why even animus-driven females such as Silla are focused on owning a home (not minding the sacrifice). Deighton's uncoordinated efforts in the marketplace yields very little and this adds to his conflicts with Silla which sets her animus at war with him. Mary Helen Washington argues that Silla's "life is a paradigm of the Barbadian community. She is the touchstone, for she proclaims aloud the chaotic trouble deep in the core of the community. Her endurance, her age, her devotion to the dollar and property, her determination to survive in 'this man country' is theirs" (315). Silla's singleness of purpose, courage and unyielding strength seem to engulf her family members. For instance, as far as Selina is concerned, Silla is at once "the mother" (a reference free of emotional attachment) and "Hitler" (184), after she masterminds Deighton's deportation. Deighton reacts after after Silla illegitimately sells his plot of land in Barbados by referring to her as a "tearcat" (120. Consciously or unconsciously, Deighton appears to be both appalled and fascinated by Silla's body – for instance, when:

> [h]e glimpsed her face in the mirror above the sink: the resolute mouth, the broad nose, the bold yet well-molded contours of the bones under her deeply brown skin – and wished that there was not this angularity about her. Then he thought of how cool her skin would be despite the heat and his fingers suddenly ached for that touch. (22)

In *The Visions Seminars Volume 2*, Jung writes that everything that falls into the unconscious is possessed by the animus. He explains that the female's animus can hurt relationships by unconsciously engaging the male's anima (497). This idea seems to be realized when Deighton approaches Silla on his way out of the house and "he saw her now as she was whenever he was near, with her clenched back and wary eyes warding him off (23). Yet, with all his ideas of Silla's unattractive angular mannish body features, her animus still engages Deighton's anima – exerting control over him. Thus, Deighton is restless at home under Silla's ever-watchful eyes. Her unique feminine disposition resonates with Ositadinma Nkeiruka Lemoha's notion of "hybributch." Lemoha explains that "hybributch is a combination of the words hybrid and butch [which] describes the femininity that is both hybridized and manlike [...] with a broad-based attitude that engenders strength and assertiveness" (26). Silla is a domineering and forceful character who is obsessed with owning a property on Chauncey Street, Brooklyn, and will stop at nothing to realise this dream.

Selina's intense reminiscences as she walks down Chauncey Street after deciding to relocate to her ancestral homeland, all she recollects of Silla, is the idea of raw strength – what she describes as the image of "the mother hacking away through like a man lost in the bush" (307) in pursuit of her objectives. This image masculinises Silla by stamping the brand of a female-man on her. Expectedly, by the end of the narrative Silla appears to be in a confused state and indeterminate state of mind – a little bit of a changed woman. She is abandoned by Selina after Ina's marriage and, hence she is left alone to confront what selina describes as "the final frightening loneliness that was to be her penance" (307). For indeed, Silla's interactions with her husband and children demonstrate certain exhibitions of mannerisms/behaviours that are considered typical of males. These mannerisms/behaviours firmly situate her in the frame of a manly woman. Regrettably, there is a weighty price tag attached to this binary identity that is also the case with her West Indian counterpart in *Season of Adventure.*

While Marshall's *Brown Girl, Brown Stones* is set in Brooklyn, New York City, *Season of Adventure* is set in the Island of San Cristobal. This island is Lamming's artistic representation of his formerly colonised territory in the Caribbean region where the reader is introduced to the character of Mrs. Agnes Piggott and her family. Agnes is the key mother character in the narrative and is portrayed as strong-willed, ambitious and an enigmatic achiever in the island of San Cristobal. She is married to a police officer and the protagonist of the novel is her daughter, Fola, who is a product of rape. Agnes is extremely concerned about the outcome of her daughter and often puts herself under unnecessary pressure in order to mould her into a respected woman in the society. Her craving for an upper class child who is well-informed and highly educated is frustrated by Fola's disinterest in her mother's upper class sentiments or association with the *crème de la crème* in San Cristobal. While she reunites with her daughter after her experience at the tunnel, she is saddened by the fact that Fola does not think much about social class and comfort.

Arguably, the character of Agnes Piggott remains the most formidable presence in *Season of Adventure.* Her imposing attitude and conduct in the domestic sphere is palpable. Thus, Mr. Piggott's status as a father and head of the family are wrestled from him and his masculinity is grossly marginalised. While her husband is a highly-placed police officer, in the entire Island of San Cristobal Agnes is a very prominent personality in her own right. For Tony Simoes da Silva, her "shadow looms large over the conflict between the powerful elite to which she precariously belongs and the powerless people of the Reserve with whom she once shared her experience (132). Agnes Piggott's position in *Season of Adventure* where she wrestles the headship of the family from her husband in the difficult fictitious post-colonial setting of San Cristobal. Individually, the two female-father characters also aim to raise well-educated, well-adjusted and highly successful children who will rise far above the failure, rootlessness and aimlessness which are prevalent among their peers.

> You had all your senses when you decided to do what you do [referring to Mr. Piggott's decision to marry her even with a pregnancy that is a product of rape]. Remember, that […] an' remember […] I didn't sit back like one o' those women too lazy to move […] and I didn't help to prove hel'. I help 'cause it was your own ambition eating up your brain. Don't forget to remember that the moment you star riding your high horse. (100)

Agnes remains saddled with her self-inflicted burden of the providing for her daughter in *Season of Adventure.* To this end, she resolutely avows as she addresses her husband, "while I got enough strength to work an' eye to see, Piggy, nothing go happen to put more strain on what I brought into this world" (338). Essentially, her main worry is not being capable or incapable of providing material things for Fola, but the kernel of her interest is to provide the girl with the necessary psychological and educational tools which will enable her to excel among the upper class citizens in San Cristobal.

Agnes's status as an embattled father in *Season of Adventure* stems from her extreme maternal gatekeeping and high-handed nature which brings tension between her and other members of her family, especially, her husband. She takes it upon herself to act as a single parent to Fola and keeps referring to the fact that the girl was born without a father to lay claim to her as his own, in her early years. Consequently, she tries to over compensate for this situation with her fierce desire for the girl to be among the upper class of the San Cristobal society without much success. The tension which exists between mother and daughter ensues from the fact that Fola prefers to identify with the lower class of San Cristobal who reside at the tonelle. Her daughter's preference to associate with the lower rungs of the island infuriates as well as frustrates Agnes and worsens their already fragile relationship. However, this hegemonic personality trait seems to be the dominant feature in the psychological makeup of Agnes – the woman Mr. Piggott has chosen to marry, because she is light-skinned (mulatto) and beautiful. He, probably, had not taken into consideration the fact that Agnes is a woman whose animus (masculine aspect of the feminine psyche or personality) is more exerting than her anima (feminine aspect). As a result, Mr. Piggott appears physically and psychologically drained by this female enigma and at a point in the narrative when he gets overwhelmed by her overbearing behaviour, he helplessly blurts out, "but why you such a bitch, Agnes?" (99). The "bitch" which he realises in the character of Agnes is the main element which drives her dogged trait and manifests not only in her inability to submit to him as her husband, but also in her lack of consideration and respect for him as a foster father to her child.

John Beebe notes that Jung addresses "anima Mercurius" in his later writings where he explores both androgynous and trickster aspects of the anima (100). This aspect of anima resonates clearly with the character of Agnes Piggott, as she manipulates and threatens her husband who, ironically, is police commissioner, to do her biddings. Interestingly, Brenda Donahue insists that the anima is a factor of utmost importance in the psychology of a man wherever emotions and affects are at work (70). Undoubtedly, Agnes has Mr. Piggott under firm grip in this direction and recurrently plays the man's inability to father children as a subtle emotional card which she often draws to her advantage in order to checkmate him. To ground the workings of the anima in a situation such as the Piggott couple, Donahue personifies this contra-sexual element when she writes that:

> She [the anima] intensifies, exaggerates, falsifies, and mythologizes all emotional relations with his work and with other people of both sexes. The resultant fantasies and entanglement are all her doing. When the anima is strongly constellated, she softens the man's character and makes him touchy, irritable, moody, jealous, vain and unadjusted. He is then in a state of "discontent" and spreads discontent all around him. (70-71)

The reader recognises most of these listed elements (touchy, irritable, moody, jealous, vain and unadjusted) at work in the character of Mr. Piggott. As a result, he comes across as a helpless troubled figure. In his private space, he appears obscured as he struggles to live under the large unyielding shadow cast over him by Agnes. Also, as Brenda Donahue succinctly puts it, "Sometimes the man's relationship to the woman who has caught his anima [the unconscious feminine aspect of a male] accounts for the existence of this syndrome [of the marginalised male]" (71). How do anima and animus as important Jungian concepts manifest in the behaviours of Lamming's female characters such as Agnes Piggott? Examining the psychoanalytic concepts such as Jung's anima/animus provides an important starting point. Perhaps, more important than the examination of these concepts in this chapter, is the explication of their workings which, more or less, challenges some long-held ideas concerning traditional/conventional parenting gender roles and dispositions.

Interestingly, from the Classical to the Postmodern periods, the image of the suffocated female who is passive, disrespected and economically dependent on her spouse, has remained a familiar portrait [in representational texts], (Osuji 48). However, the characters of Silla and Agnes are markedly different. As a result, within their individual socio-familial circles, the two wife/mother characters appear to have shattered the order of emphasised femininity by refusing to be marginalised and everyone seems to be in unconscious awe of their "unfeminine" attitudes and conducts. Both Silla Boyce and Agnes Piggott are female characters who have mastered the art of self-respect and assertiveness, and as Montagu rightly writes, both women "respect themselves as women and not to think of themselves, any longer than is necessary, as pale and submissive echoes of their alter egos (247). Interestingly, Jill Mathews...the specific nature or content of any gender order is constantly in process, being formed and changed. It is fashioned by actions of individuals who are themselves formed in that interaction, [...] the femininity and masculinity that are forged of these counterveiling forces are never constant but always changing and, more often than not, internally inconsistent if not contradictory (14-15). Mathews specifically makes reference to the idea that the "or content of any gender order is constantly in process" (14). This fluctuating nature of any gender order and in this instance, the female gender order, remains to be seen in the character traits of Silla in Marshall's *Brown Girl Brown Stones* and Agnes in Lamming's *Season of Adventure*. Both individuals remain female men all through the novels.

In literary history, there have been women whose femininities have been queried as a result of their seeming embodiment of maleness or conducts and attitudes that are commonly associated with the male gender. Chinua Achebe's character of Chielo, the priestess of the Oracle of the Hills and the Caves, is one such female character. On the night that the priestess ignores Okonkwo's plea, carries his sick daughter on her back and swiftly moves through the nine villages of Umuofia, the narrator tells the reader that "Chielo was not a woman that night" (79). While this comment on the gender of the priestess might been perceived as complimentary, it is also problematic, this is because Chielo's femaleness is contested because of the elements of fearlessness, physical strength and will power which are not often associated with the ideals of conventional femaleness.

Pro-gender inequality exponents such as Chinweizu, maintain that "[t]he African feminist must align her womanhood and feminist consciousness with the African traditional ideal of womanhood [...] she must respect and resume her status as a mother, the mother of the family, the mother of the nation, the mother goddess of the African people (108). This is the type of male chauvinism that Montagu challenges by insisting that "[t]he natural superiority of women is a biological fact, and a socially unacknowledged reality. The facts have been available for more than a century, but in a male-dominated world, in which the inflation of the male ego has been dependent upon the preservation of the myth of male superiority, the significance of those facts has simply been denied attention" (238). In this manner, Montagu, consciously or otherwise, places a stamp of approval on strong females that are of the ilk of Marshall and Lamming's main wife/mother characters in *Brown Girl, Brown*

Stones and *Season of Adventure.* Thus, Chinweizu's warning comes too late for females such as Silla and Agnes whose personality traits and well-developed animus refuse to be bridled by the seductive appellation attached to a real or imagined idea of an exalted African motherhood; an appellation that is targeted at female oppression by some exponents of gender inequality. Thus, Silla and Agnes's refusal to bow to the roles, conducts and attitudes of conventional femininity in their individual communities in Brooklyn and San Cristobal, set them apart as women whose femininity is in doubt and, therefore, contested.

Conclusion

Although hegemony is often associated with maleness and the victimisation of women, hegemony is not necessarily gender-specific, especially, in marital relationships. The two main wife/mother characters in *Brown Girl Brown Stones* and *Season of Adventure,* Silla Boyce and Agnes Piggott, *struggle* to succeed and refuse to conform to their society's demands and expectations of the idea of emphasised femininity which revolves around the ideal of the unassertive female. Their actions and conducts are read as counter-male-hegemonic efforts that are, consciously or unconsciously, directed at dismantling the yoke of socio-familial female oppression and exploitative tendencies. While marriage and motherhood are generally perceived as sites of female marginalisation and oppression, for Marshall's Silla and Lamming's Agnes, the situation is markedly different. Their strong personality trait (hyper animus) gives them agency to resist, challenge and seek to subvert/dismantle the unequal gender status and female marginalisation in their socio-familial worlds by succeeding where their men fail. Their rejection of the ideal female-box that is fashioned out for them by their communities becomes the bases for their being branded "un-female" in the two narratives. For indeed, they have crossed their societal female gender role/conduct boundary and, to some extent, did so at their own jeopardy.

Works Cited

Achebe, Chinua. *Things Fall Apart.* Heinemann, 1958.

Beebe, John. "The Father's Anima." *An Introduction to the Father: Contemporary Jungian Perspectives.* Edited by Andrew Samuels, New York University Press, 1986. 229-248.

Cheng, Cliff "Marginalized Masculinities and Hegemonic Masculinity: An Introduction." *Journal of Men's Studies*, 7: (1999): 205-315.

Chinweizu, Anatomy of Female Power: A Masculinist Dissection of Matriarchy. Pero Press, 1990.

Chodorow, Nancy Julia. *The Reproduction of Mothering: Psychoanalysis and the Sociology* of gender. Berkley: University of California press. 1978.

Connell, Robert William. *Masculinities.* (1995) Polity Press, 2005.

Donahue, A. Brenda. *C.G Jung's Complex Dynamics and the Clinical Relationship: One Map for Mystery.* Charles C. Thomas Publisher, 2003.

Gramsci, Antonio. *Selections from Prison Notebooks.* London: Law and Wishart. 1971.

Jung, Carl Gustav. "The Secret of the Golden Flower" (1931) *Commentary by C.G Jung in CW* 13: Alchemical Studies, 1968.

..........*The Visions Seminars Volume 2*, (1875-1961, Zurich: Spring Publications). Ed. Claire Douglas. Princeton, N.J: Princeton University Press 1997.

Lamming, George. *Season of Adventure.* 1960. Allison and Busby, 1979.

Lemoha, Ositadinma Nkeiruka. "Uncovering Myriad Femininities in Nawal El Sadawi's A Daughter of Isis and Love in the Kingdom of Oil." *Gender, Culture and Development in Africa.* Eds. M.E Sotunsa and O. Yacob-Haliso. Pan-African UP, 2017. 19-30.

Marshall, Paule. *Brown Girl, Brown stones.* 1958. The Feminist Press, 1981.

.... *The Chosen Place, The Timeless People.* Harcourt Brace & World, 1969.

Mathews, Jill. Good and Mad Women: The Historical Construction of Femininity in *Twentieth Century Australia*, George Allen and Unwin, 1984.

Messerschmidt, James W. Hegemonic Masculinity: *Formulation, Reformulation, and Application.* New York: Rowman and Littlefield, 2018.

Montagu, Ashley. *The Natural Superiority of Women.* 1952 New revised edition, Collier Macmillan publishers, 1974.

Osuji, Clara Ijeoma. "Stripped of the Vestiges of Dignity: Unpacking the Knapsack of Female – Suffocation in John Munonye's *Oil Man of Obange and* Chimamanda Ngozi Adichie's *Purple Hibiscus." On* Justice, Equity and Dignity: Recreating Womanbeing in Contemporary African Society, edited by Ngozi Ezenwa-Ohaeto and Ijeoma C. Nwajiaku. Prof. Ezenwa-Ohaeto Resource Centre, 2019, 47-64.

Pilcher, Jane and Imelda Whelehan. *Fifty Key Concepts in Gender Studies.* Sage Publications, 2004.

Russ, Joanna. *The Female Man.* United States and Bantam Books, 1995.

Simoes da Silva, Tony. *The Luxury of Nationalist Despair: George Lamming's Fiction As Decolonizing Project.* Rhodopi B.V, 2000.

Washington, Mary Helen. "Afterword." *Brown Girl, Brown stones,* by Paule Marshall. 1958. The Feminist Press, 1981.

CHAPTER 7

The Study of Feminism in Selected Works of Khushwant Singh

V. G. Sadh

Abstract

The depiction of women characters in Khushwant Singh's fictional world is silhouetted aligned with their enormous, panoramic backdrop, the immense human calamity of the partition as presented from men's point of view. It suggests and indicates the appalling and horrid experience of women involved in this chronological and dehumanized progression. There are stories of characters that bring out Khushwant Singh's deep insight into human psychology especially women's psychology. It is essential to evaluate Khushwant Singh's short stories to observe either female characters in his fictional world are marginalized or he has given them due credit. It is because social exclusion or marginalization is normally blight to the woman at an individual level and society at the public level which is an obstacle in the interests of women.

Keyword: Feminism, Marginalization, Social exclusion, Patriarchal, Oppression

Introduction

Khushwant Singh ranks among India's distinguish men of letters who have attained an international reputation. Even a brief account of his achievements as a novelist, short story writer, historian journalist, and editor should be enough to establish his status in Indo-Anglian writing and bring out his versatility. He is the solitary Indian author who has been writing in English for over four decades and who is capable of playing down his achievements.

In this well-known novel 'Train to Pakistan' Singh appears to be uninterested in sketching female characters. He has sketched a only some female characters that have no voice of their own. His feminine characters are feeble, passive, marginalized and above all the sufferers of family and colonial domination and they symbolize the destiny of all Indian women of the era. In *Train To Pakistan* the writer has represented feminine character not only as a second gender somewhat she has been made irrelevant all over the narratives apart from she is a corporeal and sexual entity. She is born to provide her body to the male dominion. She is dwelling without any home, country, and kith and kin. Singh's women characters plead to the compassion in the sense that they are the sufferer of the situations. India and Pakistan's partitions on religious lines, scarcity, colonial exploitations, and conventional societal configuration have destitute them of their authorized right of living as human beings. Khushwant Singh appears to be compassionate to the weaker gender and he can imply Postcolonial gender. *Train To Pakistan* does not have so many women characters but the author has competently narrated gender complications and conflicts reflecting the position of peasant women mistreated and dishonored by the social arrangement and separation.

Khushwant Singh's short stories are patriarchal in temperament. Patriarchy offers liberty to men merely and women have subsidiary positions. Eighteen short stories out of thirty-two stories are quite Patriarchal in nature where men are governing and dominating. In 'Kusum', is a Cinderella story that unpretentiously describes the healthy joy that is released with the emergence of natural feminine instincts. It is a short story about a girl, as is clear from the title. She is not a normal girl, her appearance and her way of thinking are all together are different from the other women. She does never apply anything on her face, never wears smart clothes and in a way does never try to look attractive. She feels that nobody pays any attention to her because she is ugly and that is why she has no interest in boys. She goes to college on bicycle regularly, studies well, and gets good marks every year. She is no burden on her parents but there is always a burden in her heart that nobody likes her and even notices her presence. The story is based on the patriarchal impression that attractiveness only can craft women's life significantly.

'Karma 'depicts the slavish psychology of the educated Indian in British India and is marked by irony and inversion. Sir Mohanlal, a Barrister, is a person symbolizing British aristocracy and English culture so much that he does not like Indian people who don't live a highly sophisticated life. He always travels in a first-class compartment so that he can meet English officers and talk to them in English. He wears 'Balliol tie' while traveling and reads the English paper 'The Times'. He has a packet of English cigarettes in a gold case and orders scotch and whisky. He does all these to impress the English people. Sir Mohan Lal didn't love his uneducated spouse and her companionship. He visited her rarely in a while at hours of darkness and stayed for hardly any minutes. He controlled her in anglicized Hindustani, and she follows him submissively. The dominating personality of Mohan Lal with his spouse becomes susceptible about the English soldiers who despite their low services rank are capable to govern Mohan Lal due to their racial and imposing preeminence.

'The Memsahib of Mandla' is another story on the supernatural theme. In the story 'The Memsahib of Mandla' the red brick house, situated in the center of a small clearing in a Jungle, is the scene of the tragic play of the supernatural. John Dyson his wife and their daughter Jennifer arrived at the red brick bungalow on a holiday. On the first evening at the time of dinner, Jennifer saw a picture on the wall but neither her mother nor father pays any attention to the statement. Mrs. Dyson told John that she did not like the place and she could not sleep and decided to take a stroll. Then again Jennifer saw the ghost in a white dressing gown. So both the mother and daughter are afraid and they tell about their fear to Mr. Dyson, but Mr. Dyson does not believe in such things. On the next morning, Mrs. Dyson told John that she had seen a woman in a white dressing gown. John was then taken to the lawn and was shown the footprints. The footprints came to end near the grave. The following night John loaded his gun. In the night Dyson saw the woman in white. He caught the butt and fired and instead of firing at the ghost he kills himself. John Dyson in this story is the model of male bigotry and chauvinism. He overshadowed the overall characters in the story. All the time Dyson suppresses his wife Mrs. Dyson. He is not thoughtful or responsive about her approach and emotions. Although she doesn't prefer to stay the place due to his stubborn and dominating attitude, she submits herself. Mrs. Dyson, Memsahib, and Jennifer are overlooked and marginalized.

'A Bride for the Sahib' is yet another story of a westernized oriental gentleman and his typically Indian wife. Srijut Santosh Sen, an oxonian and Indian civilian was married to Ku. Kalyani Das is in rather odd circumstances. Mr. Sen, by nature reticent, wished to behave like a cultured, polished, dignified Englishman. His mind, personality, and conduct bore the stamp of Tory England. His wife Kalyani was a very shy, unsophisticated girl. Sen was her exact opposite. He drinks whisky and soda, while Kalyani ate betel leaves.

He ate western food while Kalyani took rice and lentil curry. After few days Kalyani was found dead as she had taken an overdose of pills. *'A Bride for the Sahib'* is a story of the intense human predicament and brings temperamental, social, and marital dissonance. Mr. Sen could not fathom the depth of Kalyani's bitter frustration and pain which made her end her life. Santosh Sen and Kalyani are individuals in their own right: Yet they are also types, representing different facets of Indian Society in British India. Mr.Sen in the story is a distinctive example of patriarchy. He listens to his mother. He accepts to marry Kalyani only for his mother's contentment. He has no concern for her. On the other hand, Kalyani is a classic case of the conventional Indian woman. She is completely dependent. In the system of patriarchy, once the girl is wedded she cannot anticipate any help from her parents. Kalyani too sent for the residence of in-law despite her unwillingness and the consequence is her suicide. This situation prevails in India still today as women are concealed and suffocated.

Chisti in the short story 'The Red Tie' is delegate of patriarchal sumptuous pleasure seeking men. He defines 'wedding is like chewing gum, sugary in the starting, sticky in the end'. He is as anglicized as Mohan Lal in the story 'Karma' but much more lecherous. Men never regard as them timid. Chisti is one of them. Although he is timid, he doesn't demonstrate his timidness. On the other hand, he tries to brag over the others. He is very quiet patriarchal in his opinion.

Khushwant Singh has not dishonored the social norms of Indian culture in the protuberance of women in his work. Women appear as passive representatives in most of his work who pursue the patriarchal norms and being subjugated, marginalized and set aside second in gender level. Khushwant Singh talks of love sex, his women characters are also gets equal importance. He has a deep insight and understanding of human psychology. Singh portrays the preponderantly physical reality of woman's passion for man and man's irrepressible desire for woman and creates an effect of surprise. Whether it is Bindo or Dalip Singh in 'The Rape', or Moola Singh's pretty daughter and Hansen in 'The Punjab Patoral' or Martha the black negress and Banarjee in 'Black Jasmine' or Kusum in 'Kusum'.

Conclusion

Every character in Khushwant Singh's work primarily deals with men and women living in society. These characters possess a personality of their own and act in and out of society. We found patriarchal and marginalized attitudes in most of his work. Women in his writing have become the victim of social and family dominance and suppression. Her dependency on others was marginalized in most instances. Therefore, as are there the consequences of social barring like inferior complexity, crime, health, etc., it is not necessary to take a posture on labeling and naming of the errands complete by individuals. Not a single task is of woman and man only. It can be passed out either by women or men. And it is probably only through societal work raising the awareness of the marginalized person i.e. woman. The same consciousness of male supremacy and female subordination would not end though we want to discontinue it.

Works Cited

Dadas, AN. (2010). "Feminist Reading of 'Karma' by Khushwant Singh", *Vishwabharati* 2 148-150. Print.

Naik, M.K. (1989). *A History of Indian English Literature.* New Delhi: SahityaAkademi, Print.

Singh, P.K. (2005) *The Novels of Khushwant Singh: A Critical Evaluation.* Jaipur: Book Enclave, Print.

Singh, K. (2003). *The Collected Short Stories of Khushwant Singh.* New Delhi: Ravi Dayal and Permanent Black, 3rdimp. Print.

Singh, Khushwant. (2007). *Train To Pakistan.* Penguin Books.

........, (2007). *Absolute Khushwant: Khushwant Singh with Humra Quraishi*, Penguin Books.

CHAPTER 8

Exemplification of Apocalyptic World in Bernard Malamud's *The Assistant*

Mamta Garg

Abstract

The Assistant, published in 1957 established Malamud as one of the leading writers on the scene of contemporary American fiction. The celebration of Jewishness incorporated as an essential premise in the plot of the novel represents the transformation of essential Jewish life into a life of want and misery, aggravated by the incidence of economic discrimination and deprivation. The narrative presents a dismal picture of poverty and frustration. Frank Alpine had come to America in search of 'new life', but all his dreams and hopes of seeking a bright future prove futile. All the personages in the novel meet frustration and failure, instead of the contemplated bright future. Both Morris as well as Frank, in other words the grocer and his assistant, saint and sinner, Jew and Gentile, present interpenetration, a symbolic juxtaposition of characters and destinies. Considering the totality of the narrative in The Assistant, it can be said that the Morris – Helen – Alpine tripartite axis of suffering and regeneration, constitute the thematic crux of the novel. Everything else contributes to the same formulation. *The Assistant* can thus be called an elaborate rendition of the theme of suffering which runs through the entire Malamudian fictional cosmos.

Keywords: American World, Quest, Futile, Apocalyptic, Illusory Reality.

The Assistant, published in 1957 established Malamud as one of the leading writers on the scene of contemporary American fiction. This is the most direct and perhaps the most moving of all Malamud's novels. In this work, the spectacle of an increasing general prosperity for American Jews becomes an illusory reality. The typical Jewish figure, symbolized by the personages of a Jewish family in the novel, represents a need to redefine and reconsider the allegiance of American Jews as Jews and as Americans. The celebration of Jewishness incorporated as an essential premise in the plot of *The Assistant*, represents the transformation of essential Jewish life into a life of want and misery, aggravated by the incidence of economic discrimination and deprivation.

The Assistant also presents the most thorough exploration of the theme of suffering prior to *The Fixer* that Malamud ever attempted. This tale of the relationship between a poor Jewish grocer and an Italian boy who comes on the scene to rob the former and stays on to exchange identities, reminds one of the simplicity of the dramatic form, its allegorical motif and its ethical perspective of a morality play. *The Assistant* can also be called a fable of good and evil, warring for every man's soul. But if the term Morality play suggests an abstract sophisticated approach, it is perhaps misleading, for despite the semi-naiveté of its characters and its parable like quality, *The Assistant* becomes a highly artful exercise in the psychology of guilt, and the idea of redemption through suffering. The Jew Gentile relationship also forms an important facet in the central action of the novel.

The Assistant as the title of Malamud's novel suggests the idea of assimilation as well as alienation. Frank Alpine, an Italian Christian, involves himself in a hold-up at the grocery store of an old Jew, Morris Bober. Morris's pretty young daughter, Helen Bober, becomes the enchantress for Alpine and in order to possess her sexually, the Italian gentile offers his services as an assistant to Morris, at the latter's shop. What happens in the aftermath of this arrangement provides much of novel's action. The Bober family epitomizes Jewish suffering and deprivation in a socially and economically hostile environment. We are also provided with the pathetic description of the life of the old Jewish couple, Morris Bober and Ida Bober, with only their unrealized hopes and aspirations for themselves and their daughter, Helen.

The narrative employs the third-person limited point of view. Alpine as the protagonist of the novel, is of "Italian extraction", and "has come from the West looking for a better job". Frank as the apprentice tries to be altruistic in helping Bober to run the grocery store, but Frank's 'altruism' is only motivated by a deep desire to possess Helen. After committing the robbery at Morris's store in the company of Ward Minogue, a hoodlum. Frank repents of the heinous deed and wishes to expiate through free service at the store. While working for Morris, he is attracted by Helen, Morris's twenty three year old daughter, who works in a garment store and helps out the family with her earnings. Ida, Helen's mother becomes suspicious of Frank's designs and does not "like the way he looks on her", more so because he is a goy, a non Jew. Meanwhile, Frank has been stealing a little money; nevertheless when business is bad, puts a little of the stolen stuff back in the till. One day in the process of filching, he is caught red-handed by Morris and dismissed. The same night he rescues Helen from being raped by Ward, but almost rapes her himself, leaving Helen hysterical. The Jewish girl abhors the thought of Frank being an "Uncircumcised dog", yet he remains the main stay of the Bober family when their fortune declines. The store is kept open and Frank takes up a night job to collect enough money for Helen's admission to a college, hoping thus to win back her trust and love. The process of his inner transformation is symbolized when "after Passover he becomes a Jew". Frank's repentance and moral regeneration get climaxed by his undergoing circumcision and entering the Jewish faith. Yet the irony and ambiguity remain. Inspite of Frank's sacrifice, his being accepted by Helen Bober remains unresolved till the end.

The narrative presents a dismal picture of poverty and frustration. Frank Alpine had come to America in search of 'new life', but all his dreams and hopes of seeking a bright future prove futile. This is essentially because he willingly takes up on his back, "the same wretched store, and the same wretched life that crushes his dead employer". Alpine's quest turns absurd and his dreams prove ironic. The Bobers also become the frustrated victims of time. Morris Bober "had escaped out of the Russian army to the U.S.A., but once in a store he was like a fish fried in deep fat". The world of the Bobers is materially speaking bleak; morally it glows with a faint constant light. Morris and his wife Ida toil sixteen hours a day in a grocery store, barely eking out a living. In the gloomy world of Bobers night gives way not to day, but only to a night less dark. If time promises Bobers anything, it is only the constant anxiety of an insecure present, extending backward and forward and usurping not only memory but hope, as Malamud says, "he had hoped for much in America and got little. And because of him Helen and Ida had less. He had defrauded them, him and the blood sucking store". Morris is the quintessential instance of the Jewish sufferer, whose enemy is life itself: "I gave away my life for nothing", these words constitute the Jew's final reflection. In the depiction of the Bober family, particularly Morris, Malamud's celebration of Jewishness makes suffering the thematic core of *The Assistant.* Yet, it is not Morris

Bober's suffering that becomes most significant but the suffering of Frank Alpine on which the novel centre's. Ostensibly, suffering here in Malamud's novel is illustrated as a quality of the human world in general. It can be said that for Bober as well as for Frank, for the Jew as well as the gentile, suffering is "the thunderous truth". Morris laments his fate because "the right thing was to make the right choice but he had made the wrong even when it was right it was wrong", and for his family "he had not provided the poor man's disgrace".

Just as Morris is entombed in his grocery store, all the other souls are also imprisoned in the same situation. Helen, too, had dreamt for "a college education but had got instead a job". She tells Frank "I want a larger and better life. I want the return of my possibilities". But all these prospects she never achieves, and remains a girl "with little promise of a better future". Ida, Morris's wife also shares "unwillingly the grocer's fate". She keeps on waiting that a buyer will come and purchase the store, but that never happens and when a buyer does appear, he leaves without buying the store. Thus, all the personages meet frustration and failure, instead of the contemplated bright future. The horizon of attainment, joy and bliss seems to be an ever receding one. Both Morris as well as Frank, in other words the grocer and his assistant, saint and sinner, Jew and Gentile, present interpenetration, a symbolic juxtaposition of characters and destinies. Considering the totality of the narrative in *The Assistant*, it can be said that the Morris-Helen-Alpine tripartite axis of suffering and regeneration, constitute the thematic crux of the novel. Everything else contributes to the same formulation.

The Assistant can thus be called an elaborate rendition of the theme of suffering which runs through the entire Malamudian fictional cosmos. In the growth of Frank's vision and Morris's forbearance, the value of suffering is of crucial relevance. It is quite appropriate to call Morris the ethical centre of the novel, for he embodies in his life-style the essential spirit of Jewishness and of humanity. Bober is the selected victim of capricious fate; he is also a schlemiel, an unfortunate person, who fails, despite all his endeavors to succeed. The exhausting grind of each day starts at six O' clock in the morning, when he drags in the heavy milk carton and sells a sour – faced old polish woman, a three cent bread role:

> "The early November Street was dark though night had ended; but the wind, to the grocer's surprise, already clawed. It flung his apron into his face as he bent for the two milk cases at the karb. Morris Bober dragged

the heavy boxes to the door panting. A large brown bag of rolls stood in the doorway along with the sour faced, grey-haired polished huddled there who wanted one".

Morris continues like this till late at night. These words symbolize what is to be the final horror of Morris's predicament; dispossessed of nature he retreats into a store which represents a deeper dispossession. What we witness is a suffusion of images of claustrophobic containment, the grocery store being repeatedly referred to as a prison.

In spite of being poverty – stricken and facing harsh and brutal realities of life, the Morris family as the symbol of Jewishness never displays arrogance or atheism or ever yields to despair. The most significant point made in the narrative is that despite being poor, one can be good. Morris is luckless, but morally he is superior to one-dimensional Jewish go-getters, who flourish in business but know not the tragic qualities of life. As a Malamudian Jew, the grocer has infinite compassion for the poor who suffer like him. He always offers a glass of tea to Breitbart, the destitute peddler, who sells light bulbs. It is this quality of Morris, which finally leads to Frank's redemption. What Frank wishes to realize, first through self-purgation and later through conversion, is the meaning of being human in a life dominated by dogmas and doctrines.

Initially, Frank Alpine is a Jewish hater and makes a Jew his victim, but as the tale proceeds, "the structural pattern of moral experience grows broader and deeper. After encountering Morris Bober, Alpine the gentile discovers the affinities between a Jew and a Christian. Frank learns through another human being a law of conduct, which might give meaning to the burden of suffering. As he accepts faith, he "paradoxically eradicates the barriers between theologies". The grocery store, which is Bober's predicament becomes a haven for Alpine. It also becomes the dreary locus of his painful rebirth. A gentile becomes a Jew's spiritual son – who lives by the law. In the fictional cosmos of *The Assistant*, the Malamudian celebration of Jewishness through the figure of Morris Bober includes in its climactic phase the painful moral regeneration of a repentant gentile. Consequently, the emphasis in the narrative shifts after the early pages to Alpine whose story thereafter is one of conflict of ambivalent impulses. Finally, after making his soul a battleground where the chief weapons used are guilt, debasement and self-punishment, Alpine becomes at the end of the novel a *pharmakos*, who has to sacrifice his religion in order to strengthen the apotheosis of Jewishness. The circumcision of Frank climaxes the celebration of Jewishness:

> One day in April Frank went to the hospital and had himself circumcised. For a couple of days he dragged himself around with a pain between his legs. The pain enraged and inspired him. After Passover he became a Jew.

The catalyst for Frank's conversion to Judaism is the irrepressible love he has for Helen Bober. After committing the abominable deed of raping the Jewish girl, he wants to rehabilitate himself in the eyes of Helen, and also longs for her love, and his stepping into the grocery store demonstrate the fulfillment of his dream, because in spite of taking the burden on his shoulders, "his new identity brings him to the edge of peculiar kind of self-destruction". All the other personages also face such kind of failure and horrible nightmares, and they operate in the ironic mode. That is why in the whole narrative, Malamud piles irony upon irony which is not "dry", not, "scathing", yet produces an oppressive and suffocating atmosphere. The disparity between the "hopes, dreams and the aspirations of the characters in the novel and horrible reality that is insisted upon over and over again", as it denies the fulfillment of the character's dreams, produces the overwhelming pathos. As a pattern of fictional experience the two main personages of Malamud's novel, Morris Bober and Frank Alpine, become victims. Both are at odds with their environment. Frank is at odd even with himself, before his final acceptance of the Jewish faith. The energy of Morris and frank becomes the energy of opposition. The only difference is that the aggression in Morris is directed against poverty, whereas in the case of Frank it is directed against his own self, and consequently he becomes the victim. Both as rebel (Morris) and as victim (Frank), the American protagonist of Malamudian fiction labours in the ironic mode. As in existential fiction, the illusion of choice is maintained, though for Morris as well as for Frank choice brings no victory. Morris remains "a tragic figure fighting for life against overwhelming odds". Perhaps, because of this, Leslie Fiedler, sees *The Assistant*, as a "belated novel of the thirties, a last expression of the apocalyptic fears and Messianic hopes of those terrible but relatively simple times. Certainly *The Assistant* is a book which reminds us of ancestors rather than suggesting to us progeny….." Sidney Finkelstein is more accurate in seeing in the novel disillusion with all social promise. Charles Hoyt speaks about this dismal scenario of the novel, vis-à-vis the same ironic affinity which binds the characters: "Out of the dirt and the deprivation of the novel's slum setting there has come not the naturalistic cry of pain but an inescapable sense of mystic union the identity of the oppressor and the oppressed".

Since World War 2nd, there has been a profound and remarkable change in the nature and content of the American novel. The modernist American novel written from the beginning of the 1950's, has largely concerned itself with presenting a harsh, brutal and disquieting world in which human nature itself is at stake and society becomes a mob looking for a victim, a speaks about this dismal scenario of the novel, vis-à-vis the same ironic affinity which binds the characters: "Out of the dirt and the deprivation of the novel's slum setting there has come not the naturalistic cry of pain but an inescapable sense of mystic union the identity of the oppressor and the oppressed".

Since World War 2nd, there has been a profound and remarkable change in the nature and content of the American novel. The modernist American novel written from the beginning of the 1950's, has largely concerned itself with presenting a harsh, brutal and disquieting world in which human nature itself is at stake and society becomes a mob looking for a victim, a *pharmakos* to strengthen the forces of evil. The introspective and suffering Jew, in such a kind of society, has come to epitomize the Western man searching his soul, afflicted and disillusioned and grouping for meaning. Both Morris Bober and Frank Alpine become prototypical personages particularly Alpine, who views his condition not with anger but with pain and opts for self-laceration rather than external rebellion. Thus as an intrinsic component of the Jewish psyche in *The Assistant*, suffering becomes the primary quality, the main theme.

Works Cited

Malamud, Barnard, *The Assistant.* New York: Oxford University Press, 1957.

Dickstein, Morris, *Gates of Eden: American Culture in the Sixties.* New York: Basic Books, 1971.

Friedman, Alan, *The Turn of the Novel.* New York: Oxford University Press, 1966.

Francis, H.E., 'Bernard Malamud's Everyman', *Midstream.* 7 winter, 1961.

Waldmeir, Joseph J., *Recent American Fiction: Some Critical Views.* Boston: Houghton Mifflin Company, 1963.

Hassan, Ihab, *Radical Innocence: Studies in the Contemporary American Novel.* Princeton: Princeton University Press, 1961.

Field, Leslie A., and, Field, Joyce W., eds., *Bernard Malamud and the Critics*. New York: New York University Press, 1970.

Klein, Marcus, *The American Novel Since World War II*. Greenwich, Conn., Fawcett, 1969.

Fiedler, Leslie, *Waiting for the End*. New York: Stein and Day, 1965.

Finkelstein, Sidney, *Existentialism and Alienation in American Literature*. New York: International Publishers, 1965.

Hoyt, Charles A., "Bernard Malamud and the New Romanticism", *Contemporary American Novelists*, ed., Moore, Harry T. Carbondale, III: Southern Illinois University Press, 1964.

CHAPTER 9

Women Issues in Sarah Joseph's *Othappu*

Divya Das S P

Abstract

Sarah Joseph is marked as a realistic writer of Kerala in the literary world. The radical thoughts of Sarah find its expressions through writings while touching women's emotions, insecurity, sexuality, spirituality, relationships and subalternity in the particular structure. In *Othappu,* Sarah depicts the impact of social-cultural factors on the marginalized, suppressed, downtrodden and deprived women in a system. In addition to this, the norms of religion dominate and stretch in the lives of people at every walks of life. The author highlights various codes in the existing society which foreground in the literary pages revealing the turmoil of the marginalized sex. *Othappu* reflects the author's attitude of bringing change in the views of the common people. All her ideas and visions take shapes of various women characters and her revolutionary thoughts are represented in the actions of various characters.

Usually, we are exposed to the suffocated situations of women in the writings of many writers. As an activist, Sarah commits herself to share not only the female experiences but to give a deep insight into the feelings and psychology of women. She goes on disclosing the different female characters in the distinguished arena of social orders. A sophisticated girl's entry into celibacy and her dissatisfaction within the religious system, a married woman's distress and her way of realizing spirituality, the perception of religious dogmas among women of different age groups and discriminated conditions of men in the name of religious institution are drawn to evoke consciousness in public. As a humanist thinker, she identifies the destruction of values, integration and harmony in the human community and strongly criticizes the cruel issues of women in the name of practices. Besides, she brings forth the history of people and marks the transgression in the social strata from time. The attempt of woman's understanding of the gospel clearly reflects the potentiality of the author.

Keywords: Women, religion, society, issues and marginalize.

Sarah Joseph is recognized as a significant contributor to the Indian literary scenario. As a Malayalam writer, her focused area is the lives of women. This radiant personality fights for gender oppression and discrimination in the existing social structure. She continues this struggle not only through literary articulation but also places herself as a role model by participating in various movements against injustice. Her ideologies, thoughts and revolutionary ideas have a sense of responsibility to disassociate women from all bondages. In the contemporary world, her representation strikes each woman to realize her identity, confidence and to outgrow all short comings of life. Her concern for women is revealed through her feminist writings. It is marked that some communities in Kerala is matriarchal but the writings of Sarah propose to highlight the oppressed status and lives of women of various communities in this particular region. Sarah's activities consider some visions to bring changes in this realistic world. In this connection, she touches the women's emotions, insecurity, sexuality, spirituality, relationships and life in *Othappu.*

Othappu novel analyses socio-historical aspects of a particular community in Kerala. It exposes the women's issues, critical juncture, new possibilities and psychological conditions in the conditioned structure. Besides the traditional and conventional religious institution, family and social orders spread their power and try to establish domination over the marginalized, downtrodden and helpless women. The radical thoughts of Sarah not only articulate her demand to discard women's issues but also stress the essentiality of women's identity.

Sarah's writings find the concern for women which universally address the power of women. She deserves a remarkable status as a potential Christian woman writer in the field of Indian English literature. In *Othappu*, she presents the realities of woman's celibacy, marital life, poverty, responsibilities, single life, emotions, spiritual thoughts and psychological situations in Kerala region. Particularly her questions connects to the hegemonic norms of religion towards woman and controlling acts of the institution. Depiction of a new vision to liberate women from the clutches of religious order is reflected.

Jancy James writes:

> The Malayalam word 'othappu', which is the colloquial equivalent for *uthappu*, a word from the Malayalam (Catholic) Bible, means 'falter' or 'stumble', that is, cause someone to lose faith and turn to evil ways.[1]

With modernist perspectives, Sarah identifies the strength of a woman within the religious orders and provides a new vision to empower her. She creates such awareness through the portrayal of a reverend nun, Margalita. The structure of celibacy and norms of the cloister are presented with the striking narration of the author. Margalitha renounces her sophisticated traditional catholic family to accept the religious life. Ignoring her affectionate father's objection to nun ship, family's wealth and worldly happiness, she enters the cloister to fulfill her dream of serving the needy.

"Devine calling" is often a common feeling in every catholic girl to submit herself to the service of nunship. This instance arrives in the life of Bama, the author of *Karukku* and she joins to complete her dream of serving her society like Margalitha in *Othappu*. Binaries of situations place them at different levels. They surpass the threshold of the institutional order to realize their dream. Bama's rejection of convent life opens a way to serve her Dalit community without institutional restrictions. Margalitha's repudiation of nunnery for the sake of the priest, Karikkan, directs her to continue the mission of service with her ideologies.

Inside the sacred vocation, Margalitha dedicates herself to the religious devotion. She has denied all family relationships with a thought of selfishness. But her dream and desires are against to the restricted life of the nun ship. Her imagination of motherhood and thought of platonic love nowhere allow her to co-operate with the restricted system. She takes initiative of transgression to come out of the restricted world. The social and religious sin of Margalitha never allows to get shelter in her own reputed family. Her act is a symbol of empowerment from the bonded life inside the nunnery. On the contrary, Karikkan has no such courage to face the entire world like Margalitha.

The author delineates the grounded experiences of the living world. Margalitha's character lives out of marital system which remarks Sarah's idea of love beyond the norms of marriage. The ex-nun enjoys the motherhood of born and unborn babies standing against various obstacles of the social conventions. The past willing detachment lingers in front of Margalitha to fulfill the worldly responsibilities as a docile nun. Facing shaky situation, she travels ticketless in the train to hide herself from the public without shelter. Nowhere, she feels to end her life and boldly moves to live in this distressed world.

Service of humanity in the mind of Margalitha opens various turns. She encounters limitations in the patriarchal systems. Even she realises marginalized activities for nuns which are preserved only for the priests in the religious orders. The female spirituality is depicted as oppressive in the narration of Margalitha's ideas. Karikkan's unexpected attitude to extend emotional support to Margalitha pushes her to darkness. He never has positive mind set to protect Margalitha but leaves her in Kasseessa's house and in a Syrian Christian's family. Cowardly he manages to make settlement in her mother's and brothers' home. The unborn child in the womb of Margalitha terrifies him and takes him to the escapist world.

Besides institutional hypocritical structure, the male domination senses are displayed on her arrival into the family. Margalitha's departure from the nunnery is considered as the dishonourable act. Her brothers', mother's and family members temperaments are too cruel and thrusts her into the virtual dungeon.

The author writes:

> Bitter words. Hard voice. It was Margalitha's Amma's words and voice.
>
> Even in her swoon, these words pierced her like burning coals thrust into wounds.[2]

Insecurity haunts her at every step and brothers deny to confer family property and a job in their own school. Undying trust to live her life insists her to find a financial support. At the end of the novel, the humbleness of her mother is shown in the form of the title deed and a sophisticated family prestige is offered through the proposal of advocate Chiramel but her deep routed sacrifice and humble life liberates her from these worldly things. Such emancipated woman tries to meet her dream of serving humanity individually.

Aabelamma is also a nun like Margalitha but with different shades of background and belongs to other generation. The Author notes Aabelamma's life:

> It brought immeasurable relief to their father, immense prestige to the family and augured an economic boon for her seven brothers.
>
> The youngest sister could be married off. Aabelamma's vocation had been a sort of transaction.[3]

Margalitha's "sacred calling" has made her to renounce the richness and affection of the family willingly but Aabelamma has forced to accept the celibacy sacrificing hopes and desires. The main intention is to come out of the burden of poverty. Aabelamma is aware of Margalitha's disturbed mind. Her revolutionary and realistic thoughts regarding the convent inspire Margalitha to leave the codes and place. The coining of the word "caught" in her discourse of the institutional set up describes her awareness about the sacred vocation. Portrayal of Aabelamma itself is evident of feminist views in the novel. Inside the holy system, she is rebellious of their norms and indirectly condemns the suppressed nuns' life in the cloister. Her silent defiant nature represents psychological and emotional thoughts of a religious convent woman.

Rebekka, a powerful female character expresses spirituality in her own way. She accepts the role of a Pentecostal preacher without any religious institutional bondage. Her character is appreciable for the multiple modes of engagement as a committed wife, a cook and the god's preacher.

Rebekka is mirrored to show the level of parent's ill-treatment and tortured marital status. Unwilling wedlock with the aged vaidyar, Thomas disappoints her strikingly. The unquestioned cruelty of the husband is defended to find her way for the survival.

In the field of spirituality, she proves her own ideologies. In Kerala, the majority of people are controlled and monitored within the realm of the church and the priest. These spiritual leaders have some restrictions related to the religion and spirituality. Rebekka upholds her distinct aspect of receiving the Holy Spirit through her healing sessions without expecting monetary benefits from the public. Her resistance towards the dictators stresses the idea to have direct link with the God.

Rebekka's mission is to liberate the needy and the suffered discharging her services. Lonely she asserts the dominant institutional agents:

> 'Those who stuff their stomachs three-four times a day will not receive the holy spirit! I have suffered much. I have begged. Suffered rejection and abuse at the hands of the rich. Maddened by hunger, I have eaten paper soaked in water. Have stayed indoors for days, lacking even rags to cover my nakedness. Have suffered all these; and more sorrow; sorrow upon sorrow. Won't God come down to me in all His Majesty?[4]

Boldness of Rebekka tries to rescue Margalitha from the violence of her brothers, John and Paul. Against the tyranny of men and religious institution, a fighter – Rebekka has accompanied Margalitha in the short journey of life.

The author highlights Rebekka's identity noticing her counter with the elite preacher, Chandy Doctor. She exposes the corruptive mindset of this wealthy preacher in the public. She gains the trust of the common people with her individual's faith towards God and opposes the doctrines of the mainstream.

The discussion of sister Jereemia's act of offering the Eucharistic sacrifice to God exhibits taboos within the religious institution to limit the woman's identity. Sister Jereemia trespasses the ritual and such act victimizes her with blasphemy. Those confinements are questioned to voice their exclusion.

Yohannan Kassessa's mother, Annamkutty has entered into the marital bond with a Syrian Christian. Outwardly, she shows herself as a follower of Syrian Christian. Inside, she sincerely follows her catholic practices. Celebration of her individual freedom in connection to religion is expressed in battling to protect her deep rooted tradition.

On one side, the author attempts to show the existing limits of religion to prohibit the mobility of women. On the other side, with versatile women characters interpret the challenges and the realistic mindset of women to realize their individualistic existence. The instance of nuns' visit with gifts to Margalitha's place at the end with a secret pleasure echoes the indirect supportive attitude towards emancipation.

The author's universal message in the novel evokes spirit in every woman to seek the light of courage and confidence. She presents herself as a role model for the women's writings with her commitments and supportive voice to the women's folk. Every discussed idea in the novel inspires a movement for women's group to have a new way of life in the bounded order of this world.

Joseph's coining of the word "Othappu" itself tunnels into the idea of liberating humanity from the clutches of suffocating system. She weaves stories of Jesus with the contemporary situations to preach his real teachings which are applicable even to the present world.

Works Cited

1. Joseph, Sarah. *Othappu.* Trans. Valson Thampu. *The Scent of the Other Side.* New Delhi: OUP, 2009. xx. Print.
2. *Ibid,* p.45.
3. *Ibid,* p.05.
4. *Ibid,* p.39.

CHAPTER 10

Parveen Shakir: Master of the Art of Articulating Thoughts

Abdul Anees Abdul Rasheed

Abstract

Parveen Shakir seems to have a remarkable mastery over the communication of thoughts. Her poetry adequately translates the inner thoughts and emotions. Her words are loaded with a deal of joy, pain, wonder and inspiration. Her distinctiveness lies in her creative brilliance and belief in human emotions. Though she was highly proficient in English, Urdu had always been her first love. She used Urdu as mode of expression. Shakir was determined to make a mark of her own in the male dominant society. She was not an established feminist, but her works reflect the elements of feminism and romanticism from a purely female perspective. She can be arguably considered the first poetess to metaphorically use the word 'larki' quite often in her prose and poetry. Her writings embody all shades of human emotions from selfless devotion, love, solitude, separation to renunciation.

Keywords: Selfless love, Devotion, Subjugation, Gender Bias, Marginalization.

Parveen Shakir (1952-1994), a Pakistani third world Muslim female poet; a rare combination of beauty with brains was born in Pakistan. She is one of the finest poets of the modern era who masters the art of communicating thoughts in a very celebrated manner. Her poetry is about giving words to emotions. The words in her poetry seem to be loaded with a deal of joy, pain, wonder and inspiration. Though, much like rest of the world number of poetesses in Pakistan is relatively less, the name of Parveen Shakir beautifully makes up for this gap. Her creative brilliance and belief in human emotions make her stand out. She was highly proficient in use of English language, but Urdu had always been her first love. She majorly used Urdu as a mode of communication. She was honored with Pride of Performance by the Government of Pakistan in 1976 for her outstanding contributions to Urdu literature.

Shakir was determined to make a mark of her own in the male dominant society and she tried hard to realize this dream in all fields from education to professional to literary. She has six books on her credit which have been received by the audience and critics. These are *Qushboo* (1976) – *Fragrance, Sad-barg* (1980) – *Marsh Marigold, Qud Kalaami* (1990) – *Talking to Oneself, Inkaar* (1990) – *Denial, Maah-e-Tamaam* (1994) – *Full Moon* and *Kaf-e-Aayena* (1997) – *The Edge of the Mirror.*

Shakir was not an established feminist, but she has enjoyed writing about feminism and romanticism from a purely female perspective. She pioneered the trend of using terms that could personify women rightly. She can be arguably considered the first poetess to metaphorically use the word *'larki'* (girl) quite often in her prose and poetry.

Her writings embody all shades of human emotions from selfless devotion, love, solitude, separation to renunciation. It is widely believed that the shades of agony in her poetry are result of her failed marriage.

This paper is an attempt to deal with the selected couplets from her *Qushboo* (1997) – *Fragrance* with a female perspective. Most of the poetic works in this volume carry the autobiographical elements of the poet, but at the same time, it is the voice of all the females who have gone through the same situations that Parvin Shakir had to. Her poetry mostly deals with –

> …love, feminism, and social stigmas, though she occasionally wrote on other topics as well. Her work was often basedon romanticism, exploring the concepts of love, beauty and their contradictions, and heavily integrated the use of metaphors, similes and personifications.

Parvin Shakir lived in the patriarchal society. Hence, she closely observed how a woman has to mutely tolerate the social and cultural atrocities. Moreover, she was born and brought up in a rigid Pakistani Muslim patriarchal family. She wanted to establish her own identity. She believed in individuality, self-actualization, and to the much extent she succeeded. However, at the emotional and psychological level, she always kept pining for something unattainable. Nida Fazli has rightly expressed:

Kabhi kisi ko Mukammal Jahan Nahi Milta
Kahin Zameen to Kahin Asman Nahi Milta

Nobody can achieve the whole world (s)he aspires
Somewhere, (s)he has to lose earth, somewhere sky. (own translation)

Her poetry reflects woman's longing for the unattainable which results in that she feels herself mentally and emotionally devastated.

Dil Use Chhahe Jise Aqal Naahi Chhahti Hai
Qaana Jangi Hai Ajab Zahen wo Badan me Ab ke. (P. 226)

Heart desires for something to which wisdom denies
Startling civil war is there between mind and body. (own translation)

This couplet reflects the woman caught in crisis: the crisis between passion and wisdom. She, on one hand, at heart, extremely loves someone and for that she is ready to do anything and on the other hand, she is restrained by her wisdom. She passionately desires to seek someone's love. But she gets frustrated when she is restricted by the moral or social restrictions; sometimes her wisdom forces her to give up the idea. Woman feels herself sandwiched between her heart and mind. This crisis is always with the sensitive woman; sometimes passion triumphs over wisdom and vice versa; sometimes she leaves it to the time and just waits. It reflects a woman's helplessness because she is bonded with both the mind and heart. She can't deny either. She keeps dangling between passionate desires and the controlling wisdom.

Parvin shakir has used her poetry as the medium of expression of what she could not do publicly. Her poetry is a kind of out let of the suppressed feelings. Her poetry is full of symbols, metaphors, allegories, etc. She argues in the foreword of one of her volumes of poetry entitled *Sadberg-*

Sachhai Jab Muqbiron Me Ghir Jaaye to Guftagu Alaamaton Ke Supurd kee Jaati Hai (Sadbarg, 1997)

When the truth is found to be under the trapping surveillance, it is communicated by means of symbols. (own translation)

Parveen Shakir's poetry, has also reflected the rigid and conservative male attitudes that have always influenced the social, cultural, economical, political and domestic status of women and particularly the matrimonial ties. Apart from these, the male dominancy is the key factor. Ironically, she is subjugated and taken for granted. Many times, her flaw is that she is flawless; her crime is that she is innocent. Unfortunately, the woman seems to be the mute witness of her own emotional and psychological apathy. She knows –

Main Such Kahoongi, Magar Phir Bhi Haar Jaoongi
Wo Jhoot Bolega, Aur La-jawab Kar Dega (P. 208)

I will tell the truth, still I will lose
And his lie will leave the listener unanswerable. (own translation)

This couplet reflects how the innocence of the woman is tortured in the patriarchal society: she is emotionally marginalized; her inner voice is not listened; she is psychologically segregated, and how man enjoys the privileges gifted to him by the patriarchal society. It is man's privilege that even if he is guilty, he is set free; he, though faulty, hardly admits his fault. Ironically, the woman has to surrender; she has to undergo the sufferings for doing nothing; and it is confirmed that many times, innocent souls are agonized without any concrete reasons.

Pareveen Shakir candidly represents the woman as a subaltern character: abused and exploited by the outside world; her own husband or lover. In fact the woman is the integral part in man's life. Her marginalization, her discard and humiliations, bring her despondency. She too has an independent individuality and her own potentials gifted by Almighty. But she is identified by her male companion. She seems to be groping her identity and her individuality in the darkness of hopelessness and ultimately she has to be tight-lipped. She can only cry over the futility of her own existence.

Parveen Shakir was aware of the woman's being emotionally attached with her lover or husband. The woman/girl, feels her lover/husband at her core of heart. She tries her level best to be faithful towards him. But it is man whose fidelity cannot be fully trusted. He treats her as if she is a toy; he hardly considers her feelings and emotions; he accompanies her as long as he enjoys her company and leaves her whenever he wants.

Woh to Qushboo Hai Hawaon Me Bikhar Jaayega
Masla Phool ka Hai, Phool Kidhar Jaayega (P. 188)

He is the fragrance, may be wafted by the air
Problem is with the flower, where shall it go? (own translation)

The poet used *qushboo*, fragrance and *phool*, flower symbolically. 'Fragrance' stands for man and 'flower' for woman. The flower without the fragrance may be attractive but worthless. The flower is worthy and valid as long as it produces the fragrance. It implies that the man, as an individual may be complete without woman but without man or husband, the woman is incomplete. Flower is liked and admired as long as it produces refreshing fragrance, but once its fragrance vanishes, it is either crushed or thrown away. The woman as a wife or beloved is like a flower whose fragrance is her husband or lover.

Here, the liberal attitudes of the man are shown. Ironically, it is up to the man how long to accompany the woman and when to leave her. When man deserts woman, he, being a man, is set free to accompany another one of his choice. This male tendency is compared with the spreading of fragrance of the flower in the air. And the deserted woman is just like the flower without fragrance. She is left helpless and hapless; not free to choose another one; she is completely devastated. This devastation is at mental, emotional, social and psychological level. She becomes a silenced witness of her own apathy. Her emotional disintegration and unpredicted desertion interrogates –

Koi Sawal Jo Pooche, To Kya Kahungi Us Se
Bichadne Wale, Sabab To Bataa Judaai Ka (P. 133)

If someone questions, what shall I say?
Oh! departing fellow, tell me the reason of separation.(own translation)

Agonized woman knows that she is flawless, yet deserted. In the patriarchal social setup, nobody interrogates man. She asks man to tell her what's wrong with her side; what is her fault; why she has been left at the mercy of fate; what made him to leave her; what are the concrete and justified reasons of the separation. Shakir's *ghazalyaat* are considered – "a combination of classical tradition with modern sensitivity"

Perveen Shakir's poetry reflects how woman has to bear injustice: social injustice, cultural injustice and the injustice in the name of morality. She has presented the woman as a victim of chauvinism and the victim of gender biased male attitude.

Shahadaten Mere Haq Me Tamaam Jaati Thi
Magar Qaamosh the Munsif, Nazeer Aisi Thi (P. 331)

All the evidences were in my favour
But the judges were reticent, as it was a unique case. (own translation)

Here is the focus on the gender biased mentality of male dominated society. When the apathy of the woman is brought to the notice of the so called social justices, they know that the woman is innocent; they also know that it is the man who is faulty; but the problem is that how man can be declared guilty. They can neither say anything nor extend their helping hands to the woman. It also reflects how the falsely generated norms and conditions of the male dominated society do not take woman into consideration; how obstructions are created on the way of woman's progress and her individual development. She is subordinated. And if she tries to get herself granted, she is either taken casually or not permitted to prove her potentials. Though she has her own identity, her distinct potentials, she is recognized just a wife of husband: subjugated and dependent. She is not permitted to enjoy her life the way she likes. The patriarchal society accepts and appreciates only the woman who are submissive and that's all. The woman or *larki* in the poetry of Perveen Shakir represents all the subjugated and oppressed women/girls. And to give justice to one may mean to generalize it. Her recognition, her self-actualization, may become the ideal for the rest. That's why the self-proclaimed social thinkers and social justices intentionally keep quiet.

Shakir has also touched the susceptibility of women. One of her free verses reflects this issue:

Majboori (Susceptibility)
Hawaayen,
Daustakon Me Mera Naam Le Rahi Hain
Mai Kawad Kaise Kholun
Mere Dono Haat Pusht ki Taraf Bandhe Huwe Hain (P. 265)

Breezes,
Knocking on the door and echoing my name,
How can I open the door?
My hands are tightened at my back. (own translation)

Hawaayen (breezes), *dastakon* (knocks), *kawad* (door), *haath* (hands) *pusht ki taraf* (at the back), and *Bandhe huwe* (tightened) all these words are allegorically used. Knock of the breeze symbolically stands for provocative opportunities for the woman to prove her individuality; to prove her capabilities; to enjoy her freedom as men do. *Daustakon Me Mera Naam le Rahi Hai,* Knocking on my door and echoing my name, may symbolically mean that the opportunities provoke the woman that she too has the right to live the way she likes; the freedom of thought and freedom of living with dignity as man has. *Mai Kawad Kaise Kholun*, How can I open the door? stands for woman's subjection; her helplessness. In fact, woman is not supposed to prove herself, though she is capable enough as per the demands and needs. *Mere Dono Haat Pusht ki Taraf Bandhe Huwe Hain*, my hands are tightened at the back, symbolizes the extreme point of woman's helplessness. If she had been normally tied, she would have ultimately succeeded in loosening the knot and freed herself. But when someone's hands are tightened at back, it is hardly possible for him/her to loosen the knot so as to get himself/ herself rescued. *...tightened at the back* also symbolizes the extreme point of rigidity; the inflexibility of the rules in the patriarchal society. It focuses on how woman is treated mercilessly. She is restricted in such a way that she can only breathe. She becomes a mute observer of her own predicament. It focuses on the emotional and psychological exploitation of the woman.

Shakir also touches the segregation of the woman. Shakir dreams of having a society in which the woman and man should have the equal privileges. Like man, the woman wants to be recognized, to be appreciated, and to be valued on the basis of her own qualities and distinct potentials. But it is impossible unless the social setup is restructured.

We can also have women's peculiar emotional implications which Shakir has very romantically reflected in her poetry:

Who Shaher Me Hai, Yahi Bahot Hai
Kis Ne Kaha Mere Ghar Hi Tahere (P. 328)

That he is somewhere in my town is enough for me,
Who forces him to stay at my home. (own translation)

Shakir has presented a very unusual aspect of woman's personality. She may be alone at home and pining for her lover. When she becomes to know that he is somewhere in the same town, she hankers to be with him. But she also knows that it is impossible for him: either he does not want to be with her or he may be restricted by someone or something from doing so. That's why she can only console herself saying *'Who Shaher Me Hai, Yahi Bahot Hai,* that he is somewhere in my town is enough for me. She is ready to adjust with the situation. Her love for him has made her submissive. Her adjustment is unconditional and selfless. She doesn't want to condition or blackmail him emotionally. Her love is pure and selfless. That's why for her, his very presence in the town is enough.

Shakir's poetry also covers a unique and mind-boggling feminine emotional implication. It reflects one of the aspects of woman's personality, though it is beyond her endeavor. Shakir writes –

Kamal-e-Zabt Ko Qud Bhi to Aazmaaungi
Mai Apne Haat Se Uski Dulhan Sajaaungi (P. 212)

I shall taste the culmination of my tolerance
I shall titivate his bride with my own hands (own translation)

Shakir focuses on the meekness of woman or a beloved. Instinctively, a beloved or a wife can bear anything, but it is beyond her tolerance that some other woman is sharing the love of her husband/lover. It may be due to the excessive sense of possession. But sometimes very odd situation occurs within which it is only the woman/beloved who is tasted and expected to compromise. Here, Shakir presents the woman as a submissive. She, only for the sake of her lover is ready to undergo the unbelievable ordeal in which the wife/beloved silently and reluctantly allows the another woman to share her husband. It shows very heartbreaking situation for the wife/beloved. But her emotional and psychological agony is reflected in the very following couplet.

Badan Ke Karb Ko Who Bhi Samajh Na Paayega
Mai Dil Me Roungi, Aankhon Me Muskuraungi (P. 212)

He too will not understand my physical torment
At heart, I will be crying, but externally pretend to smile. (own translation)

Though for the woman/beloved, such situation is soul-pricking, she has to bear. What may happen if the man has to face such odd situation? Man can hardly think about such devotion. The social construct shall not approve it as it is beyond imagination in male dominated society. *Mai Dil Me Roungi, Aankhon Me Muskuraungi,* At the heart, I will be crying, but externally pretend to smile. Parvin Shakir focuses on the selfless devotion of the woman. Only for the sake of her lover/husband she will pretend to be happy and her husband/lover may not realize it. But at the heart she will be completely devastated; at emotional level she will be broken; psychologically she will be extremely agonized. A most prominent literary figure, Iftikhar Arif has praised Shakir for impressing-

> "the young lot through her thematic variety and realistic poetry," for adding "a new dimension to the traditional theme of love by giving expression to her emotions in a simple and pellucid style," and using a "variety of words to convey different thoughts with varying intensities.

Shakir's poetry also reflects the woman's quest for freedom. Suppressed and agonized woman wants freedom from the tyranny of man and man-made social norms and conditions. She wants to have her own world of freedom; the world that may approve her identity and recognition. And for the fulfillment of this urge, she can pay any price, even separation from her husband. Shakir writes-

Bichadte Huwe Dilon Ko Agar Che Dukh to Huwa
Khuli Faza Me Magar Saans Lena Achha Laga (P. 288)

The moment of departing, though brought heavy pains to our hearts
But it was rather pleasant to breathe in open air (own translation)

Shakir focuses on the woman's urge for freedom: freedom of thoughts; freedom of expression; freedom of living without botheration and fear; freedom of choice. But in the patriarchal society, it is just like a mirage in the desert. But the secret of happy life lies in freedom. On one hand, the quest of freedom slowly ignites the woman and on the other hand, husband wants her to be dominated. Woman's immense desire for freedom has beautifully been summed up in the couplet of Wasim Barelvi –

Main Bhi to is Baagh Ka Ek Parinda Hun
Meri Hi Awaaz Me Mujhko Gaane De (Barelwi, Wasim. 2007, p.43)

I am too one of the birds of this garden
Let me sing only in my own voice. (own translation)

Wasim Barelvi has allegorically used *Parinda* and *Baagh*. *Parinda*, the free bird stand for the woman and *Baagh* stands for the human world. The woman wants to enjoy the freedom and a liberty in the society as the man does. She interrogates that she too has the potentials; she too has her individuality; she too has distinguishing attributes. Then she must be set free to prove herself. She should be allowed to articulate. She wants to exhibit her won god gifted qualities. *Meri hi Awaaz me Mujhko Gaane De,* Let me sing only in my own voice. She urges to let her prove these qualities, as these uncommon qualities can expose her uniqueness.

But she is unheard and even suppressed. Ultimately it causes the crisis between woman and husband/lover. And such crises ultimately lead to divorce/separation. The idea of divorce/separation is detestable for the woman, because it is the woman who has to bear the consequences of separation. Man is free to choose another partner. But, as an individual, the woman who is in pursuit for freedom has to scarify something or take some perilous decision, i.e. separation from husband.

No doubt, the separation or divorce causes unbearable pain. But *Khuli Fazaa me Magar Saans Lena Achha Laga,* but it was fairly pleasant to breathe in open air. It may occur for the woman when she is trapped in such crucial situation. In such cases, for a woman who is extremely lured by the idea of freedom, prefers even to be separated from her husband. It is because there is no other option left for her. Her pangs of separation are compensated by the sense of being rescued from the suffocating and stifling situations. Now she can console herself that at least she can now breathe in an open air; she is no more subjugated, she feels like a free bird flying and singing in its own world that knows no restrictions.

This is the time to consider the woman sympathetically as an individual. A renowned Urdu poet, Kaifi Azmi expresses in his poem entitled *Aurat* (the Woman):

Tu Haqeeqat Bhi Hai, Dil-chasp Kahani Hi Nahi
Teri Hasti Bhi Hai Ek Cheez, Jawaani Hi Nahi

Oh! Woman, you are too a concrete being and not only an interesting story,
Your being is too worth living and not only your youth. (own translation)

Works Cited

Barelwi, Wasim. *Mera Kya*, Maktaba Jamia Ltd. New Delhi, 2007.

http://hamariweb.com/newsdetails.aspx?id=2184 Archived 30 May 2013 at the Wayback Machine, Retrieved 18 Jan 2016

Shakir, Parveen. *Qushboo,* Fareed Book Depot, New Delhi, 1997.

CHAPTER 11

Altruisticc Nature of Women in Literature

Sindhu V. Jose

Abstract

If a person wants to find out the real meaning for mother, it is infinite. The mother is a shielder, strict authoritarian, peer, unselfish, loving human and so on. Altruism can be defined as a "unselfish regard for or devotion to the welfare of others; behaviour by an animal that is not beneficial to or may be harmful to itself but that benefits others of its species" (merriam. com.n.pag). Altruism is nothing but the incarnation of the mother. Altruism or the self sacrifice is none other than the Mothers of Nissim Ezekiel, Prof. A. Arunachalam and Dr. A.P.J. Abdul Kalam, the Former President of India. The self-effacing love of Nissim Ezekiel and Prof.Aruna's nobility of motherhood and Dr. Kalam's mother's piety have been portrayed as an avatar of virtues in their poems. In India, motherhood is thought as a celestial thing. The above mentioned three mothers sacrificed their whole life for the sake of their children and does not have desires of their own without expecting in return. They done all the duties without mussitation and vexation. They had been the epitome of the motherliness and the selected poems are the best examples of mothership.

Keywords: Altruism, self-effacing love, nobility, piety.

Introduction

Motherhood in India is considered as an ethereal, ambrosial and god like thing but still few mothers are not empowered. Mothers are made to forfeit their own happiness for the sake of their children. A good mother does not have a story of her known, for her everything, her living itself is her children. One who offers their endless, silent, undemanding love for her children is a good mother. Anyone can provide food, accommodation but all will not be tagged as mothers. A true mother is someone who cares and rearing her children with deepest and sincere love. If her child is in hurt or in fear a true mother alarms; she supports her child's dreams and paves them to the way of success. Righteous mother is a tutor, trainer, cheerer and a real fan of her child at all times.

Critical Analysis

Nissim Ezekiel is an Indian born Jew of Bene – Israel origin. He is one of the notable post-independence English poets and he belongs to the new poetry in Indian English poetry of the fifties. His most famous poem *Night of the Scorpion* portrays the solid forthright explanation on the passion of self-effacing love, the high-minded love of the Indian mother. This poem is in the form of a monologue that is in the form of first-person narrative of the agony that a son had to undergo watching his mother suffer due to a scorpion sting. The poet depicts the Indian ethos and cultured richness through a simple incident and exemplifies the typical Indian motherhood which illustrates sacrifice and affection. The poet cum the narrator remembers the night when the scorpion had bitten his mother. "I remember the night my mother/ was stung by a scorpion. Ten hours/ of steady rain had driven him/ to crawl beneath a sack of rice," (Lines 1-4). Heavy rainfall caused the scorpion to crawl under a sack of rice in the poet's home to keep itself away from water. Regrettably, a scorpion bites his mother's toe, parts with its poison and leaves the house.

The farmers and neighbours of villages come like legion of flies to sympathize with the poet's family. Here the bond between the individual families and the neighbourhood is perceptible. The relationship between the poet's family and the neighbouring grazier is vigorous. In metropolis life, perdurable relationship between neighbours is rare. The neighbours of the poet hunt for the scorpion with lanterns and lights and they start chanting the name of God with hope hundred times so that they can paralyze the scorpion. If the mother moves with pain, the poison will also spread. They chink their tongues so that the mother's sufferings may decrease the misfortunes in her next birth. "May the sum of evil/balanced in this unreal world/ against the sum of good become diminished by your pain, they said (Lines 23-26). They even pray that quantity of evil of her present may be balance against the sum of good of her past. They also implore that the poison of the scorpion must purify her desires and ambitions. Though the pain is the symbol of sins it also enacts as the sign of purgatory. The villagers was sitting around and in the centre his mother moaning and squirming with pain on the mat.

Being a rationalist and a practical man, Ezekiel's father tries cursings, blessings, powders, mixtures, herbs and hybrids. He pours a little paraffin upon his wife's bitten toe and put a match on it, hoping to burn the poison away. The poet as a little son watches the flames feeding on his mother. The holy man performs his rites and rituals to subdue the poison with a chant. One can explicitly see the rational belief of the poet's father and the irrational belief of the neighbours. The poison diminishes the mother after twenty hours and relieves from the pain. The nature of the Indian mother has been clearly depicts in the concluding lines of the poem. "After twenty hours /it lost its sting. My mother only said/Thank God the scorpion picked on me / And spared my children" (44-48). Here underlies the ecumenical truth that every Indian mother is ready to anguish all types of pains and tortures with a smiling face. Despite she will not bear any pain aggregate on her children.

As a woman, as a mother starts to undergo the gestation and cesarian pain, and later she sacrifices everything for the sake of her children that depicts the maternal and selfless love. The mother bears the pain and suffering for nearly twenty hours, twisting and groaning in pain. After recovery, she immediately thanks Almighty God that she was bitten and not her children, and for protecting her children. Children would not have tolerate the pain. She even hands over her life to the superstitious villagers and to her rationalist husband. The mother of Nissim Ezekiel is the representation of the Indian mothers who choose themselves to undergo pain before their children. The poem brings out the mother's love and sacrificial thoughts, the maternal instinct, caring love and so on. The mother is an unexpected winner of selfless love in the middle of the superstitious peasants and the villagers.

Avul Pakir Jainulabdeen Abdul Kalam served as the Eleventh President of India and affectionately known as the People's President and the Missile man of India. He comes from a poor family. His father, Jainulabdeen, a boat owner and imam of a local mosque and his mother, Ashiamma, a home maker. He was much affectionate towards his parents, especially towards his mother. His mother was a tall, good looking and deeply attached towards her children and an perfect spouse to her husband. Abdul Kalam wrote several books including an autobiography *Wings of Fire*. He won numerous awards including two prestigious awards of the country the Padma Vibushan and the Bharat Ratna.

Abdul Kalam has written many poems about his mother. This poem entitled *My Mother* depicts how he was loved by his mother than his brothers and his sister. Abdul Kalam was the youngest of five siblings. The eldest one was his sister, Asim Zohra, followed by three elder brothers namely: Muthu Meera Lebbai Maraikayar, Mustafa Kalam and Kasim Mohammed. "Sea waves, golden sand, pilgrim's faith, / Rameswaram, Mosque street, all merge into one, / My Mother!". (Lines 1-3) Abdul Kalam was born in the Pilgrim Centre of Rameswaram in a Muslim family. It is situated on Pamban Island. One can view the site of sea waves, golden sand under the sun light, the faith of pilgrims; his ancestral house was situated on the street where the mosque is situated. In front of his mother's love, all has been integrated into one. Nothing is high before mother's unending love.

The mother of Kalam come to him like Heaven's caring arms. During the second world war, the life become become very challenge and toil. Before sunrise, at four a.m., he has to walk many miles to take lessons from the saint teacher, Swamiyar and then to Arab school. His mother used to get up before Kalam and will give bath to him. The financial condition of the family forced him to work at a very tender age. Then, he used to climb sandy hills to railway station to collect and distribute newspapers to the temple city citizens. Because of the second world war the trains were all stopped and with the help of his cousin, Samsuddin, Kalam collect the newspaper bundles. After sunrise, it is the business time for Kalam. There was a great demand for tamarind seeds during the war time and he used to collect tamarind seeds and sell it for an anna. Thus he earned his first wages.

> "My mother you transformed into pious strength/with kneeling and bowing five times/ For the grace of the Almighty only, My Mother" (Lines 14-16).

Ashiamma, the mother of Kalam was gentle, reverent and a devout Muslim like her partner. She prayed namaz five times a day for the grace of the Almighty. Her children's strength was her strong piousness. She seems to be angelic during her namaz. His mother naturally a generous lady and feed limitless numbers of people. She always distributed the best to the needed.

It was full moon night and Kalam was ten years old, sleeping on his mother's lap. His elder brothers and sister envied when they saw this but the poor and the only soul who know about him is his mother. "When at midnight I woke with tears falling on my knee/ You knew the pain of your child, My Mother." (Lines 24-26) At midnight, the tears fell down his knees, and Kalam wake up. The tears are none other than but his mother. His mother with her soft, caring hands used to remove the pain. The love, the care and the faith of his mother gave him strength and gave him enough courage to face the world without fear. He concludes the poem by saying that he would meet his mother with the same strength during the Last Judgement Day i.e. after death. He has addressed six times as "My Mother" in this poem. The 'm' in Mother has been capitalized which shows the high esteem and accolade towards his mother.

Aruna, the assumed name of Prof. A. Arunachalam has published three volumes of poetry and a novel in English. The poem *My Mother* is a tribute to the poet's late mother. The poet succeeds in highlighting the nobility of motherhood in this poem. NOBILITY THY NAME IS MY MOTHER./FRAILTY NEVER HAD SHE ANY BUT/ ABILITY HAD SHE IN ALL. (Epigraph) In the above Epigraph, poet Aruna states that his mother's name is nobility and she had no weakness in her but she had the ability, that is, the talent, the power to do something. The epigraph at the beginning of the poem, the stanza format and the lengthy sentence show the style of the poem.

Aruna's mother uses to wake up at five in the morning. She uses to go to kitchen and start preparing various kinds of dishes. Taste will be delicious. She will do it by herself and no one will be there to aid her. There were totally nine members, six males and three females and she packs them to different spots: schools, fields and businesses. As a son, Aruna has never seen a complaint, neither an anger on her face nor an irritation in her mother's eyes. Throughout her life journey, she endeavour hard for her family members. In addition, her husband, the poet's father will take heavy strain of her physical strength and mental stamina. He troubles her for all the small things. Nearly for thirty years i.e. from the prime age of forty and to the seventy, the poet's father was bed ridden. But his mother took utmost care of him without pulling the long face.

The mother of Prof. Arunachalam has no desire or greed. She never demand for jewel or silk. The poet wonders whether she had opinions of her own. The children's demands are hers. Her whole world ended within the whole house. She is very strict in her morals, but she never imposes them. She, as a cliff, remains like an impressing personality. When the sons start growing up, the family starts disintegrate and she meekly agrees. Suddenly poverty predominant at home, but his mother take care of the family very modishly.

"Poor soul! Solely depended on me in her last days./ I proved thankless, seething with rage at naught and finding no time to indulge her."(lines 24-26) During the final days, the poet's mother entirely depends on him. The poet finds no time to pander her and he agitates with anger for no reasons. He remained ungratefulness to the poor soul. She goes to coma stage and comes into conscious occasionally. She contorts in pain. She became lean as skeleton and her body become shrink. The poet begins to behave like a dissembler. In the past, she was like an angel but now she is lying like joint sticks with sores and stench.

The poet starts to show his uncontrollable fury on the lady doctor and compels her to put his Mom to permanent sleep. After the demise of his mother, the poet realizes his mistake, his ungratefulness and so he wants his mother to be his mother in all his births and he will replace it by giving much love. "Mother! My Mother! Be my mother in all births." (Line 47)

Conclusion

To conclude, a mother can be the symbol of epitomize love, altruistic mother like Nissim Ezekiel's Mother where she even bears the pain of the sting of the poison for a long twenty hours and tolerates all the customs and rituals steered by her neighbours, holy man and her husband. Ashiamma, the mother of Kalam, the woman of piety knows the pain of her sons and daughter especially, her youngest son. Even at midnight, she uses her soft, caring hands to remove Kalam's pain. One full moon night, he sleeps in his mother's lap which seems to be a corking solace to him and cracking envy to his siblings. The mother of the poet Aruna who does not know the outside world except her family members and the Kitchen. She was the striver, who wakes up at five and works till her husband goes to sleep. During her terminal stage, depending on the youngest son, who behaves like a dissimulator without understanding the feelings of his mother. He even goes to the extreme to put his mother to deep sleep. Later he understands his blunder and he prays to God that he wants his mother to be his mother in all his births to replace by his love. Thus, the altruistic nature of Nissim Ezekiel's mother, Kalam's mother, Ashiamma and Poet Aruna's mother have been beautifully exemplified in their poems. Hence the title is proven.

Works Cited

Aruna. "My Mother." *Ripples, A Selection of Poems,* edited by Board of Editors, Macmillan Publishers, 2009, p.29, 30.

Ezekiel, Nissim."Night of the Scorpion". *Ripples. A Selection of Poems,* edited by Board of Editors. Macmillan Publishers, 2009. p.25, 26.

https://www.englishstudystore.com/my mother-Kalam. Web. October 02. N.Pag.

https://www.learn cram.com/ definition-altruistic nature. Web. October12. N.Pag.

https://www.literary yog./ nissim Ezekiel-night of the scorpion. Web. October 4. N.Pag.

https://www.countryliving.com/mother's happiness. Web. October 5.N.Pag.

https://www.houseofkalam.org.mymother. Web. October 5. N.Pag.

CHAPTER 12

Understanding the Shades of Marginalisation in Afro-American Writings: A Study of Alice Walker's *The Color Purple*

Rima Nambata

Abstract

Afro-American writings have portrayed the long-standing sufferings of its women community through the central fictional characters. The texts from the 'womanists' are representational of themes that have underscored shades of marginalisation through racism, black feminism, gender discrimination, lesbianism, female genital mutilation and incest with overlapping tones. These have ripped apart the humanistic ideals of society. This entire episode of inflicted misery has been depicted through Pulitzer winner, Alice Walker's *The Color Purple*. Chronicling the history and the events, an enslaved woman Celie having gone through the brutality of debauchery and seduction, rises above the evils of the society. This paper ends with a note of hope and optimism, where the mutilated women (here Celie) symbolic of the maltreated Black women, instead of submitting to centuries' old depravity and humiliation, rise against all odds as awakened souls to negotiate with the forms of injustice. Liberation of minds and emancipation of life find its truest ardour in Walker's female characters.

Keywords: woman subjugation, womanists, gender discrimination, female genital mutilation, emancipated souls

Introduction

> "I only know that other people call me a feminist whenever I express sentiments that differentiate me from a doormat or prostitute."
>
> Rebecca West's The Young Rebecca

Literature for ages has been representational of societies and human civilisation with an underlying message. This idea gets reinforced with the writings of the marginal to 'by' and 'for' the marginals. Literature weaves the story of hindrances that are the fallacies of fate, fallacies of society, worse still discrimination against mankind. The cries of the marginals are tailored into the literature to underscore the wounds inflicted on humanity by the dominant, privileged class acting as the puppeteer, the black women community as the puppet. These neglected souls championed causes to release themselves from psychological scars imposed for centuries. The writings attempted to brave the odds by the cursed-upon individuals and be a part of the mainstream. The proceeding paragraphs cement the idea as to how representational writing has a redemptive voice of credibility and is not looked down upon.

Is there any definition of literature of the marginals? To me, it is understanding the literature of the people surviving in the geographical and psychological margin, as written by Kamala Das in *The Dance of the Eunuchs*, reflecting colour differences (dark skin) and racism as in Toni Morrison's writings *The Bluest Eye*, and *Beloved*, incest (sexually abused children) as in the writings of Alice Walker, Maya Angelou or even Pinki Virani with her faction *The Bitter Chocolate,* literature by and for the LGBT Community with tones of homosexuality as in Osborne's *Look back in Anger*, Walker's *The Color Purple*, Toni Morrison's *Sula* to name a few. Slave Narrative, literature by and for the Dalit class, literature by the aboriginals are some of the other areas of marginalisation, but the list can be more.

Themes of Marginalisation

The paper focuses on shades of marginalisation as and when demanded by tradition, culture, race, tribe, and nation. The layered discrimination and consequential marginalisation are evident in one of the best-sellers in Afro-American writings, *The Color Purple* by Alice Walker. Winner of the Pulitzer Prize and American Book Award, where Walker quotes, "... I gathered up the historical and psychological threads of the life my ancestors lived, and in the writing of it I felt joy and strength of my own continuity..." (453). The words resonate with the scarred pains of Alice Walker and her community. The power structure of the society raises questions at large of the inequalities prevalent along the length and breadth of the novel and inquire the stereotype in relationships, class division, sexual liberation, humanistic ideals, and the mores and manners of the society.

Walker's *The Color Purple* is having all-pervasive marginalised themes on colonisation, racism, sexism, black feminism, gender discrimination, lesbianism, female genital mutilation and incest with overlapping tones. The following paragraphs reveal the hidden layers of marginalisation which is reinforced in the essay *The Resisting Reader*, where Fetterley writes, "Literature is political" and its politics is "male" (561-569). Further reflections by Guerin et al. in *Feminisms and Gender Studies* critique on the "recent decades" where "tendency has changed, in part because of the efforts of feminist critics but also because of social changes such as mass education, the Civil Rights Movement, the Vietnam War, increasing urbanization, and the growing liberalization of sexual mores" (223).

Examples of marginalisation proliferate in the novel. The 'male gaze' is based upon voyeurism and fetishism, the only available pleasure (usually) being the male one of looking at women's bodies for sexual cues. . . According to Mulvey, a woman is an image, the man and bearer of the look, the voyeur: "In a world ordered by sexual imbalance pleasure in looking has been split. . . [and] the male gaze projects its fantasy onto the female figure, which is styled accordingly" (Qtd. in Guerin et al. 237). An illustrative negative tone in the novel would substantiate how a character in the novel, Albert's lustful gaze on Nettie exemplifies the above-quoted words. Albert before getting married to Celie always had his (male) gaze on Nettie and sexually fulfilling his desires through eyes. The body here is objectified into a subject of pleasure without sexual gratification and mutual understanding of the parties.

Observations by Madison on Walker's essay *In Search of our Mother's Garden*, addresses how "Black women are called, in the folklore that so aptly identifies one's status in society, 'the mule of the world,' because [they] have been handed the burdens that everyone else – *everyone else* – refused to carry. We have also been called "Matriarchs," "Superwomen," and "Mean and Evil Bitches." Not to mention "Castraters" and 'Sapphire's Mama"' (519). The above lines replicate what Walker or her ancestors' have dealt with in the history of their lives. Their characters have been mutilated, prayers for love have been granted with children, and yearnings for care have been treated with 'inspirational appellations'. Further Madison corroborates Alice Walker's views "to be an artist and a black woman, even today, lowers [their] status in many respects, rather than rais[ing] it". . . But she firmly asserts, 'artists we will be' (519). The author moans the pain of loss that her clan, her mother, her grandmother (generic for the black women community) has endured and 'died with their real gifts stifled within them'. The plight of forced childbearing, maltreatment in the hands of the male as well as the white coloured people, subjugation in the form of physical abuse, sexual abuse, hard labour before sunup to late sundown, selling bodies, and throwing away their spirituality are the extreme examples that marginalise Walker's black women community.

Racism

The above thoughts synthesise in the forthcoming paragraphs to understand the themes of marginalisation as and when found in the writings of Afro-Americans with Walker's *in* context. 'Racism' undeniably is a major factor of marginalisation in the Afro-American setting of the Southern peasants. In 1970, when cultural nationalism was at its peak the most of the Black literary activity was focused on the defiant urban Black in conflict with white society. In the novel, *The Third Life of Grange Copeland*, Walker brings out the relationship between the racist sharecropping system and the violence the members of the family mete out on each other. In the writings of Walker through *The Color Purple*, *The Third Life of Grange Copeland* and the contemporary writers of Walker, Marshall's *The Chosen Place, the Timeless People,* and Morrison's *The Bluest Eye* seem to wage war against racism only. The novels act as a continuous reminder that much of the Afro-American population is still under a 'feudal sharecropping system' (Christian 459).

Sharing sentiments with the above paragraph, let us anchor what racism is? *Encyclopedia of Race, Ethnicity and Society* defines "racism [as] a belief or ideology that all members of each racial group possess characteristics or abilities specific to that race, especially to distinguish it as being either superior or inferior to another racial group or racial groups." (Schefer 2008) An article by Lysik, refers to oppression in *The Color Purple* as "themes of an antebellum slave narrative and implicitly refers to the legal system of chattel slavery while telling a traumatized tale of sexual oppression and violence" (22). The above words identify with the kind of historical oppression that has been transferred to generations of Africans that led to the mention of racism either implicitly or explicitly in major Afro-American writings. This necessitates understanding the history of the Black communities that unfold the reasons behind racism as prevalent in the lives of the Black people.

We find agonising and realistic illustrations of North America's chattel slavery in the literary genre of Afro-American writings. The fictional central characters of the genre observed by Rushdy, portray the slave status either as 'narrators, subjects or ancestral presences' (533). Words from Nettie to Celie in *The Color Purple* excerpted from Rushdy's writing illustrates:

> Millions and millions of Africans were captured and sold into slavery – you and me, Celie! And whole cities were destroyed by slave catching wars. Today the people of Africa – having murdered or sold into slavery their strongest folks – are riddled by disease and sunk in spiritual and physical confusion. . .

Why did they sell us? How could they have done it? And why do we still love them? (533)

In various essays Walker acknowledges the African-American literary tradition and names the black writers (several of whom wrote or dictated slave narratives) and activists whose life and works have been an inspiration to her, including Lucy Terry, Phyllis Wheatley, Nat Turner, Harriet Tubman, Sojourner Truth, Frederick Douglass, Malcolm X, Martin Luther King, Jr., and Nella Larsen. In the essay *Saving the Life that is Your Own: The Importance of Models in the Artist's Life* writes scholar Lysik:

> .. . black writers seem always involved in a moral and/or physical struggle, the result of which is expected to be some kind of larger freedom. Perhaps this is because our literary tradition is based on the *slave narratives,* where escape for the body and freedom for the soul went together. [*In Search* 5, emphasis mine] (19)

The 1960s marked the Civil Rights Movement era. In reflection to the above lines, the universities opened the gates for Black scholars to bring into their writings the history of slave narratives portraying American slavery. Voluminous numbers in novels were written in the post-Civil Rights Movement that brought in the neo-slave narrative. According to Rushdy, the theme of neo-slave narrative is the chronicle of chattelhood "as a historical phenomenon that has lasting cultural meaning and enduring social consequences" (533). If this feature is explicitly evident in Toni Morrison's *Beloved* or in Margaret Walker's *Jubilee*, then Walker's *The Color Purple* is overtly evident of the after and the unending effects of slavery where "Celie is enslaved by her husband, because he has internalized the racist stereotypes of the master-slave position as exercised during the times of slavery." (Lysik 20)

Gender Discrimination

Overt gender discrimination or sexism is another theme of marginalisation which is interrelated to racism and impacts major Black writers. The term sexism denotes when particular sex 'enjoys rights or privileges over the other sex and even to an extent dominates, abuses, subjugates, ill-treats the other sex can be rightly defined as sexism. In many of Walker's writings, key of them being *In Love and Trouble, The Third Life of Grange Copeland, Meridian, One Child of One's Own*, her collection of short stories *You Can't Keep a Good Woman Down* (1981), emphatically looks into the 'twin afflictions' of Black Women's Lives (Christian 467). The Black woman is oppressed first in form of womanhood and second in colour. The miseries are inflicted by white feminists and also Black people. This emphasizes how sexism is innately present in Afro-American lives. The societal evils subordinate one race to another, one class to another, one sex to another, ultimately fragmenting and ruining the meaning of living (existence). Sexism and racism in America are critically related.

Thoughts on the comparison – contrast between male-female relationships in Africa and the Black South suggest that sexism for Black women in America does not derive from racism, though it is quantitatively affected by it. And Nettie's community of missionaries graphically demonstrates Afro-Americans' knowledge of their ancestral link to Africa, which, contrary to American myth, predates the Black Power Movement of the 1960s (Christian 470).

In most of Walker's fiction, there is a meeting of Black women in the South. They are simple, plain, honest women who know to grow Petunias and quilting. They are harmless as they know no wrong; mostly just 'Churchgoing' or 'Church-been' women. But their tales are very much personal, real, bleak, and dismal. These women keep on repaying dues for no or little fault of theirs. In an article Smith studies, the plight as:

> Different though they may sometimes seem they all push against the same barbed-wired wall of racism, sexism, age, ignorance and despair. Often they are reduced to a level lower than themselves (frequently analogous to animals and insects), become frustrated, and operate on the level consistent with their reduced state. They are trapped by circumstance and this entrapment is the result of their sense of powerlessness against the structure of the dominant society. . . Therefore, in day-to-day existence,

> they carry out plots constructed by white society (male and female) and choreographed by Black men. Walker's characters' mirror allegations about Black women in relation to their pain and suffering. (479).

Further, the fiction adopts the epistolary form of weaving narration through facts, piece by piece exemplifies the womanist process that Walker has advanced. To this reflection, scholar Christian observes, "In using the epistolary style, Walker is able to have her major character Celie express the impact of oppression on her spirit as well as her growing internal strength and final victory" (469) is excerpted in *The Color Purple*:

> Dear God,
>
> Me and Sophie work on the quilt, Got it frame up on the porch. Shug Avery donate her yellow dress for scrap, and I work in a piece every chance I get. It's a nice pattern call Sister's Choice. (Qtd. in Jovanovich 53)

Rise of Black Feminism

Chronicling Black Feminism has its roots in one of the great anti-lynching crusaders, Ida B. Wells. The literature by the Black Womanists focuses on the convoluted connection between rape and lynching, sex and race, that constitute to this day" (Christian 469). The work of Walker spans generations of one poor rural Southern Black family where the weaving of the plot is personal with history, with the image of quilting being the central plot of the novel. In the novel, *The Color Purple,* the emphases remain on subjugation which the Black Women folk experience in their relationships with Black men– be it fathers, brothers, husbands and lovers– and share an open relationship with the black women folk that liberates them. *The Color Purple* exemplifies themes that are forbidden, but Walkers' approach seems radical, rational and clean. The marginalised themes find focus in her novels and the epitome of examples include," incest in a black family and portrays a Black lesbian relationship as natural and freeing" (Christian 470). Conclusively, I would like to suggest that the body of Black Feminist writings' honest approach to the maltreatment of the Black women won their stature in the later part of their struggle (through the writings). They stood for their cause that changed the minds of the readers and voices were heard for the oppressed class of black women.

Alice Walker however has refuted the term Black feminist and instead coined 'womanist' to represent herself; she writes, "she has replaced *feminist* with *womanist,* remarking that a womanist does not turn her back upon the men of her community" (Guerin et al. 233). She refuted her charges against black male critics responding to the portrayal of black men in The *Color Purple*.

Resistance to the established order leads to revolution. A change for the betterment is the objective of many such institutions. Black feminism is also one such class of writers who protested the stereotyped anarchical order that dominated the lives of Black Women. Black Feminist Thinkers have stood apart for the discovery of free country order, considered as a must for growth. All of Walker's writings are a reflection of the subjugation manifested in the protest writings of the Black Feminists. The more they protest, the more marginalisation in society. Gender discrimination in *The Color Purple* are illustrated through the excerpt:

> I curse you, I say. What that mean? He say.
>
> I say, Until you do right by me, everything you touch will crumble.
>
> He laugh. Who you think you is? He say. You can't curse nobody. Look at you. You black, you pore, you ugly, you a woman. Goddam, he say, you nothing at all. (75)

The broad thematic areas of Walker's writings *In Love and Trouble* and *You Can't Keep a Good Woman Down*, are – societal attitudes and mores that women have, and challenged – includes the themes of pornography and male sexual fantasies in "Porn" and "Coming Apart"; abortion in "The Abortion", sadomasochism in "A Letter of the Times", interracial rape in "Luna Advancing." The forms Walker invents to critically reflect these issues are as unconventional as her subject matter. Many of the stories are process rather than product. Feminist thinkers of the seventies asserted a link between process (unravelling of thought and feeling) and the way women have perceived the world. In keeping with this theory, Walker often gives us the story as it comes into being, rather than delivering the product, classic and clean. The author then not only breaks the rules by writing about "womanist" issues, but she also employs a womanist process" (Christian 468) voicing against the society made rules. And there lies being honest about their opinion bearing the name of 'marginalised' in the society. They are the Black-feminist thinkers – independent, honest, clean, and self-made that makes them receive differential treatment from the mainstream.

Homosexuality as a Marginalised Theme

The theme of marginalisation deal with the issue of homosexual relationships between two women, giving the tone of marginality at once to the esteemed class of rationalists, intellectuals and politicians. What remains distant from our understanding is the blooming of sisterhood and their strength in the relationship. Rightly explained through Showalter's *biological model* that "if the text can be said in someway to mirror the body, then does that reduce women writers merely to bodies?" Yet Showalter praises the often shocking frankness of women writers who relate the 'intimacies of the female experiences of the female body' (Guerin et al. 225). The lines visibly explain the relationship status:

> She say, I love you, Miss Celie. And then she haul off and kiss me on the mouth. Um, she say, like she surprise. I kiss her back, say, um, too. Us kiss and kiss till us can't hardly kiss no more. Then us touch each other.
>
> I don't know nothing about it, I say to Shug.
> I don't know much, she say. (47)

Feminist scholar and critic, Beauvoir in the essay *Prime of Life* express '[her] feminine status. . . is a given condition of [her] life, not an explanation of it' (292). This is why she finds it unjust if she is reduced to her sex. (Qtd. in Marso 64) Stripping of sexuality is as good as repression of reality. This note will give us insight into the liberalisation of black women even in terms of sexuality. Breaking conventions of stereotyped sex roles need courage from within to follow sexual mores of choice and orientation.

Further, Beauvoir puts it quite simply by stating that "we need others in order for our own existence to become founded and necessary." (Qtd. in Marso 74) The words aptly describe the arousing pleasure of Celie for Shug Avery. Shug acted as a muse for Celie to become independent in life – sexually, financially and as a woman. This relationship is better described as having and wearing a lesbian identity where racism, sexism and oppression are rampant within the Afro-American community. The sexual openness of revolutionary Shug and docile Celie stemming from the flame of their relationship brings strength and independence in 'Celie'. The broken body and maimed spirit of Celie from sexual slavery shows the only indignation of heterosexuality better to say rape (here abuse) from the menfolk. In contrast, Celie enjoyed her sexual life after having met Shug Avery. This calls to question, do we see lesbianism as the cornerstone to basic human rights or curtailment of freedom in its conservative and stereotyped practices?

Female Genital Mutilation

In 1989 and 1992, the consecutive publications of the two books, *The Temple of My Familiar* and *Possessing the Secret of Joy*, Walker took on the issue of female circumcision in Africa. This is an insight into another area of marginality where a segment of race and culture is still in the ritual of brutal practice and under the wrap of marginality in a civilised world. Even at the level of naming, we must question – "From whose center are we operating?" In both *Possessing the Secret of Joy* (a sequel of sorts to Walker's 1982 *The Color Purple*) and *Warrior Marks: Female Genital Mutilation and the Sexual Blinding of Women*, Walker's fictional depictions of female circumcision in "Africa," portray "Africa" and consequently African culture and people, in light not dissimilar to colonial explorers, scientists, anthropologists and missionaries – as backwards, primitive and in need of salvation' (Blay 7). There are reflections which otherwise is considered outside the mainstream. Walker concentrates with an open and accommodating approach on these reflections. And FGM is one of them.

Walker has challenged the existing norm of Initiation Ceremony (FGM), in *The Color Purple*, where Tashi did not want to be a party to the initiation ritual (to be read as FGM and scarring of the face) that the Olinka race (tribe) practices in Africa. Adam was too circumcised. Tashi and Adam loved each other. The ritual determined purity, manhood and womanhood. Initiation accompanied by scarring of the face! The characters may be fictitious but the practice is not. It is very much prevalent in our society and the populace still yields to it. 'There is a sense in which the "forbidden" in the society is consistently approached by Walker as possible route to truth (Christian 458) and Walker has this unwavering honesty to reveal those sticky issues.

Walker demystifies even her nation by citing some of the rituals of Africa which are considered barbaric and the system and race as being another marginalised section of the society. It is the process, but that which is scrutinised is the continuation of this barbarism that horrifies any modern existence or civilisation. And Walker just points at the brutality of the ceremony. It can be ritualistic for a tribe but in the days of globalisation and advancement of the nation, being a part of that ritual that scars the vital organs of the body is nothing but a disgrace to humanity, and Walker did not flinch from what she saw – she did not glorify the ritual, but made it an eye-opener for the human race. She "challenged the idealistic view of Africa as an image. . . in pursuit of racial pride" (Christian 459). The practitioners of Initiation Ceremony, who considered FGM as symbolic of purity and womanhood is still under the smoky screen of uncivilised and brutal forces of religion. Literature, the reflection of society is not behind in propagating the cruelty involved in FGM. Alice walker's writings are examples.

Conclusion

The Color Purple has invariably the setting in a black milieu, with overwhelmingly black characters in a black environment. The thesis to understand the various shades of marginalisation has been interspersed across the paper as experienced by Walker's community or the Afro-American women, but the novel does not end in submitting to the forms of marginalisation meted out, instead, the characters challenged this ongoing deformity of the race boldly and rescued themselves from years of rape, violence, isolation, sexism, racism, drudgery, mutilation, abuse, oppression, sexual exploitation and class conflict by sheer skill, grit, determination, tolerance, patience and importantly awakening to negotiate with the forms of injustice. In conclusion, as an academic practitioner and a reader, I would take a step beyond to look not into the marginalised status of the Black community, women in general, instead embody the awakened souls of Walkers characters who outdid the pain and mutilation and rose to engulf the dark and embrace the dawn of their lives. It heralds a meaningful beginning of surpassing the woes and germinating hope for mankind even. Celebrating the freedom against the years' long physical and mental afflictions, Walker respects the womanists. She pays:

> homage to the Black feminists by portraying a woman who struggles through adversity to assert herself against almost impossible odds. She pays homage to the lesbians by portraying a relationship between two women that reads like a schoolgirl fairy tale in the unconventional happy resolution. She pays homage to black nationalists by opposing colonialism and to Pan Africanism by suggesting that yes, indeed, a black American does understand and sympathize with the plight of her black brothers and sisters thousands of miles across the ocean. (Qtd. in Harris, pp.155-161)

The writing ends with the following lines of the poem *Still I rise, And Still I Rise* (1978) in which the poem anchors self-liberation by conquering the afflictions and reflecting the beacon of the enslaved souls who are now the artists, the exalted poets. The poet glorifies the writer, the artist, the selfhood of the free-thinking Afro-American writers through the lines:

> Bringing the gifts that my ancestors gave,
>
> I am the dream and the hope of the slave.
>
> I rise
>
> I rise
>
> I rise. (Angelou, 1978)

Works Cited

Angelou, Maya. *Still I rise, And Still I Rise.* 1978.

Schefer, R, "Racism." *Encyclopedia of Race, Ethnicity and Society*, Sage, 2008.

Bell, Bernard W. *The Afro-American Novel and Its Tradition.* The University of Massachusetts P, 1987.

Blay, Yaba Amgborale. "All the 'Africans' are Men, all the 'Sistas' are 'American,' but Some of Us Resist: Realizing African Feminism (s) as an Africological Research

Methodology." *The Journal of Pan African Studies*, vol. 2, no. 2, 2008, pp. 6-7.

Christian, Barbara. "Alice Walker: the Black Woman artist as Wayward." *Black Women Writers (1950-1980): A Critical Evaluation*, edited by Mari Evans, 1984, pp. 457-477.

Fetterley, Judith. "On the Politics of Literature." *The Resisting Reader.* Indiana UP, 1978. Fulton, David, B. "A Plea for Social Justice for the Negro Woman." *The North Carolina Roots of African American Literature: An Anthology*, edited by William Andrews. The U of North Carolina P, Issued by Negro Society for Historical Research, 2006, p. 303.

Goldman, Emma. "A Feminist Search for Love (Emma Goldman on the Politics of Marriage, Love, Sexuality, and the Feminine)." *Feminists Thinkers and the Demands of Feminity – The Lives and Work of Intellectual Women,* edited by Lori J Marso. Routledge, 2006, p.113.

Guerin, Wilfred L, et al. *Feminisms and Gender Studies: A Handbook of Critical Approaches to Literature.* 5th ed., Oxford UP, 2005, pp. 222-274.

.... *Cultural Studies: A Handbook of Critical Approaches to Literature*, 5th ed., Oxford UP, 2005, pp. 275-349.

Harris, Truder. "On The Color Purple, Stereotypes and Silence." *Black American Literature Forum*, vol. 18, no. 4, 1984, pp. 155-161.

Lysik, Marta. "You have seen how a [wo] man was made a slave; you shall see how a slave was made a [wo] man: Alice Walker's The Color Purple as a Neo-Slave

Narrative." *American Studies*, edited by Agnieszka Graff, vol. XXI, The American Studies Center, Warsaw University, 2004, pp. 17-34.

Madison, Soyini. *The Literature and Culture of Contemporary Women of Color,* St. Martin's P, 1992.

Marso, Lori J. *Feminists Thinkers and the Demands of Feminity – The Lives and Work of Intellectual Women: Women's Situation, II (Existential Experiments with the Feminine)*, Routledge, 2006.

Parker-Smith, Bettye J. "Alice Walker's Women: In Search of Some Peace of Mind." Black Women Writers (1950-1980)': *A Critical Evaluation*, edited by Mari Evans, 2004, p. 479.

Rushdy, Ashraf H A. "Neo-slave Narrative." *The Oxford Companion to African American Literature,* Editors, William L. Andrews, Francis Smith Foster, and Trudier Harris. Oxford U P, 1997, p. 533.

Walker, Alice. "Writing *The Color Purple* (1984)". *Black Women Writers (1950-1980)*': *A Critical Evaluation*, edited by Mari Evans, Anchor Press, 1984, p. 453.

West, Rebecca. *The Young Rebecca*, edited by Jane Marcus, Virago, 1982, p.219.

www.infoplease.com/spot/bhmquotes1.html

www.asc.uw.edu.pl/theamericanist/vol/21/21_17-34.pdf

CHAPTER 13

From Silence to Global Citizenship: A Study with Reference to Jhumpa Lahiri's *In Other Words*

Rima Chakraborty

Abstract

In human history, migration has always involved multiple affiliations and identities. Diaspora refers to people or ethnic groups who have left their homelands and have settled in other parts of the world.This situation has traditionally been equated with longing for a lost home. An analysis of the South Asian diaspora, however reveals that, migration experiences are different for men and women. But migration discourses are rarely viewed solely from the female perspective. This paper intends to highlight how the diasporic space slowly but surely creates transnational as well as global identities which are not restricted to any national, cultural or ethnic boundaries. Reading and understanding Jhumpa Lahiri's works as well as her personal experiences of being second-generation diasporic citizen, which are well-recorded in *In Other Words,* help us to understand the process of metamorphosis of the diasporic women from being hybrids to trans-nationals to Global Citizens. Moreover, it may also be reasonably assumed that in the near future 'Global literature' would take over the Indian, African, Chinese, Australian or Caribbean Diasporic literature, and the documentation of the idiosyncrasies of a particular ethnic or diasporic community would become extinct. This perhaps can be considered to be the future of the diasporic writings and Jhumpa Lahiri's *In Other Words* certainly corroborates the probability of such a future.

Keywords: Diaspora, Ethnicity, Hybridity, Transnationality, Global Citizenship

"The Present epoch will perhaps be above all the epoch of space. We are in an epoch of simultaneity. We are in an epoch of juxtaposition" (Foucault). Problems concerning Identity have always been difficult to resolve and have also been an intriguing study for social scientists since time immemorial. The term, 'Identity', refers to the meanings attached to an individual by his/her own self and also by others, and it develops as a consequence of his/her interaction with the complex yet organized socio-cultural framework in which he/she is born and brought up. In this regard, the Social Identity Theory[1] should be mentioned, which suggests that membership in social groups and categories are important components of a person's identity. People's belonging to these groups in a way define who they are. Considering this, it would be riveting to take up the cases of diasporic citizens who voluntarily or sometimes involuntarily depart from their respective homelands under diverse circumstances. However, an analysis of the South Asian diaspora reveals that, migration experiences are different for men and women. Moreover, migration discourses arerarely viewed solely from the female perspective. Scholars and researchers tend to generalize the diasporic condition without acknowledging the peculiarities of diasporic women's experiences. Thus, my aim is to inspect how communal and ethnic displacement eventually transforms the diasporic women from being hybrids to trans-nationals and finally Global Citizens. Thousands of miles away from their homelands, and freed from all forms of socio-ethnic expectations, they do get the chance to re-define their territories and in the process, do even gradually transform into global citizens who can dwell with ease everywhere and hence 'belong' to nowhere. Jhumpa Lahiri's latest memoir *In Other Words,* helps us to understand the process of such a metamorphosis. Accordingly, the paper will concentrate on the life and literary works of Nilanjana Sudeshna Lahiri aka Jhumpa Lahiri. But before that, it is of much relevance to look through the history of South Asian women's writing in English.

Historically speaking, it was unusual for South Asian women to write in English, because proficiency in English was a skill that was specific to men. Despite the promotion of women's education, it was only offered in the native language of the time. In fact, the South Asian women who acquire English education are still a privileged minority in the present era. Thus, men have been the torch-bearers of South Asian literature in English, and over the years, the modest literary pieces of the women writers have been totally shadowed by the works of authors like R.K Narayan, V.S Naipaul, Salman Rushdie, Upamanyu Chatterjee and many others, who are globally acclaimed. However, during the 1960s and 1970s a couple of genuinely unskippable women's voices gained prominence. The works of Anita

Desai, Kamala Markandaya, Attia Hosain, Nayantara Sahgaland numerous others exhibited the authors' commendable command over the English language, along with potency and sophistication. The issues which they took up for their writing were fairly distinct from the male writers and also from the British authors. They offered the readers their perspective of their 'home and the world', as South Asian women writers. Indeed, theirs was a unique position of being 'doubly othered', first as the colonized citizens and then as women. Hence being 'doubly marginalized', these eloquent women authors utilized the germane methodologies of disruption, deconstruction, and recreation in order to end their quietness and voice their convictions. It therefore comes out loud and clear that the South Asian women writers, alongside the male literary giants, have contributed considerably to the advancement of South Asian writing in English.

It is intriguing to take note of the fact that the different phases of South Asian Women's writing in English bear likeness with the development of European women's writing, as elaborated by Elaine Showalter in her seminal work *A Literature of Their Own: British Women Novelists from Bronte to Lessing.* But then, in the case of South Asian women authors, one ought to remember their postcolonial inheritance. Therefore, the Euro-centric stages of development of women's literature which Showalter depicts, in spiteof bearing semblance, cannot completely capture the nuances of South Asian women's writings in English. Nevertheless, following Showalter, the initial stage of (European) women's literature is the 'feminine phase'. During this phase, the women protagonists were presented as docile individuals, conforming to the social restrictions imposed on them on grounds of their gender. They would perpetually endure ill treatment and deprivation for their families, or sometimes for the society at large. We may find a comparative model in Kamala Markandaya's *Nectarin a Sieve*, published in 1956. The novel features Rukmani, who is a simple villager, enduring indigence. But in spite of that, she stays a supporting mother and spouse, constantly working for her family's welfare.She follows the directs of Indian society, which expects that the women should meticulously adhere tothe dos and don'ts prescribed for them by the society. In Indian culture, a 'good woman' has to be an amenable daughter, a compliant spouse, and a nurturing mother. Among other things, she rarely has autonomy over choosing her soul mate, her home and even her profession. Therefore, the women rights in Indian society are usually sacrificed for the benefit of family and community. Duty takes precedence over individual desires. South Asian women's fiction however contains few heroines of this kind. Because of their passivity, the self-sacrificing characters generally play secondary roles, and are not oftenportrayed as protagonists.

The second stage of women's literature in South Asia is strongly reminiscent of Showalter's 'feminist phase'. In this stage, the authors challenged thepatriarchal social order and demanded recognition and equal rights. Their writings challenged the authoritative forces, which have dictated women's lives for centuries. Among many eminent South Asian women writers who have taken up the 'feminist cause' emphatically and brilliantly are Anita Desai, Rama Mehta, Shashi Deshpande and Arundhati Roy. In this regard, one is reminded of Arundhati Roy's *God of Small Things* in which Amu, the protagonist, disregards thetraditional dictates of the Indian society by leaving her husbandfor a worthy reason and engaging in an extra marital relationship with a man from lower caste. As a consequence, however, the retaliatory society charges, punishes and even kills Amu's loverVelutha, unfairly.

There is no denying of the fact that, in the Postcolonialera, the socio-economic condition of South Asian women has changed to a great extent. But in spite of that, the set social norms, still endorse gender inequality as a prerequisite for a 'happy' society. Nevertheless, the growth of the middle class has been parallel to the growth of the economy in the South Asian countries. For this reason, women are now the target customers for various commercial products. Patricia Jeffrey has clarified how:

> Women are being wooed as privileged consumers, urged to spend money on themselves for an endless flow of nondurable goods that undercut the traditional domestic values of the self-effacing woman who lives not for herself but for her family. A rather aggressive new consumerist individualism is generated, and a new identity fashioned. Significantly, the new Hindu upper-caste, upper-class woman nowhas the ability to respond independently to the seductive calls of the advertising culture, since she is often educated and employed (Jeffrey 103).

The contemporary South Asian women authors also reflect this trend in their novels, which feature economically independent middle-class women. Theprimordial crisis in the lives of these women, is to choose between loyalty to set social norms and the desire to forge a distinct, independent identity. Thus, more often than not, these women find themselves in a state of quandary, as they are expected to preserve their traditionand customs, while being simultaneously mindful of the course of globalization which is an unavoidable reality in the present era. It is definitely a fragile equilibrium, on the grounds that the South Asian women are relied upon to maintain, save and shield their ethnicity, while they additionally make endeavors to get away from the limitations forced on them by the same culture and society, which they are safeguarding and preserving. The resultant pressure puts the women in a position, where they need toreframe their identities as the traditional norms fail to incorporate all elements of their multidimensional selves. The last phase of South Asian women's writing, is therefore reminiscent to Showalter's 'female' stage, which is also the period of self-revelation and a journey towards independence.

Indeed, in the postcolonial period, with the ascent of the middle class, women novelists from South Asia weren't restricted to the aristocracy anymore. This branch of literature has been enriched with new subjects and concerns, and also with new writing styles.To be explicit, the books (particularly those by the diasporic writers) have become progressively reflective and open-ended. There are no black-or-white issues, no stereotypical answers and no obvious antagonists. Although men are no longer seen as foes, native/homeland societies are time and again perceived as obstacles, hindering the growth and development of women.Subsequently a fresh consciousness appears to be emerging out ofthe fast-changing financial condition of women, the breaking down of enormous joint families, and movement from native lands to unfamiliar nations in the current era of globalization. The women, as portrayed by the postcolonial South Asian Women Diasporic authors, constantly seek self-resilience, while being surrounded by multitude of familial as well as social tensions. In this context, Edward Said's commentin *Intellectual Exile: Expatriates and Marginals* becomes relevant. Following him, the condition of marginality, which might be the outcome of being an expatriate or exile, "Frees you from having always to proceed with caution, afraid to overturn the apple cart, anxious about upsetting fellow members of the same corporation..." (Said 124). Said's comments definitely hold relevance for the South Asian women who are, liberated with their immigration. The ubiquity of the foreignness and the need to change in order to adapt with the new and unfamiliar culture, remake their characters and free them from the shackles of their hostland customs and traditions.

So, to sum up, in the history of South Asian Women's writing in English, the primary stage was, 'writing from the Empire'. It is important to understand 'Empire' from the point of view of the South Asian Women writers.Being doubly marginalized, the term might be thought of (in their situation) to be a signifier for all the oppressive factors (native and foreign) which hindered them from flourishing as successful authors. It cannot be denied that both the colonizing as well as the native social forces together forestalled the women writers from gaining prominence as creative writers. The couple of them who still penned their feelings, while dwelling in such oppressive environment, chose to follow thedictates of the 'Empire'. The following stage was, 'writing back to the Empire', which implies, protesting against the oppression which the South Asian Women and the South Asian Women Writers have endured for centuries. But then the postcolonial women authors from the South Asian countries write neither from nor back to the 'Empire'. One may rather detect their absolute insouciance towards the Empire. The diasporic authors of the South Asian heredity endeavour to liberate themselves from the shadow of colonization while portraying the changing manners inwhich the Diasporic condition has impacted the lives and strugglesof the women, post-migration. However, in this regard, Derek Gregory's reminder of our colonial present holds much significance, as it is a fact that, even though the South Asian Women authors of the present era consider themselves liberated from every single influence of the colonizer, yet the impact of the colonial power politics on their writings cannot be blatantly ignored.

There has been a noticeable increase in the number of South Asian women writers over the last two decades, but there has been a substantial lack of serious literary criticism addressing this development. This indicates that the South Asian Women's literature is still not incorporated within the mainstream literary canon. The absence of scholastic consideration can be due to the problem of defining what constitutes South Asian culture. In fact, the very concept of 'Indian' has become complex in the global context. Salman Rushdie in *Imaginary Homelands* states, "The word 'Indian' is getting to be a pretty scattered concept. Indian writers in England include political exiles, first-generation migrants, affluent expatriates whose residence here is frequently temporary, naturalised Britons, and people born here who may never have laid eyes on the subcontinent" (Rushdie 80). Due to their varied experiences, it isn't simply hard to define Indians, but also impossible to expect that a vast range of people with South Asian ancestry would fit neatly into a single category. Thus, one group of South Asians might feel that the term 'South Asia' itself is a political construct, developed with the purpose of homogenizing their experiences, though they have little in common with the other South Asian groups.

Another pressing issue concerning South Asian Women writers is their positive reception by the Western World. Indeed, South Asian women writers face the problem of benignant imperialism throughout their careers. They are commended just for composing books, and not for the merit of their works. Numerous South Asian women writers have also pointed out that frequently their compositions are thought to be autobiographical, even when they are not. Although some authors prefer depicting their personal experiences in their writings, many of them dislike their work being interpreted biographically. In addition, they disapprove of the mixing of their public image with their private lives.South Asian women writers are also subject to the danger of being 'tokenized,' as representatives of Third World writers, or Indian writers, or postcolonial writers, rather than being esteemed as litterateurs who are capable of writing about any and every subject of relevance and interest. In this regard, Chandra Talpade Mohanty's comment seems to be of much relevance: "Being a woman has political consequences in the world we live in; that there can be unjust and unfair effects on women depending on our... marginality and/or privilege" (Mohanty 3).

South Asian women's literature faces yet another major problem, as there is a set number of subjects, which the majority of authors repeatedly address. In contrast to the previous writers of the 1960s, they don't mirror the political ambiance of their protagonist's homelands. Rather the prevailing issues are generally relating to custom, marriage, connections, family, food and home. The women are shown for the most part as survivors of constrained relationships and widowhood, who suffer mainly because of their subordinate position in the patriarchal society. Considering the fact that South Asian nations had had a turbulent political history and keep on being politically unpredictable, this trend may seem a bit strange. India's partition, which had a variety of social, political, and economic ramifications, is often recounted in novels as merely a backdrop, and referred only in the context of how it affected the women and their families. *Cracking India* by Bapsi Sindhwais one of those pioneering works which explores the multiple effects of Partition on women from diverse backgrounds, ethnicities, and faiths. However, there have been no successors to Sindhwa, and the contemporary South Asian writers portray Partition simply as a historical backdrop in their works.Oddly for sure, South Asia's vast regional diversity is scarcely emphasized in the literature of this region. Especially the Diasporic authors apply expansive brush strokes to separate between the East and the West, without caring much about the regional diversity of their subjects' homeland.

As the South Asian women novelists time and again depict very similar issues in their works, they have become an easily identifiable voice in International Literature. In an ironic turn, the readers have now built an expectation that this branch of literature must exclusively deal with a limited number of themes and concerns. South Asian literature is therefore at risk of becoming stereotyped. It is therefore fascinating to study how emerging diasporic, South Asian women writers are challenging stereotypes and constraints of topics to carve out their own niche in this field. There is absolutely no denying that the South Asian women writers of today tend to explore newer horizons and narrate untold stories. This may explain why, despite the obstacles mentioned above, South Asian women writers of the present era have gained global acclaim. In the light of what has already been said concerning the positionality of South Asian women novelists, it is now important to elaborate my central concern. I intend to study *In Other Words*by Jhumpa Lahiri, a renowned second-generation South Asian author and portray how the diasporic circumstance in the postcolonial period have freed thewomen from the colonial, familial as well as ethnic restrictions, and have offered them a space in which they can redefine their identities as independent global citizens.

Jhumpa Lahiri was born in the year 1967 in London. She was born NilanjanaSudeshna Lahiri (her good name), but when she was enrolled in school, the teachers decided that Jhumpa (the nickname) was shorter and easier than her Indian name. Hence 'Jhumpa' became her school/good name and gradually she emerged as one of the elegant and discerning creative writers of our times. Lahiri spent her childhood in Kingstown, Rhode Island. Her father was a librarian and her mother worked as a teacher. Many a time she visited India along with her parents who could never emotionally sever themselves from their homeland. Such journeys impacted Lahiri's young impressionable mind. She became conscious of her unique position as a second-generation diasporic citizen and eventually these experiences became the principal subject of her writing.

Jhumpa Lahiri's career as a literary figure took off in 1997, when she started working as an intern for Boston magazine. During this period however, unfortunately her writings were not properly evaluated by the magazine. Her international fame came after the publication of her short story collection *Interpreter of Maladies* in 1999. Then in 2003, Lahiri published her first novel *The Namesake.* Written initially as a novella for *The New Yorker, The Namesake* was later developed into a gripping novel by Lahiri. Her second short story collection, *Unaccustomed Earth* was published in 2008. Her next novel *The Lowland*, published in 2013 further enriched the gamut of her creative work. Her recent publication *In Other Words* (*In alter Parole* in Italian) (2015) is her impactful debut in the field of non-fiction. The book poignantly depicts her struggles to gain command over the Italian language which never really 'belonged' to her.

In a conversation with Mary A. Dempsey, Jhumpa Lahiri elaborates, "When I first started writing I was not conscious that my subject was Indian-American experience. What drew me to my craft was the desire to force two worlds I occupied to mingle on the page as I was not brave enough, or mature enough to allow in life" (Lahiri). Being a second-generation diasporic citizen, Jhumpa Lahiri grew up as an ABCD[2] and could never completely relate to her homeland. Born and brought up in America, she gradually perceived that, "for immigrants, the challenges of exile, the loneliness, the constant sense of alienation, the longing for a lost world, are more explicit and distressing than for their children" (Lahiri). In other words, when, Lahiri's parents could never break the umbilical cord which kept them connected to India, Lahiri herself could never feel this connection. India was never her 'home' as she visited the country occasionally and could not keep up with the events happening there. She did not even find her parental home in Calcutta to be comfortable and welcoming, "[b]ecause growing up in America is different-I have my own room, I can shut the door. There, we became part of other families, lived according to their schedule" (Lahiri). But even then, Calcutta played a significant role in chiselling

Jhumpa Lahiri as a successful novelist that she has become. The fact comes out prominent from her online interview (published in *Bookbrowse.com)* where she states:

> I spent much time in Calcutta as a child-idle but rich time-often at home with my grandmother. I read books, I began to write and to record things. It enabled me to experience solitude ironically, because there were so many people, I could seal myself off psychologically. It was a place where I began to think imaginatively. Calcutta nourished my mind, my eye as a writer, and my interest in seeing things from different points of view. There's a legacy and tradition there that we just don't have here. The ink hasn't dried yet on our lives here. (Lahiri)

It is therefore evident from her comments that, like numerous immigrants living in the foreign soil, Jhumpa Lahiri too felt marginalized. In *In Other Words,* she states unambiguously: "I write on the margins, just as I've always lived on the margins of countries, of cultures" (Lahiri 89). Dwelling thousands of miles away from India and being surrounded by the all-pervasive American culture, she could certainly not preserve her Bengali identity, the way her parents have done. Talking of her experience as a hybridized Indian-American, Lahiri comments: "I am conscious of the unpleasant sensation of having to be two different people at the same time – an existential condition that marked my life" (Lahiri 114). Deducing from her comments it becomes apparent that Jhumpa Lahiri had to live with dilemma of her hyphenated identity for very long. She was definitely more inclined to the American ways of living but at the same time could not disown the Indian (Bengali) side of her identity. She was a hybrid second generation diasporic citizen who was fighting hard to build up 'a room of her own'.

Now, 'Hybridity' is one of the most debated terms of the postcolonial studies. It signifies "The creation of new trans-cultural forms within the contact zone produced by colonization" (Ashcroft 118). Robert Young pointed out that it has often been used to highlight the negative results of the mingling of different races. He explained that the colonial discourse "[a]ttaches the accusation of impurity, monstrosity and illegitimacy to thosc who are the products of miscegenation" (Young 122). The concept however has been differently dealt with by the postcolonial studies where it is "[C]elebrated and privileged as a kind of superior cultural intelligence owing to the advantage of in-betweenness, the straddling of two cultures and the consequent ability to negotiate the difference" (Hoogvelt 158). Following Bill Ashcroft, Hybridism has been seen as a strength and not a hindrance by a majority of postcolonial writers. It is no longer perceived as a process of the oppressive colonizer forcefully muting the colonized. Rather it is comprehended as a happy amalgamation of multiple cultures, which "[C]an have its impact on both the colonizer and the colonized" (Ashcroft 118). Presently the name Homi K. Bhabha is often attached with the concept of 'hybridity'. Bhabha assumed hybridity to be a procedure in which the colonizer attempts to alter the identity of the colonized in order to fit the latter into a convenient and familiar mould. But the process eventually backfires, producing something similar but not identical. In his own words: "A new hybrid identity emerges from the interweaving of elements of the colonizer and colonized" (Bhabha146). Bhabha further argues that Hybridity invariably procreates an 'in-between state' which he calls the 'third space'. He elaborates that it is "a space of production of new forms of cultural meaning, beyond the limitations of existing boundaries of culture and identity" (Bhabha 207). Such an elaboration can be well applied in the context of the postcolonial diasporic situation, though the terms 'colonizer' and the 'colonized' are to be substituted with the hostland and the homeland cultures respectively.

Coming back to Lahiri, with years such a severe identity crisis in her gradually paved the way for a better comprehension of her own situation. She came to realize that being a hybrid was not a flaw. Rather it was a dynamic condition which she was privileged to have. She eventually decided not to follow the footsteps of her mother for whom any sort of change post migration was unwelcome. She allowed herself to mutate, being surrounded by the dominant American culture, in the due course of time accepted her hybrid, diasporic identity with elan.

> When my mother returns to Calcutta, she is proud of the fact that, in spite of almost fifty years away from India, she seems like a woman who never left.
>
> I am the opposite. While the refusal to change was my mother's rebellion, the insistence on transforming myself was mine (Lahiri152-153).

This is perhaps the reason why Lahiri chose to write her stories in English and not Bengali, which depict the various facets of South Asian diasporic experience, and as the reader journeys with her from *Interpreters of Maladies* to *The Namesake,* he/she can invariably perceive the progression of the Diasporic mind from 'expatriation' to 'hybridization'. *Unaccustomed Earth* further traces the progress of the diasporic sensibility to acculturation, and ultimately assimilation with the omnipresent American Culture. Finally, in Lahiri's latest novel, *The Lowland*, we see how the diasporic condition of the characters capacitates them to shape unique and independent identities irrespective of their ethnicities.

Curiously, Lahiri has composed her latest memoir *In Other Words* in Italian. The book is an honest record of the author's struggle to gain proficiency over Italian language. While being in Rome, learning to communicate in Italian was a necessity and yet a challenging task. And thus began an immensely arduous period of Lahiri's apprenticeship in Italian. Time and again she felt abashed when her teacher found numerous faults in her composition. To quote her from *In Other Words*:

> I've never tried to do anything this demanding as a writer. I find that my project is so arduous that it seems sadistic. I have to start again from the beginning, as if I had never written anything in my life. But, to be precise, I am not at the starting point: rather, I'm in another dimension, where I have no references, no armour. Where I've never felt so stupid. (64)

Onemight wonder at Lahiri's desperation to gain command over a new language, especially when all her English publications namely, *Interpreter of Maladies*, *The Namesake*, *Unaccustomed Earth* and *The Lowland* have gained immense popularity and appreciation. The author herself solves this mystery by claiming: "I think that studying Italian is a flight from the long clash in my life between English and Bengali. A rejection of both the mother and the stepmother. An Independent path" (144).

Lahiri's words may be further understood by looking at the works of two eminent French philosophers – Deluze and Guattari – who had systematically developed the idea of territorialization in their two volumes of *Capitalism and Schizophrenia: Anti-Oedipus and A Thousand Plateaus*. Guattari defines territorialization as the separation of people based on their geographic, cultural, or ethnic locations. Individuals feel a sense of belonging to such territories and their personality is also shaped by them. In this era of deterritorialization, however, diasporic studies have proven without slightest ambiguity that no ethno-cultural boundary can constrain an individual for long. Hence, it is quite a normal sight to find a Japanese entrepreneur enjoying American delicacies like Cobb Salad, Pot Roast or California Roll, more than his native food. In the same way, a conservative Indian Hindu family staying in the USA may be seen participating in

Christmas celebrations with their acquaintances with much pomp and enthusiasm. Adaptations of this kind certainly lead to the fashioning of 'new' diasporic identities. Such examples are numerous and varied and they also aid in understanding the malleable nature of postcolonial diaspora. Jhumpa Lahiri's attempt to write in Italian is perhaps another step towards the transformation of her diasporic identity. From her biography as well as her publications, it is apparent that Lahiri has learnt to be at peace with her transnational self. It is evident from *In Other Words* that Lahiri has successfully crossed a number of huddles to gain proficiency in Italian. Only time will tell whether she will continue to write in Italian or not, but it is obvious that she has overcome her initial stages of identity crisis and today can profess to be a global citizen, who is neither Indian, nor American, but Italian by choice.

In this regard, if we follow Preston's model of citizenship, then Global citizenship cannot be expressed in any legal sense as there is no global bureaucracy to give sanction and protection to the global citizens.[3] However, in response to the escalation in the number of global citizens, anti-global activities are on the rise in the present decade. Demonstrations in Seattle in 1999,[4] Genoa in 2001[5] and in dozens of other sites brought activists together from all around the world. They have argued that, Globalization strengthens the strong and weakens those who are already weak. Here it is also relevant to mention that, although the technological advancements of today's trans-cultural world have facilitated the interaction between the cultures from all over the world, the individuality of each culture has begun to fade. So as to say, the process of Globalization eventually leads to annihilating the feeling of 'displacement' and cutting off the ties of an individual with his/her native land and culture. Any discussion on Global Citizenship certainly incorporates both its positive and negative aspects. But the fact remains undeniable that Global Citizens do exist and are growing in number. And asa representative South Asian women novelist of our time, Jhumpa Lahiri's biography and her works provebeyond doubt that the diasporic space, which acts as a foundation to global citizenship does offer new resources and opportunities to the women to refashion their identities with an absolute unconcern for any and every ethnic expectation of the homeland as well as the hostland societies. However,at the same time, it may be reasonably claimed that in present era, 'Global literature' would inevitably take over the Indian,

African, Chinese, Australian or Caribbean Diasporic literature, and the documentation of the idiosyncrasies of a particular ethnic or diasporic community would become extinct. Such a future invariably awaits the diasporic literature and Jhumpa Lahiri's *In Other Words* corroborates this idea in incontrovertible ways.

Notes

1. Refer to "The Social Identity Theory of Inter-Group Behavior" by Tajfel and Turner.
2. ABCD refers to American – Born Confused Desi
3. Reference is made to P.W. Preston's *Political/Cultural Identity: Citizens and Nations in a Global Era.*
4. The 1999 Seattle WTO protests (also known as the Battle of Seattle) were protests directed against the WTO Ministerial Conference of 1999. The movement is considered to be a strong anti-globalization movement which took place in the USA. The protesters were known as N30 and were a large group. Thousands of people protested outside the hotels where the delegates from around the world stayed, as well as outside the Washington State Convention and Trade Center. The demonstrators protested against 'world meetings' pertaining to economic globalization.
5. Genoa, Italy, was the site of the 27th G8 summit, held July 21-22, 2001.In the anti-globalization movement, it has been hailed as a significant milestone.

Works Cited

Ashcroft, Bill, Gareth Griffiths, and Helen Tiffin. *Post-Colonial Studies: The Key Concepts*. London: Routledge, 2003. Print.

Bhaba, Homi K. "The Third Space." *Identity: Community, Culture, Difference.* Ed. Jonathan Rutherford. London: Lawrence and Wishart, 1995. Print.

Deleuze, Gilles, and FélixGuattari. *Anti-Oedipus: Capitalism and Schizophrenia.* London: Continuum, 2003. Print.

.........*A Thousand Plateaus: Capitalism and Schizophrenia.* London: Continuum, 2004. Print.

Foucault, Michel. *Of Other Spaces: Utopias and Heterotopias.* Trans. Jay Miskowiec.*mit.edu.* N.p., n.d. Web. 30 October 2019.

Hoogvelt, A. *Globalization and the Postcolonial World: The New Political Economy of Development.* Baltimore: The John Hopkins University Press, 1997. Print.

Jeffery, Patricia, and Amrita Basu, eds. *Appropriating Gender. Women's Activism and Politicised Religion in South Asia.* New York: Routledge, 1998. Print.

Lahiri, Jhumpa. *In Other Words.* Trans. Ann Goldstein. India: Penguin Books India, 2016. Print.

.........*Interpreter of Maladies.* New Delhi: Harper Collins, 1999. Print

.... *The Lowland.* London: Bloomsbury, 2013. Print.

.... *The Namesake.* New York: Mariner Books, 2003. Print.

.... *Unaccustomed Earth.* India: Random House India, 2008. Print.

.... "A Conversation with Jhumpa Lahiri." *bookbrowse.com.* Book Browse. n.d. Web. 07 June 2016.

.... "Jhumpa Lahiri in Conversation with Mary A. Dempsey." *wbez.org.* NBEZ News, 09 October 2006. Web. 07 June 2016.

Mohanty, Chandra Talpade. *Feminism without Borders: Decolonizing Theory, Practicing Solidarity.* Durham: Duke University Press, 2003. Print.

Rushdie, Salman. *Imaginary Homelands.* London: Granta Books, 1991. Print.

Said, Edward W. "Intellectual Exile: Expatriates and Marginals." *Grand Street* 47.1 (1993): 112-124. Print.

Tajfel, H. and J.C Turner. "The Social Identity Theory of Inter-Group Behavior." *Psychology of Intergroup Relations.* Eds. S. Worchel and L.W Austin. Chicago: Nelson-Hall, 1986. Print.

Young, R.J.C. *Colonial Desire: Hybridity in Theory, Culture and Race.* London: Routledge, 1995. Print.

CHAPTER 14

Liberation of the Trodden Blossoms: A Study of Taslima Nasreen's *My Girlhood*

Anupriya Roy Srivastava

Abstract

The predicament of women we see now in today's world is marked by contrasting gaps in all realms. Women's concerns are still neglected. They continue to face discrimination and marginalization, but understated and brazen. To a varying degree the presence of patriarchy is still felt. Histories of most cultures and countries are about what men have achieved in this world. Male dominance over women is the product of historical development as women are systematically disadvantaged and oppressed with time. Autobiographical literature has granted women a scope to voice their need. It would provide them a space for introspection, self-expression, and relief from the pressures of living. To confront the patriarchal domination and hegemonic structures, a woman in her autobiography exposes her discrimination in society. This paper analyses how Taslima Nasreen's *My Girlhood: An Autobiography* (2001), invariably questions the subaltern existence of middle-class Bangladeshi women of the late 60's and 70's through the story of the life of the author. This paper also scrutinizes the close observations of Nasreen about how the Muslim society of Bangladesh acknowledges religion that finds precedence and how the saints and the mullahs are greeted with respect and reverence than the educated elites, why women are mostly home bound, hardly sent to school, married at an early age, and hardly get justice when subjected to violence in and out of their homes. This paper thus undertakes to show how Nasreen's autobiography has denounced the anti-patriarchal stance of the society and how it has provided women a space to voice their demand of basic human rights to live.

Keywords: Religion, Bangladeshi society, Autobiography, Patriarchy, Subjugation

Autobiography provides an individual the space for self-examination, self-actualization, exposition of self, expression of self, pursuit for identity, relief from the compressions of living. The process of construction of self of a woman is different from that of a man in autobiographical literature because feminine involvements, understandings and sensibilities are mostly different from what men experience in their lives as these are unquestionably shaped by factors like gender, class, category, politics, region, and religion. When real life-experiences of a woman are faithfully recognized and put forth in print and made public, to confront the patriarchal domination and hegemonic structures, it maneuvers her autobiography. This process of composing her autobiography requires an act of scripting down her 'self' that brings into being her individuality truthfully, decently, and honestly before her readers. An examination of the creation of her 'self' in her autobiography would certainly validate that a woman in her life-narrative exposes her exploitation, discrimination, oppression, repression, subjugation in society and humiliation in public sphere, and more often she documents her social exclusion and erasure from the mainstream life, thus re-generating her fractured self to question the masked and suppressed issues of women in society.

A woman writer writes her life either at some moment of catastrophe in her life or at a certain time when she achieves fame and recognition in public sphere. Most of them usually write to assuage the pain of their distressing circumstances born out of some unpleasant and acrimonious life-experiences that require a vent to counterpoise the push of living. The writing of autobiographies and scripting of their selves became an empowering device for women. In the Indian scenario, women creative writers progressively switched to the autobiographical mode. Earlier they looked upon themselves through the eyes of men, but with time, they have learnt to become authors of their own stories, as Ranjana Dwivedi writes:

> Autobiographies written by Indian women in English show how difficult it has been for them, the ones subjected to metonymy from time immemorial, to grow out of that metonymy and to find a real metaphor of self for themselves. Over centuries Indian women were looked upon as metonymy by men and by society. This practice was so over-powering and their social conditioning to self-effacement so strong that at one stage of social history they too started believing in the metonymical tags stuck to them by the male dominated society. Indian women's progress from metonymy to metaphor has been a heart-breaking hard journey for them. (117)

This paper analyses how Taslima Nasreen's *My Girlhood: An Autobiography* (2001), invariably questions the subaltern existence of middle-class Bangladeshi women of the late 60's and 70's. Originally written as *Amar Meyebela* (1998), a term in Bengali meaning my girlhood, this autobiography depicts the observations of the author about Muslim society where religion finds priority and the saints and the mullahs are hailed high with respect and reverence than the educated elites, where the women are hardly sent to school, married at an early age and often subjected to violence in and out of their homes. It also delineates how her individual self is merged with the collective selves of the women of her society and how it is deeply embedded in their customs and conventions as almost all women undergo similar form of oppression. This transforms her life-narrative into a socio-biography. *Amar Meyebela* when translated into English from Bengali by Gopa Majumdar in 2001, it transcended all the regional boundaries and linguistic barriers and reached to the global readers opening their eyes as it portrayed the hapless condition of the women of her society very much like the trodden blossoms before their blooming.

A woman constantly attempts to depict every minute detail of her life in her life narrative as she contemplates many things in her life to express, even those miniscule events which men often renounce considering them as trifle anecdotes, unsuitable to be archived in the pages of their autobiographies. The consequence leads to the fact that women's autobiography is multidirectional, non-chronological and disjunctive whereas men's autobiography is linear and unidirectional. This is more distinctly stated by Estelle Jelinek in her essay "Introduction: Women's Autobiography and the Male Tradition", that women's autobiographies are non-linear in structure (90-91). Jelinek notes that this back and forth movement and fragmented narration, often lacking coherence is a special characteristic of women's autobiographies. Taslima Nasreen's *My Girlhood* opens during the War of Independence in 1971, when Nasreen was only nine years of age. She has given a detailed picture of the war stricken area of her locality, the havoc and massacre she has witnessed. The narrative is disjunctive, not linear, as it is found in most of the women's autobiographies.

Women's consciousness of her 'relational' self brings to her awareness of others who are part and parcel of her life. The possibility of women's autobiography lies there where "the individual does *not* feel herself to exist outside of others but feels she is included in an independent existence that asserts its rhythms everywhere in the community" (Bree 174). This is elaborately explained by Nancy Chodorow in *The Reproduction of Mothering: Psychoanalysis and the Sociology of Gender*:

> .. . growing girls come to define and experience themselves as continuous with others; their experience of self contains more flexible or permeable ego boundaries. Boys come to define themselves as more separate and distinct, with a greater sense of rigid ego boundaries and differentiation. The basic feminine sense of self is connected to the world, the basic masculine sense of self is separate.
>
> .. . Masculine personality, then, comes to be defined more in terms of denial of relation and connection (and denial of femininity), whereas feminine personality comes to include a fundamental definition of self in relationship. (169).

This is obvious as Nasreen narrates that her mother was married at a very early age to her father, who was then studying medicine. Nasreen has pointed out that her mother wanted to study as well but had to conform to the norms of the society and therefore had to leave her studies after marriage. Through and through, as the story moves, she unfolds that the marriage of her parents did not work as one day, her mother found her father in bed with another man's wife, Razia Begum. To keep herself away from the conjugal discord, her mother used to pass her time in the movie theaters leaving her children to their uncles and aunts after their schools. Nasreen writes in her autobiography that she was molested many a times at the hands of her uncles, but being fearful, she kept it a secret.

It is anticipated that women should never talk about themselves candidly being the victims of molestation, their subjugation and marginalization in society and if they do at all, like Taslima has done, there is every possibility of inviting trouble for themselves. Patriarchal burdens have always disenchanted and restrained women's creativity and made them suffer in silence. Writing has given women an opportunity to undermine the man-made prognoses of female identity. In their autobiographies, women creative writers refashion and modify their selves based on their own conception. They vandalize and destabilize the conventional and stereotypical notions of age old female identity created by the male hegemonic discourses. Usha V.T. comments: "By writing the self, the woman writer could challenge accepted notions of the female and redraft general opinion on the feminine mystique" (1-2). The open declaration of her molestation in Taslima's autobiography had brought her into controversy as this outrageousness is unexpected from the part of a woman in a very conservative Bangladeshi society. But what can a woman do? How long can she suppress her desire to express what truth is? Why should she suffer in silence? These questions tend to be very disturbing as Bhagyashree Varma writes:

> Living life in a very limited world, women view their life-story more intensely. For them, autobiography is a literary mode rather than an aesthetic experience, the personal reflection of 'self' with an impersonal viewpoint. . . Theirs is essentially a suppressed self-trying to explore its psychic potential so far neglected, negated and nullified in the male world. (97)

To escape the harsh realities of life, as mentioned before, Taslima's mother soothed herself in movie theatres. When cinema could not bring her comfort, her mother took refuge in the lap of religion. She became an ardent follower of Hazrat Baba (Amirullah), a Muslim Guru who though suggested perverse practices to follow, had a long line of women followers. Almost every day the women used to drink the water after cleaning his feet; not only that, but they also often gobbled his mucus and cough, and repeatedly there are cases of molestation followed by harassment. The father of the author and her maternal uncle Siddiqui, these two people who claimed themselves as such Muslims who are "different" from other people mentioned in her autobiography condemned Amirullah's supremacy as both are learned. Uncle Siddiqui is disappointed with the misinterpretation of the preaching of Islam though he studied Arabic and theology at Dhaka University. He discards the "superstitious" rites and rituals that are accepted, implemented, and often followed by the members of his family, that includes their blind faith on baba Amirullah and often is at daggers drawn with her sister Nasreen's aunt Fajli. Nasreen's father, a doctor by profession, dreams big for his children and expects them to study subjects that may inculcate some secular values in them, never wants them to be pulled towards the religious instruction of Amirullah like her mother and expects his wife Idulwara to be there during midday to take care of the children. But he is a womanizer, does not reciprocate love to his wife or his daughter, sends the major share of his earnings to his father who used to work as a farmer and to his poor siblings and sleeps with Razia Begum, the wife of Chakladar, as Nasreen states that: "Ma simply failed to grasp how Baba's mind worked. She was convinced that no one in the world has such a complex character...

The truth, Ma thought, was that he was devoted to Razia Begum" (*My Girlhood,* 88). Describing the condition of her mother she writes in her autobiography:

> This was the kind of man Ma lived with. People saw her as a doctor's wife, her life full of joy and happiness. Only Ma knew how the scent of another woman wafted up from her husband's body and doused her dreams and desires....What kept Ma company during her sleepless nights were her own long, deep sighs (*My Girlhood,* 90)

The book depicts the incapacity of the mother to recognize the love of her daughter, fondness and favouritism towards sons than to the daughter, the benevolent indifference bestowed to the children by their mother. Nasreen has openly criticized all these practices and says that all these rites of the Peer especially do not belong to Islam rather misinterpreted. Now, the question arises why the followers are always women? The answer is evident from her autobiography that voices of women of our society are hardly heard. Her mother and Nasreen herself are representatives of the women of our society, where, often they are asked to put a stop to their education as soon as they are married. Can marriage be the last nail on the coffin of desires of the women of our society? Nasreen systematically criticizes Islam here.

Nasreen states in her book that most of the Muslims of South Asia learn about their religion on hearsay because according to the author, the Muslims are taught to read Quran phonetically as it is written in Arabic and most difficult to understand. So they have to depend on translations, but very less number of people actually read them. In her book, she has portrayed how people always used religion to justify their actions, may it be better or worse, as they lack in conceptions and proper knowledge. Wherein this book, every bitter action (of ignorant people) can be traced back to Islam.

Taslima Nasreen brings into forefront some relevant observations about Muslim society – its patriarchal nature, the Peers, mullahs and Imams who are revered and respected more than doctors and engineers or any other learned men, references of polygamy, women are married early at a very low age, women suffer from very low status in society owing to illiteracy, less alternative to justice to women, etc. A string of profound pessimism features in her autobiography, because of her futile anticipations from the members of her family, from her society, and even from the religion she embraces, most specifically based on gender discrimination.

This paper thus undertakes to show how autobiography has provided women a space to voice their demand of basic human rights to live. It has provided women a space to expose their marginalized condition through the pen of the author. One such example is Sharan-Jeet Shan, an Indian woman writer, whose expressions in her life narrative seem very similar to what Nasreen states in *My Girlhood.* She re-creates her split selves in her writing to overcome her marginality in the world of men, as she states in her autobiography:

> I had started writing it [the autobiography] while I was still imprisoned in my own situation. Unable to bear the pain of physical and mental abuse. . . I remember hitting my head against walls. When nothing worked, I sought refuge in writing.... If my book awakens awareness in just one woman's heart, that inside all of us there lies a latent courage, a whole host of inner resources, then it will have served its purpose. (76)

Writing has a dual impact on women: a cathartic effect of mollifying their sufferings and of refurbishing their selves to normality. In this context, Gail Chester and Sigrid Nielson state that: "Writing plays a vital part in forming our perceptions of our lives as women, in working out our feminist views and in communicating them to others" (9).

Similarly, Nasreen's writing has smashed down all the conventional norms and social taboos to establish her own autonomy and has thus created a state of permanency in the heart of the readers. Nasreen has bravely raised questions whenever she finds a flaw in the social setup. She has written to neutralize the pressures of her living. She has written to unburden her heart clogged with pains. She has written in order to escape from the loads of worries of this mundane world that a woman is compelled to bear. Her too much frank confession has led the readers to be flabbergasted as hardly any such woman writer previously had the courage to do so leaving one or two. Her confession straight-from-the-shoulder has taught the society that a woman too has tales to tell; she can be bold and forthright in narration and society should change its outlook towards the stature of a woman. *My Girlhood* has emerged as a priceless treatise for the posterity because her dissension and discordance with the harsh realities of life and her decry of the forceful imposition on women in the name of tradition substantiate that she has objurgated the patriarchal norms through her writing. Her voice is the voice of her subjugated counterparts who are duped and dumped at the periphery of human conglomeration, silently suffering under the cruel and dominating fangs of patriarchy, fearful to express their desire and are assaying to set forth their own identity. Taslima Nasreen's *My Girlhood* has always been an inspiration to them. In one of her works, *All About Women*, Taslima says:

> We women are sent by nature.
> Nature does not create women from men's ribs.
> We women are sent by nature.
> Nature does not place women under men.
> We women are sent by nature.
> Nature does not put women's heaven under
> men's feet.
> Nature says women are human beings-men
> have made religions to deny it.
> Nature says women are human beings-society has cocked a snook at it.
> Nature says women are human beings-men cry
> out NO! ("We Women" 39)

The depiction of her pains through her life story has taught women to wage the war of life with their pen, to show the almightiness of their pen, because the process of writing can save women from self-subjugation and stabilize her identity. Taslima Nasreen has shown that autobiographical literature serves as the best medium through which a woman can relieve the pain and anguish of her life and this journey from silence to expression can empower them. Therefore, through this autobiography *My Girlhood*, she has called for the emancipation of the suppressed voices of women of her society, the liberation of the trodden blossoms.

Works Cited

Bree, Germaine. "Autogynography." *Studies in Autobiography*, edited by James Olney, Oxford University Press, 1988, pp. 171-179.

Chester, Gail, and Sigrid Nielson. Introduction. *In Other Words: Writing as a* Feminist, edited by Chester and Nielson, Hutchinson Press, 1987, pp. 9-20.

Chodorow, Nancy. *The Reproduction of Mothering: Psychoanalysis and the Sociology of Gender*. University of California Press, 1978.

Dwivedi, Ranjana. "Autobiography: A Metaphor of Self." *Between Spaces of Silence: Women Creative Writers*, edited by Kamini Dinesh, Sterling Publishers, 1994, pp. 115-125.

Jelinek, Estelle C. *Introduction: Women's Autobiography and the Male Tradition*, edited by Trev Lynn Broughton, Vol. 2, Routledge, 2007, pp. 78-93.

Nasreen, Taslima. *My Girlhood*, translated by Gopa Majumdar, Kali for Women, 2001.

.... "We Women". *All about Women*, Rupa & Co., 2005, pp. 39.

Shan, Sharan-Jeet. *In My Own Name: An Autobiography*. The University of Michigan Women's Press, 1985.

V. T., Usha. "One Woman's Autobiography: Kamala Das's *My Story*." *Kamala Das: A Critical Spectrum*, edited by Rajeshwar Mittapalli and Pier Paolo Piciucco, Atlantic Publishers, 2001, pp. 1-9.

Varma, Bhagyashree. "Feminine Concerns: Autobiographies of Amrita Pritam, Kamala Das and Jean Rhys." *Modern Indian English Fiction*, compiled and edited by T. S. Anand, Creative Books, 2002, pp. 95-109.

CHAPTER 15

Astha's Journey toward Emancipation in Manju Kapur's *A Married Woman*

Sandeep Kumar Nandlalji Saraiya

Abstract

The contribution of women writers in the enrichment of English literature is extremely noteworthy. In this movement Manju Kapur has created her own place by contributing the novels *Difficult Daughters, A Married Woman, Home, Immigrant* and *Custody*. All of her novels have the common theme of the time. The Woman and her problems are at the centre of her focus. As the life of a woman is gaining significance today, she has depicted the life of a woman with minute details in all of her novels. She has explored the position of male chauvinism and violence committed against women. Manju Kapur has focused her deep insight in to human nature and her understanding of day-to-day problems faced by woman in this male dominated society. She has presented the female protagonists in her novels as educated individual caged within the boundaries of traditional Indian society aspiring for emancipation. This research paper aims at finding how Manju Kapur has presented the problems faced by Astha in the novel *A Married woman.*

Keywords: Woman, Self-identity, tradition, modern.

Introduction

Manju Kapur has given a noteworthy contribution to Indian writings in English by writing the novels *Difficult Daughters, A Married Woman, Home, Immigrant* and *Custody*. There is a female protagonist in each of the novels she has contributed and through each female protagonist she has tried to bring forth the problems faced by the woman in Indian male dominated traditional society. She has delineated the woman characters with minute details describing the problems of women and the novel *A Married Woman* is no exception to this. Astha is a middle class working woman in the novel *A Married Woman.* She imbibes the middle class values and latter experiences a sense of incompleteness in her married life. Manju Kapur gives her the valuable insights into the feminine consciousness through her protagonists. Astha is the protagonist of the novel. The novel is the story of her life. Astha, being an educated woman displays the capacity to determine her priorities for self-discovery. While struggling for the desired status in the society which is dominated by the males in India, she strives to the best of her capacities.

Astha was a single child of her parents. Her parents were always concerned about her education, her character, her health, her marriage etc. *"His daughter's future lay in her own hands, and these hands were to be strengthened by the number of books that passed through them. At least once a day he said to her, why aren't you studying?"(P.2)*But she was dreaming a handsome young man holding her in his robust manly embrace and always thinking of the romantic fancies. This common thing is skillfully depicted about her adolescence of a school going girl Astha. She falls in love with Rohan, a boy of her age due to which her daily routine was disturbed. This relationship does not last longer as the boy moves for the Higher education to Oxford. This was for the first time she had lost her individuality. She was married to Hemant. At first her marriage she enjoyed the most but after giving birth to two children, she was fed up with the married life. She wanted to shoulder the responsibilities on her own. Hemant didn't like this and gets irritated and blames her for not trusting him. Here Astha finds that she was a stupid to believe him and anticipate him to appreciate her. She identifies well that Hemant never endeavors to be a good companion –

> "She has a good life, but it was good because nothing was questioned. Astha was pleading now, begging Hemant to understand. She meant nothing personal. She didn't want to feel dependent that was all. Surely equals could relate better than master and slave?" (*AMW*, p.99)

Her natural inappropriateness with her corporate husband forces her to play the role of both the mother and a father for her two children. Her dissatisfaction is the root cause due to which the institution of marriage is collapsed. She has a lack of self-esteem in facing the challenges of life. Her guilt feelings and negativity is the product of the anxiety, uneasiness and isolation she developed out of the frustration in her married life.

Astha is suffocated with growing needs of the family and adjusting everybody's needs. However she concentrated on her duties as a daughter, wife and a mother. She recognizes the place of a married woman and compares herself to the unpaid servant or a slave. She thinks of a divorce which brings social and economic damage to her status in Indian social system. Due to the continuous tension she develops migraines.

In this novel Hemant as a husband is shown as the master of Astha's fate. He expects her to fulfill the needs of the family directly attached to the duties and responsibilities of husband. The moment she fails to perform these duties she is blamed for that. Here the woman character Astha is suppressed at the hands of her husband. When she brings books from her father's house Hemant says – "*Are you mad? We don't have room,' declared Hemant.* She has no freedom even in the house of her husband. On the trip to Goa also she is not allowed to purchase an antique box. This trip was planned by her husband and with the money earned by Astha herself and without her own consent. She is not satisfied with the trip to Goa because everything has been done at her husband's accord: *"their money spending was decided by him, not by her."*(*AMW*, p.167)

She feels suffocated and subjugated. After her suffocation she turns to the outer world where she comes across with Aijaz Khan, the theater artist and activist who performs the street shows. As Astha had a teaching job, Her first meeting with Aijaz takes place at school as she was assigned to work with him. Meanwhile they become intimate friends but after the sad demise of Aijaz Khan, once again Astha becomes frustrated as she comes to that he was burnt alive along with his crew. After this incident she meets Pipeelika Trivedy, a widow of Aijaz. There is a development of intimate relationship between the two. Here Manju Kapur projects the lesbian relationship. Astha's passion with love and lesbianism, a mismatched marriage and consequent frustration are evidently visible here. However, Astha claims her to be happy with her married life and two children but Pipee recognizes her sorrow. Pipee is able to sense the sorrow behind her confident smile – *"So? Are you telling me you are happy, fulfilled, and what have you? Unexpected tears came to Astha's eyes."* (*AMW*, p.219)

Here Manju Kapur has been successful in presenting the changing image of woman moving away from her traditional role of enduring, self-sacrificing woman towards ambitious, assertive and self-assured woman. She presents the more demanding woman making society aware of their demands and in this way providing a medium for self-expression. Pipee is shown more demanding and asks for more time to be spent with her as a result Astha starts ignoring her children and family. Even she could not pay attention to her own health. Astha does not want to leave her husband and children. This shows her attachment towards her family. Here her traditional outlook is clearly seen. I the due course of time this relationship comes to an end as Pipee goes to USA for pursuing her Ph.D. This lesbian relationship was a kind of step toward emancipation from the traditional role of a daughter, wife and mother. The writer concentrates on the destiny of a woman that she is forced to accept again the traditional threshold only for the benefit of familial harmony.

Manju Kapur has stressed on the externally appearing safe and protected pattern of life of a woman. Actually, such type of life of a woman not only enslaved her but also made her dependent. Now, it through education she has become aware of her position in the society. As a result she started thinking liberally and she could know the significance of self-reliant life of woman. With this intention she started struggling against the taboo issues related to woman in the male dominated Indian society. Though this struggle is hard-hitting, but it has begun. Binod Mishra writes in his article, *Obsession to Ovation: A Thematic Study of Manju Kapur's A Married Woman* –

> "The new generation of women delineated in A Married Woman shows the split in their personalities. They are highly educated and are accustomed to the sound and furies of the world. Their eyes and ears, ascertained to the ups and downs of the fast changing world long to experiment something unusual to satisfy their suppressed ego. And in their venture to do so, they feel a prey to false temptations. These temptations distance them from their practical responsibilities and they burg on forth a tree of detachment. The urge to lead their own lives and the impulse to galvanize them drive them ultimately to disappointment." (*Mishra*, p.205)

Astha represents a modern Indian woman who exhibits courage to fight against the problems of woman in male dominated Indian society through her journey towards emancipation.

Conclusion

In this way it is a great success of Manju Kapur as a novelist in contributing to Indian writings in English and through the character of Astha in *A Married Woman* bringing forth the problems faced by the woman in male dominated Indian society. She has also been successful in projecting Astha's journey towards her emancipation.

Astha does all this for the sake of her identity and self-esteem and becomes a new modern woman as well as proves her own capability.

Works Cited

Ali, Farzana S. *Novels of Manju Kapur-A Critical Study*, Nagpur: dattson, 2015.

Kumar, Ashok. *Novels of Manju Kapur: A Feministic Study:* Sarup Book Publishers, 2015. Print.

Kumar, Ashok. "Social Web and Cry for the Self: A Critical Analysis of Manju Kapur's A Married Woman," *New Lights on Indian Woman* in *English Vol.4*. Ed. Amar Nath Prasad, New Delhi: Sarup and Sons, 2008.

Kapur, Manju. *A Married Woman,* New Delhi: India Ink Pvt. Ltd. 2002. Print.

Mishra, Binod. "Obsession to Ovation: A Thematic Study of Manju Kapur's *A Married Woman.*" *Studies in Woman Writers in English, Vol. IV*. Ed. Mohit Ray and Rama Kundu, New Delhi: Atlantic Publishers and Distributors, 2005.

Nitonde, Rohidas, *In Search of a Feminist Writer,* India: PATRIDGE

CHAPTER 16

Feminist Reading of Myth: A Study of Amish Tripathi's *Shiva Trilogy* and *Ram Chandra Series*

Ayushi Zina

Abstract

Mythical narratives have been androcentric from the ancient times. Women have been presented as the weaker sex, in need of protection from their male counterparts. A popular trend that can be seen, is the revisioning of the myth. This aims at retelling mythological tales to accommodate and represent the perspective of the women characters and bring them at the center of the action. "Feminism can be defined as a political, cultural, pedagogic and theoretical response to the patriarchal structures of power that seek to subordinate women's lives, interests, bodies and sexualities." 66 Amish Tripathi has aimed at changing the narrative of the mythological tales in his well-acclaimed works, *Shiva Trilogy* and the *Ram Chandra Series*. In this book chapter, the themes of feminism have been explored in relation to all the women characters introduced by Tripathi in the two series.

Keywords: Feminism, Gender Roles, Mythologies, Narrative shift.

From the ancient times mythological tales have represented the patriarchal narratives. This can be exemplified by looking at the great mythologies of Indian culture like Ramayana – which means 'Rama's journey'. It has not been termed Sitayana – which would mean 'Sita's journey', though the story clearly states the hardships faced by both. Similarly, if we look at Mahabharata, it is seen as a monumental work with characters like Arjuna, Bhima, Yudhishtir, Karna who have been portrayed as heroic, brave, courageous and strong, while the women characters have been presented as the sufferers of their fate. Mythologies are made up of heroes, who protect the heroine/ the women characters.

Amish Tripathi aims at changing the narrative of the mythologies in his retelling of the tales, be it the Shiva Trilogy or the Ram

Chandra Series. He has presented a balanced view of the characters. In the Shiva Trilogy, Sati has been depicted as a glorious warrior, a courageous person who fought till her last breath and died valiantly in the battle ground. Similarly, the book written on Sita is called; *Sita – Warrior of Mithila.* The name itself hints at the characterization of Sita and her portrayal as a warrior. If we look at the other women characters also created in the two series, we find a plethora of strong-willed women who fought and lived their lives on their own terms. They did not need a hero to save them.

> "Since the early twentieth century feminist criticism has grown to encompass a vast series of concerns: a rewriting of literary history so as to include the contributions of women; the tracing of a female literary tradition; theories of sexuality and sexual difference, drawing on psychoanalysis, Marxism, and the social sciences; the representation of women in male literature, the role of gender in both literary creation and literary criticism (as studied in so-called gynocriticsm); the connection between gender and various aspects of literary form, such as genre and meter (it is clear, for example, that certain genres such as epic embody masculine values of heroism, war, and adventure, while lyric has sometimes been seen as feminine, expressing private emotion)….And how do women confront the task of being historically coerced into using a language dominated by male concepts and values?" (Habib:668)

Thus, we can see a retelling of mythologies taking place to re-interpret the role of women in the stories. Mythologies were mostly seen as a masculine body of literature. The new writers have taken this masculine body of literature and shifted the narrative to women centric novels as in the case of Chitra Divakaruni, who in her story – *The Palace of Illusion and The Forest of Enchantment,* tells the story from the perspective of Draupadi and Sita respectively. The novels recount the incidents of the original epics, but introduce elements which would portray the anguish, courage, strength of the two ladies.

Shiva Trilogy as the name suggests is the story of the Hindu mythological god, Lord Shiva and his quest to find evil in the world. What sets this retelling of Lord Shiva's life apart from the previous renditions is the portrayal of Goddess Sati. When Shiva sees Sati for the first time, he falls in love at the first sight. Amish Tripathi describes the scene gloriously,

> "In a flash Shiva drew his sword and stretched out his left hand protectively, to pull the object of his fascination behind him. She however deftly side-stepped his protective hand, reached into the folds of her angvastram and drew out her own sword" (Meluha: 49)

> Thus begins the description of Sati as a self-sufficient warrior. When Shiva sees her prowess, he is left stunned and unintentionally remarks, "it's just that in our society, women don't fight. You don't wield your sword too badly for a woman" (Meluha: 52)

This brings to our notice the common belief that women are not supposed to be warriors. They are not expected to know sword fighting. Their place is the home and the hearth. Tripathi intricately weaves incidents where Sati would be required to wield her sword. Even as a child of six, she had gone against the gender stereotypes and saved the life of a woman by fighting with a pack of wild dogs. She is praised for her bravery at that tender age by her grandfather. Tripathi has also broken gender stratification by showing that King Daksha had no male progeny to continue his royal lineage. It has always been seen that kings or emperors needed male heirs to ascend the throne after their deaths. But King Daksha dotes on his daughter and had no other wives or children. As the story progresses, we see that there are other women characters who have been presented as strong, independent women, contrary to the notion that women were born to be wives and look after their children. Lady Ayurvati is considered the best doctor in the land. She is a lady of dignity who was a savior of the people and commanded immense respect. "She was used to being obeyed. She was a doctor." (Meluha: 21)

Here we are forced to see the role gender classification plays in the society. She was respected not because she was a woman but because she was a doctor. It makes us question whether she would have commanded equal respect, had she not been a doctor and been just an ordinary wife. Similarly, we find an important position, that of the Prime Minister of such an illustrious place being given to a woman; Kanakhala "She takes care of the administrative, revenue and protocol matters" (Meluha:67). It is surprising to note that the first female prime minister of the world was elected in 1960, too late as compared to the men of the time. But in the mythological tale, way back in time, Tripathi presents women characters in important roles. What strikes us the most is the wide range of characters Tripathi has woven into the story. Anandmayi is an intriguing character. She likes flaunting her sensual side, but it does not lessen her authority or chastity in any way. She dresses voluptuously and likes being admired by others. But at the same time, she learns sword fighting to win the heart of a warrior-Parvateshwar.

Feminist criticism explores the concept of the different types of women presented in literature. Women were mostly withheld from positions of power or speaking their voices; males made decisions for them and their lives were dictated by the men that ran the society.

Women had to take up one of the following roles – Mother, the Virgin, The Witch or The Whore.

> "The woman is typecast as 'Mother Nature', thus reducing her to the role of the perpetual 'giver'. Religious doctrines aid these representations. Language makes it appear permanent and 'natural' through the use of patriarchal terms like Mother Earth and Mother Nature." (Nayar:67)

In the Shiva Trilogy, women have not been put under any of these classifications. Just because Anandmayi likes dressing provocatively, it is not hinted that she was the witch or the whore. Instead, she falls in love with a valiant fighter whom she ultimately takes as her husband. The husband-wife relationship is also worth observing. Unlike common representation, where husband is the patriarch of the family and thus, controls the running of the house and the lives of everyone around him, in the relationship of Shiva and Sati or Anandmayi and Parvateshwar, we find a bond of equals. No one is the master of the other. They have a marital life which is equal for both and they mutually respect each other.

> "Feminism looks at all the representational strategies in popular and other cultural forms, drawing attention to the masculinist/ patriarchal constructions of women within these representations, and acquiring a political platform from which such an agenda can be articulated and justice fought for." (Nayar:67)

The idea that has been circulated for long is that 'women are subservient and inferior to men such as the Virgin, which portrays females as passive and weak, or the mother whose very life circles around making a better life for her family and especially for her husband.' Tripathi breaks this concept when he writes that Sati left behind a three-year-old Kartik to go and unearth the mystery behind the going away of the king to the eastern part of the palace. A similar thing happens when, she goes away to find the man-eatingtigers and kills them, getting severely wounded in the process. Her motherhood doesnot keep her from taking up dangerous tasks. When she faces Ganesha and Kali for the first time, she is resolute that she would not give them up, even if she would have to stay away from her husband and the society. Kali is yet another fierce female character created in the novel. Kali had lived an ostracized life because she was a Naga.

Yet despite her hard life, she is feared by all. She is a righteous character. 'She is tough but fair'. This asserts the fact that women have been given important roles throughout the story. Tripathi also expresses his views on the masculine and the feminine traits of life, "The feminine way of life is life by probabilities. There are no absolutes. No black or white. People don't act as per some preordained law, but based on probabilities of different outcomes perceived at that point of time.... Feminine civilizations, like Swadweep, are comfortable with contradictions. And the code for success in such a system? Unmistakably, Passion, Beauty and Freedom." (Nagas:45) He asserts that both masculine and feminine ways of life are needed to balance each other. World needs both in order to exist. With this explanation Tripathi has clarified that men and women occupy equal importance in the world and both must exist in harmony. "Both types of civilizations must exist, because they balance each other." (Nagas:46)

> "I have heard that on an average, the female of the species is smarter. But it's a little more complicated. Elephant herds are matriarchal and its usually the oldest female who makes all the decisions in the wild; when they will move, where they will feed, who remains in the herd and who gets kicked out." (Vayuputras: 94)

These anecdotes throughout the story emphasize on the importance of both the genders.

Towards the end of the story the vivid description of Sati's heroic and tragic death leaves the readers awestruck. She is face to face with the most fearsome murderers, who take her for granted and look down upon her. The most fearsome of them all was named Swuth, who considers her to be 'stupid baby-producing machine'. As the fight progresses, she singlehandedly fights them all.

> "Swuth stared at Sati, dumbstruck. She was completely soaked in her own blood, there were cavernous wounds all over her body... her soul must know that death was just minutes away. And yet, her eyes did not exhibit even the slightest hint of fear. She stared directly at Swuth with only one expression. An expression of pure, raw, unadulterated defiance." (Vayuputras:477)

He acknowledges her indomitable spirit and decides never to fight against anyone else after his battle with Sati. Tripathi concludes the novel with the valiant death of Sati and Shiva's wrath to avenge her murder. Thus, we can conclude that the Shiva Trilogy has a wide range of women characters who have not been created keeping in mind the traditional and narrow scope of women representation.

This is a novel experiment by Tripathi as in the ancient mythologies we have seen that women were mostly characters who needed to be protected. Here in this trilogy, women are the saviors.

In the Ram Chandra series, we find a similar representation where the first time Lord Ram sees Goddess Sita, she is seen fighting for justice and truth. She is adept at stick fighting. In the original mythology; the epic – Ramayana, Sita has been presented as a princess, a wife and later a mother, who has to face many hardships in life. She is abducted by Raavan and taken to Lanka where she saves her honour and is ultimately rescued by Lord Ram, her husband. Her hardships don't end here. After being rescued, she has to go through agnipariksha to prove her chastity. She comes out safe and is taken back by Lord Ram. Eventually though, she is again abandoned by her husband because of some gossip doing the round on her character. So, we see how the woman character had been delineated. Now, if we look at the description of Sita given by Tripathi, we see that he does not create her as a submissive, docile girl, subversive to her fate. Right from childhood she breaks the gender-stereotype,

> "Vishwamitra observed Sita with a keen eye. Tall for a thirteen-year-old, she was already beginning to build muscle. She flicked a spear up with her foot, catching it expertly in her hand. Vishwamitra noticed the stylish flick. But he was more impressed by something else. She had caught the spear exactly at the balance point on the shaft. Which had not been marked, unlike in a normal training spear (Mithila: 51)."

Tripathi brings out the legend of Vishnu and Mahadev in his books. According to the legend, Vishnu is a male character, a reincarnation of God. In the second book of the Ram Chandra series, we see that after observing the intellectual genius and warfare prowess of Sita, 'Vishwamitra chooses her as the next Vishnu and the title of Vishnuhood is conferred upon her'. Apart from Sita we see many other women characters of importance. She was the adopted child of King Janak and Queen Sunaina. Sunaina has been endowed with pragmatic excellence and fighting spirit. "But the new queen Sunaina who had married Janak two years earlier was not of the ideal sort. She planned to restore Mithila to its old glory. Janak was spending more and more time lost in the world of philosophy (Mithila: 21)." This line highlights the general belief that women were not expected to have the acumen to run a kingdom. They were supposed to be silent observers and look after the needs of their husbands and children. It is Sunaina who was efficient enough to run Mithila. Janak was too engrossed in philosophy to be a good ruler.

Sunaina takes control of the running of the kingdom but it is Janak who is the king and the ruler in the eyes of the public. Sunaina also trains her daughter to be efficient to look after the citizens of her land. She makes her the Prime Minister and Sita works wonders for the people of Mithila. She in turn has a confidant who helps her in every work-Samichi. She is again an intriguing character who is too ferocious and rough and is quite opposite to the accepted 'feminine' traits.

In the third book of the *Ram Chandra Series*; 'Raavan-Enemy of Aryavarta' tells the story from Raavan's perspective. Here again we find a woman being at the centre of the story-Vedavati. She is portrayed as a goddess throughout the story though she does not possess any supernatural attributes. She is considered a Kanyakumari. She is the symbol of love and hope in the life of Raavan. Though he is too cruel to the world, she manages to convince him to come to the path of goodness. She has the power to turn a hardcore criminal into a man with a good heart. This shows the power of women.

Feminist critics have been advocating for the rights of women. Their concern is that women have been falsely presented in the narratives created by men. They have been voiceless for a long time. With writers like Amish Tripathi, this concern is being addressed. Women characters are being re-written. The question of gender is being answered. "Indeed, the depiction of women in male literature – as angels, goddesses, whores, obedient wives, and mother figures – was an integral means of perpetuating these ideologies of gender" (Habib: 667) It is said that gender is a socially constructed notion. Thus, there has been a need to deconstruct the notion of gender roles and the present writers of the myths are doing so, by placing women in the center of the text and by 'decentralizing the male superiority in the myths, portraying the uncelebrated glory of free willed ancient woman, demythifying the portrayal of woman in ancient myth and subverting the power structure which provides the space for them to show case their talents'.

Works Cited

Habib, M.A.R., *A History of Literary Criticism and Theory*. Wiley Blackwell, 2015.

Nayar, Pramod K, *An Introduction to Cultural Studies.* New Delhi: Viva Books Pvt. Ltd, 2016

Tripathi, Amish *Scion of Ikshvaku.* Chennai: Westland, 2015.

_____. *Raavan Enemy of Aryavarta.* Chennai: Westland, 2019.

.........*Sita Warrior of Mithila.* Chennai: Westland,2017.

.........*The Immortals of Meluha.* Chennai: Westland, 2010.

.........*The Oath of the Vayuputras.* Chennai: Westland, 2013.

.........*The Secret of the Nagas.* Chennai: Westland, 2011.

CHAPTER 17

Vikram Chandra as a Modern Feminine Realist

Shitalbabu Ambadas Tayade

Abstract

Many current Indian writers deal with a realistic portrayal of modern life. Vikram Chandra is the most well-known contemporary author among them. Feminine exploitation is a feature of the modern society that Vikram Chandra observes. Vikram Chandra characterizes the society's dominant class as those who have a privileged position in society and wield authority over their subordinates by displays of money and power. Vikram Chandra highlights the reality, stating that women face the negative and unpleasant parts of life. The writer accurately describes the suffering many women face at the hands of their husbands. Vikram Chandra depicts domestic harshness and unfaithfulness in equal measure, mirroring the realities of women's lives.

Keywords: Vikram Chandra, Women issues, Modernity, Exploitation

Literature always reflects society. It is the reflection of the various social situations that imprints some pieces of evidence on the personal mind framework of the writer, who is influenced by the conditions of the surroundings. Many a time the revelation of the impression is not far away from the reality and the facts. It is the real representation of what exactly it is. While creating such sort of literature writer by no means moves away from the fact of the facets, on the contrary, he always sticks to the situation and elaborates it through the sly touches of his imaginative characters and situations. Indo Anglian literature always deals with such factual pragmatism. Dorothy M. Spenser rightly affirms, –Indo-Anglian fiction is a major source for a systematic study of cultural contact and cultural change with the Indian worldview as a focus of the Westerners to increase their knowledge of acculturation processes. (Spenser, 10-11) Realist writer at all times deals with the authentic picture of the society whichever good or bad. The motif of the realist writer is no more tutoring rather it deals with the rational. Different thinkers have a diverse opinion about realism in the literature some are pro with the factual presentations whereas some are not. Wole Soyinka writes, – a writer records the experience of his society and is the voice of vision of his time. He has to function as social conscience. . . or else, he will have to withdraw to the position a post mortem surgeon. (Killam 89) whereas Velmani states 'writer is designated based on the socio-geographical community and culture to which he belongs and those traditions, life and language he utilizes in his writings. The Indian English novelists of the 1980s are assimilated with the western culture and they establish an independent cultural and literary identity exposed to the experience of life in India and abroad'. (Velmani, 336)

Many of the modern Indian writers deal with the realistic picture of contemporary life. Vikram Chandra is leading among contemporary writers. Brother of noted filmmaker and screenwriter Tanuja Chandra, Vikram Chandra is Indian-American Writer. *Red Earth and Pouring Rain* (1995) his first novel which was inspired by the autobiography of James Skinner, legendary nineteenth-century Anglo-Indian soldier. The novel won both the Common Wealth Writers' Prize for Best First Book in the year 1996 and the David Higham Prize for Fiction in the year 1995. He published collection short stories in the year 1997 titled as *Love and Longing in Bombay.* His short stories set at the backdrop of the social events intertwined with contemporary modern life. It won the Commonwealth Writers' Prize for Best Book in the year 1998. *Sacred Games* another work published in 2006 which won the Hutch Crossword Award for 2007. His other work is *Geek Sublime: Writing Fiction, Coding Software* published in the year 2013. Vikram Chandra a keen observer of the society of Mumbai, the then Bombay. He deals with the keen and the sharp realities of the society of Mumbai. He pens down the realities of the surrounding society. Commenting on the presentation of realities of the life Dorothy Figueira remarks: The novelist is a new kind of god, who loves people, who overcome his isolation, puts his knots alongside theirs, grows with them, manifests himself in the multiplicity of their beings and releases them into their own unique life, and co-exists with them in the joys and sorrows of their human life (Dorothy 41).

Vikram Chandra describes the dominant class of the society who possess the privileged position in society and create a sense of the power on the subordinates through the show of wealth and power. He describes the character of Chetan Bhai Ghanshyam Patel in the *Love Longing in Bombay* who owns the rich house like an old feudal lord with the grand show of Elephants outside the house. He owned Contessa Car and Rolex watch worth 218000/- Description of the aura of his house bring before us the real feudal picture before our eyes. In the contemporary lifestyle, we can have the lavish show of the wealth among the high class of society. Even he has the concept of the parties which he celebrates as a weekend with his design programme and with his own erected structure of fame and name. Society is made up of with the continuous flux of the contradiction of the views between husband and wife. He has an encounter with his wife. Write states one of the events in the novel where husband and wife went to Daman and had quarrel between each other. The cause of it is the way word attitude and the lifestyle of the Chetan Bhai Ghanshyam Patel which he initiates against the backdrop of his white collar. Vikram Chandra brings out the realities and states that women have to bear the adverse and rotten aspects of life. Women have to suffer at the hands of the husband is well described by the writer.

In cities and the urban life husbands and wives are involved in the individual, social and corporate assignments. It leads to social gatherings which includes fun and food including drinks and dance. The writer describes the club culture in the novel where the character named Sheila throws a cocktail party. In the contemporary world, the club culture is at rising where we find that the involvement of the women is parallel to that of men. The business encounter of the feminine world is aptly described by the writer. He describes the counterpart as Bijlani and Boatwalla. These two are continuously influx of conflict with each other. Each one tries to establish herself as a part of the top brand of success but Sheila being the higher in the social hierarchy she never allows anyone to be at the top.

Independency in form social status is well described by the writer. It is the real character of toady's women. Women got an equal way of life status to that of the men. A researcher states: "Arranged marriages have long been the norm in Indian society. Even today, the majority of Indians have their marriages planned by their parents and other respected family-members. Recent studies suggest that Indian culture is trending away from traditional arranged marriages". (Nanda, n.pag/web) Sandhya is the representative of the superwomen in the novel who has her ideology of life. She is projected as an independent woman possessing all required and essential amenities. She is aware of her existence. She rebels against all odds and establishes her world against all odds. She never thinks of the forceful acceptance of the views struck by the other on her. She knew that the world is cruel and she has to bear herself against all odds so she divorced from her husband and create her visionary world and compel her husband to live away from her. She accepted to troll her path without begging at the other doorsteps. She has her liking for creative art. She wants to know the world outside of the four walls. She doesn't want to live in the bondage of the limited livelihood. For the sake of her son, she takes care of everything. She divorced from her husband to roll on her views on the horizon of the world. She opts for her liking at the cost of money. She buys painting without thinking of money. She spends money as much she wants. She never bears infidelity of the other towards her. She has keen eyesight for her existence. She put herself out of the house and establishes her own reliable house. She always looks forward to the best position. She always tries to get the top position in the company in which she is working and she becomes successful in her view. Today we can see the perfect scenario where the women are always playing a very leading role and create their world of existence.

Parallel to the reality of the women existence Vikram Chandra describes the domestic brutality and the unfaithfulness in an equal manner. The modern world has changed the scenario of the relationship. In today's modern world the relationships are not the same as they were in the past. Relationships between parents and kids, husband and wife, boy and girl and even social relations have changed. Things have changed and to be successful in a modern relationship, one needs to use a modern approach to understand the undercurrent of the relationship. Metro cities we find multiple reasons for personal violence and dislike for each other. The dominance of the women over the men is one of the basic reason, Both are working and sometimes women lead in the earning creates the inferiority complex among the men which gives space to the fire of conflict. Another reason modern time create a haphazard way of life. It creates the way to the multiple tasks which one has to handle at any time which breaks the silence of the relationship. Late-night arrival of the women in the house, continuous engagement in the work, higher-earning, wayward lifestyle, copying of the western culture, different parties, high aim, visiting different worksites for the sake of the duty creates a distant relationship in the metro cities. Such lifestyle gives space to the extramarital relationship. Vikram Chandra being in touch with the culture of the city is aware of the new trends of the metro life which he reflects in his writing. Kamla Pandey in the *Sacred Games* is the representative of the metro culture. She faces the violence from her husband but she is bold enough to undertake the challenge and become successful in treating the violence. She shows her masculine power and treats the attitude of her husband and make it correct. Her husband always roams around her as a spy who cooks the view in his mind that his wife has an affair with someone and her doubt became true as she has an affair with pilot Umesh.

Feminine exploitation is another reality of the contemporary world which remain unhidden from the observation of Vikram Chandra. He portrayed the fashion and the film industry and bring out the basics of exploitation of the concerned industry Commenting on it famous fashion critic Eric Wilson says, "Popular culture has always played an enormous role in what fashion is and the fact that so many celebrities have started fashion lines speaks to that". (Wilson, n. pag) India has a tradition of the fashion industry where the involvement of the society towards the fashion industry is remarkable. From the outer side, the fashion world is very glamorous but it has the very dark and shocking inside story of the suffering. Sexual exploitation is the key aspect that is hidden under the red carpet of the fashion industry. Many incidents have proven the heinous and the gloomy side of the industry:

> Karen Mulder's startling claims came on 31 October 2001 while being interviewed on Tout le monde en parle (Everyone is Talking About It) on French TV. In front of a live studio audience, Mulder made bold claims of sexual misuse at the hands of her modelling agency, Elite Model Management. She claimed executives at the agency had attempted to rape her. (Mulder)

Another even comes out in form Louise Gagnon. An editor of a French fashion magazine and herself a former model since the age of 18, who now lives in southern California, where she runs her own business making designer wedding dresses. In one of the interviews she says:

> I was raped regularly. Sometimes multiple times per week. I was depressed all the time and the only thing that made me feel better was the heroin. It didn't stop when I stopped modelling either. I was in some bad

> relationships with the photographers who I had met years earlier and I was involved with them professionally so I had to ignore my feelings. It was complicated and I became more and more disgusted at myself every day. I finally decided I needed to quit before I killed myself. (Fringemedia.Net.)

Aspirants are always ready to join the industry by hook or crook. Without looking beyond the frame of the fame they try to establish themselves in the industry with eager readiness for the physical surrenders. He sketches the character of the Jojo Mascarenas, in *Sacred Games* as a model coordinator, who suggest the contract of the model to the different modelling agencies. She is in the touch of the needy girls who want to establish in the industry and to become famous. She too had an aspiration for actor in the film industry but exploited at the cost of the opportunity. Gaitonde projected by the author as an exploiter of the society who helps to Zoya Mirza at the cost of financial assistance. He supplies money to Zoya for the plastic surgery by which she wants to uplift her face value. Thus the women characters of Vikram Chandra deals with modernity which reflected through their course of action and the cult of behaviour.

Conclusion

Vikram Chandra reflects the life of the metro city. He describes the way of life of the women in the city. He focuses on the reality and the attitude of the women characters. The characters which he presented are a very ordinary human being. He portrayed the attitude and the modern metro feminine mentality which is ubiquitous in the contemporary modern world.

Works Cited

Figuiera, Dorothy. "Anand's war novel – An essay." *The Journal of Indian Writings in English* 28 (2000): 41. Print.

Fingemedia.net. "Sexual Exploitation and the Fashion Industry." N.p., Web. 26 May 2016. <https://www.fringemedia.net/sexploitation-and-the-fashion-industry>.

Killam, G. D. *African Writers in African Writing*. London: Heinemann, 1973. Print.

Mulder, Karen. Interview by French TV. n.p., Web. 29 July 2016. <https://en.wikipedia.org/wiki/Karen_Mulder>.(IV-29)

Nanda, Sarena. "Arranged Marriages in India." *Bartleby.com*. N.p., 30 Apr. 2010. Web. 17 Oct. 2015. <https://www.bartleby.com/essay/Arranged-Marriage-in-India-F3CUA6N3VJ>.

Spenser, Dorothy M. *Indian Fiction in English: An Annotated Bibliography*. Philadelphia: University of Pennsylvania, 1960. Print.

Velmani, N. "Ethnicity in the Novels of Vikram Seth." *The Criterion* 4.6 (2013): 336-340. Web. 20 Apr. 2020. <http://www.the-criterion.com/V4/n6/Velmani.pdf>.

CHAPTER 18

Depiction of Women in Shashi Deshpande's *The Dark Holds No Terrors*

Prachi Bhongale and Varsha Vaidya

Abstract

The status of women in post independent India was that of a subaltern one. However, earlier when people lived in tribes, the culture was inclined towards matriarchy. Woman was the head of the tribe. She enjoyed a high and respectable status. Hence, we normally identify one's language as 'mother tongue' and not father tongue.Women in these times had no binding for marriage. They were worshipped because of the fact that they bore the miracle of giving birth which people considered as gift to women. Various religious texts were created to degrade and mock the status of women in order to establish stronger roots of patriarchy. Hence, these days we normally name things as 'man-made'. This is the impact of such religious texts which ensured the deterioration of status of women.Shashi Deshpande is one of the iconoclastic writers of post independent India. She is known for the realistic representation of middle class educated modern women. Her women protagonists are at the crossroads of tradition and modernity. Initially, we see her protagonists confused. However, after going through process of internal struggle and self-realization, they emerge confident and strong from their traditional cocoons and are determined to face the realities of their lives audaciously.

Keywords: Women, Tradition, Patriarchal, Marriage, Internal struggle.

Introduction

Literature is the mirror of society. The culture of any society is governed by the traditions and rituals that the society follows. The same philosophy is applicable to the depiction of women in the society. There are reasons to believe that erstwhile society was matriarchal. The status of women in any society is determined by the culture and social behavior of that society. History has witnessed this from many years. In order to understand this, one cannot ignore historical facts. The status originates from the man-woman relationship in the history of mankind. The history of mankind is divided into three tiers namely ancient, medieval and modern. Ancient period starts from the stone age period where hunting was of prime importance. The tribe was the owner of property. Man and woman relationship was quite different then. They used to live in caves. When fire was invented, they tried to burn the wooden sticks so that there is sufficient light in the cave. The continuous burning of fire was a necessity and this led to cutting of nearby trees. Thus land was available. Women, while staying in the caves, tried to plough the land with the help of bones of animals and sharpened stones. They got to understand the fact that when seeds are sown, plants can grow. These instincts are carried by women since birth. It was women who discovered agriculture. The strength to conceive a baby is bestowed upon woman as she is the strongest one. The primitive man used to live in tribes. Robert Briffault in his '*The Mothers*' quotes,

> The females in a polygamous herd are more or less kept together by the males, but that control has reference to sexual relation only. The actual leader which guides the herd in its movements and keeps watch against possible dangers is usually an old female (Vol I, 185).

In tribes, there was no restriction on selection of partners. Polyandry was quite common. Robert Briffault quotes,

> The social unit is the maternal clan, defined practically by the ocular consanguinity of birth from a common line of mothers. Each clan is headed by a clan-mother, and comprises a hierarchy of daughters and grand-daughters, collectively incarnating that purity of the blood which is the pride of the tribe. The indigenous name of the tribe is 'Kunkak,' which means 'womanhood,' or 'mother-hood. (Vol I, 185).

Hence, it is clear from the above quotes that status of women was high during the times of tribes. When people lived in tribes, there was no system of marital life as such. Also, woman was the head of the clan. As Robert Briffault in his *'The Mothers'* quotes,

> In primitive Greecethe women did, as a matter of fact, give their names not only to their children, as the Athenian tradition mentions, but to their families, clans and tribes (Vol I, 293).

This justifies the clans like Maurya dynasty from name of mother, Aditya clan from Aditi etc.

Trauma faced by Saru

Shashi Deshpande in her novel *The Dark Holds No Terrors* introduces us to the protagonist, Sarita (Saru) and her internal struggle. Saru, during her childhood, faces a lot of humiliation at the hands of her mother. She is rejected because of the only reason that she was a girl. Her younger brother, Dhruva, is the apple of her parents' eyes. She faces severe gender discrimination during her childhood. She is made to feel that her birth was a terrible experience for her mother as it was pouring cats and dogs on the day she was born. It is only later that she realizes that it was her birth as a girl that was horrible and not the rain. The birth of a boy is ceremoniously welcomed in Indian families whereas a girl's birth is looked down upon. The main reason for this discrimination is that girls bring upon burden to the lives of parents as they take away dowry whereas in case of boys the case is reversed. Saru was no exception to this treatment. Her mother treated her as a second sex. She is reminded every time of the fact that she is a liability whereas Dhruva is an asset. She recalls the excitement in the house on the occasion of naming ceremony of her brother. Dhruva's birthdays were always celebrated with joy and excitement with all the religious rituals. Later, after the death of her brother Dhruva, her birthdays went unacknowledged as if it was she who killed him. Even small scale celebration on her birthdays stopped after his death. There was none in the family whom Saru would share her feelings to. Her father never spoke to her except urgent matters. This indifferent behavior from his end implies the fact that daughters are mother's business and have nothing to do with fathers. Saru's brother Dhruva died due to drowning and this was a major loss in the life of her mother. She couldn't bear the loss of her son and blamed Saru for his death. This is evident from following lines.

> You killed him. Why didn't you die? Why are you alive, when he's dead? (*The Dark Holds No Terrors*21).

As Sarbjit Sandhu observes:

> The mother is very attached to her son. Her attitude is a typical one, all he is a male child and therefore one who will propagate the family lineage. In another sense also, the male child is considered more important than a girl, because he is qualified to give 'agni' to his dead parents. The soul of dead parents would otherwise wander in ferment (*The Images of Woman in the novels of Shashi Deshpande* 72).

Saru's mother's Kamala's biased attitude towards her can be attributed to her own unhappy childhood. Saru's maternal grandmother was deserted by her husband, leaving her with the burden of raising two daughters. They were sheltered unwillingly by her parents. The ways with which she was treated like a burden had conditioned her to such an extent that she started considering girl child as burden. She suffered from stomach cancer and never complained about it to her husband. She never ate her food properly and never revealed the same to her husband. Even when she was asked to visit a doctor, she refused to do so and Mai Kaki appreciated her refusal just because Kamala was not like new generation women who rushed to see a doctor for petty reasons.

Her mother's constant criticism got on Saru'snerves. Hence, Saru decides to work hard and become a successful doctor. This decision is not appreciated by Saru's mother. Had she been a boy, her parents would have taken pride in her achievement of passing the exam with the first class. Behind Saru's fortitude was the internal aspiration to prove her mother wrong and her unquenchable thirst for acknowledgment. She had to literally fight for her career. The exhaustive list of dos and don'ts made Saru more obstinate. She reminded Saru of her dark complexion every now and then. This depicts the inclination of our typical Indian society towards fair complexion. Everyday we witness various advertisements endorsing the fairness creams. The newspaper column for matrimony even mentions the need for a fair complexion bride. The stress is given on passivity and sublimity.

Vern Bullough observes:

> "The very word woman... emphasized [a] passive anonymous position. It derives from the Anglo-woman separate from wifehood. As individuals, with few exceptions, women did not account. They are mothers, wives, daughters, sisters." (*Subordinate Sex: A History of Attitudes towards Women*3)

Marriage on the Rocks

Rules mentioned in the Manu were created for behavior of women. According to The Laws of Manusmriti translated by George Buhler,

> By a girl, by a young woman, or even by an aged one, nothing must be done independently, even in her own house (83).

> In childhood a female must be subject to her father, in youth to her husband, when her lord is dead to her sons; a woman must never be independent (83).

Stringent rules like Sati were introduced. A widow had to throw herself on the burning pyre of her husband. Child marriage became prevalent. Girls at a tender age were married to men twice their age. Thanks to Raja Ram Mohan Roy who crusaded such practices along with the help of British government. However, the humiliation didn't stop. Since widows were not allowed to follow sati, they were tortured to a great extent. They were sexually exploited as widow remarriage was not allowed under the guise of so called laws of Manu. Some widows were even barred from their own houses both from maternal and in-laws house. Such group of women had to succumb to prostitution to earn money to survive. This is how prostitution must have come into picture.

A woman's menstruation is considered impure to such an extent that she starts hating herself. Simon De Beauvoir quotes in *The Second Sex*, "Anglo-Saxons call menstruation "the curse" (62). Basically, all movements of a woman were controlled (rather are controlled even today) by the male chauvinist patriarchal society.

Marital discord is as old as the organization of marriage itself, even if it has diverged from time to time and from person to person. In the pre-industrial period, men and women who came jointly in marriage shared intellectual values, mutual dedication, belief and hope which subordinated the interests of the individuals resulting in the smooth relationship of the family. There were tensions in their marital relationship too, but the ethical and religious convictions, economic belief and the fear of social condemnation kept them together. (*Sharma* 86).

As rightly stated above, modern educated women are no exception to it. Saru met Manu and fell for him. They both admired each other which is why they tried to culminate their relationship to marriage. When Saru disclosed her affair to her parents, her mother asks,

> What caste is he? I don't know. A Brahmin? Of course not. (*The Dark Holds No Terrors*96).

Saru had no right to choose her career initially and now her better half. One must not forget the fact that Swayamvar was allowed even in the history. If a girl decides to marry by her own choice or marry outside the caste, she is labelled as threat to the family's reputation and honor. However, a man is free to marry as many times as he wants. This portrays the double society standards. If a well-educated Saru is not allowed to marry the partner of her own choice then one can very well imagine the plight of illiterate women in Indian society.

Shashi Deshpande reflects the typical attitude of post independent Indians where caste consciousness prevailed. It was obvious for disapproval of their match. Despite the disapproval, they got married. Saru felt that she got free from the clutches of shackles of tradition by marrying the person of her own choice.

Marriage is a union of two souls. It's like two wheels running in parallel and the burden has to be shared by both husband and wife together. Both husband and wife are equally responsible to hold the relationship together. However, there is always subaltern treatment towards women in male chauvinist society.

K.M. Kapadia, while discussing the concept of marriage, writes: "Marriage was a social duty towards the family and the community, and there was little idea of individual interest. The social background provided by the authoritarian family afforded no scope for the recognition of any personal factor, individual interest and aspirations, in the relation between husband and wife." (*Marriage And Family In India*169). Thus, Saru's individual interests remain unacknowledged.

There is one such life turning event in the life of both Saru and Manu. Saru is called upon in the neighborhood due to an accident in the factory. Saru's total dedication in treating the victims of an accident in a nearby factory gained her fame and there are greetings and smiles. People looked up to Saru because of her profession. These smiles had brightened up on people's faces due to highly respected profession of Saru. In contrast, this made Manu frown upon his own low earning profession of a lecturer in a not so famous college. This was because Manu had been moulded in a way where women never had a supreme position than men. A woman on birth becomes a daughter of her father and then wife to her husband. There is no individual identity as such. Tradition has bounded women to be dependent on men. This was not Manu's fault but the culture into which he was brought up into.

Internal struggle and Self-realization

We see Saru as a new woman who challenges traditional norms and shows sheer disapproval towards them. The deprivation of love and affection from parents pushes her to take the decision of marrying Manu. Her dream of a successful marriage shatters. Manu turns into a sadist due to Saru's respectable medical profession. She submits to her husband's torture without even discussing about it. She has a guilty conscience that some way she is also responsible for her husband's failure. She even thinks of parting ways with Manu, but the thought of her children is unable to let her do it. Saru wished a refuge is her husband's home as she was deprived of the affection at her parents' home. However, the same feeling of suffocation surrounds her with Manu.

When she pays visit to her home she carries out an honest appraisal of self. She detaches herself from all the relations of mother and a doctor. She tries to ponder upon her situation. This process leads to an internal purge of her thoughts leading to a self-discovery. That Saru who was initially identified as a daughter and later a wife is now just Saru who tries to search her own identity. She realizes that there is no point in running away from the problems. The only way to get out of the same is to face them audaciously.

She is able to perceive her faults against Manu, only after her going away from him. Her fight against the age-old shackles of tradition ends up in accepting the reality. Her story is the story of every Indian woman. It is her education which teaches her to show resistance to unreasonable and irrational things. Thus, Saru no longer is scared of the terrors of the dark. She learns to accept her faults and flaws and is firmly determined to return to her husband on a positive note. She learns that the only way out is to learn how to balance her professional and personal life. Marriage to Manu turns Saru timid and gentle who unquestionably follows the traditional ethos. However after much introspection of the self, she attains a stage of looking towards life with an optimistic approach.

Thus, we see that even if a women is highly educated, she cannot get rid of her roots. Basically, a man can get rid of his family for spiritual salvation but for a woman it is difficult. A woman loves her child even if it is legitimate or illegitimate. However, in case of a man, the case is not so. He can anytime reject the illegitimate child. Nature itself is responsible to create women with strong instincts, lest its existence would cease.

Conclusion

The internal struggle of the protagonist, Saru, in *The Dark Holds No Terrors*, goes from the life of an unhappy childhood to facing her husband with courage and confidence. Saru is treated as an unwanted daughter. She is criticized for her complexion. Later after marriage, she is treated as an animal just because of highly respectable profession. Saru undergoes humiliation, neglect as a child, and after marriage as a wife. Saru is humiliated emotionally during childhood at her parental home and physically by her husband after marriage. Saru is neglected during her childhood and after meeting Manu she looks forward to find refuge in him. However, her bliss is short lived. Being a rational thinker, she marries Manu out of caste this rejecting traditional norms. At the end of the novel, we see Saru emerging quite bold and strong. She prepares herself to face her husband audaciously. Thus, Shashi Deshpande believe in cohesive existence and does not suggest parting ways as an option. Saru makes herself ready to face the upcoming challenges and derives harmony in her marital life. Shashi Deshpande tries to convey that women should no more be treated as subaltern and they should try their ways out and surpass all the obstacles without losing their individuality. She believes in equal opportunities to both men and women to make the world a better place to live in.

Works Cited

Deshpande, Shashi. *The Dark Hold No Terrors*. New Delhi: Penguin Books, 1990.

Briffault, Robert. *The* Mothers: *The Matriarchal Theory of Social Origins*. New York: The Macmillan Company, 1931.

Buhler, G. (1886). *Manusmriti: The Laws of Manu*. Trans. G. Buhler.

Bullough, Vern. *Subordinate Sex: A History of Attitudes towards Women*. New York: Penguin, 1973.

De Beauvoir, Simone. *The Second Sex*. New York: Vintage Books, 1989.

Kapadia, K.M. *Marriage And Family In India*,2nd edition, Bombay: Oxford University Press,1958

Sandhu, Sarbjit K. *The Images of Woman in the novels of Shashi Deshpande*, New Delhi: Prestige, 1991.

Sharma, Mohini. "Marital Discord in Anita Desai's Novels." *Global Journal of Human Social Science Linguistics and Education*, vol. 13, issue 10, Version 1.0, Publisher: Global Journals Inc. USA, 2013, pp. 86.

CHAPTER 19

Gender Aesthetics in Abimbola Adunni Adelakun's *Under the Brown Rusted Roofs* and Molara Wood's "Gani's Fall"

P. Ibrahim Firdaws Oyebisi

Abstract

Issues concerning gender have continued to prevail in global feminist discourse and its evolution is evident in the postulation of various notions of feminism that are situated within the African cultural context. The purpose of this study was to add to the critical works in the field of gender studies by adopting African Feminisms to the analyses of two contemporary Nigerian female writers, Adelakun's *Under the Brown Rusted Roofs* (2008), and Wood's "Gani's Fall" (2013) in order to identify the feminist perspectives of these writers. Findings derived from the analyses of these texts, showed that the feminist perspectives of the writers are not exactly similar as Adelakun is more diplomatic than Wood in her approach, however, both writers project similar gender issues like patriarchy and polygamy, which are obtainable within the Yoruba African cultural setting. The study, therefore, concludes that the feminist perspectives of the selected writers are situated within the notion of the selected theory for the study, African Feminisms, as both writers succeed in contextualising their projection of gender issues and solutions within the Yoruba cultural setting.

Keywords: Gender, Culture, Adelakun, Wood.

Introduction

Nigerian literature comprises numerous works, written by female and male writers of Nigerian origin, in all the genres of literature. The works are used by these writers to present and represent gender, environmental, socio-economic, and political issues as they affect Nigerian societies at specific points in time, either in the past or the present, and how these issues can sometimes influence the future. A look at some of these Nigerian writers concerning their projection of gender would be done briefly in subsequent paragraphs.

The earlier generation of Nigerian female writers like Flora Nwapa, Buchi Emecheta, Mabel Segun, Zaynab Alkali, and Tess Onwueme (Aliyu, 2013, p.22) according to Okonjo-Ogunyemi (1988), mainly focused on attempting to correct the negative "stereotypes of female characters" (p.61), projected by the earlier male writers. Flora Nwapa, for example, on her writings, states that "a major aim that motivated her works was the need for women's voices to be heard, presenting aspects of women's lives that were ignored, under-represented, or distorted by men" (qtd. in Kolawole 1997, p.107).

In an attempt to debunk the negative projection of female characters by male writers, the early generation of female writers end up, mostly, idealising their female characters, and presenting them as the only victims of the oppressive structures (mainly patriarchy) that exist in society. These female writers, present chiefly female protagonists along with female-related issues, and the "impact of social change on only women" (Kolawole 1995, p.198), in their writings. Examples of some of these characteristics can be found in Flora Nwapa's *Efuru* (1966), Buchi Emecheta's *The Bride Price* (1976), and Zaynab Alkali's *The Stillborn* (1984), amongst other texts.

However, a later and contemporary generation of Nigerian female writers have joined the budding list of writers in Nigerian literature. These writers fall under, the third generation of female writers. This third generation of Nigerian female writers are those that started publishing in the 1990s and are "... 'new' (in comparison with the older Nigerian female authors)", and, "in the sense of just starting to gain literary significance…irrespective of the age of the writers and the number of their publications" (Aliyu 2013, p. 21). Examples of the female writers that fall under this category include, Chimamanda Ngozi Adichie, Sefi Atta, Kaine Agary's, Abimbola Adunni Adelakun, Lola Shoneyin, Chika Unigwe, and Molara Wood.

This latest crop of female writers, unlike the older generation writers, have moved beyond idealising their female characters to presenting them as less of victims, and more of choice-makers who have to deal with the consequences of their actions. The reason for this depiction, according to, Chimamanda Ngozi Adichie, in an online interview with Claire Cohen, is that women no longer want mere "simpering heroines" (Online).

African Feminisms

It is a label ascribed to one notion of feminism and was postulated in the year 2013. The reason for its being labeled in the plural form, as, "Feminisms", is due to its recognition of the diversity of cultures in Africa as it "espouses its feminism from tenets derived from African culture" (Aliyu, 2013, p.86). Therefore, texts with various African cultural settings can be analysed using the features of African Feminisms. Ogundipe (2007), anticipates Aliyu's line of thought on the need for this type of "Feminisms" in African literary criticism, in her assertion that "...we need to speak of 'feminisms' rather than 'feminism' due to the various forms that feminism takes worldwide to express the differing cultural and national objectives and needs of women"(p.10). The analysis of gender issues in literary texts, as specified by African Feminisms, refers to, "the power relations between the two sexes and how this is challenged" (Aliyu 2013, p. 97).

Having examined the background to this study, the study aims to add to critical works in the field of gender studies by adopting the new feminist notion, African Feminisms, as a model of analysing to investigate the feminist perspectives and to bring to the fore two contemporary seemingly unpopular Nigerian female writers: Abimbola Adunni Adelakun and Molara Wood, through the analysis of their works: *Under the Brown Rusted Roofs* (2008), and the short story "Gani'sFall" (2013), respectively. The similarities and differences that exist in the themes and style of these writers in their projection of these gender issues would also be identified after the analysis of the texts.

The Role of Women in the Public and Private African Cultural Spheres

African Feminisms does not distinguish between the private and public spheres as it considers both females and males as active participants in the sustenance of all aspects of society (Aliyu, 2013, p.91). It also embraces other struggles for liberation into feminism, and views women as being important to the African society (Aliyu, 2013, p.91), therefore, supporting the notion of most African feminists like Nutsukpo (2011), that "women's rights is human rights"(p.90).

Women in many African societies play an active role in the public sphere, and this is illustrated in Adelakun's *Under the Brown Rusted Roofs*. The female characters in the novel illustrate Taiwo's (1984) stance that African women are hardworking and are economic assets to their husbands and children. In the critic's words:

> Not only is the African woman hardworking, she is also an economic asset to her husband and family. Without the money she makes from her petty trading, fishing and farming, her husband will hardly be able to cope with all the needs of the children (Taiwo, 1984, p. 4).

In Adelakun's *Under the Brown Rusted Roofs* (2008), the hardworking nature of women is reflected in the portrayal of characters like Afusa and Sikirat. Afusa, is reported to be selling, "fast-moving consumer goods" (*Under the Brown Rusted Roofs,* 2008, p.23), while, Sikirat:

> sold pepper at Ojaoba and usually left early for Sasa market where pepper was bought wholesale from the Hausas who brought them from the North. Thereafter, she took the purchases to Orita Merin where she would sell them in retail quantities (*Under the Brown Rusted Roofs,* 2008, p.23).

In Wood's "Gani's Fall", this theme of women's activeness in the public sphere is illustrated through the importance of education for women as a tool for their liberation. Ezeigbo (1996) asserts that "many African women writers see education as the basic tool to bring about the emancipation of women" (p.108). Wood belongs to this group of African female writers who see education as the basic tool for the liberation of women from oppressive structures and systems. She illustrates this through her portrayal of Clara one of Gani's wives.

Clara is presented as a drop-out student from the Teachers' Training College, who due to her unplanned pregnancy (for Gani) was "kicked out of school" ("Gani'sFall", 2013, p.28). Clara despite being a young twenty-two year old ("Gani'sFall", 2013, p. 28) lady, is more exposed than Sariatu, Gani's first wife, who is in her forties ("Gani'sFall", 2013, p.23 & p.27). Wood links Clara's exposure to her level of education, which is higher than Sariatu's, whose schooling "ended after secondary school" ("Gani'sFall", 2013, p.27).

Clara's high level of exposure and education also makes her confident enough to stand on her choices in Gani's house as she boldly confronts Hafsanat ("Gani'sFall", 2013, p.27) Gani's sister, who usually has "a domineering attitude towards women that married into Gani's family" ("Gani'sFall", 2013, p.25). Thus, Sariatu begins to see Clara, as less of a rival and more of a symbol of liberation, for herself and other wives in the family, from oppressors like Gani, Hafsanat, and the rest of their in-laws.

Polygamy

Aliyu's (2013) stance on polygamy in her African Feminisms is reflected in her statement that, "...while polygyny may be abused in certain cases, the institution, generally, can be liberating for African women rather than inhibitory" (p.56). She adds that "some of its advantages for women include child care sharing, emotional and economic support, sisterhood and companionship" (Aliyu, 2013, p.56).

Scrutinising gender as it relates to specific issues like polygamy, Emecheta (2012) asserts that polygamy, unlike what people believe it to be is not always oppressive to females. She cites Nigeria as a case-study, where "some women now make polygamy work for them" (p.553). She further states that some of these women deliberately encourage their husbands to marry other wives to help relieve them from household chores and to allow them to focus more on their businesses. In addition, Ogundipe-Leslie (1994) asserts that "polygamy is not always oppressive to the woman. It has its economic role in guaranteeing women the autonomy and human dignity they need" (p.53).

The theme of polygamy is one of the major issues that Adelakun addresses in her *Under the Brown Rusted Roofs* (2008) as the plot of the novel is woven around various polygamous homes in the traditional Yoruba setting. Adelakun presents how the female characters in the novel, "have navigated around the disagreeable parts of polygamy even, as they benefit from some of its positive aspects" (Aliyu, 2012, p.5). The majority of the families in the novel are polygamous, from Alhaji Arigbabuwo to Baba n'sale and Chief Akeweje, amongst others.

Adelakun presents the satisfaction of Alhaji's wives with their night arrangement, as it enables them to have more time for themselves and their children, and also helps them discuss important matters with their husband. The women in the household manage their time by sharing the nights they spend with Alhaji, through the following arrangements:

> Motara, being the most senior wife, the Iyale Agba, took the first two days, Sunday and Monday. The next two days were for Afusa while Sikira took Thursdays and Fridays. Alhaji rested on Saturdays…It was not a time to be missed because that was the only opportunity to talk to Alhaji without interference and to a large extent, get his attention (*Under the Brown Rusted Roofs,* 2008, p.20).

On the other hand, Adelakun (2008) also portrays the stress involved in living in a polygamous home through her presentation of the jealousy, quarrels (*Under the Brown Rusted Roofs,* 2008, p.17), and even ageing of women, in some polygamous settings. An instance is given through Adelakun's illustration of Alake, who is Baba n'sale's "eighth wife or so..." (*Under the Brown Rusted Roofs,* 2008, p.42). The author describes Alake's ageing, through her depicting her as a woman who "could not be more than twenty-eight but looked at least a decade older" (*Under the Brown Rusted Roofs,* 2008, p.42), and she partly blames, "the politics of living with Baba n'sale and his wives" (*Under the Brown Rusted Roofs,* 2008, p.42) for this.

Complementary Gender Roles and Female Bonding

Another area of gender that scholars have examined, is the relationship between female and male members of society. Adelakun, for example, states that "men and women are created equal, hence, they should be treated that way" (A.A. Adelakun, personal communication, 2014). She explains that the relationship between them should be "equal, respectful, and balanced" (A.A. Adelakun, personal communication, 2014). Also, Osofisan (2001) opines that "…the world will be saved neither solely by men nor by women fighting alone, but by both sexes working together hand in hand, struggling together shoulder to shoulder, and investing together grain by grain" (p.23). Osofisan, like Adelakun, advocates a complementary relationship between males and females. This, according to these scholars, is necessary to achieve the full definition of feminism and to ensure the attainment of a progressive society.

The stance of these two critics (Adelakun and Osofisan) is relevant to this paper as African Feminisms conceives the relationship between females and males as complementary. It is accommodationist in nature and "does not see men as the enemies but rather as being both beneficiaries and victims of the oppressive structure, and that, it is these structures that need to be changed" (Aliyu 2013, p. 90). In addition, African Feminisms also prescribes collectivism against individualism, which is founded in the communal spirit present in most African indigenous cultures. This collectivism includes female bonding, and the complementary relationship between females and males (Aliyu 2013, p.92).

On the other hand, Nwapa (2012) asserts that a "woman should be independent of her husband" (p. 528) and further encourages the type of women that can say, "To hell with men and marriage. ...I want to be free to do just as I please" (p. 530). Nwapa's opinion does not obtain in the African context and is more Western in orientation. The African woman normally is not hateful of men. Nwapa's idea of the African woman doing as she pleases is not feasible in the African setting.

This theme of a complementary relationship between men and women is further portrayed in Adelakun's *Under the Brown Rusted Roofs* (2008). Adelakun signifies her support for the complementary roles in the society, as she presents it as a means of fostering and ensuring a progressive home, and society. This is illustrated through the eventual success of Afusa's son, Kazeem, who ends up as a lawyer. Alhaji points out that this success is due to Afusa's persistent, and unrelenting contributions. In his conversation with Kazeem, he states that "thanks to her (Afusa) shoulders that didn't let clothes fall off my body" (*Under the Brown Rusted Roofs,* 2008, p.248).

Females as Problem of their Folk

One of the biggest challenges faced by females are females themselves, and Adelakun's *Under the Brown Rusted Roofs* (2008) presents this issue through various instances. One of such examples is illustrated in Alake's sour relationship with her co-wives who refuse to assist her in carrying out household chores but were always ready to start a fight if she failed in doing these chores (*Under the Brown Rusted Roofs,* 2008, p.42). Also, Iya Agba and Motara's deliberate "long evenings plotting" (*Under the Brown Rusted Roofs,* 2008, p.51), to cause a rift between Alhaji and Afusa, is another instance of how females could pose as enemies of one another.

This theme of females as problems of their folk is presented in Wood's "Gani's Fall" (2013) through the portrayal of Sariatu's mother-in-law and sister-in-law (Hafsanat), who both pose as threats to Sariatu in her matrimonial home and her relationship with her husband. Sariatu's mother-in-law restricts and watches her (Sariatu's) every step ("Gani'sFall", 2013, p.23), while Hafsanat, according to

Sariatu, was beginning to "crowd me (her) out in my (her) own home" ("Gani'sFall", 2013, p.25).

Militancy as an option in Women's Liberation

African Feminisms, advocates a non-confrontational stance that only applies to the relationship between females and males, but does not imply that militancy cannot be used as a weapon to challenge other oppressive systems and structures. This outright disapproval of a non-confrontational stance in African Feminisms should not be seen as constant. This is evident through characters like Gani in Molara Wood's "Gani's Fall (2013), whose confrontation by one of his wives serves as a wake-up call for him to treat his first wife better. Hence we, therefore, differ from this feature of African Feminisms and posit that individuals should be treated based on the characteristics they exhibit. Hence, a confrontational stance could be applied to settle disputes between females and males. Although, this stance should be used only as a last resort after all other forms of subtle approaches (like dialogue and external intervention), have been applied and failed.

Conclusion

This paper has examined gender aesthetics in Adelakun's *Under the Brown Rusted Roofs* (2008)and Wood's "Gani's Fall" (2013). The analysis of the selected primary texts was done using African Feminisms-a notion of Feminism derived from the African culture – as a guide. Both Adelakun and Wood address patriarchy in their prose works through their identification of the patriarchal nature of the Yoruba culture. In projecting these patriarchal values, they both employ the figure of old male characters, (Baba n'sale in *Under the Brown Rusted Roofs*) and (Baba in 'Gani's Fall') to symbolise the patriarchal structures. Unlike Wood who limits the negative use of patriarchy to its oppression of females, Adelakun on the other hand extends hers to its oppression of male characters as well.

Polygamy is another similar gender-related theme that both authors address in their writings. Both writers weave the plot of their stories around the lives of females and males in Yoruba polygamous settings. Wood, on her part, condemns the practice of polygamy and emphasises its negative effects on female characters, while Adelakun on the other hand, although also addressing the negative side to polygamy, is more diplomatic in her approach. Her diplomacy is reflected in her illustration of how her female characters make polygamy work for them.

In proffering solutions, Adelakun in her *Under the Brown Rusted Roofs* (2008) advocates a complementary relationship between the genders, as well, as female bonding, while Wood only examines the importance of female bonding, in her "Gani's Fall" (2013). However, both authors also portray the negative effects of the lack of co-operation among females and how this poses a great threat in the affairs of the female characters in the two prose works.

Also, the use of education as a liberating tool is illustrated in the writings of both writers. The difference, however, lies in Adelakun's examination of the use of education to liberate both females and males, which differs from Wood who limits hers, to its (education) use to liberate the female folk.

The study, therefore, concludes that the feminist perspectives of the selected writers: Abimbola Adunni Adelakun and Molara Wood, are situated within the notion of the selected theory for the study, African Feminisms, as both writers succeed in contextualising their projection of gender issues and solutions within the Yoruba cultural setting.

Works Cited

Adelakun, A.A. (2008). *Under the brown rusted roofs.* Ibadan: Krafts Books Limited.

Afolabi, J. (2002). Of womb-men, we-Men and woe-men: Feminist aesthetics, theatre practice and the democratic process in Nigeria. In A.Yerima & A.Akinwale. (Eds.), *Theatre and democracy in Nigeria.* (127-35). Ibadan: Kraft Books Limited.

Aidoo, A.A.(2012). To be an African woman writer – an overview and a detail. In T.Olaniyan & A.Quayson. (Eds.), *African literature: An anthology of criticism and theory.* (Rev.ed.), (513-19). U.K, U.S.A. and Australia: Blackwell Publishing Ltd.

Aliyu, F.R. (2013). *Contextualising women's writings in African culture: feminist perspectives in selected emerging Nigerian writers* (Unpublished Doctoral dissertation). University of Ilorin, Ilorin, Nigeria.

Alkali, Z. (1984). *The stillborn.* London: Longman.

Emecheta, B. (2012). Feminism with a small 'f'!. In T.Olaniyan & A.Quayson. (Eds.), *African literature: An anthology of criticism and theory.* (Rev.ed.). (551-57). U.K, U.S.A. and Australia: Blackwell Publishing Ltd.

Emecheta, B. (1995). *The Brideprice.* England: Heinemann.

Ezeigbo, A.T. (1996). Women's empowerment and national integration: Ba's *so long a Letter* and Warner-Vieyra's *juletane. Gender and development in Africa: Journal of the centre for gender and social policy studies*, 1 (1), 103-115. Ile-Ife: Obafemi Awolowo University.

Kolawole, M.E. (1995). Gender and changing social vision in the Nigerian novel. In S. Afonja & B. Aina, (Eds.), *Nigerian Women in social change.* (193-205). Ile-Ife: The Programme in Women's Studies Obafemi Awolowo University.

Kolawole, M.E. (1997). *Womanism and African consciousness.* New Jersey: Africa World Press, Inc.

Kolawole, M.E. (1997). Gender myths, self-image and metaphor in Flora Nwapa's *One is Enough* and *Women Are Different.* InE. Eko, et al. (Eds.), *Flora Nwapa (Critical Perspectives).* (107-23). Calabar: Department of English and Literary Studies, University of Calabar.

Nutsukpo, M.F. (2011). The pioneer female writers of the Niger-Delta: A feminist study of the works of Flora Nwapa, Zulu Sofola and Mabel Segun (Nee Imokhuede). In C.Nwahunanya, (Ed.), *From boom to doom: Protest and conflict resolution in the Niger-Delta.* (88-108). New Owerri, Imo: Springfield Publishers Ltd.

Nwapa, F. (2012). Women and creative writing in Africa. In T.Olaniyan & A.Quayson.

(Eds.), *African literature: An anthology of criticism and theory.* (Rev.ed.). (526-32). U.K, U.S.A. and Australia: Blackwell Publishing Ltd.

Nwapa, F. (1966). *Efuru.* Ibadan: Heinemann Educational Books.

Ogundipe, M. (2007). *Indigenous and contemporary gender concepts and issues in Africa: Implications for Nigeria's development.* Lagos: Malthouse Press Limited.

Ogundipe-Leslie, M. (1994). *Re-creating ourselves: African women and critical transformations.* New Jersey: Africa World Press, Inc..

Okonjo-Ogunyemi, C. (1988). Women and Nigerian Literature. In *Perspectives on Nigerian literature: 1700 to the Present,* 1 (1), (60-67).

Osofisan, F. (2001). *Literature and the pressures of FREEDOM: Essays, speeches and songs.* Ibadan: Opon Ifa Readers.

Shoneyin, L. (2010). *The secret lives of Baba Segi's wives.* Abuja: Cassava Republic Taiwo O. (1984). *Female novelists of modern Africa.* London: Macmillan Publishers.

Wood, M. (2013). *Indigo.* Lagos: Parresia Publishers Ltd.

CHAPTER 20

Panorama on Kinship through the Characters of Arundhati Roy's *The God of Small Things*

S. Preethi and M. Premavathy

Abstract

Kinship or relationship not only implies the bonding between members of family or friends but also the psychological attachment or belief among human souls. It was well portrayed in the semi-autobiographical novel *The God of Small Things* by Arundhati Roy. Perspectives of readers and critic may differ on characters of novel. But the depiction of circumstance which caused the behavior of novel personae could not provide distinguished thought or sympathetic ideas among readers and critic. Association of generations and their corresponding laws of heredity gave frame look to the readers through picturization of relationship between Pappachi and Mammachi; Chacko and Margaret Kochamma; Ammu and Baba; Ammu and Velutha; Estha and Rahel and so on. Those scaffolded and paralleled love laws would be analysed in this paper.

Keywords: Forbidden Love, Affinity, Expression, Gender Discrimination.

The God of Small Things (1997) was a debut novel of Arundhati Roy which brought Booker Prize (1997) for her. She wrote this literary piece for five years with the touch of autobiographical elements. Novel revolved the story of generations of Ipe family. Rahel and Estha fraternal twins gave the storyline to the readers. Rahel was the narrator of the novel. She narrated the story between her age seven and her age thirty one. It initiated the years 1969 and 1993. Pappachi and Mammachi were first generation couple of 1950s.Their children Chacko and Ammu. Couples Chacko and Margaret kochamma; Ammu and Baba were belong to second generation. Rahel and Larry McCaslin were third generation couples. Main plot of phenomenon around Ammu and her children Rahel and Esthappan; Ammu's divorce with Baba; Ammu and Velutha Relationship. In sub sections

Margaret and Joe kinship; Baby Kochamma and Father Muligan love were discussed. Those things made the novel's consequences, climax and denouement. Now this paper is going to analyze their kinship between themselves.

Pappachi and Mammachi

Sir Bennan John Ipe (Pappachi) was an imperial entomologist who had found a new species of moth. But he died before getting recognition for that. During his lifetime, whatever stress he had, he showed off on Shoshamma Ipe (Mammachi) only by beating her with brass vase, torturing her and not even listening of her tears. He practiced male dominating patriarchal claims in the Ayemenem house. Mammachi lead unhappy married life in that house with their children Chacko and Ammu. Chacko prevented Pappachi of beating Mammachi once. Because of that he stopped talking with her for the rest of his life. Instead of physical violence he gave mental violence to Mammachi by stopping conversation with her. To get rid of this Mammachi started Paradise Pickles and Preserves. She got success in it through her Mango Jam, Bottled Pineapples and Preserves. Again she felt tormented when she became sleeping partner of Paradise Pickles by handing over it to chacko. Relationship between Bennan Ipe and Shoshamma Ipe became patriarchal mentality of Pappacchi and unfruitful dependence of Mammachi. Here Paradise Pickles played symbolized role.

Baby Kochamma and Father Muligan

Navomi Ipe (Baby Kochamma) was the younger sister of Pappachi. During her teenage fell in love with Father Muligan, Irish priest who came to Ayemenem to understand the Hindu Scriptures. He became devotee of Lord Vishnu. Baby Kochamma converted herself from Syrian Christian to Roman Catholicism for Muligan. She started to live in convent. But she could not express her love to him. Her father wanted to ruin her idea of conversion. So he sent her to America for studying Ornamental Gardening. She remained unmarried throughout her lifetime. Because of her unrequited love, unfulfilled desire she became sadist in character by tormenting others by making unlawful arrangements to drop other family members' wishes. She loved to watch television and used to register it in her diary. Even she behaved horrible to the kids Esthappan and Rahel. She treated Ammu Ipe as an unwelcome guest to Ayemenem house. She was the prominent reason for the death of velutha. Psychologically she became ill of unrequited love. To escape from that she showed off her as supremacy.

Chacko and Margaret Kochamma

Chacko only son of Mammachi, he went to Oxford for studies. There he met Margaret and married her. They gave a birth of Sophie Mol. But Margaret felt detachment with Chacko who was inexpressive and lazy in manner. But he had strong affinity on his wife and daughter which he had never exposed to them. This made Margaret to divorce Chacko. After their divorce also Chacko invited them to Ayemenem which made reader to regret for him.

Margaret and Joe

After the divorce from Chacko, Margaret felt attracted towards Joe. From Joe she received her expected love and comfort. Unfortunately Joe met with an accident and died. Margaret and her daughter Sophie Mol returned to Ayemenem. There she lost her only daughter by drowning in Meenachil River. So, Margaret became so miserable. Rapport among Joe and Margaret concluded fatefully.

Ammu Ipe and Baba

Since the childhood, Ammu wanted to be away from Ayemenem. Once she went to her aunt house in Calcutta for summer holidays. She planned not to return Ayemenem. So, blindly she accepted the love proposal of Bengali Hindu Baba, tea plantation worker. She married him. But she lead stressful marriage life. Baba became drunkard and more violent. They had fraternal twin children named Esthappan and Rahel. Baba wanted to save his job, for that he tortured Ammu to share her bed with Mr.Hollick, an English employer. So Ammu assaulted her husband and returned to Ayemenem with her children. She was unwelcomed guest there. Because of her own decision on her marriage her parents refused to provide honourable position to her. Baby Kochamma used to insult her always. Here we would see the gender discrimination crystal clear. Ammu and Chacko's parents accepted the love marriage of Chacko and even accepted their divorced daughter-in-law who was invited there by Chacko. But Ammu's marriage and her separation from her husband could not be accepted by her family in Ayemenem. This was the picturization of marginalized pitified condition of womanhood in both parental and in-laws house. Correlation between Ammu and Baba made Ammu in search of consolation.

Ammu Ipe and Velutha

Ammu was Syrian Christian by birth. Velutha was Paravan by birth. Velutha and his predecessors worked for Ipe family. Racism was in peak at the years of 1960s. At that time, a love between two rational classes would be a great disaster in society. Eradication of racism was sprouting just here and there at that time by the name of communism. During that period in Ayemenem, Ammu felt her consolation from Velutha. Ammu was just 27. Velutha found recovery of Ammu along with him. Velutha was so kind to Ammu's children Estha and Rahel. He taught them swimming, building boats and making toys. Ammu was attracted towards him. In sunlight Velutha showed his fondness towards children. In moonlight Velutha and Ammu shared their consolatory love. Simply, they did not think about rifts which may happen in future. They thought their scaffoldings by sharing the words "Tomorrow? Tomorrow". (page 339). "Even later, on the thirteen nights that followed this one, instinctively they stuck to the Small things. The Big things ever lurked inside. They knew that there was nowhere for them to go. They had nothing. No future.So they stuck to the small things." (page 338).

Their Relationship provided the injured death of Velutha and Ammu's suicide by hanging. Due to the correspondence between racism and marginalization and unaccepted love and death of Ammu, her funeral was not held with proper respect. It was not informed to Estha (her son).Churchyard didn't allow Chacko to bury Ammu in graveyard. So Chacko wrapped her with worst dirty bed sheet. Her funeral held in electric crematorium where beggars' bodies were burnt. Finally, Ammu became the receipt number Q498673. These were witnessed by Rahel terribly with her helpless age. These were the ugly reality of marginalization and racism in the world.

> "The God of Loss
> The God of Small Things
> He left no foot-prints in sand, no ripples in water, no image in mirrors."
> (page 265).

Rahel and Larry McClasin

Rahel went to study Architecture in Delhi. And she went to America for visit. There she met Larry McClasin and fell in love with him at first sight. Eventually, she married him and started life in America. But they felt totally disconnected. They divorced each other. She never thought of any connectivity between them after their marriage. This depicted the immature attraction among them.

Esthappan and Rahel

From the childhood Esthappan used to call Rahel as a Refuge Stick Insect and Rahel called him as an Elvis the Pelvis as nicknames. Estha and Rahel didn't get proper parental brought up. Blood father was alcholic and arrogant. Their mother Ammu was helpless. In Ayemenem comparing to Sophie Mol they didn't get proper response. Once, Estha was molested by Orange drink Lemon drink man at theatre. So, Estha was affected psychologically. After the death of Sophie Mol and Velutha, Ammu was kicked out of house by Chacko. Being children Estha and Rahel could not save their mother and they were insecured. Estha became speechless. He muted himself from talking to anyone. Estha and Rahel were separated. Once, he wrote in pickle bottle "Anything can happen to Anyone, Best to be Prepared". This showed his affected and dreadful mind during his childhood. He was sent to his father Baba under compulsion who lived in Assam. There in Assam Estha was tortured a lot by his step mother. He didn't utter a single word even. He didn't get proper education as well as childhood. He lead a life in very pathetic condition. During the childhood Estha and Rahel liked and hoped each other. But they were separated unexpectedly. So, he became drifted mentally. Rahel was sent to America. At the age of thirty one Esthappan was returned to Ayemenem in half-insane condition. His father left him and went to Australia. After hearing the news of Esthappan presence in Ayemenem, Rahel returned to Ayemenam. Now Estha finds in Rahel both his sister and his lost mother. He uttered words after 24 years. He got secured feeling after 24 years. He felt intimacy after 24 years. Those things he felt only with his fraternal twin sister Rahel. His depressed mind got slight sunshine through Rahel.

Arundhati Roy drew a large canvas of characters which belong to three generations. All the characters have a story of lost dream to tell. She portrayed a social satire on contemporary society. She dealt issues like homeless, hunger, alcoholism, violence, racism, urbanization, cultural decadence, marginalization of women, religious institution, family relation and sexuality in this novel. Relationship played vital role in this novel. Conclusion of the novel which showed the intimacy of Estha and Rahel made some differences among readers.

As a reader, I would like to exclaim that Estha became mute because of torments and psychological tortures which he received since his childhood. Moreover his separation from Rahel made him insecure. After 24 years, at his age of 31, he saw his twin Rahel to whom he could feel secure, hope, love and everything. So, he exposed his suppressed feelings whatever he had within himself for 24 years. In my opinion, their intimacy of reunion was an expression like our tears, anger, smile, mirth and stubborn not at all a dealings.

Ayemenem house is a "TREASURE OF HUMAN EMOTIONS AND CIRCUMSTANTIAL PHENOMENON".

Works Cited

Roy, Arundhati. *The God of Small Things.* New Delhi: India Ink Publishing Co., 1997.

Singh. R.A. *Critical Studies on Indian Fiction in English*, New Delhi: Atlantic Publishers, 1999.

Singh.R.A. *Arundhati Roy's The God of Small Things a Critical Study*, Bareilly: Prakash Book Depot, 2004.

CHAPTER 21

Snapshot of Women in Literature

A. Geetha and M. Shanmugathai

Abstract

Literature is the collected creative writing of a nation, people, group or culture. It is rightly said that literature is the reflection of the culture and the society. We acquire knowledge from the past and bring it into practice with the present culture. The role of women and their transformation have been observed for ages. Their journey has been very decisive, contemptuous, condemned which they have managed with pensiveness and equanimity. This paper discusses the progress of women from the Chaucer period to Modern period. The paper also exposes the freedom of women, their difficulties and the representation of women centric characters in literature. Women are controlled to comply with the expectations of men uncooperatively due to their submissiveness in the male supreme society.

Keywords: Characterization of women, typecast, befree

Introduction

Ancient literature describes women as both complementing and supplementing their spouse. This inspires and persuades the writers to mould the women characters in their works. Yet, one person's thinking is different from others and similarly one's creation too. A few writers portrayed women as a glyph of power and oneness, and some described them as an object of gratification. Women have been typecast for ages because the mentality of men believes that the virtue of women is always old fashioned. The stereotypes of women are true, says Tanner (1986). Women are criticized for being talkative and they are often expected to be silent. According to Olsen (1999), man is the breadwinner to uphold the family while the duty of a woman is to do household chores and to bring up the children at home.

Characterization of Women

Character is a distinctive trait or attribute that makes a person different from others. It serves as an expression, establishment, interpretation and portrayal that demonstrates the behaviour, responsibilities and class of everyone in the community. Until recently, in the history of literature, most writers were male and their depiction of women in literature was undoubtedly partial. Nevertheless, the women's contribution to folk songs and tales, rhymes and stories should not be undervalued.

The oral culture is a tradition of handing down information, belief or custom from one generation to another and in due course it passed into written culture. Women in literature have been represented in various ways from Chaucer period to Modern period. The portrayal of women in literature is frequently persuaded by the writer's own personal experiences or with the conventional image of women in society. The interpretation of male writers about women's view is totally dissimilar to the female authors. For instance: F. Scott Fitzgerald delineates his prime women characters as a person subjected to oppression, deceived whereas Zora Ncale Hurston represents her female characters as determined, someone who is uninhibited by traditional society structures and self-reliant. Though women trait mightily in the early work of Chaucer, we can only observe a few women characters like nun, prioress and the wife of Bath are described in *The Canterbury Tales*. Women are elucidated as sinful, unkind, courtesan, spouse, skin and blister, fraud and companion. To be specific Shakespeare and Webster present female roles on stage after the renewal of drama during the 16th Century. Women were disguised as men which shows that there were lesser parts written for them. To mention a few famous characters are Rosalind, Viola and Portia. Shakespeare's heroines showed a boundless variety of female roles as mother, wife, daughter etc. Webster's female roles were overtly sexual. Though common stereotypes are still widespread, there is an extensive variety of female representation during the 17th Century. Mistresses still emerged as bashful in the poems written by Donne, Herric and Marvell.

In short, women have been observed as good and as well as bad. They are considered an inevitable partner for men. Life is meaningless without women. Man, generally, considers that female owns submissive nature when compared to male and these were womanly standards. However, this is not the same in all cases. In some situations, there were women who held the qualities of male even more than their spouses. Mr. Bennett in Jane Austen's *Pride and Prejudice* doesn't have the ability to cope with difficult situations like his wife to settle their five daughters with a happy married life. Molly Gibson, the only daughter in Gaskell's *Wives and Daughters,* turns out to be a better child to her father than a son like Osborne Hamley who neglected his parents. Edgar Linton in Emily Bronte's *Wuthering Heights* is a true depiction of manliness. George Eliot's female character Maggie Tulliver in *The Mill on the Floss* has been portrayed as unyielding, courageous and resilient than her own brother Tom. Despite the fact of being naïve and beautiful, Britomart was disguised as a knight and fought actively to save the lives of people. This shows the strong character of Spenser's heroine.

Jane Austen's female characters in *Pride and Prejudice* are certainly portrayed in a positive manner. It can be observed through their dialogues and from the description given by the author in the novel. One can conclude that being a female Jane Austen used more positive vibes rather than negative. Women authors use more positive terms for the purpose of saving their character's faces and to bring harmony. Even though women have lower honour than men it does not mean that they are vulnerable. The courtesy of women's communication points out women's moral behaviour and that has been broadly accepted by the male dominated society. They were raised and expected to speak less and to be polite always.

In addition, Coates (2004) declares that the middle-class women tend to be more fragile to reputation. Jane Austen is one such author who employs standard forms to prove her honour and to acquire good opinion and admiration from society. Apart from novels, the portrayal of women in poetry also plays a vital role. Speaking of Indian poetry, Mahadevi Varma, a mover and shaker and revolutionist turned into the reflection of the problems faced by womankind. Her works expressed the idea of women's freedom. It is important to mention Kamala Das whose writings are mainly on the analysis of bond between man and woman. This approach was then followed by other women poets like Chitra Narendran, Gauri Deshpande and a few more writers.

The portrayal of women in literature by male and female authors are different. The female authors know the needs and problems faced by women rather than a male. A M Irvine's *The Probationer* is a notable example to showcase the position of women in the post Victorian age. Specifying the dawn of modernism, the fiction also exhibits the rights of each modern woman through the protagonist character and by narrating her as a free-spirited and her personal adulthood.

Amidst the contemporary Indian writers Shobha De is one of the most profound writers who can proclaim her notion in a forceful and modish way through her works. In her writings, women are depicted in an unusual and eccentric way. Her fictions are a combination of exoticism, love, desire, hatred and extra-marital relationship in an exaggerated way. Indeed, she tries to picturize the truth and real life of metropolitan and cosmopolitan society. The female characters in her fictions are futuristic and have no trust in doctrines and traditions. They also break all kinds of proscriptions and feel out of the ordinary. She reveals the actual truth and brings awareness of women's sufferings and despotism done to them by their life partner in the male dominated society through her novels. Lately, the most admired fictionist, Chetan Bhagat has unveiled the new kind of women in his works. He presents his female persona as a precursor of social and cultural transformation. This theme is visible in one of his novels named *One Night @ the Call Centre*. Both men and women have been treated in the same manner while working night shifts.

Conclusion

The roles of women have been developed in the history of literature. Without any doubt the characterization of women was prejudiced since most writers were male and the society was ruled by those kinds of men, till now. Hence, the process of women being disregarded and controlled has been happening in every part of literature. Before the 19th century the women were subjugated due to their insignificant roles in literature. When women started to gain their equality, their main characters in novels continued to be transformed. By observing these modifications, it is noticed that not only the characters represent the woman's personality, but also the main characters change into the reformed figures that women aim for in their real life.

Works Cited

Coates, J. (2004). *Women, Men and Language.* 3rd ed. Harlow: Pearson Education Limited.

K. K. Ruthven, *Feminist Literary Studies: An Introduction.* Cambridge, 1990.

Olsen, K. (1999). *Daily Life in 18th century England.* Westport: The Greenwood Press.

www.iosrjournals.org.

CHAPTER 22

Transgression of Masculinty and Regeneration of Idyllic Female Space in Christina Georgina Rossetti's *The Goblin Market*

N. Poonkodi Shrri

Abstract

Christina Georgina Rossetti, a writer of romantic, devotional, and children's poems, depicted Goblin Market as a poem, which narrates the story of Laura and Lizzie who are enchanted by Goblin Merchants. Goblin Market recounts the adventures of two sisters, Laura and Lizzie, and their experience with Goblins. This chapter aims at bringing out the temptation encountered by two sisters and they find ways to get rid of the temptation and transgression created by the goblin merchants. The poem begins with the cries of the goblin merchants, selling their fantastic fruits in the twilight and their call was heard by Laura. She longs for the goblin fruits but without money, she puzzles and then, ready to offer a lock of her hair for the fruits. When Laura exchanges a lock of her golden hair for the chance to taste the goblins' enchanted fruit forbidden, she stoops herself to knock on the death's door. Laura returns home in an ecstatic trance, with one of the seeds. She narrates to her sister the delights she indulged in. Her sister tries to resolve by giving away a silver penny and escapes from the goblin men. But they forces her to eat the pulp of enchanting fruits. With the pulp of fruits, Lizzie reaches home and the dying Laura consumes the pulp and juice from her body, the taste spurns rather than satiates her, in the morning, Laura is fully restored to health. They both live to tell their children of the evils of the goblin's fruits, and the power of sisterly love. This chapter documents the idea of how unregulated, unprincipled capitalism becomes a masculinist menace and how that destroys and can potentially destroy the idyllic space of female. The poem ends with various acts of sacrifice, self-sacrifice, and regeneration.

Keywords: Temptation, masculine mercantile space, transgression, idyllic female space, regeneration.

Christina Georgina Rossetti, a writer of romantic, devotional, and children's poems, depicted Goblin Market as a poem, which narrates the story of Laura and Lizzie who are enchanted by Goblin Merchants. Initially, it is comprehended as children's literature but because of sexual images, it is included in the feministic writing. Goblin Market recounts the adventures of two sisters, Laura and Lizzie, and their experience with Goblins. A goblin is a monstrous creature that appears in the folklore of multiple European cultures, first involved with the stories of the Middle Ages. This chapter aims at bringing out the temptation encountered by two sisters and they find ways to get rid of the temptation and transgression created by the goblin merchants.

Though the sisters are young, they live in a house themselves and used to get water from an adjacent stream. The poem begins with the cries of the goblin merchants, selling their fantastic fruits in the twilight and their call was heard by Laura. Rossetti warns that the 'goblin men' resemble animals with faces like wombats or cats and with tails. Laura longs for the goblin fruits but without money, she puzzles and then, ready to offer a lock of her hair for the fruits. Even though it is set in a fairy-tale world; it explores themes of temptation sacrifice and salvation. The idea of male merchants, the masculine, mercantile space, the bazaar, or the market corrupts the idyllic female space. The poem clearly depicts the permanence and purity of the idyllic world and is destroyed and invaded by the impermanence and temporarily of the mercantile male world.

When Laura exchanges a lock of her golden hair for the chance to taste the goblins' enchanted fruit forbidden, she stoops herself to knock on the death's door. The whole idea of exchanging and purchasing the goblin's fruit for a lock of her hair could be symbolically drawn as a form of the sexualization of consumption. A form of prostitution where selling the lock of her hair becomes a sort of selling off the sexual self in the hope of getting the commodity from the market. The female sexuality is being exchanged for male commodities.

Laura returns home in an ecstatic trance, with one of the seeds. She narrates to her sister the delights she indulged in, but Lizzie is reminded of Jeanie, another girl who contacts with the goblin fruits, died at the beginning of winter after a pathetic decline. It is strange no grass covers her grave. But Laura wipes out her sister's worries and assures the next night to get more fruits for herself and Lizzie. The sisters slept in their shared bed.

The next day, as Laura and Lizzie are busy with the household chores, Laura dreamily wishes to meet the goblins. She could not buy more of the forbidden fruit, Laura grew sickening. She withers and feels too weak to do her routine. Suddenly she has remembered the seed, which she plants but nothing grows from it. As days and months pass by, Lizzie realizes that Laura is wasting her days and age. She decides to resolve this and buy some of the goblin fruit for Laura with a silver penny, she goes down the brook and is heartily greeted by the goblins and invited to dine. But the merchants came to know she has not come to eat but to buy in exchange for a silver penny for her sister. They attack her, force her to eat their fruits. But Lizzie denies consuming and is drenched with the juice and pulp.

Lizzie escapes from there and reaches home. The dying Laura consumes the pulp and juice from her body, the taste spurns rather than satiates her, in the morning, Laura is fully restored to health. They both live to tell their children of the evils of the goblin's fruits, and the power of sisterly love.

Christina Rossetti has chosen up the skill to be metrically consistent specially to make the public clear about the meter and metrical consistency. The formal subversive quality of the poem is intense, apart from being thematically subversive, even the rhythm, the metrical clarity, and the metrical consistency too. As a subversive text, this interruption of metrical consistency is to be taken into account. The compelling narrative of the poem is animated surprisingly and it never confirms a set rhythm scheme, rhyme scheme, or metrical pattern. The goblin merchants cry in the opening tries temper not through lavish verbal the opening description but forms.

Apples and quinces,
Lemons and oranges,
Plump unpick'd cherries,
Melons and raspberries,
Bloom-down-cheek'd peaches,
Swart-headed mulberries,
Wild free-born cranberries,
Crab-apples, dewberries,
Pineapples, blackberries,
Apricots, strawberries: –

This does not give splendid descriptions of fruits and where they came from, but it gives a bullet list of different commodities of different fruits which are offered in the market and the hard-hitting quality of the words. The description of the hard commodity and the consumption of these are some of the interesting things in modernist and post-modernist literature. The screaming out of the commodities makes it more appealing and sensational in quality. The goblin market is essentially a bazaar, which has different fruits from different parts of the world especially from Britain, Australia, Africa, Asia, and the whole bazaar becomes a metonymic creation of the empire in a way. This is symptomatic of the economy, the quality of the economy in Britain, the quality of the bazaar in Britain. The British bazaar does not have only British commodities anymore, but it has opened up to different commodities from different parts of the world. This idea of outlandish commodities, the idea of the foreign commodity or foreign body which is inhabiting the bazaar space makes it exotic as well as dangerous. The whole idea of a dangerous commodity, a dare commodity, is portrayed here and it particularly talks about the incantatory reputation of berries and the seductive sibilance that hints at the fruits' dark properties, so there is a menacing quality about these commodities as well. This is the world of flowers, plucked from bowers, where bowers came from a place where summer ripens at all hours, always Summer, endless Summer. There is a sense of perversion involved in the idea of endless Summer, permanent Summer. A perverted sense of abundance that does not follow the cyclicity of seasons – Summer, Winter, Autumn, etc. There is a degree of pathological quality or unnatural quality in this process of ripening. The artificial, inorganic quality about this process of ripening. The artificial, inorganic quality includes the dangerous modes of production becomes a menace for the consumer. This poem could also be analysed as a caveat to the consumer, a caveat against contaminated consumption, or the contamination which comes out of consumption.

Jeanie also appears in this narrative as a warning story, as a caveat narrative, as a caveat figure something which tells us what not to do. She went and looked for the goblin men in search of an antidote presumably, but she could not find them because they have disappeared. They are not quantified clinically, so different kinds of fruits come in – some very exotic, some familiar, some unfamiliar and so the bazaar, being a space, which accommodates a combination of familiarity and unusualness. A bazaar is a process or a drama of defamiliarization so the whole poem could be observed as an act of defamiliarization where known virtues, known movements, known recognitions, known mechanisms of manners get defamiliarized with the arrival of different objects from different parts of the world. The essence of idyllic Britain, an idyllic pastoral Britain is feminized. Rossetti creates a disorienting fairy-tale atmosphere, simultaneously seductive and alienating. It offers a variety of literary genres including gothic, fantasy, biblical, children's literature, and fable.

The bazaars cause a sense of the uncanny, a sense of something which is outside the home. It is literally and geographically outside the home. The Bazar is a made-up of Adhoc public space. It is the space of hybridity wherein different things come together and are sold simultaneously. It becomes not just a space for need classification, but it becomes a space for the production of hybridity among other things. The hybridity could be seductive, alienating, dangerous which we quite do not know what we are consuming, it is beyond cognitive radar.

Rossetti wrote the poem in 1859 while volunteering at the saint merry Magdalene penitentiary for fallen women at Highgate. Dedicated to the reform, and rehabilitation of prostitutes, this Anglo-Catholic institution was remarkable in the period for its conviction that women who had transgressed sexually could be redeemed. Instead of taking a very blunt, moral stand on prostitution, it offered a possibility of redemption and rehabilitation. These people would be reintegrated into civil society through different kinds of practices, economic practices, moral practices, etc. Rossetti was actively involved in this institution existentially as well as an Associate Sister at Highgate. Initially, it appeared to have elements of fairy-tale cadences but it is noted as it had adult themes of enticement, transgression, and redemption which also appealed to mature readership. The two themes, the two tensions, the two trends keep mixing and the poem gives a very interesting colour. The poem also resonances with the feministic classic *The Madwoman in the Attic* 1979, one of the canonical books in feministic writing. This also documents the female resistance, female solidarity, and a generation of female agency against the attack by male merchants.

The twentieth-century revival of interest in the poem opened the flood gates for feminists, Marxists, Freudian, Queer theory, and the New Historicist critiques which variously interpreted the poem as the warning about the dangers of the free-market economy, a protest against hazardous practices of the nineteenth century, food adulteration, Christian tale of sacrifice and salvation, a parable of lesbian empowerment, a fable about anorexia, an expression of incestuous yearning and a tribute to the delicious oral and aural pleasure of poetry.

The goblin market becomes a metaphor for consumption, the grand narrative of the mercantile economy. In this grand narrative, the poem flags up and foregrounds the theme of female consumerism. Laura is the fallen woman in the poem, she goes and establishes an exchange between the commodity and her sexuality. She gives a part of her sexuality by symbolically giving a lock of her hair with hope, with the expectation of getting some commodity out of the market. That becomes an interesting exchange and that commodifies Laura as well. The whole aspiration for a commodity is then itself commodified. The idea of Laura offering golden hair in exchange for a fruit becomes quite an allegory of prostitution, allegory of female disempowerment. She gives in to the seduction of the man with her sexualized body and that golden curl becomes the metonymic marker for that kind of sexualized body. She sucks the golden fruits. The fruits are:

> Sweeter than honey from the rock,
> Stranger than man-rejoicing wine,
> Clearer than water flow'd that juice;
> She never tasted such before.

So, they are something that she never tasted before. The idea of something new, exotic, forbidden, and fascinatingly foreign but at the same time menacing and dangerous and contaminated in quality is brought out.

> How should it cloy with length of use?
> She suck'd and suck'd the more
> Fruits which that unknown orchard bore;
> She suck'd until her lips were sore;

The understanding of sucking gives a sense of intoxication which she is completely addicted and completely intoxicated with the partaking of that kind of flavour, that kind of taste. The intoxication and the seduction become part of the fallen woman narrative in the poem.

> She suck'd until her lips were sore;
> Then flung the emptied the rinds way

But gather'd up one kernel stone,
And knew nor was it night or day
And she turn'd home alone.

She did not know it was night or day and she lost the sense of spatiotemporal recognition. She becomes the prey of the unhomely, uncanny space. She defamiliarized and deterritorialized herself. This becomes the beginning of her loss of embodiment, loss of agency of her embodiment, loss of agency over her own identity as a female. In contrast with Lizzie's more sensible and more judicious, more pragmatic and more subversive idea of going to the market with the actual penny, not a metaphorical, sexual object, not a metaphorical extension of the self but the actual penny which will let her enter the exchange mechanism in a very objective way. The woman with the penny, the woman with money, the woman with agency, the symbolic agency that annihilates or unsettles to a great extent the mechanism of the market, because the market in the poem is essentially male, essentially masculinity. The masculine quality of the poem, that marketplace is undercut by Lizzie's refusal to consume anything without the penny. The refusal to consume anything without paying for it also becomes a resistance against commodification. With Lizzie, it is different because Lizzie goes to the marketplace with a clear difference, with a clear externalization between herself, her biological self, and the currency with which she will purchase the commodity. She holds the penny in her hand and the penny is outside of her. It does not become a part of herself and it becomes the protective mechanism against self-commodification. She does not get commodified because of the penny that she is holding. The body of the goblins is non-human in quality. There is an unfriendly quality about the goblins. There is a rat-like quality and their physiognomic features are not human. They are not familiar and they are dangerous outsiders. They are outsiders who come and consume the purity of the British Idyllic landscape.

The violence on the body of the women is metaphorically viewed as violence on purity, violence on cultural purity, violence on cultural hygiene. Hygiene means biological hygiene, bodily hygiene, and also moral and cultural hygiene. From a Marxist perspective, it is a cautionary tale against open capitalism or unregulated capitalism.

Golden head by golden head
Like two pigeons in one nest
Folded in each other's wings,
They lay down in their curtain'd bed:

Like two blossoms on one stem,
Like two flakes of new-fall'n snow
Like two wands of ivory
Tipp'd with gold for awful kings,
Moon and stars gaz'd in at them,
Wind sang to them lullaby,
Lumbering owls forbore to fly,
Not a bat flapped to and fro
Round their rest:
Cheek to cheek and breast to breast
Lock'd together in one nest.

A lot of bird metaphors could be seen in the description of the particular intimacy between the two sisters. It is a sense of kinship, a sense of biological kinship but it is also an erotic quality about how this intimacy is described in the poem. They lie together, they symbolize tranquillity, sense of absolute intimacy. The poem uses a combination of natural metaphors like snow, blossoms on the stem, ivory, tipped with golds, etc. Ivory was a very common colonial commodity that often became a metaphor for greed, a metaphor of lust, a metaphor of colonial expectations. They are like two birds that are huddled together in absolute intimacy in one nest. A construction of a perfect home, a perfect protective home where Laura and Lizzie find themselves nested at this point in time. They are taking part in domestic idyllic activities, fetching honey, milking the cows, kneading the cakes with wheat, churning butter, whipping cream, feeding the poultry, and sewing and sitting together.

The idea of sisterhood which is present in the poem throughout is very complex. It is not quite clear whether they are talking about sisterhood as biological kinship or sisterhood as friendship or sisterhood as something quasi-erotic in quality, that is never quite spelled out but what is quite palpable is the intimacy between the two female protagonists in the poem and that intimacy is extended onto the future as well, in the sense that they marry and become wives. But there is no mention at all about the husbands and we get to know that they sit with the children, and tell them the warning tale of what happened with the goblin men and how one sister stood up for the other sister, and then they rescued each other in a tale of fall and restoration.

Days, weeks, months, years
Afterward when both were wives,
With children of their own; Their mother-hearts beset with fears,
Their lives are bound up in tender lives.

Laura would call the little ones
And tell them of her early prime
Those pleasant days long gone
Of not-returning time:

So obviously, when they become mothers and wives, then they call the children sometimes and tell them stories about their prime, tell them stories of what the events have happened which will not come back, not return in time.

Would talk about the haunted glen,
The wicked, quaint fruit-merchant men.

The wicked outsiders, the evil outsiders again, the goblin men over here represent alterity, they represent a sense of otherness, a fearful otherness, menace, which comes with otherness, etc.

The wicked, quaint fruit-merchant men,
Their fruits like honey to the throat
But poison in the blood;
(Men sell not such in any town):

The sentence 'Men sell not such in any town' has appeared already once in a poem, so it comes from outside, they come from an alien land. This degree of fearful foreignness, about these goblin men, becomes an embodiment of a certain kind of menace, which comes from the outside, which does not quite have a name. They come from places where things are perversely pleasant, things are perversely abundant. And they come with fruits that are grown in such inorganic, unnatural conditions. And that is the tale, a tale of caution, a tale of almost morality fable, which is told to the young children of Laura and Lizzie subsequently and how they encounter the goblin men and how one sister fell for the enchantment and the seduction the goblin men and the other sister, Lizzie, rescued her through great pain and difficulty, and this is what the moral of the fable is. This story is told to the children.

Certain critics read, bring in the lesbian angle into this poem in terms of how the whole idea of sisterhood becomes a sense of solidarity, becomes a community of solidarity, which is quite sexualized in quality. But then what is more important for us to remember is how the binary between the menacing men or the men who are carriers of menace, the men who are markers of menace, and their sisters or females who stood together in terms of regenerating themselves is captured in the poem. How the binary works out in very interesting ways. It is also a tale about a feminist critique of masculine, mercantile behaviour, masculine mercantile invasion, and how the feminist critique undercuts to a certain extent the menace of the marketplace which is a very masculinist peril. It is about fearful men who look very fearful, come from the outside. There is an outlandish quality about these men and the merchandise. The outlandish quality defamiliarizes and reterritorializes the known landscape, the known idyllic landscape of this very English countryside.

The space again becomes a very important symbol in the poem, in the sense that the spatial metaphor, the spatial mappings are very interestingly done. So, we have the home space, the idyllic space that has their cows and honey and butter have been churned. That is very idyllic and domestic and familiar and there is a virtue quotient about the home. And in contrast to that of the marketplace where things come and go, where everything is temporal in quality, where everything can very quickly change into something else, there is no permanence at all and the lack of permanence, the lack of virgin quotient of the marketplace, makes it a complete and perfect other of the home. So, the market is the other of the home spatially speaking and that spatial otherness, obviously extends onto the physiognomic otherness in terms of how the goblin men look like, they look like people with whiskers and tails and nails and they have cat-like features, they have rat-like features, and they fly in, they hobble in, they crawl in, the role in, their movements are not very human at all. So again, that becomes a part of the uncanny that is created by the marketplace, and the men in the marketplace, and how the poem becomes an example, how the domestic can be consumed by the uncanny. The poem is about consumption, contamination, sexual deprivation, regeneration, and sisterhood, and sisterhood, of course, is a very-very loaded term, a very complex category of identification of this poem because it could be a sort of biological kinship. The temptation and transgression are overcome by the two sisters and they emerge successful females. They warn their own children to overcome the same in the future.

The idea of unregulated, unprincipled capitalism becomes a masculinist menace and how that destroys and can potentially destroy at least the idyllic quality of hygiene, cultural hygiene, oral hygiene, sexual hygiene, etcetera and how that becomes the problem in a menace that is done away with by the time the poem ends with various acts of sacrifice, self-sacrifice, and regeneration.

Works Cited

Bovey, Lee-James. "Goblin Market by Christina Rossetti". *Poem Analysis*, https://poemanalysis.com/christina-rossetti/goblin-market/. Accessed 18 November 2021.

Pouliot, Amber. "Goblin Market Themes." LitCharts. LitCharts LLC, 7 Jun 2019. Web. 7 Aug 2021.

Rossetti, Christina G, and Martin Ware. *Goblin Market.* London: V. Gollancz, 1980. Print.

Shmoop Editorial Team. "Goblin Market Themes." *Shmoop.* Shmoop University, Inc., 11 Nov. 2008. Web. 23 Nov. 2021.

Rossetti, Christina. "Goblin Market by Christina Rossetti." *Poetry Foundation*, www.poetryfoundation.org/poems/44996/goblin-market.

CHAPTER 23

The Portrayal of Female Characters in the Various Literature of Different Cultures

Ayesha Khatun

Abstract

Literature is considered the mirror of the contemporary society. It reflects the contemporary issues, challenges that are existing in the society focusing on economy, political, social and religious matters through characters. Not only that, it also reflects the perceptions, believes, practices, observations and opinions of the writer also about the particular issues. The paper is a presentation on how women, half of mankind are portrayed in the literature in different cultures, ages and different continents from the male writers' perspectives. When we consider about issues women, we think of their lovely appearance, responsibility, dedication, sacrifice, heavy chores, and excessive talking without intelligence. For generations, these stereotypical views of women have prevailed. The study also shows the attitude, the conception of society towards female fraternity.

Keywords: Woman, Different cultures, Gender gap, Society's conception, Male's perception

Introduction

Women are chastised for babbling excessively having verbosity in their conversation. The old society had certain expectations of women, and one of the English Proverbs states that "quietness is the finest ornament of a lady" (Coates, 2004: 25). In the previous days, women were expected to stay passive, and they were constantly accused of babbling excessively no matter how much they even said (Coates, 2004). There is a lot of information saved as hints if we wish to discover the history of our grandfathers and great-grandfathers. They might be government leaders, business owners, or authors. In their past, there has always been distinction and honor.

However, if we want to learn about our grandmothers' or grand-grandmothers' lives, there is little to go on. All we know is that they could be gorgeous, talented at cooking, or anything along those lines. Everything is only a custom (Woolf, 1966: 2)."The history of England is the history of the male line, not the history of the female line," Virginia Woolf (1966) asserted (Woolf, 1966:2). That is appropriate. Moreover, some male writers have represented women as incapable of making their own judgments. This may be found throughout their literary works. They portray girls as weak and failures incapable of forming proper and autonomous judgments. The status of female characters and the manner of their representation in Classical, Elizabethan, African, American even in Modern literature are surely significant in terms of female social marginalization in male-written literary texts. Womanists and feminists have criticized the portrayal of female characters in these literature. The critique is based on the roles that female characters perform, which all reflect society's attitude toward women.

Methodology

This paper employs the interpretative method to examine a variety of academic critical studies on various elements of literary works. However, there are still few researchers who have studied the representation of female characters in male-written works. The interpretative research technique focuses on the nature of the views that have had the most effect on male playwrights' writings in isiXhosa theatre works. Taylor (1984:153) considers the interpretative method of research as a fundamental form that primarily interacts with texts.

The Characterization of Women in Different Literature

English Literature

Shakespeare's female characters are developed in a way that reflects the Elizabethan attitude toward women in generally. Despite the fact that the Queen was a female persona, women's places in society were severely restricted. Daughters are the property of their fathers and are handed over to their future husbands after marriage. In Elizabethan times, women were viewed as the weaker and more hazardous sex since their sexuality was reportedly unexplained and hence feared by males. Women were supposed to embody values like as obedience, stillness, sexual virginity, piety, innocence, fidelity, and endurance during the period.

Girls and women in his plays, such as Ophelia in Hamlet, face isolation, brutality, and death. All of the female characters, most significantly, appear to suffer the same tragic fate, which is an early death (Hamilton, 2003, pp. 69-70). The female characters in Hamlet, Ophelia and Queen Gertrude, have almost no power or activity (Gibson, 2002, p.72). This section will concentrate on Hamlet's female character Ophelia, who is Polonius' daughter, Laertes' sister, and Hamlet's occasional love. Ophelia is a gorgeous, innocent young girl who is subservient to both Polonius and Laertes. She is a lovely, young girl whose life has been changed forever by tragic fate, lunacy, and death (Berensmeyer, 2007, p. 38). Because of his hatred for Gertrude, Hamlet feels that all women are deceitful – 'Frailty, thy name is woman.' Regardless of how we perceive Hamlet's guilt, Ophelia suffers as a result of his archaic views on women. 'Frailty, thy name is woman.' Ophelia bears the cost of Hamlet's feudal views on women, regardless matter how we define his guilt.

It could also be asserted that the play *Othello* originates from patriarchal conventions and assumptions. Gayle Greene explains this point of view by claiming that *Othello* is a tragedy caused by "men's misconception of women and women's inability to shield themselves from society's view of them." Desdemona's feminine traits of meekness, softness, and submission, for example, are in no way comparable to Othello's masculine virtues of dominance, aggression, and authority. Desdemona says Iago, "I am a kid to chiding," after Othello had beaten her and spoken harshly to her out of jealously. Women are safeguarded by a system that weakens them. Desdemona, as a subservient female, is incapable of dealing with such harshness; she is defenseless against Othello. Desdemona consequently resorts to infantile conduct in order to escape reality. Shakespeare perfectly portrayed the true picture of the contemporary society.

American Literature

The Scarlet Letter is usually recognized as Nathaniel Hawthorne's greatest and one of the unequivocal classics of American literature. As a woman in Puritan society, the novel's protagonist, Hester Prynne, challenges authority and struggles diligently against colonial tyranny coupled by church and state. Hawthorne explores the narrative of Hester Prynne's terrible existence, revealing women's precarious situation in seventeenth-century Puritan New England while cruelly exposing the brutality and discrimination towards women in Puritan culture (Analysis of *The Scarlet Letter*). Hawthorne describes society as it was in 17th century Puritan America, which has been seen as a portrayal of women's issues at the period. It depicts not just the Puritans' animosity and the women's misery, but also the Puritans' strength of conscience and the women's low position. By the end of the story, Hester has evolved into a proto-feminist maternal figure to the women in the town. According to Meng (2003), the guilt associated with her scarlet letter is lost forever. Women perceive that her sentence was influenced in part by the town father's chauvinism, and they seek refuge with Hester from the sexist pressures they face. This statistic implies that Hester's mental independence has acquired acceptance amongst women.

A *Doll's House* an excellent literary piece of modern period published during the nineteenth century. Henrik Ibsen's renowned play *Doll's House* highlights the confined position of women at the time of its creation, as well as the issues that come from a significant imbalance of power between men and women. The other characters' treat Nora like a kid throughout the play. Torvald refers to her as his "pet" and "property," implying that she is neither knowledgeable nor reliable enough to be trusted with money. Mrs. Linde refers to her as a "kid" and neither Krogstad nor Dr. Rank take her seriously. While this treatment appears to irritate Nora, she accepts it and refers to herself as "little Nora." It displays the playwright viewpoint on women's rights. Ibsen stresses in his work that women's role is in their families, that working outside the house causes issues for women. Furthermore, Ibsen emphasizes that in this universe, males are dominating and women are subordinate. Men govern every aspect of life, and as a result, women's roles are diminished. Ibsen's presentation of female characters shows that women are subordinate to males and that women are objects rather than subjects. When Torvald accuses his spouse for the falsification and Nora says Torvald is not the one to teach her how to be a proper wife for him, he is certainly a critic of everything from Ibsen to patriarchal society. Michael Meyer was astounded that "a grown woman like Nora, however well-sheltered, could be so ignorant of the law" (104). Finally, Nora broke all the boundaries and took a stand for herself, left home to make her own identity.

Indian Literature

In the Indian literary world, Kalidas is considered as the most critically praised classical playwright. Shakuntala's characterization provides a remarkable level of literary exclusivity to the drama. The thematic essence centered around the traditional approach to Indian Womanhood and patriarchal economy demands closer investigation. Shakuntala extensively projects the patriarchal social system established in the post-Vedic period. In the drama, the female heroine Shakuntala, along with Priyambada and Anusuya, is an innocent victim of masculine persecution. Over ages, stereotype Indian women in Indian culture bear a striking resemblance to the heroine Shakuntala, whose ideal womanhood is usually defined by shyness and fidelity. Regarding the societal worth of women, King Dushyanta remarks, "“Hermit girls are by their very nature timid" (Act-2). Female socialization has deprived women of their economic liberty since the classical period. They appear to be utterly reliant on males for security and advocacy. A woman's marriage is controlled by the patriarchal authority's approval or rejection. In response to Clown's request that she marry King Shakuntala, Dushyantaspells out – "She is reliant on her father" (Act-2. This historical presumption about how women should be treated might probably be traced back to the Mahabharata, when Gandhari's rigorous compliance to her father's didactic command paralyzed her self-conscious statement to oppose the marriage with Dhritrasthra.

Bengali Literature

Kazi Nazrul Islam the national poet of Bangladesh, an eminent writer, musician was well aware of the societal negligence that had led to women turning to prostitution as a way of subsistence. He claims that our collective failure as a country has resulted in a failure to give women with the welfare and protection that they so well deserve. To despise the crime but not blaming the criminal who was compelled to commit it. He lived in a such society and ages that were very challenging times for women who lacked knowledge and opportunities to grow. He weeps for the thousands of lonesome women on the street who are beggars and have street children. In an editorial headed 'Temple and Mosque' (published circa 1926) for his journal Dhumketu (The Comet), he tells the story of a beggar lady carrying a kid and then throwing the dead infant into the garbage. When Nazrul looks about at the men going around the streets, he suspects to himself that one of them is the father of this kid, but he has taken no responsibility, leaving this poor mother to carry the entire burden. His empathy and compassion for women are unrivaled, as he elevates them to the greatest position in the world and believes in their inherent power. Here he reflected the attitude of society, their treatment towards female community.

Sarat Chandra Chattopadhyay analyzed the unfavorable attitude toward women in a male-dominated culture throughout history in his essay 'Narir Mulya' (Women's Value). A 5,000-year-old dead rule said that "if a wife dislikes her husband and says, 'Thou art not my husband,' they should throw her into the river; if a husband says to his wife, 'Thou art not my wife,' he shall weigh out half a mina of silver to her and let her go." This terrible legislation exemplifies the humiliation that women faced in ancient times.

African Literature

Chinua Achebe's *Things Fall Apart* is a patriarchal literary masterpiece in which women are ascribed very low social position. Female characters are considered as secondary in this book, and their excellent activities are not rewarded. Even though Ezinma exudes brilliance in Achebe (1958:44; 45-122), Okonkwo continuously wishes she was a man. Due to the obvious community scale in which the female characters are placed, they remain silent throughout the novel. This indicates how Chinua Achebe and other male-oriented writers regularly place female characters in disadvantageous positions. Stratton (1994:126) asserts that female characters in *Things Fall Apart* are subdued in the presence of masculine oppression. Hardly any of the female leads in this literature aim to oppose patriarchal rule, which is undesirable to females in a number of ways. Similarly, Ogunyemi (1988:66) deems African literature to be "phallic" since it is controlled by men writers and critics who deal nearly solely with male protagonists and male themes, and is thus aimed primarily at men. According to Schipper (1987:35), this is "the male heritage in African literature and criticism."

Men and women are indelibly significant aspects of society, each contributing to the solidification of a nation's backbone. However, almost in every culture and society women have a common history of patriarchal subjugation. On the basis of myth as well as in old and modern society identifying women as an inferior – silent creature, disadvantaged, subaltern subjects, subject to patriarchal control.

Social and cultural biases are still recognized as features for evaluating ideal femininity. As a result, the root of this social hierarchy is so firmly established in our social structure that the downtrodden and destitute can scarcely afford to define the purpose of life outside this long-running ideology. Concerning this biased attitude toward women, I concur with de Beauvoir's argument that women lack a "positive definition." "Humanity is male, and man defines woman not in herself but as relative to him......he is the subject; he is the Absolute – she is thc other," she asserts in *The Second Sex*. (1988:16)

Conclusion

The image of women's predicament was nearly same in every nation and culture throughout the world. Living under the iron bars of patriarchy, women had no voice to speak up against the injustice they had endured for decades. The situation began to change gradually as a group of educated women from many nations gathered to inform the world that women had the same rights as men to represent themselves in society. It should be also mentioned that the opinion, treatment and point of view of male writers are shaped up by the societal norms and ideals, of the society in some extent which are obviously reflected in their writings because they are not isolated from societal structure.

Works Cited

Chew & Shirley. (2010). *A Concise Companion to Postcolonial Literature*, Wiley-Blackwell.

Coates, J. (2004). *Women, Men and Language.* 3rd ed. Harlow: Pearson Education Limited

Cowie, L.W. (1973). *A Dictionary of British Social History*. London: G. Bell & Sons Ltd.

Beauvoir. D & Simon. (1953). *The Second Sex, London,* Jonathan Cape

Hasnain & Nadeem (2013). *Indian Society and culture*. JPD, New Delhi

Kumari & Sunalini (2017). Women Perspective in Henrik Ibsen's A Doll's House. The Criterion: *An International Journal in English Vol.* 8 (4).

Ghorai. A. (2020). Patriarchal Values of Indian womanhood and Its Legacy in Kalidas' Shakuntala. *International Journal of English Literature and Social Sciences, 5*(5). |Available online: https://ijels.com/ ISSN: 2456-7620 https://dx.doi.org/10.22161/ijels.55.17 1445

Graddol, D. & Swann, J. (1989). *Gender Voices*. Oxford: Blackwell.

Waldron, M. (1999). *Jane Austen and the Fiction of Her Time.* Cambridge: Cambridge University Press.

Woolf, V. (1966). *Women and Fiction.* London: Hogarth Press.

W. Ryder, Arthur (1999). Shakuntala (originally by Kalidas) Cambridge, Ontario

Wollstonecraft, M. (1792). A Vindication of the Rights of Women. 3rd ed. London: the Everyman Library

Hopper, P.J. (1999). *A Short Course in Grammar.* New York: W.W. Norton.

Jackson, H. (1990). *Grammar and Meaning.* London: Longman Press.

Kirkham, M. (1997). *Jane Austen, Feminism and Fiction.* London: The Athlone Press.

Newton, J. L. (1981). *Women, Power and Subversion: social strategies in British fiction.* New York: University of Georgia Press.

Meng Xueqin. (2003). Does Hester Get Rebirth? – Reexamination of the Heroine in The Scarlet Letter. *Journal of PLA University of Foreign Languages 26*.6, 79-82.

Nina, B. (2000). The Scarlet Letter: A Reading. Boston: Twyne publisher.

Wang. Y. (2010). A Representative of the New Female Image – Analyzing Hester Prynne's Feminist Consciousness in The Scarlet Letter. *Journal of Language Teaching and Research, Vol. 1*, No. 6, pp. 893-897. ACADEMY PUBLISHER Manufactured in Finland. doi:10.4304/jltr.1.6.893-897.

Olsen, K. (1999). *Daily Life in 18th-century England. Westport*: The Greenwood Press.

Persson, G. & Rydén, M. (1996). *Male and Female terms in English.* Umeå: Umeå University.

CHAPTER 24

A Study of Blanche *DuBois'* Exhibitionism and Fetishism in *Tennessee* Williams' *A Streetcar Named Desire*

Gopinath Khutia

Abstract

The present article studies *Blanche DuBois,* the central character in Tennessee Williams' 1947 poetic play *A Streetcar Named Desire as an embodiment of* exhibitionism and fetishism. Blanche DuBois is female exhibitionism personified. Blanche's "nonsexualized" exhibitionism is tacit in her name while her "sexualized" exhibitionism is a desperate attempt to fill her empty heart with kindness and with male company. Moreover, Blanche substitutes her loss with inanimate fetish objects. Blanche develops fetishism, holds on to the fetish objects out of her fear that she has lost much and is going to lose many more. The obsession with material items substitutes the need or the lack of real-life objects of desire. Blanche's exhibitionism and fetishism are part of her mental mechanism of coping with post-trauma. Williams' purpose is not to present Blanche as a disordered person. He places Blanche in the "plague of violence and horror" of this world and by his empathetic presentation seeks to know and understand the grim influences and circumstances, the variables, the storm of crisis that drive Blanche towards "disorder" and insanity.

Keywords: Blanche *DuBois,* Exhibitionism, Fetishism.

Introduction

In his introduction to *The 1940s: Profile of a Nation In Crisis*, Chester Eisinger opines that America in the 1940s was the decade punctuated by – war, postbellum neurosis, the fear of the bomb, and the government, xenophobia, and Communist threat. These resulted in depersonalization and dehumanization which got reflected in the art and literature of the period. And the literary representations of the time dealt with the themes of "quest for identity", the crisis of identity, separation of the individual from the self and the society, and the like. *While dramatists like Arthur Miller have shown social consciousness, Tennessee Williams has delved deep into the psyche of the individuals. Williams' plays are not so much socially concerned as Miller's. Williams' plays have turned inward to depict the isolation, alienation, and quest for identity of the individuals.* Williams' aim in his plays is not to offer philosophical discourse but to probe into the psychology of his characters. His character portrayal intends to portray the "interplay of live human beings in a thundercloud of common crisis" (qtd. in *Adler 1-2)*.

Noted American dramatist Arthur Miller in his Introduction to *Tennessee* Williams' modern tragedy *A Streetcar Named Desire* (1947) foregrounds the foremost themes Williams' play discourses about – *Streetcar is "the cry of pain" of Blanche DuBois; it is a lyrical play, "planting the flag of beauty on the shores of commercial theatre" (Miller ix); it is the tragedy of those who are tenacious to "desire"; it prophesies the "fate of the outsiders in America" (Miller x). A Streetcar is an episodic play consisting of eleven scenes and the plot revolves around* the "desire" of the Southern belle, *Blanche DuBois* who is based on Williams' troubled sister Rose and around the "desire" of other characters. *Blanche who always has to depend on the "kindness of strangers" arrives in the Elysian Fields with a desire to find the "visionary company" of love but her hope of happiness is nipped into the bud, and she finds to her deep dismay that the tower of vision has turned into a "broken world". My humble endeavour in this article is to look at Blanche DuBois as an embodiment of* exhibitionism and fetishism; she suffers from such psychosexual disorders as fetishism and exhibitionism. First, I shall shortly discuss relevant critical literature, and then I shall introduce and illustrate exhibitionism and fetishism.

Review of Literature

Daniel Jacobs in "Blanche, Stella, Tennessee and Rose" explores how in *Streetcar* Williams gives voice to his psychosis regarding his "ambivalent" relationship with his sister Rose and overcomes the said crisis through his writing and Blanche-Stella relationship. Joseph R. Silvio argues that the troubled childhood of the playwright and his traumatic relationship with his family members have a significant bearing on the thematic aspects of the play. In "On the Psychological Realism of *A Streetcar Named Desire*" Xuefei Wang and Shuai Han attempt to analyze the "setting", "characters", and "dialogue" of *A*

Streetcar Named Desire to show the psychological realism in the play. Farida Ratna Wiweko in her thesis "A Study on Blanche Dubois's personality disorder as seen in Tennessee Williams's *A Streetcar Named Desire*" looks into the psychological disorder by using conflict and schizophrenia and tries to understand the cause of Blanche's insanity. "The Creation of Tennessee Williams' Blanche Dubois: a Biographical Psychotic Neurotic" by Fizzah Ali orients the neurosis and psychosis of Blanche and other characters to the counterparts in the personal life of the dramatist. *The current article aims to show how the lead character Blanche DuBois is an embodiment of* fetishism and exhibitionism. She suffers from such psychosexual disorders as fetishism and exhibitionism, and a great deal of who she is and what she does is marked by these disorders.

What is Exhibitionism?

Simply speaking, exhibitionism is an inclination towards exhibiting one's capabilities or the nature to act in such a manner to seek attention. Primarily, exhibitionism "does not imply the presence of a disease entity or illness, but simply indicates the presence of a particular kind of behaviour" (Rooth 135). Exhibitionism as a disorder was first recognized in 1877 by the French psychiatrist Charles Lasègue. Since then, exhibitionism has been considered to be a psychosexual disorder, a deviant [sexual] behaviour in which one feels the irresistible desire to exhibit their private parts, especially genitals. There are different dimensions and kinds of exhibitionism. There are "sexualized" and "nonsexualized" exhibitionisms, though both types are pathological and both are triggered by a sustained "attempt to overcome shame as well as to attain admiration. Exhibitionism involves a repetition compulsion" (Silverstein 34). Thus, there is "healthier" kind of exhibitionism that come out through the display of one's abilities, e.g., acting, painting, writing, flaunting cooking skill or dress in social media. There is also "unhealthy" exhibitionism that, as Judith Silverstein points out, "has compulsive and often hostile components. Genital exhibitionism includes both a hostile and a compulsive quality" (34).

Culturally, historically and traditionally men are considered to be behaviourally maladaptive while women are taken for granted as socially and behaviourally very adaptive. So, it is generally assumed in psychiatric literature that "the occurrence of female exhibitionism…is an extremely rare phenomenon (Grob 256).

Blanche's Exhibitionism

Blanche DuBois is female exhibitionism personified. In her life Blanche has lost more than she has gained – the loss of her parents, the loss of her ancestral property, the loss of her young lover, the loss of her job. And these losses may have triggered her exhibitionism. She has made a desperate effort to compensate her losses by her deviant behaviour. The disordered world she lives in pushes her to a disordered pattern of behaviour. Moreover, her exhibitionist behaviour is necessitated by her extreme need for attention.

Blanche's "nonsexualized" exhibitionism is implied in her name. *The very name Blanche is reminiscent of Matthew Arnold's coinage "moon-blanched night". Besides suggesting purity, the name implies showiness.* Nicholas Pagan interprets "blanche" as a verb meaning "to bleach by excluding light" (qtd. in Bloom 66). *Blanche* prefers the dark. She must "avoid a strong light". Pagan further points out that colloquially Blanche means "white-washing, glossing, or more bluntly, lying" (qtd. in Bloom 25). Despite her destitute, she exhibits her haute status by showing her dress and jewellery. And in doing so, she shows off her bodily charm and her apparent chastity. Her first appearance in a "white suit with a fluffy bodice" suggests a moth and it underscores the fact that she has anxiety that her youth is waning. Blanche is as delicate as a moth. The moth analogy makes it clear that she has an exfoliated identity and she is not who she appears to be. Moreover, the analogy indicates her intense urge and her obsession with objects and men.

Blanche's "sexualized" exhibitionism becomes evident in Scene Three of *Streetcar. While* the four men – Stanley, Mitch, Mr. Gonzales, and Mr. Hubbel are playing poker at Stanley's small apartment, Stella and Blanche return around 2.30 am. After formally introducing Blanche with Stanley's friends, especially Mitch, Stella and Blanche start undressing, and Blanche steps into the light, wearing only a bra:

> [She takes off the blouse and stands in her pink silk brassi`ere and white skirt in the light through the porti`eres. The game has continued in undertones.]…
>
> Stella: ….You're standing in the light, Blanche!
>
> Blanche: Oh, am I! [She moves out of the yellow streak of light….](III 39-40)

A few moments later as Stella steps into the bathroom, Blanche "*moves back into the streak of light. She raises her arms and stretches, as she moves indolently back to the chair*" (III 40). Blanche stretches like a cat. Blanche's purpose is to distract with her semi-nude silhouette the men especially Mitch who appears to be "superior", "sensitive", "unmarried" in his first appearance. Mitch seems to be a possible saviour for Blanche from her past shame. Blanche is desperate to gain the attention and admiration of Mitch. Mitch is her last bus. So, the bodily exhibition of Blanche is like a cat's mating call. Stella warns her but Blanche pretends that she has done it inadvertently. Blanche here exhibits her "reflectoporn" tendency.

The dramatic narrative appears to be an exhibitionist one. The narrative brings our attention to the vulnerability and "unmask[s] the violence involved in victimization of Blanche" (Vlasopolos 322). To Anca Vlasopolos, the first name Blanche means both "white" and "blank" which indicates that her breakdown is preordained. Again, Vlasopolos points out that Stanley's remark that Blanche is "no lily" prefigures Stanley's final win. Moreover, in Scene Ten of the play Stanley while opening the beer bottle "The bottle cap pops off and a geyser of foam shoots up" (X 107). Then, "The barely audible "blue piano" begins to drum up louder. The sound turns into the roar of an approaching locomotive. Blanche crouches...Stanley takes a step toward her, biting his tongue which protrudes between his lips" (X 111). In Scene Eleven, Stanley menacingly approaches Blanche, "seizes the paper lantern, tearing it off the light bulb and extends it toward her. She cries out as if the lantern was herself" (XI 121). These stage details are deterministic and photographically exhibit mental and physical onslaught on Blanche.

What is Fetishism?

Originating in the anthropological discourse, fetishism ramified into history, Marxist economy, and psychoanalysis. Etymologically, fetishism comes from the Portuguese word "feitico" ("sorcery"/"magical art"/"images"/ "relics of saints") which in turn derives from Latin "facticius" ("to do"/ "manufactured"). The term was applied by the "Portuguese seamen to manufactured objects which they thought West Africans worshipped" (Pool 114).

Fetishism was a pejorative term referring to the cultural practice of using talismans in African societies, and in the colonial discourse it came to represent the crux of African society. Fetishism became tantamount to African identity and a means by which the "enlightened" Europe defined itself. Nineteenth-century onwards, fetishism was used in other discourses than the colonial and anthropological ones, and assumed different connotations in the hands of Karl Marx, Alfred Binet, Sigmund Freud, and others. While in African culture fetishism has been demonized; in Marxist interpretation it has been commoditized and socialized; in Binet, Freud, and others' interpretation fetishism has been psychologized and sexualized. Thus, fetishism has been used to refer to – "a form of enchantment"; "obsession with an "object"; "value relation"; "sexual attachment", and finally "mental illness".

Blanche's Fetishism

Ruby Cohn in "The Garrulous Grotesques of Tennessee Williams," suggests that DuBois the last name of Blanche (anglicized "doboys") might refer to her obsession with men. She is a "lover of boys and under her chaste surface, Blanche lusts for boys" (qtd. in Bloom 25). Blanche substitutes her dead husband Allan and "replaces and preferably to his sexuality" (Mountian 725) inanimate fetish objects. By this substitution, the fetish is almost "spectralised", and "its presence becomes even more oppressive and all-pervasive, as if, there is no way the subject can escape its hold" (qtd. Mountian 725). Blanche develops fetishism, holds on to the fetish objects and things out of her fear that she has lost much, and at the same time, the fear that she is going to lose many more. The obsession with material items substitutes the need or the lack of real-life objects of desire. Following Freud, we can say that Blanche's sexuality is "castrated". Her narcissistic drive tries to compensate her inner void and the void caused by her losses.

Blanche is so much obsessed with her appearance so that she needs continuous validation. On her very first meeting with Stella, she says: "You haven't said a word about my appearance" (11). She suffers from how-do-I-look anxiety. That is why, she loves to masquerade her life with dream, magic, expensive dress, jewelry, and refrains from "glaring" light so that her femininity does not feel insecure. Blanche is a "clothing fetishist". And "her sartorial autoreification" can be seen "as the symptom of an extended, projected affirmation of female ontology" (Kocela 103).

If fetishism is read "as a figure for hostility toward the social order" and "as a fundamentally conservative strategy of disavowal"

(Kocela 31), then both Stanley Kowalski and Blanche DuBois have shown "hostility" and "disavowal" to the world each belongs to. On each occasion, Stanley almost pounces upon Blanche breaking into pieces her delicate glass of illusion and magic. He tracks Blanche as a bloodhound does; unclothes her convoluted and mysterious past, ripping off all her lies. For Stanley and Blanche, Blanche's expensive dress becomes more than mere commodities. They assume a social meaning identical with the so-called upper-class Blanche belongs to and this comes close to Marx's "commodity fetishism". For Stanley, Blanche's costume acquire different value, moving away from its relation to utility. In Scene Two we find Stanley's violent surge:

> Stanley: Look at these feathers and furs that she come here to preen herself in! What's this here? A solid-gold dress, I believe! And this one! What is these here? Foxpieces! [*He blows on them*] …
>
> Pearls! Ropes of them! What is this sister of yours, a deep-sea diver? Bracelets of solid gold, too! Where are your pearls and gold bracelets? And diamonds! A crown for an empress! (II 26)

In his initial presentation of Blanche, Williams draws our attention to Blanche's haute appearance, "delicate beauty", her "valise", "dainty" dress – "white suit", "fluffy bodice", "necklace", "earrings of pearl", "white gloves", "hat" etc. And this focalization on the regalia and her outfit at the cost of other identifying descriptions places the playwright and the readers as well in the position of fetishists.

Besides, the narrative is fixed on such referents and habitual focalization as bathing in hot water to bring to the fore Blanche's fetishism. Whenever she feels distraught and overwrought she applies "Hydro-therapy" to soothe her nerves: "Blanche: I take hot baths for my nerves" (VIII 93). And as soon as she is "freshly bathed and scented" she feels "like a brand new human being!": "Blanche: "A hot bath and a long, cold drink always give me a brand new outlook on life!" (VII 89). Blanche's recurrent urge to bathe is an attempt to cleanse the problematic spots from her life; an attempt to purify herself; an attempt to start life afresh; an attempt, as if, to drink the water of the mythical Lethe and erase the precarious and questionable past.

Blanche lives as she ought to live and says what she ought to say. She creates different "veils". The idea of the "veil" is elaborated by Jacques Lacan "whereby with the presence of the veil; that which is beyond, as lack, tends to actualize itself as image. On the veil, it is painted the lack" (qtd. Mountian 725). From Lacanian perspective, her fondness for costume, "magic" is the "veil". Another such "veil" is the imaginary Shep Huntleigh who is Blanche's symbolic fetish, the Lacanian "veil" who is beyond, whose image helps her fulfill the lack albeit in wish-fulfillment.

Another obsession of Blanche is with "magic". Reality is associated with light and it is tantamount to exposure. Reality has caused many bruises to Blanche. Hence, a life of "magic", "misrepresentation" and might-have-been. In Scene IX, Blanche says to Mitch:

> Blanche: I don't want realism. I want magic! [*Mitch laughs*] Yes, yes, magic! I try to give that to people. I misrepresent things to them. I don't tell truth, I tell what *ought* to be the truth. And if that is sinful, then let me be damned for it! – *Don't turn the light on!* (IX 101).

Quite ironically, these will have an opposite impact than Blanche has expected – she will indeed be "damned". Blanche wants to drive out reality the "damned spot" of her life but as the "damned spot" haunts Lady Macbeth to insanity, the "damned spot" of her past haunts Blanche like a ghost and drives her insane.

Conclusion

Though Tennessee Williams unearths the psychological complexity, the crisis, and "disorders" of Blanche DuBois, we do not feel distanced from her. Rather, Williams "makes us see and hear like Blanche, and perhaps feel like her" (Vlasopolos 338). Williams has not offered any judgement on Blanche; she has not been presented either as a "heroine" or a "villain". The playwright has externalised the "right or wrong ways that [Blanche has] taken, not by choice but by necessity or by certain still-uncomprehended influences in [her life], [her] circumstances, and [her] antecedents" (Williams 126). Through Blanche, Williams shows us the imperiled condition of truth in Post-war America and the "plague of violence and horror in this world and time that we live in" (Williams 125).

Exhibitionism and fetishism are Blanche's post-traumatic countermeasure or strategy – "a mental strategy or defense that enables a human being to transform something or someone with its own enigmatic energy and immaterial essence into something or someone that is material and tangibly real" (qtd. Kocela 131). The inflated exhibition of the self-created fragile glass world of Blanche made of dreams, magic and artificiality is fated to shatter to pieces. The truth of heart had no place in Post-war America. Unavoidably,

Stanley and his kind are to rise and Blanche and her kind are to fail and fall.

A Streetcar Named Desire has a therapeutic and cathartic impact on Williams himself and the audience. Williams himself says that his work "has always been a kind of psychotherapy for [him]" (124), and at the same time by dramatizing the "brutal" and "ugly" instincts, he helps release our "increasing tensions, verging on the psychotic" (Williams 125). *A Streetcar Named Desire* poetically urges us not to hate, fear, and abrogate people, as Stanley Kowalski does to Blanche, but to give a try to arrive at full cognition and understanding of persons like Blanche.

Works Cited

Adler, Thomas P. *A Streetcar Named Desire: The Moth and the Lantern*. Simon & Schuster Macmillan, 1995.

Bloom, Harold. *Tennessee Williams's A Streetcar Named Desire*. Chelsea House, 2009.

Grob, Charles S. "Female Exhibitionism." *The Journal of Nervous and Mental Disease*, vol. 173, no. 04, 1985, pp. 253-256.

Jacobs, Daniel. "Blanche, Stella, Tennessee and Rose." *The Psychoanalytic Study of the Child*, vol. 61, no. 1, 2006, pp. 320–333., doi:10.1080/00797308.2006.11800777.

Kocela, C. *Fetishism and Its Discontents in Post-1960 American Fiction*. Palgrave Macmillan US, 2010.

Miller, Arthur. "Introduction." *A Streetcar Named Desire*, A New Directions Book, 2004.

Mountian, Ilana. "Fetishism." *Encyclopedia of Critical Psychology*, Edited by Thomas Teo, 2014 Edition, Springer, pp. 723-727.

Pool, Robert. "Fetishism Deconstructed." *Etnofoor*, vol. 3, ser. 1, 1990, pp. 114-127.

Rooth, F. G. "Some Historical Notes on Indecent Exposure and Exhibitionism." *Medico-Legal Journal*, vol. 38, no. 4, 1970, pp. 135-139., doi:10.1177/002581727003800405.

Silverstein, Judith L. "Exhibitionism as Countershame." *Sexual Addiction & Compulsivity*, vol. 3, no. 1, 1996, pp. 33-42., doi:10.1080/10720169608400098.

Vlasopolos, Anca. "Authorizing History: Victimization in 'A Streetcar Named Desire.'" *Theatre Journal*, vol. 38, no. 3, 1986, pp. 322-338., https://doi.org/10.2307/3208047.

Wang, Xuefei, and Shuai Han. "On the Psychological Realism of A Streetcar Named Desire." *Advances in Computer Science Research (ACSR)*, vol. 61, 2017, pp. 457-460., doi:10.2991/emcs-17.2017.90.

Williams, Tennessee. "'The World I Live In'." *A Streetcar Named Desire*, A New Directions Book, 2004, pp. 124-127.

.... *A Streetcar Named Desire*, A New Directions Book, 2004.

CHAPTER 25

Mahesh Dattani's *The Girl Who Touched the Stars:* Story of an Unwanted Girl Child

Rashmi Varma

Abstract

Although the various feminist movements have worked towards gender-sensitization and equality of sexes, misogyny and gender-discrimination continue to exist. An obvious manifestation of gender discrimination is preference for a boy child over a girl child in a family. Mahesh Dattani, an eminent Indian playwright, is known for his plays on controversial subjects like religious tension, sexuality and gender issues, subjects which continue to plague the Indian society. His popular play *Tara*, published in year 1990 was about the fate of an unwanted girl child in an Indian family. By the end of the first decade of the new millennium, Dattani, found the issue still burning as ever. In the year 2010 he published a play titled *The Girl Who Touched the Stars*. The play is a sorrowful story of a woman astronaut, Bhavna, who in the proud moment of her career, shockingly realizes that she has been an unwanted girl child for her parents. Her father had wanted a boy child who would grow up to be a pilot. Bhavna has to face the disturbing fact that her family had never accepted her as a girl child. The play shows how gender discrimination continues to eat into the socio-cultural fabric of Indian society.

Keywords: girl-child; gender-discrimination; Mahesh Dattani, radio play

Despite all the feminist movements, stories of equality of sexes and women's achievements, gender-discrimination remains a sad reality of the modern world. In India women are born in a misogynistic society where birth of a child is expected to be of a boy child and birth of a girl child is considered to be a bad luck! Dr. Rekha Samuel, professor of Pathology observes, "the unwanted girl child is India's greatest shame. The fixation for a male child transcends socio-economic status, religion, education and gender. A girl is dispensable in the world's largest democracy." Mahesh Dattani's play *The Girl Who*

Touched the Stars is a sorrowful story of a woman astronaut, who in the proud moment of her career shockingly realizes that she has been an unwanted girl child in her family. Her father had wanted a son who would grow up to be a pilot. Dattani, in the play deals with the serious subject of gender discrimination and depicts the plight of an unwanted girl child.

Any discussion about the status of Indian drama in English would definitely look forward with great expectancy towards a reference to the works of Mahesh Dattani. He is responsible for the rejuvenation of Indian drama in English as he started writing plays in 1980s about controversial subjects like religious tension, sexuality and gender issues, subjects which continue to plague the new millennium India. Similarly, his innovative stage techniques also helped him in the effective dramatization of these issues. However his most important contribution is his unapologetic acceptance of English language – the language of common urban middle class educated Indian – as a medium of expression. Adventurous enough to experiment in all the aspects of drama writing, Dattani moved on to explore the medium of radio and cinema, exploiting the potential inherent in them for the dramatic representation of his observations on issues close to his heart. One such issue is the much condemned yet universally prevalent question of gender discrimination. Although the subject keeps emerging in his plays, his popular play *Tara* published in 1990 was exclusively devoted to the fate of an unwanted girl child in an Indian family. By the end of the first decade of the new millennium, Dattani, found the issue still burning as ever. This paper attempts an analysis of a radio play titled *The Girl Who Touched The Stars* which Dattani published in year 2010 showing how the malaise of gender discrimination is far from being cured as we would like to believe and continues to eat into the socio-cultural fabric of Indian society.

The Sahitya Akademi Award citation mentions that Mahesh Dattani's plays 'probe tangled attitudes' in contemporary India. His preference for contemporary issues is also noted by a scholar who comments that "his dramatic art is the faithful and authentic expression of his firsthand experience and knowledge of socio-cultural environment in which he breathes and lives" [Parmar30]. Dattani himself accepts this when he says "social issues move me and I like to examine an idea from different angles."

Gender discrimination is one such issue that Dattani has been deeply interested in. A very obvious manifestation of gender discrimination is preference for a boy child over a girl child. Simply said, a son is wanted and a daughter is unwanted. Dattani had dealt with this aspect of gender discrimination in one of his earlier plays titled *Tara* written in 1990, where in a liberal and educated family a girl child's life is sacrificed in favour of a boy child. The implication of the play was that a patriarchy ruled society creates such a social system in which the birth of a girl child is denied and her existence is threatened.

Written in 2007 and published in 2010 Dattani's play *The Girl Who Touched The Stars* shows that despite all the claims of progress, development and equal opportunities nothing much has changed as far as the status of a girl child is concerned. Beti Bachao and Beti Padhao still remain just political slogans. The play examines the issue from the point of view of a girl child. The play opens in year 2025 when the protagonist, Bhavna, a successful astronaut is ready for a space journey to reach Mars. Unfortunately, after the take-off, her space craft explodes. Out in the space, Bhavna confronts her childhood self. Through her younger self Bhavna keeps delving deep into her past only to discover that her achievement in being the first Indian woman to reach Mars was a result of her father's wish for a male child, who he would have liked to become a pilot. Living in a society where women are not only made victims but also perpetuators of patriarchal tyranny, it is no wonder that Bhavna's mother too is a party to her husband's schemes.

The play being a radio drama is an acoustic performance, with first broadcast on 6th March 2007 on BBC Radio 4. As Tim Crook in his book on radio drama says 'this medium of drama offers the dramatist considerable control and a fast route to the centre of human consciousness and psychological engagement" [Radio Drama]. Dattani too uses the medium to its maximum effect as he unravels the doubt buried deep in Bhavna's subconscious. With the help of dialogue, music and sound effects he dramatizes the process through which Bhavna comes to face the bitter truth of being an unwanted child. The process consists of exploring the innermost recesses of Bhavna's mind where the confinements of time and space do not exist. Dattani introduces a technical innovation in plot structure when he presents the entire plot of the play as an interaction between the world of reality and the world of Bhavna's doubt ridden thoughts. It is also an interaction between past and present as Bhavna talks to her younger self and makes her recall the events as early as her own birth. The noise of cheering journalists interviewing her in the present is interspersed with the mother's lullaby for a son and a father shouting at the unwanted daughter in the past. Finally the reality of the past shown through flashback technique illuminates the nature of reality in present.

In the opening of the play Bhavna is irked that the journalists are highlighting the fact of her being a woman rather than her achievements as an astronaut. Therefore when asked about her belief in God she emphatically says, "I thank God that being a woman or an Indian has nothing to do with my journey…." [Dattani 58]. With the help of flashback scenes, three images of reality about Bhavna's existence are simultaneously presented in the play. Bhavna is aware of all the three images and is finally enabled to confront the harsh reality of misogyny.

When a journalist questions about the role of her parents in her success she acknowledges their help but ironically in the background –which may be Bhavna's psyche-the sounds of a mother's lullaby for a son and a father promising to marry her to a man of her own choice keep playing. In the space when Bhavna faces the younger Bhavna, they find their identities in conflict. There is Bhavna, the astronaut in 2025 and young Bhavna in 2006 dreaming of becoming an astronaut. The first image of reality of Bhavna then, is the astronaut, the first Indian woman to go to Mars. The second image of reality is the young Bhavna 'who dreams about spaceship all the time 'and 'wants to be the first woman on the moon' [Dattani 60]. But as Bhavna says "you see the images may be real but we still don't know the truth. Because it doesn't give us the time or the right sequence" [Dattani 63].

Taking a deep plunge in her past memories, young Bhavna provides the 'right sequence' of the shameful misogyny practiced by her parents. As Bhavna basks in the glory of her success she confesses, "I rebelled, I went to NASA against all odds, took all the jibes, passed all the tests, passed the physicals and finally my dream comes true" [Dattani 63]. She had to rebel because the parents did not approve of her so called 'unfeminine' interests such as watching cricket game on T.V. and climbing up the mango trees in school or for that matter studying maths. Sex and gender are two different concepts. Edgar and Sedguick rightly say that sex is biologically determined, a matter of nature. Whereas gender is cultural, a learned pattern of behavior and action [Bijoy Kumar Das 93]. Bhavna's parents did not want a female child and when they have one they try to mold her in the socio-culturally accepted 'feminine' behavior. Naturally, amidst all the jubilation, surrounded by the journalists and their flashing cameras, her father too showing pride in her achievement, Bhavna is disturbed by an uneasy doubt. She has an inkling that perhaps it is not her own but her father's dream that she has fulfilled. The young Bhavna refuses it as an impossibility saying, "Father never wanted me to study further. He wanted me to marry his best friend's son when I'm twenty-two and live in Bhuj for the rest of my life! How can you even think that this was his dream?" [Dattani 65]. Both Bhavna and young Bhavna become one in tracing the source of their dream to travel in space. The ugly and suspected secret that they finally unravel is the parents' desire to have a son and their denial to acceptance of a daughter. The young Bhavna recalls her humiliating shock over onset of menstruation because the mother had never educated her about it. She had ignored Bhavna's identity and had pretended having a boy child. Towards the end of play we come to know that her father-in-law had threatened to throw her out of the house if she did not give him a grandson. She had to expect a son and even sing lullabies for him. After giving birth to a daughter, for five years she passed on the female child as a male child. The father happy over having a son joyfully plans his future, "when Bhuvan grows up, he will become a pilot and fly near the moon" [Dattani 76]. Bhavna therefore is actually fulfilling her father's wish to have a son who would become a pilot. She had survived because the father took her to be a son. If he had known her identity he would not have allowed her to be born, making one more case of female feticide, so rampant in Indian society. This then is the third and real image of Bhavna –a girl child, unwelcome and unwanted by her own parents, who claim to be liberal, educated and modern enough to allow their daughter to become an astronaut. The end of the play provides an insight into mother's helplessness, reinforcing women's plight. Bhavna's mother could not do anything to liberate herself but wishes her daughter to overcome the barriers saying, "Go, Bhavna! Set yourself free. Go where I could never go! [Dattani 77].

Jeremy Mortimer rightly observes that Mahesh Dattani does not seek to cut a path through the difficulties of his character's encounter in his plays, instead he leads his audience to see just how caught up we all are in the complications and contradictions of our values and assumptions [Introduction]. Bhavna's story is an example of this.

The producer's note on the play mentions that the play is inspired by the life of Kalpana Chawla, the first Indian woman astronaut. However, the similarity ends there. The play is about Bhavna's story who while reveling in her own success also goes back to past memories to get enlightened about why she became the girl who touched the stars.

Writing in an English which is almost the first language for many middle class urban educated Indians, Dattani, "probes and unearths some compelling realities that are otherwise silenced by an orthodox narrative patriarchal order' [Shafiq Farah 52]. As the play takes up the issue of uncomfortable but widespread practice of misogyny, Dattani effectively dramatizes the disturbing fact that with all the feminist movements, talks of gender equality and strategies for women empowerment, a girl child still fights a long and losing battle to make her presence felt as important, if not more, as a boy child in this world. A journalist confirms the fact saying, "Unwanted Girls, a phenomenon and a stigma that refuses to leave the Indian society!" [EurAsian Times Desk]. Dan, a character in Dattani's play *Tara* observes that "...those who desire even a moment of freedom, find themselves hurled into space, doomed to crash with some unknown force"[Dattani Collected Plays 379-80]. Bhavna too meets the same end.

Works Cited

Crook, Tim. *Radio Drama; Theory. and Practice* Samples Sainsbury-sebooks.co.uk. 97811346069 – 48-sample – 485326.pdf.

Dattani, Mahesh. *Collected Plays,* New Delhi. Penguin Publishers.2000

.... *The Girl Who Touched The Stars in Brief Candle; Three Plays.* Penguin Books; India, 2010.

Edgar Andrew and Peter Sedgwick. *Key Concepts in Cultural Theory.* Routledge, 2004.P.158. Quoted by Bijoy Kumar Das in Form and meaning in Mahesh Dattani's Plays. Atlantic, New Delhi 2008.

EurAsian Times Desk. *The Sorrowful Tale of Unwanted Girls in Progressive Indian.* Jan 31, 2018. eurasiantimes.com

Mortimer, Jeremy. 'Introduction': *Collected Plays'* vol. ll. New Delhi. Penguin Books. 2005.

Parmar, B.R. *A Critical Study of Dramatic Works of Mahesh Dattani.*

Samuel, Rekha. *India's Greatest Shame: 'Unwanted Girl Child'.* www.outloookIndia.com

Shafiq, Farah Deeba. *Revitalizing the Tradition; Mahesh Dattani's contribution to Indian English Drama.* www.thecriterion.com

Shodhganga.inflibnet.ac.in\bitstream\10603\2296\06

CHAPTER 26

An Analysis on Modern Women Characterization in Shobha De's *Sultry Days*

S. Rajeswari and T. Manason

Abstract

Shobha De's *Sultry Days* is a novel about metropolitan elite men and women, their obsessions, frustrations, disappointments, fears, and sexual pleasures. Shobha De processes naive realism and realistically determines and portrays the characters as they are in society. She wrote the work with the intention of awakening society by exposing the rotten truth that exists among the urban elite class of India's metropolitan cities, particularly Mumbai. The novel delves into the characters' inner psyches, exposing their hidden conducts and immorality, which they have embraced as a result of western civilization.

Keywords: Emancipation, Self-Identity, Marginality, Patriarchy.

Sultry Days is claimed to be a unique work that may be classified as both a women's and a men's novel. Deb, the male protagonist, and Nisha, the female protagonist, are college students who meet in a Mumbai college canteen on a hot day. They are effervescent, impressive, adamant, arrogant, and unconventional young characters. They are also devoid of culture. They both fell in love with one another. This event sets the stage for the novel's title. Readers are enticed to be a part of the writer's involvement and enable themselves to desire an imaginative and empathic awareness of their emotional conditions through their fiction since Indian woman writers scrupulously fictionalise their experiences in their work.

The main characters Deb, the so-called God, and Nisha occupy a major and important position in the novel. It depicts an impressionable adolescent named Nisha, who comes from an upper middle-class family and is both gorgeous and intelligent. Deb works in an advertising business, but she is in charge of an art journal called 'Plume'. Nisha has a strong desire to live a bohemian lifestyle. She holds Deb (God) in high regard and loves him lavishly. She is attracted by him because of his externally attractive appearance, despite the fact that he is a combination of opposites. She is certain that she feels like a "total misfit in God's arty circle" (SD 32) She appears to be unobtrusive.

Nisha's involvement with Deb and the art magazine 'Plume' leads her into an unfamiliar environment. To be sure, she takes advantage of the opportunity to observe everything that happens in society's upper echelon. She begins to uncover her own commitments by refusing to be a part of God's fictitious promises. It is reasonable to conclude that morals have no value. Women, without a doubt, are just as promiscuous as males. Sabina Ghai et al (2017) writes: "The neo-rich Indians in De's novel, particularly educated, beautiful, competent, and confident socialite women seem to define marriage," (678)

Nisha's desire for belonging finds refuge in God's presence. She wishes to orbit around him in the same way that the moon does around the earth. Nisha appears to be a reasonable woman with concerns about her health. She is deeply concerned and is attempting to investigate the possibilities for personal commitment, growth, fulfilment, and emancipation. She is a feisty young lady who breaks everything and is unfazed by adversity. Nisha's longing for a role model becomes to be overwhelming. She refuses to identify with her home's loneliness, monotony, and complacency. She would be neither delightful nor peaceful as a result of her fake parental house. She enjoys taking on new jobs and putting on fresh outfits. She requires a source of consolation in the form of a friendship relationship. She is plunged into a state of despair. She aspires to be self-sufficient in the long run. Nisha, on the other hand, is enthralled by Deb, an unusual little kid.

Sujata is the character who draws the reader's attention next to Nisha's characterisation. Hers is a sexual role. She depicts the modern woman's desire to make money through sexual gratification. Sujata is a prostitute who does what her mind tells her to do. This makes her happy. She defines her life on her own terms. A more thorough examination of Shobha De's work demonstrates her opposition to the traditional image of a woman who can never live her life as she wishes and instead chooses to do things her own way. Women's lives are described in terms of their psyches, careers, oppression, psychological traumas, and sexual urges. Her frank narration and use of sexual matters in excess may create discomfort, while her frank narration and use of sexual topics in excess may bring discomfort.

Pramila, another female character, is a victim of Yashwantbhai, a well-known male character who is depicted as a womaniser. She travels from Nagpur to Mumbai in order to make a name for herself as a poetess. Yashwantbhai triumphs in order to realise her ambitions and passions. Pramila is a rebellious and outspoken woman. With her husband, she has a possessive personality. Unfortunately, she falls prey to Yashwantbhai's schemes because of his power and influence, which would provide her with credit and prosperity. The actuality of what occurs is uncommon. Yashwantbhai makes no attempt to be responsible towards her. He simply sees her as a conduit for his out-of-control licentiousness. His obscene behaviour worsens. When Pramila makes a claim, he avenges the plot to physically harm her. Pramila learns about it from Nisha. As a result, she resolves to vanish. Pramila is portrayed by the novelist as a woman who suffers and fights for freedom in a superior manner. Her portrayal of cruel and insistent masculine supremacy and sexuality as the driving forces behind the transformation of innocent women into rebellious warriors for their identity and independence is razor-sharp.

Pramila, being a nonconformist, comes to Mumbai with a specific goal in mind. She wants to be faithful to her husband and live a good life, as she has two daughters and a son. As a result of her personal experience, she realises that the world is full of unreal and dishonest people. Deb finds fulfilment in her physical pleasure. Moreover, Yashwantbhai treats her as if she were his property. Despite her efforts, she finds little comfort and rapport from either of them. As a result, she frequently acts as if she is a woman of reason, substance, and dignity. She gives birth to a child, and Yashwantbhai is the father. She has never liked it to the core because Yashwantbhai is a well-known political broker. He plots to murder her because he is afraid of the consequences of the scandal. Nisha rescues her from danger.

Another female character is Pratimaben, the wife of an Ahmedabad businessman, whose activities include bringing "a mocha to Yashwantbhai's house with prominent placards calling him murderer, sadist, scoundrel and other names" (SD 104). Pratimaben plays a significant role in the novel. She is portrayed as a "saviour of lost souls" (SD.145). Others who are hopeless are consoled by her. Her husband has been unfaithful to her. He is always preoccupied with his business. Her children are getting married. Her husband used to visit her once a week, so she refers to him as her "weekend husband" (SD 62). She volunteers in the community. Nisha's mother joins her as well. She always keeps her busy with trivial tasks. In fact, the worst thing about these women is that they are thrust into difficult situations and completely fail, leaving them unable to sully their spirits. At any critical event, a traditional constraint forces them to become enduring mothers or wives. They are unable to instil values in their daily lives. As a result, they violate socially prescribed patriarchal norms. It is too difficult for them to exercise in their social and professional lives.

The three female characters Nisha, Pramila, and Pratimaben become well-known as a result of Yashwantbhai's evil acts. In the face of adversity, they challenge themselves to become empowered women and winners in the realm of womanhood. In the delineation of characterization, men victimise women's lives for sexual pleasure, while women enjoy sex and earn money from men in patriarchal society, particularly in cities like Mumbai.

Nisha's mother is the subject of yet another De's tale. She is well aware that her daughter is far from content to live out her married life in peace. To her husband, who is a frequent womaniser, she acts as a subservient and traditional wife. As a result, she is irritated by her husband's rudeness and thinks him unduly interested with his secretary. She decides to live with her friend Pratimaben since she wants to be away from him. As a result, she grumbles:

> My world was collapsing and you were with that Sindhi whore… I am sick of living this false life. … So, you can go to hell with your lectures and your Sindhi girlfriends – you don't deserve me. And God knows what sins I committed in my last birth to be stuck with you. Whether you like it or not henceforth I will make the decisions about my life (SD.60)

The novel also sheds light on various facets of female society. Shona, another female character loves Anil. Shona and Anil met at a major presentation. After some consideration, they decided to marry. He, like all typical male characters, believes that his wife should not work after they stay married. He didn't want to know her wish. When Nisha asks about Shona's desire, he implies that she can take some hobby classes to pass the time creatively or open a grooming school to train young models. She should not be allowed to leave the house.

Nisha's inquiry reveals Anil to be a dormant man who is either afraid of his wife's career advancement or does not believe in her. It is widely acknowledged that husbands serve as guardians, breadwinners, and mentors. Their treatment of wives, on the other hand, is abhorrent and hurtful.

Despite the fact that the society is riddled with chaos and redundant value systems, women strive to be forerunners of togetherness and truthfulness. Power, as well as the economy, prevents people from retaining values in their daily lives. The reader's mind is deeply moved by women characters projection. In this novel, the novelist contends on the unique feature of characterization that all of the women are victims of male oppression and thus the exploitation of life.

Shobha De validates the women's virtue in the midst of an economic crisis and terrible circumstances through the depiction. They believe that 'self' is their top priority and that 'self-admiration' is their religion. Shobha De's women aspire to feel sensuous and seductive in their genuine feminine reign, in order to create an aura around themselves and reinforce their status in society as the beautiful ones. The protagonists are endowed with feminine characteristics, which is a noteworthy element of characterization. Shobha De's viewpoint that sex fosters absolute loving human relationships and sensory pleasure is one that one may agree with. The woman is not expected to be a social or moral offender; instead, she wishes for a shift in the customary thinking. Shobha De considers how she encounters these personalities in real life. Marriage is the key issue for modern educated women like Nisha and Pramila.

De's female characters refuse to be silent because they are educated individuals who claim their own space and challenge traditional values. They place emphasis on the 'self,' which should be free of various stigmas and evils. Women's self-discovery enhances free thinking. They tear the solitude and freely interact with each other because they have no qualms. They crave sympathetic listeners. They also expect their longing and voice to be heard indefinitely. Their ability to express themselves hallucinates the people's minds and provokes their thinking capacity about womanhood.

Shobha De examines modern women's search for identity and the patriarchal cultural pressures that stifle women's advancement. Although the female characters are depicted as helpless, support-less, cultural, conventional, and immature at the start of the work, they are eventually revealed as a type of "new woman" with hard experiences and self-realization. These women show that they can hold on to their power and achieve great things. They are particularly immune to male arrogance's victimisation. They encounter anti-elements and make concessions without fear or trouble through self-recognition and self-awareness, according to Sangeetha Yadav (2003), and "as mature and experienced humans they ultimately accomplish their aims of self-hood" (100).

Sultry Days is one of Shobha De's most remarkable attempts to spread the message that female subjectivity is not only a servile submission to male authority, but that every woman is a fierce feminist at heart, fighting against male injustices. Like Shobha De's female characters, the modern woman strives to be a champion of her female ego, eager to redeem women's place in the age of liberalisation. Equally fascinating is the novelist's portrayal of women and their attitudes toward marriage.

Shobha De tells how a woman fights the patriarchal dominance that suffocates her uniqueness in *Sultry Days*. The defiant and brave women in the novel enjoy beating males at their own game. The story depicts the dark aspect of Mumbai society's upper crust. Deb, the protagonist, demonstrates his callous attitude regarding women. He has no desire to ever be married. It's easy to see how Nisha and Deb's connection develops. Nisha senses her days are becoming increasingly sultry as she realises Deb is no longer dedicated to their relationship, so she starts to live life on her own terms. In general, a woman feels sultry in her life when males ignore her emotions and claims. It everything comes to a tragic end. Their goal and ambition have yet to be realised.

Sultry Days, a well-known fictional piece by Shobha De, ends on a positive note, implying that women who are in control of their lives are content. The work appears to be "humanistic for God, therapeutic for Nisha, and cathartic for the readers," (212) according to Anita Myles. There is little doubt that the novel depicts a world of beauty, sophistication, affluence, advertising models, movie stars, and other glitzy features of what is known as high society. Love, dependency, and emotional fulfilment with a defined identity are all fulfilled to the woman's complete delight. It aims to bring to light women's attitudes toward men, as well as their struggles to survive in society. Shobha De's exquisite perception of men and matter adds a new dimension. Her novels herald the arrival of new Indian women eager to rebel against the patriarchal social system's entrenched moral orthodoxy.

Works Cited

De, Shobha. *Sultry Days.* Penguin Books. India, New Delhi.1994.

Ghai, Sabina. Singh, Krantipel & Singh,Vikrangit. "*The Study of Feminism in Selected Works of Shobha De*". IJASOS. Vol III Issue 8.August 2017 p.678.

Myles, Anita. *Feminism and the Post Modern Indian Women Novelists in English.* New Delhi. Sarup & Sons. 2006.

Yadav, Sangeetha. "From Tradition to Modernity: Women in the Novels of Bhabani Bhattacharya and Shobha De" *Readings – A Biannual Journal of English Studies*, Vol 1 No.1 April 2003.

CHAPTER 27

Patriarchal Domination in Vijay Tendulkar's *Kamala*

R. Devendiran and B. Kathiresan

Abstract

This research paper is to study the domination of the patriarchal society in the play *Kamala* by Vijay Tendulkar. The play was based on a real life incident that happened to women in rural India, where women were not treated as human beings and were exploited and dominated in many ways. They were not given equal rights to take their active roles both in society and also in their home.

Keywords: patriarchy, womanhood, exploitation, cruelty, violence, inequality.

Vijay Dhondopant Tendulkar was born in Maharashtra, India in the year 1928. He was a playwright and a journalist who wrote plays in the Marathi language. He usually wrote plays based on real life incidents concerning the harsh realities of Indian society. The present play *Kamala* was originally written in Marathi by Vijay Tendulkar and was performed in some of the regional theatres in Marathi and Hindi languages. The play was translated into English by Priya Adarkar and was published in the year 1995. The play *Kamala* was based on a real life incident where a journalist named AshwinSarin of *The Indian Express* had bought a girl from a market in Rajasthan for Rs.2300 (Two thousand and three hundred rupees) to present her in front of the media to show the harsh realities of the society and the cruelties towards women.

The play *Kamala* was about the inequality and cruelty faced by women even in modern society and the exploitation of women by the patriarchal setup in the society. It also brought out the struggles faced by women in independent India. The women were not given equal rights to take part actively in society and also they were not free in their homes. In their homes, they were treated as slaves by the denial of freedom to stand on their own. They were treated as mere objects of sex and laborers used to fulfill the domestic needs of men. In this play, Kamala is an Adivasi woman bought for two hundred and fifty rupees from a flesh market in Luhardaga Bazaar in Bihar by Jaisingh Jadhav a young journalist and protagonist of the play. Jaisingh, a journalist by profession, did this to show the condition of women in rural India. But the fact behind this was that he used her as a milestone in his professional life to become famous. Jaisingh treated his wife Sarita as a slave in his house, by not giving her equal rights to speak and to make her own decisions. Jaisinghkept his wife Saritajust for doing household works. When Saritasaw the women Kamala been brought by Jaisingh to their home, she took pity on her and tried to help her. But she couldn't help Kamala in the presence of her husband. She was dominated by her husband and lived as a slave without having any freedom to make decisions on her own. Later, the character Kamala opened the eyes of Sarita, and Saritaat the end of the play is determined to question the patriarchal society starting from her husband. At last, she did nothing butonly tells that she was waiting for a better chance.

Patriarchal Domination

Patriarchy can be defined as a system of male dominance or a social system in which men hold the primary power to dominate women and reserve the predominant roles in politics and social privileges. In modern society, men were given more importance than women and men had all rights to take part in societal and political affairs, whereas women did not. Men were considered superior and women inferior or subordinate to men.

There was a practice during ancient times where only men were allowed to inherit property. In Indian society, women were and are always the victims of humiliation, torture, and exploitation. The social setup encouraged men to participate actively in society and hence they became more powerful in making decisions, thereby depriving women the right to decide and also naming them as the weaker sex.

Family is the first space where exploitation of women started. Men assumed that women were enjoying more freedom in their home but women only faced more humiliation and exploitation soon after getting married. Society gave men ownership over their women and allowed them to do whatever they wanted to do including physical and psychological abuse and humiliation.

Since literature was also a medium of expressing real life incidents, such exploitations against women could also be found in the literature. While talking about Indian literature there were many feminist writers like Arundhati Roy, Shashi Deshpande, Anita Desai, Mahaswetha Devi, Chitra Banerjee Divakaruni, who fought for the freedom of women through their writings. Vijay Tendulkar despite being a male writer voiced for the women community through his plays. He brought out the hypocrisy of the patriarchal society and attacked the patriarchal minds of the Indian middle-class society. The destinies of all his women characters were the same whether they were educated or illiterate; they were helpless in front of the patriarchal oppression. The prominent themes found in his plays were violence against women and the sufferings of women. Tendulkar in some of his plays including *Kamala (1981), Silence! The Court is in Session (1967), Kanyadan (1983),* treated his characters with understanding and compassion by attacking the hypocrisy and criticizing the patriarchal society as in *Kamala.*

In the play *Kamala,* the character Sarita was doing some of the domestic work regularly in a routine manner. Though she was not interested in doing those works, she was forced to do them by her husband, and also in the absence of her husband she kept doing the same fearing her husband. When she came to know that her husband is about to return from a trip she prepared everything without fail fearing that he would shout at her. Thus she sacrificed all her life and energy in supporting and serving her husband. This was the condition of women in all houses who worked as slaves for their husbands.

When Jaisingh brought an Adivasi woman named Kamala to his home everyone in the home stared at her because of her appearance. Everyone saw her appearance but no one considered her as a woman, or even as a human being.

> "Kamala...
> KAMALA [Indistinctly].Sir?
> JAISINGH. How are you? All right?
> [she nods her head.]
> Want some more tea?
> [she shakes her head.]
> Something to eat?
> [she shakes her head.]

> Look, think of this as your own house. you are quite safe here.
> [she moves her head to show she has understood.]"(*Collected Plays*, p. 11)

This shows that Kamala consideredJaisingh who bought her from the market as her master and obeyedhim politely without speaking anything against him.

When Jaisingh's wife Saritacame to know that Kamala was bought from a flesh market, she was shocked to hear that from her husband and even surprised to know that it was done by her husband.

> "JAISINGH. I bought her – in the Luhardaga bazaar in Bihar.
>
> SARITA. Huh? [she can't understand.] Bought her?
>
> JAISINGH. Yes. For two hundred and fifty rupees. Even a bullock costs more than that.
>
> [Sarita is stunned.]"(*Collected Plays*, p. 14)

Here a reader can observe how Jaisingh had portrayed the woman whom he bought from the market saying that a bullock costs more than that. Women were treated as a commodity that anyone can buy at a low cost. Here Kamala is a commodity according to Jaisingh who can be bought if one has money.

When Jaisingh is about to take Kamala to the press conference to present her in front of everyone; he asked his wife Sarita to bring Kamala, but Saritatold that she was sleeping. Jaisingh did not consider that and ordered Sarita to bring her at once. He behaved like a rude person controlling them without any humanity and he thought that he was the master since he had bought her.

> "SARITA. She's asleep. She isn't feeling well.
>
> JAISINGH. Wake her up.
>
> SARITA. She's only just gone off to sleep.
>
> JAISINGH. Never mind. Wake her up and send her here. I want to talk to her". (*Collected Plays*, p. 19)

Kamala considered Jaisingh as her master and obeyed him in every response. "KAMALA. I'm your servant, master." (Collected Plays, p. 20). Jaisingh's motive was really not to fight for the exploitation of women but he did all those things only to gain fame in his profession. Thus Jaisingh threw off Kamala after getting fame. "Once today's press conference is over, she has no business here." (*Collected Plays, p. 26)*

After the press conference was over Jaisingh became very happy as he had successfully finished the drama on the stage by putting the innocent woman amidst the crowd who mocked her and laughed at her because of her appearance and innocence. Some people in the press conference asked her irrelevant questions regarding politics, economics which she had never heard about and someone in the crowd asked "if there is free sex among you, what do you do with the illegitimate children?"(*Collected Plays*, p. 29) and the other person asked "you must be having free sex too. How many men have you slept with?" (*Collected Plays*, p. 29) At home, Jaisingh and his friend celebrated their success at the cost of Kamala's suffering, and at the psychological agony, she had felt in the press conference. They did notconsider the sufferings of Kamala; instead, they made fun of it.

The same night Kamala and Sarita shared their experiences and Saritatook pity on Kamala and she was ready to keep Kamala with her forever. Saritaspoke in a way that gives her hope and also she extended sisterly concern for Kamala. When Jaisingh asked Kamala to leave the house she refused and Sarita also supported her saying that Kamala will not be going with Jaisingh and she will stay in the same house. This irritated Jaisingh and he shouted at Sarita and took her away to an orphanage. Sarita spoke against her husband for the first time saying "SARITA [with greater determination]. Kamala is not going to come with you."(Collected Plays, p. 41) for that Jaisingh replies "It's I who takes decisions in this house, and no one else." *(Collected Plays, p. 42)* This clearly shows that he treated everyone in his family as slaves working only for his benefit and they do not have any freedom. Thus the freedom of a woman was in the hands of the man who dominated everyone.

Sarita started questioning the patriarchal society starting from her husband thereon and at a point, she asked if a man is great why not he stayed in the same position, rather than turning into a master to control over everyone. She also questioned why men were always masters and why they did not allow women at least to fulfill their small desires in life.

> "If a man becomes great, why doesn't he stay a great man? Why does he become a master?" *(Collected Plays, p. 47)*

The arrival of Kamala to her house was the turning point in the life of Sarita which has made her realize her power and it also gave her a new thought to think about her own life. Sarita wanted to be an independent woman who can live life in her way. But she postponed seeking independence because of several reasons such as considering the society, shelter, and protection. She just postponed it by staying with and tolerating her husband, anticipating the day when Sarita will become a new woman. "But a day will come,...when I will stop being a slave." *(Collected Plays, p. 52)* Sarita was waiting for the day to come when she would willingly question all the problems; she had faced as an epitome for all women.

Man exploited women in many ways as Jaisingh in this play exploited Sarita and Kamala. The play clearly pictured that the two characters Sarita and Kamala were the victims of the patriarchal society and they were nothing more than a property of men. At the end of the play, the major character Saritahad changed drastically, thus the passive woman at the beginning of the play turns to be more active and becomes a new woman. She was then able to speak against her husband and question her husband for the needs of her own life. Empowering Sarita and Kamala, Tendulkar left out the conclusion of the play to the readers.

The Play was a poignant voice of the marginalized and the oppressed class of the society who were exploited by social norms, patriarchy, and age-old practices within and outside the family.

Works Cited

Chakravarti, Uma. Conceptualizing Brahmanical Patriarchy in Early India: Gender, Caste, Class, and State. *Economic and Political Weekly*, Vol.28, No. 14 1993.

Kamala. En.Wikipedia.Org, 2019, https://en.wikipedia.org/wiki/Kamala.

Tendulkar, Vijay. *Collected Plays in Translation*. New Delhi: Oxford University Press. 2003.

CHAPTER 28

Institutional Atrocities and Poile Sengupta's *Mangalam*

Prashant Raosaheb Shinde

Abstract

Family and marriage institutions of Indian society are the major institutions. Both are interdependent. They play significant (adverse) role in the preservation of the society. As stated misogyny remains the perpetual nuisance in the lives of the female community members. Institutional discrimination means the atrocities have been awarded upon them. It is a state sanctioned discrimination where state cannot intervene in the matters of the marriage and family institutions. Even the female members could not withstand the unjust practices imposed upon the female characters in the play, Mangalam. It is notional these institutions treated as the pious and auspicious. As a result Poile Sengupta has ironically christened Mangalam, an eponymous play dominated by the victimization of the protagonist Mangalam. It is very difficult to raise voice against the life partner due to auspicious nature and place of husband in one's life. There is a great line of victims (Survivals) in the society but they have been crushed and suppressed under the notional load of the marriage and family institutions.

Keywords: Institutional atrocities, family and marriage institutions, patriarchy, misogyny

The drama *Mangalam* consists of two acts and its dramatist Poile Sengupta utilises the famous technique of play within the play, like Hamlet, to form discussion and put forward her narration throughout the characters. The playwright through this technique demonstrates the promptitude of violence against women. The objective of the technique is to highlight the intensity of the in-house violence. As per the play is concerned even homeliness becomes the den on of atrocities. For instance Mangalam stoically stomachs the unjust treatment given by her husband. To quote Sengupta, "It (the device) is used as a means to lend perspective to an issue. But in *Mangalam* I have used the same actors in both 'plays' as an indication that nothing really changes, the sameness of it all, to me, is deeply disturbing".

The play's title belongs to the protagonist who is not present physically in the act, but pervades the drama and the action throughout the first act. The first act revolves around the unsuccessful and devastating marriage of Mangalam and Dorai. They are married of to each other for urgent, confidential and practical reason. There is not any sort of mutual affection, communication or understanding between them. Both consider themselves victimized by the other and so are at constant war each other. Dorai, being a husband has been given an upper hand in a patriarchal societal structure. His extreme harassment of Mangalam leads to her death rather than living with him. The play progresses and its audience comprehends Mangalam as the victim of the sordid crime; however, Mangalam fails to pour out herself. The odious incidence act of her rape by her floppy brother-in-law transmutes the course of her life perpetually. She marries to the economically poor Dorai but he knows about her pregnancy after their marriage and thus she becomes the victim of the atrocity on her. Her husband Dorai, who fails to understand her state and silence and interprets her silence as betrayal, is hurt by the betrayal by Mangalam and her father; and thus, considers her as characterless for the rest of their life and spoils and punishes her in all ways to avenge. Mangalam is taunted, humiliated, abused emotionally and physically her whole life by her husband.

Mangalam suffers everything silently, because she has to keep her family's reputation. She knows that she cannot control her destiny and dreadful happenings in her life. distressed past keeps stopping her from seeking assistance. This kind of protection of family name the brings domestic violence. Kishwar and Vanitha state in their article *Initiative Against Dowry Deaths*, "She (the woman) has been made to think of this (violence) as 'normal', 'a woman's fate', religious, films, her elders, her own and her mother's experience-tell her that if a woman is unhappy, nothing can be done about it. It must be her own fault" (John 45). So, Mangalam's life has never ending assaults not only on her mind but also her body; that is why, she determines to end up her life.

Thangam, Mangalam's elder sister, a strong character, dominating in nature, controlling others, is presented as a representative of orthodox and old generation. Being a traditional woman, she imposes her old values and truss on other women around her. As the most straightforward character, she patently criticises Dorai's ill-treatment to Mangalam in an extremely vociferant manner. She takes her side as Dorai blames Mangalam as characterless. She denounces Dorai mistreating and torturing her as she says: Thangam: "...... But what else can I except from my brother-in-law? He has been like this since the day he tied the thali around that poor girl's neck! That! It was more like a rope".

The use of the word Thali briefs a woman's experience in the marriage system in India, indicating how she is forced against her will to be a subordinate object or puppet in the hands of patriarchy. "Any traditional custom that places women in the subordinate positions within society or in the family has the potential to turn violent".

In traditional societies, marriage was universally deemed to be the significant point in a girl's life with no care of her caste, religion, class, and ethnicity. Marriage in India brings inequality to a woman's life. The woman is supposed and forced to forget an intrinsical part of her own identity and has to confirm to an extrinsic one with asking no questions. She is to perform her roles of a dutiful wife and daughter-in-law. She is not supposed to show her individual existence, her view point becomes secondary and if she strives to show independence, her own opinion, it is considered rebellious and is generally looked down upon by her in-laws. A woman's suppression in a traditional of her in-laws at several levels and it is assumed that she will accept all the changes occurred in her position post-marriage. Majority of women accept this kind of sacrifices are expected and demanded from women.

Thangam finds resemblance to Mangalam's marriage. The poor woman has to live a dissatisfied and distressed life, as a widow of a man, of an abuser, abusing her own younger sister. To save her family's name and her sister's honour, she fails to protect her own innocent sister against her husband's brutality. She knows both Mangalam and she is the victim of domestic violence equally. Her marriage abandons her from asking for justice. Keeping quiet, she must go through all this for the so-called prestige. She cannot ask for separation from her husband for her own and her natal family's sake. A separation could have followed by loss of honor and grin prospects for her natal family with a younger sister still unmarried. This way, both the sisters have become victims of this so-called patriarchal institution. They are left with no hope of justice or even express their agony. This kind of marriage system makes women helpless, powerless, confidenceless and insecure they have to endure all the pain inflicted on them in the private space called 'home' and the family. "An analysis of the power hierarchy within the conjugal home would suggest some identifiable features – a gendered division of labor, the fact that in most Indian marriages women enter as stranger into an already structured world, the creation of a permanent inequality in the relationship of the natal and conjugal homes, and overarching domestic ideologies that legislate gender status and role".

Due the holy nature of the institution it becomes a notional legacy of suffering where daughters, mothers, great mothers and great grandmothers, etc. have never escaped from the suppressers and oppressors. To B. R. Ambedkar to deny the Shastra based institutions in order to breathe freshly, such institutions seem as the gas chambers to suffocate the Jews during Holocaust.

In this way, one cannot imagine the institutional or organised crimes against women in the Indian society. Poile Sengupta has tried to show the helpless and hopeless women in the society only of the patriarchy built misogyny.

Works Cited

Ambedkar, Bhimrao. *Castes in India.*

.... *Annihilation of Castes.*

Sengupta, Poile. *Mangalam.*

.... *The Dramatist and the Play.* Routledge, New Delhi. 2010.

CHAPTER 29

The Angel and the Spice Mistress: A Study in the Positions of Women

Rajiv Kumar and Himadri Shekhar Dutta

Abstract

The history of literature has witnessed multidimensional portrayals of the fair sex across its domain since its inception from the oral over to the printed tradition of dissemination. Though the world has strived to abide by an egalitarian framework of social sphere since the beginnings of human history, the reality has often failed to live up to this ideal conception. There has been a continuous dethronement of the female subject from its platonic pedestal of worship to the status of an anonymous and subordinate self without an identity. The additional attachment of a third world postcolonial subjectivity has done further damage to this already dehumanised existence. Happily, this situation has not been unanimously prevalent. Despite the patriarchal hegemonies, this condition of the empowered feminine self has been distinctly projected forward by many literary figures over the times and cultures, women's writings constituting a majority of this corpus. The position of women has been fairly resurrected with such endeavours and the future is promising in this regard.

Keywords: Woman question, Gender roles, Representation, Third world, Diasporic feminism

It would be imperative to start with the age-old resonant statement that literature is a mirror of the society. A careful or casual perusal of any form of literature across times and forms would assert this. When it comes to the structural notion of society, both men and women constitute it and complement each other equally. The all-inclusive presence or absence of one of these sexes would render the concept of a society impossible and incomplete. This practical situation extends itself to the world of literature quite, naturally which cannot be imagined without women. An argument might present itself in this context throwing in a pool of texts where the fair sex does not feature in the role of a protagonist or major character. In spite this fact being affirmed, it does not and cannot rule out the presence of women completely. It is a fact that women cannot be whitewashed from a narrative domain however male centric it might be. They will be found in the fringes and aporias if not any better. In short, all men are born out of women and that itself is a circumstance enough to locate the fair sex in the literary as well as the cultural domain if not as a direct existence, then in aporias and absences. The biblical situation of paradise as described by John Milton in relation to the creation of the first man and woman has an alternative circumstance in this respect as God himself creates Adam whereas Eve is a product of Adam's rib. That is to say that woman is not shown as directly responsible for the creation of man in the first instance. But she starts and continues to be so since the event of the fall within the same narrative trajectory.

As far as the presence of women is concerned, Adam initially is quite self-sufficient for both the existential as well as the literary domain within the narrative for a significant duration of time. His state of loneliness, incompleteness and incompetence emerge prominently with the passage and progress of time and the inescapable need of a complimentary female self is soon realised and fulfilled. Interestingly there have been works like *Vanity Fair* by William Makepeace Thackeray which has its subtitle as 'A Novel without a Hero' suggestive of a scenario of prominent male absence within the narrative. It matters a lot and had in fact created an inquisitive storm after its publication at the height of the Victorian age during the mid-nineteenth century that was technically a man's world. This novel centres on the lives of its two female protagonists namely Amelia Sedley and Becky Sharp in the form of a female bildungsroman where men feature in important but subsidiary roles when compared to the space and characterisation allocated to these two women. After going through the book, one would be compelled to accept that there are literally no male heroes or heroic figures in this story. Contemporary female novelists of that age in their novels as well which had led to a welcome consolidation of women's position and female characters in the social and literary fabric simultaneously had attributed this focus and position of eminence to women.

The position of women as a literary theme has been a major area of critical study and understanding of the feminine self and world in relative juxtaposition to the world of men specifically during the

Victorian age and beyond. This discourse has offered crucial insight into the multifaceted play and politics of power equations between the two sexes tracing its history from time immemorial until recent times. The nineteenth century in British literature is a major point in this chain because of its significant location in the post-enlightenment age fuelled by the ever-flourishing industrial revolution empowered by the rising consciousness in realms of science and rationality. The encroaching air and aura of empowerment inevitably touched the domain of female subjectivity and feminine world and made its sustaining impact throughout. This erstwhile controlled and essentially domestic world started to delimit itself and mingle with the outer circle and space possessed by men till date.

This phenomenon could be traced in the ground-breaking works pouring from women's pens marvellously but mostly anonymously during that age with the likes of Jane Austen, the Bronte sisters, George Eliot, Mrs. Gaskell and so on whose fictional women stand side by side with equal elegance and dignity with the heroes of Dickens or Hardy. Novels such as *Pride and Prejudice*, *Wuthering Heights*, *The Mill on the Floss* and *North and South* are some among numerous literary endeavours by female writers of the Victorian era which foreground the daring concept and character of the new women that does not quite fit in the stereotype of 'angel in the house' thereby moving on towards carving a niche for the female subject prominently in literature, culture and society. The female protagonists in these works have consolidated their position in western and world literature as characters of strength and individuality that compel men till date to accept and respect them.

The names of Elizabeth Bennet, Jane Eyre, Catherine Earnshaw and Margaret Hale have an aura of their own that have acquired the status of adjectives over time. These names stand for all the attributes that are desirable in an empowered female self and continue to inspire and strengthen female folk towards ideals of self-respect, self-sufficiency, indomitable willpower and the courage to break the shackles of restrictive hegemonic traditions of the past. Elizabeth Bennet is the prototype of the ideal progressive woman who is smart, confident, well read and well-spoken which get reflected in her demeanour so naturally and in a dignified way. Even a man like Darcy has to bend before her out of his own will. Jane Eyre on the other hand is a woman of perseverance who ends up as the guiding force for Rochester as a result of her dedicated will-power, passion and selfless love. In the novel she becomes a saviour for the hero on two crucial occasions, once while he falls from his horse and the second time when his bed is set on fire at night by his mad wife. Jane reappears as saviour for a third time at the end of the story and Rochester's life is changed for the better forever. Catherine Earnshaw is the typical rebellious girl on the face of men and the society of men at large. Her characterisation is one of the rarest in the history of literature and continues to haunt readers and critics alike. Margaret Hale is quite the opposite of Catherine but no less than her or any of the aforementioned heroines when it comes to the question of strong and empowered womanhood. One thing that connects all these women and establishes them on their esteemed pedestal is their indomitable spirit and progressive zeal, which foregrounds them at an equal or rather a higher level than menfolk of that age.

At a time when women were designated as subordinate and subservient to men, both in literature and society, such portraits paved way for a new era of hope for the feminine self and subject. It will not be too farfetched to trace the effect of this phenomenon in the changing characterisation of women by mainstream authors like Dickens or Hardy where one can find characters like Agnes Wickfield or Bathsheba Everdene finding place and prominence replacing earlier subordinate models such as Nancy or Miss Havisham. At the same time, one must not rush into the happy conclusion that women's position in art and life had changed completely and forever with a handful of literary works reflecting this positive scenario in a representative manner. Things were yet quite bleak and on the darker side for the fair sex in general. In other words, a few instances of empowerment and emancipation like that of Elizabeth Bennet or Jane Eyre did not ensure that this phenomenon had acquired the status of a universal reality. As mentioned, such cases of breaking the shackles were still meagrely numbered and the reality maintained its status quo without any alterations per se.

The 'angel in the house' was still the accepted and expected social syndrome for women across all strata of society. The lady of the manor house was practically no different than the lady of the slums in her day-to-day existence in terms of an independent life and self. The position of the fair sex had been generalised and coerced into a stereotype as per the suitability of the male domain that looked upon this situation as highly normal, correct, practical and desirable which suited best for the recipient of these gender roles and the society at large. The obedient and dependent woman devoid of an identity was regarded as the perfect example of womanhood during the peak of the

Victorian era, which was seen as being in the best interest of both men and women. The situation was therefore this that the subordinate and voiceless self-ascribed to the woman of the household was regarded as the best possible existence for the female self that promised and simultaneously offered her the best life in this world. Thus, it was by default a man's world and there was nothing wrong in this world where the better half of man had been systematically erased into oblivion. This state of affairs was universally accepted as the norm and enforced with greater zeal every time by men at large with a handful of exceptions that hardly mattered or were taken into cognizance. Rather, such rare instances of humane men would be regarded with the bitterest scorn and subjected to mockery by the rest of the society. An interesting and very unfortunate circumstance in this respect was the fact that this aforementioned 'rest of the society' which had been apparently critical of the few benevolent striving for the betterment and emancipation of women's position in society consisted of women and that too in majority. That is to say that women were largely content to live in their subordinate existence and had accepted as well as internalised this way of life as the norm, the alteration of which would negatively affect the position of their sex as per their system of rational belief.

This, according to later feminist critics and scholars, would turn out as the biggest hindrance in the path of women's progress and emancipation where not only men but women too would emerge as a social threat and challenge for the members of their own sex who would aspire, dream and strive towards the slightest of individuality and independence. Literature overflows with instances related to this phenomenon and brings into light the fact that women have been equal if not sometimes bigger enemies of progressive women in society across ages and cultures. In the very classical age in a text none other than The Iliad, we see Aphrodite setting the ball of troubles rolling for Helen as she promises Paris regarding her. The previous argument positioning women as enemies of women acquires a more serious implication in this context as the woman in concern, that is Aphrodite, is a goddess although pagan per se. In more recent literary contexts, we have characters like Emilia playing a major role in the fall of Desdemona or Lear's first two daughters whose equations with the youngest Cordelia is not on the better side. A century later, we see the rape of Belinda's locks but it is to be noted that the scissors are placed in the hands of the perpetrator by Clarissa, a woman. The world of Victorian novels has countless and diverse instances in this category. In the very narrative where we have Elizabeth Bennet at one hand, we have characters like Mrs. Bennet on the other who is in an impatient rush to get all her daughters into becoming obedient wives of rich men at tender ages for the rest of their lives. Then, we have Lady Catherine who herself belongs to the category of powerful womanhood but would not like the likes of Elizabeth thereby creating hurdles for her at every possible step. Lady Catherine contents herself with subservient women like Charlotte Lucas who are born to be at the mercy of men for their whole lives. In Jane Eyre, we have several such female figures throughout the story who act in antagonistic ways for Jane.

Feminine hurdles continue to create obstacles in the path of progress for women who cease to be angels in their houses and a careful perusal of the latest literary canons and popular narratives would indicate the sad continuation of this situation till date although one can safely claim that things are much better at present and this statement is true to the utmost extent. This set of argument never rules out the element of male factor and its oppressive hand on the female subject which has been a constant presence till date simultaneously though matters have altered for the good in this domain as well and that too at a significantly visible level. Writers of the twentieth century experimented with the position of women attempting to provide an empowered and respectable niche to female subjects, both as protagonists and in minor roles within the narrative. Virginia Woolf is an important name in this regard alongside male novelists especially D.H. Lawrence who painted very bold portraits of the feminine in his works. The concept of the 'new woman' emerging out as a prominent figure by this time was a welcome departure from the angelic woman of the inner household circle. It was the demand of the times, all the more so because of the two world wars that brought out the woman from the confines of private sphere in the literal sense of the term and made the human race realise her real worth. The arena has expanded over the decades, women have found better positions in life and literature transcending the British boundaries to the Eastern literary zones of the postcolonial and the diaspora.

The study of the position of women in the postcolonial or third world countries, or in other words beyond the boundaries of the English territory, has become an interesting pursuit in the present times as new cultural theories keep on surfacing rapidly and substantiate us with modern perspectives to look into this particular field of social existence. A critical pursuit of literary texts from these geographical domains opens up fresh angles to observe and understand the existing and changing phenomenon in this particular area that is the position of women in these civilisations since the earliest traceable instance up to the most recent times. A comparative study of the east and the west in this context enlightens researchers further as well as the entire discourse of woman-centric and gender studies in general at the global level. Following the orientalist perspective, the state of life in postcolonial nations is by and large at a lower stratum in comparison to the first world nations. An aura of primitivism, darkness and existential backwardness are attributed as generalised characteristics of these societies. Therefore, when it comes to locating the position of women in these locales, the 'second sex' is popularly designated as doubly and perhaps triply marginalised. This concept rests on the theory that if women live in a marginalised state in the west which is a term synonymous with progress and modernity, the women living in the east would by default be marginalised a step further downwards as the idea of the east has been always constructed in a position of binary and subordinate to the west.

This pathetic existential and social condition naturally becomes an area of humanitarian concern as well as urgent critical study for scholar across the globe, predominantly from the west with their western occidental male gaze. The problem greatly lies here. The cultural, geographical and emotional distance between the researcher and his subject often tends to foreground erroneous and fragmented conclusions on this particular topic, that of the position of women in the oriental world. A good way to avoid falling into this trap of stereotypical study and judgement would be to pursue the third world literature through the cultural and feminine lens of that particular land. In other words, if someone is willing to look into this domain from an alternative and fresh perspective, it would be a wise step to study the works on women by women preferably from the recent times as modernity often alters an author's gaze as well while dealing with traditional structures and cultural narratives. One would locate a clear and positive departure from the past structures of narration in the field of women's saga by modern female authors who prefer to portray their heroines in empowered and divine attributes rather than depicting them in an age-old dark light as was quite popular with the women writers of the past. It is a welcome change to highlight the greatness instead of showcasing the depravity of women in art, the latter often tending to be a construct transcending and solidifying its roots into popular belief. Nevertheless, this does not rule out the subordination, subjugation and all the pains that women are subjected to in these spaces. The argument is simply to shift one's focus for good to the positive attributes at least for once rather than remaining stereotypically stuck in the pursuit of women's miseries.

The Indian subcontinent takes pride in its glorious past and present in the realm of both life and literature that has its tradition of consecrating the female subject and self to the pedestal of divinity in the form of an all-powerful and benevolent goddess. This could be traced throughout the history of literature produced within the nation across different times and cultures and also beyond the borders to the domain of diaspora. Especially, works by female authors make this cult of discourse all the more enriched and empowered. Starting from Akka Mahadevi to Mira Bai from the medieval times up till the recent times when globally acclaimed writers such as Jhumpa Lahiri, Anita Desai, Kiran Desai, Chitra Banerjee Divakaruni, Bharati Mukherjee, Monica Ali and their likes are dominating the literary scenario, the study of the position of women both at the authorial and textual level becomes a vibrant phenomenon. Among the aforementioned writers, Chitra Banerjee Divakaruni has carved a special niche for herself during the course of past few years with back-to-back publications of popular canons that have garnered wide public appeal among the masses within the nation and all over the world. Her renderings of the great Indian epics and tales from history in alternative narrative voices and structures have made way for novel approaches and perspectives to our classical sagas.

What make these re-workings all the more special is the fact that the narrative voice has been entrusted with the female protagonists of these tales who narrate or rather retell the stories from their feminine perspectives and experiences. Thus, the reader gets to know the events of the tale as seen and felt by the women which fill in the gaps left by the male voice consciously or unconsciously. To elaborate, we can visualise the Ramayana story from Sita's eyes and the Mahabharata through the lens of Draupadi which render these tales multidimensional. Similarly, the tales from the everyday life of the national and diasporic worlds are catered to the readers through female voices that allow us to look into life as our mothers and sisters have to go through every day. A glance at some of the major works by Divakaruni would offer further insight into this spectrum. To begin with the two national epics *The Ramayana* and *The Mahabharata*, the respective renderings of these two tales as *The Forest of Enchantments* and *The Palace of Illusions*, the former unfolding through the narrative voice of Sita and the latter by that of Draupadi take on these tales from history from the perspectives of their two heroines.

In the first instance, Sita retells the story as seen and experienced by her thereby bringing in the feminine touch to the authorial voice of the tale. She not only replaces the male narrative voice but also supersedes the male authority which has been controlling the whole domain of the narrative starting from characters, their characterisation and destiny since the first records of the existence of this epic tale. Similar is the case with the other novel which has been retold by Draupadi. These innovative structural and narratorial experiments by the author depict the woman in history and literature in an entirely new and positive light which had been erstwhile overshadowed and obliterated by a sense of male hegemony and superiority. It simultaneously helps in bringing forth a holistic picture of the woman and her true position, both at the level of the individual and social. For instance, both Sita and Draupadi have been generally stereotyped as women at the merciful hands of their male counterparts whose fates are continuously decided by men surrounding and dominating the scenario. Their lives literally evolve and revolve around men. Divakaruni's versions portray a different picture altogether. Her Sita and Draupadi are in full command of their narrative as well as socio-historical arena and emerge as the women they are in reality. The ideal notions of Indian womanhood and femininity as divine and powerful subjects are correctly realized and justified in these versions which additionally help towards upholding the nation's image in relation to its attitude towards women in general. The traditional Indian cult worships its female subjects and citizens at the divine pedestal that is applicable to women from every section of the society regardless of its various creeds. It ought to be mentioned here that the idea of divinity in this context is synonymous to a position of power, prestige and respect that envisages the woman as a goddess.

The other novels of Divakaruni dealing with non-epic female protagonists per se follow the same ethos as regards to their portrayal of women who belong either to the national or diasporic zone. Some popular titles in this category are *Sister of my Heart, The Mistress of Spices, One Amazing Thing, The Vine of Desire* and so on. In the first one, we come across a typical Bengali household in Calcutta from the 1970s that has been withholding fast to its traditional way of life of the 19th century Bengal and expects its ladies to conform to the norms from the past. The novel interestingly centres entirely on its women in the fashion of Thackeray's *Vanity Fair* and men have a marginal space throughout the narrative. But, it is sadly true that the women within the novel are confined to their domestic limits despite being the majority whereas men dominate their lives and fate though they are insignificant in number and character. At the same time, the good thing about this story is that the two female protagonists of the modern times, Sudha and Anjali are quite progressive in nature and behaviour that ushers in a fresh ray of hope in the narrative which is unfolded through the narratorial voices of these two girls. They grow up together to cross their threshold of restrictive traditions towards a modern life of freedom and individuality. Their life saga is continued in the sequel *The Vine of Desire. The Mistress of Spices* later adapted into a popular Hollywood movie of the same name in 2005 takes the readers to a world of fantasy and oriental mysteries within the very heart of the American subcontinent where the narrator cum protagonist, a woman of Indian origins possessing certain magical charms, is shown to be a phenomenal power who heals her clients with spices that apparently have mysterious medical properties.

Looking through the lens of critical theory, white western men have to come to an immigrant woman of the east seeking remedies for ailments that cannot be cured by the advanced tools of California. A more powerful designation for a woman could hardly be imagined in the postmodern and postcolonial context. Chitra Banerjee Divakaruni takes her women to the zenith of power and glory and this is particularly very inspirational at a time when women especially from the third world have been struggling for their due position in life and art.

When it comes to 21st century saga of women narrated in their own voices, notable names like Anita Desai, Monica Ali, Kiran Desai, Anita Nair, Devdutt Pattanaik and Jhumpa Lahiri feature at the forefront. Devdutt Pattanaik's *Sita* (2013) offers a new angle to the character and concept of Sita. He emphasises that Sita, who is generally shown as a submissive character, was a woman of strength and stood equally in mettle and merit alongside her husband. Kavita Kane's *Lanka's Princess* (2017) tells the story from Ravan's infamous sister Surpanakha's point of view. This novel explores whether Surpanakha was really to be blamed for starting all the chaos which led to the destruction of Lanka or was she an innocent victim of circumstances? The narrative is her version of *The Ramayana* which throws a volley of thoughts to reconsider for the reader. Another novel by Kavita Kane titled *Karna's Wife* (2014) is a great instance of retelling of classic epics. The depth given to the non-central characters like Kunti is exceptional along with the character central to the plot that is Karna's wife Uruvi. Outside the purview of myths and histories, authors like Monica Ali have brought forward the erstwhile marginalised and voiceless woman into limelight as the protagonist and narrator of her tale where she has been given infinite freedom and space to relate her life story in her own words as well as shape it according to her choice outside the line of control of her male counterparts.

Brick Lane (2003) is one such instance that relates the story of a woman finding a niche for herself away from her homeland in an unknown land as a diasporic subject. Anita Nair's *Ladies Coupe* (2001) narrates the journey of a middle-aged Indian woman who travels to Kanyakumari in search of her independence and swaps stories with other women inside the train during the journey. Kiran Desai's Man Booker Prize winning novel *The Inheritance of Loss* published in 2006 centres around an orphaned girl named Sai and her life in the mountainous Kalimpong where she continuously struggles to consolidate her identity and self-respect.

The roots of the problem lie in the concept and politics of representation. As per popular notion, women have to be depicted, represented and given a position in art and culture by some external agent; be it a male or a female artist, be it the east or west. The day when women come out of these shackles of subalternity and when their voices and selves would no longer have to be handled by a second self, this second sex would stand with par with the first sex per se. It would be a woman's world too then.

Works Cited

Divakaruni, Chitra Banerjee. Sister of my Heart. Anchor, 2000. Print.

.... *The Mistress of Spices.* Black Swan, 2005. Print.

.... *The Palace of Illusions.* Picador, 2008. Print.

.... *The Forest of Enchantments.* Harper Collins, 2019. Print.

Pattanaik, Devdutt. *Sita.* Penguin India, 2013. Print.

Kane, Kavita. *Karna's Wife.* Rupa Publications, 2013. Print.

.... *Sita's Sister.* Rupa Publications, 2014. Print.

.... *Lanka's Princess.* Rupa Publications, 2016. Print.

Delap, Lucy. *Feminisms: A Global History.* Pelican Books, 2020. Print.

Knott, Kim and McLoughlin. *Diasporas.* Rawat Publishers, 2011. Print.

Milton, John. *Paradise Lost.* Penguin Classics, 2000. Print.

Thackeray, William Makepeace. *Vanity Fair.* Wordsworth Classics, 1992. Print.

Austen, Jane. *Pride and Prejudice.* Penguin, 2021. Print.

CHAPTER 30

Reweaving the Tapestry of Femininity in Neo-mythological Works of Mahasweta Devi's *Draupadi* and Kavita Kane's *Lanka's Princess*

Nandini Anand Vyas

Abstract

The mainstream patriarchal discourse has used mythology as a vehicle to propagate the phallocentric conception of 'Femininity' in society; and the ancient Indian epics, *The Ramayana* and *The Mahabharata,* exemplify this phenomenon of creating a discursive image of womanhood to subvert women. Mahasweta Devi as a notable activist advocating for the rights of the marginalized tribes, initiated the journey of re-analyzing the patriarchal mythological narratives from a contemporary feminist lens, by situating the mythical damsel in distress, 'Draupadi', the queen of Hastinapur into a tribal santhal woman Dopadi Mehjan, a comrade fighting in the Naxalite movement of the late 1960-70s. Following this tradition, Kavita Kane, the author of a new era of feminist re-telling of mythology, reflects upon the socio-cultural ethos of the current times by bringing the women from margins to the centre.

This paper examines the aspects of Subalternism, female resistance as well as undertones of gynophonocentrism by deconstructing the mythological stigmatization of womanhood, female sexuality and 'gender perfomativity; along with Lacan's phallic womanhood and Helene Cixous' *Jouissance* at locus in Mahasweta Devi's short story *Draupadi* and Kavita Kane's novel *Lanka's Princess.*

Keywords: Subalternism, gynophonocentrism, gender performativity, phallic womanhood, Jouissance

Introduction

The mainstream patriarchal discourse has used mythology as a vehicle to propagate the phallocentric conception of 'Femininity' in society; and the ancient Indian epics, *The Ramayana* and *The Mahabharata,* exemplify this phenomenon of creating a discursive image of womanhood to subvert women. In Indian mythology, the stereotypical ideal women characters such as Sita, Savitri, Kunti, Gandhari, Draupadi, Mandodari and others, foregrounded the feminine codification imposed by the misogynist society; are universally found in other cultural myths like Penelope in *Odyssey* as well. In *The Penelopied,* a feminist re-telling of mythology, Margarete Atwood states that the character of Penelope as an ideal wife was used as a stick to punish other women who dared to break the feminine social code. Helene Cixous, in her theory of *Ecriture feminine* or 'women's writing' says:

> Woman must write herself: must write about women and bring women to writing from which they have been driven away as violently as from their bodies – for the same reasons, by the same law, with the same fatal goal. Woman must put herself into the text – as into the world and into history – by her own movement. (*The Laugh of the Medusa*)

This feminist resistance against the phallocentric conventional narrative can be found in the re-telling of mythology in India in the works of Mahasweta Devi, Chitra Banerjee, Kavita Kane, Suniti Namjoshi, Volga (Popuri Lalitakumari), Madhavi S. Mahadevan. A pioneer to this, Mahasweta Devi, an Indian writer in Bengali, as a notable activist advocating for the rights of the marginalized tribes, initiated the journey of re-analyzing the patriarchal mythological narratives from a contemporary feminist lens. Awards like Padma Vibhushan, Padma Shri, Sahitya akademi, Ramon Magsaysay and Jnanpith are bestowed upon her for her novels and short stories voicing the unspeakable misery of the marginalized women by creating a deconstructive counter-historical narrative of postcolonial subjugation and exploitation on the bases of caste, class and gender. She de-mythicizes the objectification and humiliation of 'Draupadi', the queen of Hastinapur into a tribal Santhal woman Dopadi Mehjan, a comrade fighting in the Naxalite movement of the late 1960-70s through her short story *Draupadi* first published in her collection *Agnigarbha* in 1978, later in 2010 it was republished in *Breast Stories* with a deconstructionist forward by Gayatri Chakravorty Spivak. Mahasweta Devi's rationale behind rewriting the mythology is:

> It is essential to revive existing myths and adapt them to the present times and following the oral tradition, create new ones as well. While I find the existing mythologies, epics and 'puranas' interesting, I use them with new interpretations (Untapped Resources 17). P7

Following this tradition, Kavita Kane, the author of a new era of feminist re-telling of mythology, reflects upon the socio-cultural ethos of the current times by bringing the women from margins to the center. Earlier she served as a feminist journalist and later, in 2013, she started her writing career as a full-time novelist. Her novel *Lanka's Princess* published in 2016 uncovers the unheard life story of Surpanakha, the sister of Ravana, the mythological deviant woman, dismantling the patriarchal idea of *'Stree Dharma'* by presenting the Sita-Surpanakha dichotomy. In an interview to *The Hindu*, Kane emphasizes the importance of re-writing mythology to portray contemporary issues and sensibilities:

> If myths reflect the socio-cultural ethos of earlier times, they can also be used to contemporaries those same issues in today's world. Actually, nothing has changed. Love, rivalry, disappointment, war, anger, greed, all these emotions still exist. There's a chance of an alternative perspective by looking at the epics through the women and minor characters at that. (The Hindu) p5

Mythological subalternity v/s modern feminist resistance

The etymological roots of the word "Subaltern" were laid down in the Latin words – *Subalternus,* meaning a person "next below every other". Thus, the modern term "Subaltern", popularized by Gyatri Chakravorty Spivak in her essay *Can the Subaltern speak?* (1985), identifies an inferior position in terms of class, caste, race and gender. Carl Jung's conception of 'the collective unconscious' based on the set of shared knowledge of human existence derived from myth advocates the age-old internalization of subalternity; as the patriarchal mythologies propagate the willing subjugation of women alongside stigmatization of the self-determining womanhood as deviant behaviour.

In contrast to Vijay Tendulkar's male-centric outlook in his two-act play *Kamala,* reflecting upon the consensual subjugation of the tribal woman Kamala, a victim of flesh-trade, Mahasweta Devi's Dopadi, though entrapped in an adverse situation of draught, tribal exploitation and physical mutilation by the power politics of Senanayaka, her actions are a voice of resistance. In response to Spivak's assertion that subaltern females are not heard or read, Devi's Dopadi not only speaks loudly, literally and metaphorically, rather her "voice…is as terrifying, sky splitting, and sharp as her ululation", as through her resistance she breaks the stereotype of docile femininity. Similarly, Kane's Surpanakha is a gendered subaltern and a racial victim whose aggression is in contrast to the idea of femininity. Thus, the Aryan hegemonic society stripped her off her identity as Meenakshi, a beautiful princess of Lanka by fixating her as the demoness Surpanakha due to her resistance towards the patriarchal status quo.

Gender Performativity and feminine deviance

The Psychologist Robert Stoller was the first one to challenge Freud's believes on gender dynamics in his book *Gender and Sex* (1968). According to him, 'sex' represents a person's biological orientation while 'gender' is constructed through socio-psychological imprints. Judith Butler introduced the idea of "Gender Performativity" as a critique of the socially constructed rigid notions of sex and gender divided on the bases of performative roles in her book *Gender Problem* (1990). Furthermore, talking about the concept of 'true gender' and the sexed body on one hand and the gendered behaviour, Butler says:

> "If sex and gender are radically distinct, then it does not follow that to be a given sex is to become a given gender; in other words, 'woman' need not be the cultural construction of the female body, and 'man' need not interpret male bodies" (Butler 1999, 142).

In continuum to this sociology of gendered roles, a violation of the same leads towards the accusation of social deviance. This relative term of 'Deviance' is often universalized when comes to women defending their 'true gender'. The deviant actions are characterized by two Latin phrases, *malum in se* (evil in itself) and *malum prohibitum* (evil because it is prohibited).

Devi's protagonist, Dopadi Mejhen is subjected to triple marginalization on the bases of class, caste and gender as a farm labourer of Santhal tribe, she is oppressed by the local *Zamindars* and police officers on socio-economic, sexual and political grounds. During draught, struggling for survial, as an act defense, she, along with her Naxalite comrades, kills the landlord Surja Sahu and his son as they were hording the water reserves. This act of violence and violation of the socio-political code made her "the most wanted" and "the most notorious woman" on the police record. She sacrificed her right to motherhood and a stable family life as the couple fought for a greater cause. Devi's Dopdi as a child of nature longs for freedom and detests the individual as well as national power politics of internalized subalternism, stimulating her defiant revolt against such operations. Thus, her character can be seen as an illustration of modern feminine resistance, deconstructing the stereotypical myth of "gender performativity".

In sync with Mahasweta Devi's Dopdi, is Kavita Kane's Surpanakha The character of Surpanakha has been condemned on the grounds of body, colour, choice and gender. since her childhood, she was rejected by her mother because of her gender, even her father did not allow her to study or learn different combat tactics alongside her brothers. Her dark skin and lean body made her inferior and unnoticed to her strong brothers; only her grandmother Taraka showed love towards her but soon this acceptance and love were ripped her off. When Ravana killed her pet lamb, Maya, out of anger, she brutally wounds him. Ravana, bleeding profusely cried out in pain and fury with his masculine ego hurt, 'you ugly wretch…Surpanakha, that is what she is…a witch with long, sharp claws'. (8)

Similarly her half-brother Kuber tries to abduct her as a leverage to protect his thrown in Lanka; in absence of any masculine protection from his brothers or father, she herself uses her 'sharp nails' (*surp nakha*) to defend herself. Kaikesi, her mother, also criticized her for not behaving like a girl due to her indulgence in fights like a man: 'Surpankha that is the right name for you, you monster'. Therefore, it can be observed that Surpanakha's deviance or monstrosity was not a *malum in se* rather an imposed *malum prohibitum.*

Later, she finds love in Vidyujiva but her family schemes to kill him for power and unable to bare this loss of a loved one, the Lanka's princess Meenakshi impersonates the infamous role of the demoness 'Surpanakha' out of vengeance. In the Indian mythology she was the first woman who dared to express her desire for love to a man without any remorse and to subvert her idiosyncrasy, Ram instructs Lakshman to "maim her". Therefore, her physical mutilation was a forewarning for women to surrender their freewill to the patriarchal notion of predestined gender roles. She is a personification of Helene Cixous' gyno-phonocentric voice. Here, in contrast to the dominant phallocentric discourse of the "good woman" and the "bad woman", Surpanakha voices her freedom of expression through her atypical individualistic actions as well as her body; articulating a powerful personality.

Stigmatization of Female sexuality

In the misogynist society, the female body is both the object of desire and the subject of control and this power over the female sexuality is controlled by the patriarchs to suit the purposes of their social code. According to Henley and Freemen the society constantly reminds women of their 'place' as gendered subalterns and if they deviate from the mainstream, they are sternly put back in their place; this social construct of the devaluation of the women's individuation is exercised through stigma laden norms. Alicia Gasper de Alba says:

> Sex empowers the body. Sex is agency, the enactment of desire, and in patriarchy, the only ones permitted to enact their desire are men; women's sexuality has to be scrutinized, proscribed, protected, or punished at all times. (2014, p. 161).

Mahasweta Devi's Draupadi, unlike her mythological namesake, is disrobed, threatened, beaten and stripped off her feminine shame, rapped by many and made to bleed in pain; she is pushed in this vulnerable situation by Senanayak to gain her compliance to curb the individual feminine as well as collective Naxalite resistance. The character of Senanayak is the most intellectual as well as contradictory one. As a leftist, he sympathizes with the Naxalite tribes though as a Bengali Combatant Specialist who understands the Naxalbari Revolt and he schemes to entrap them like Shakespeare's Prospero as he believes, "In order to destroy the enemy, become one" (394); though aware of the ingenuity of the two resistances, Senanayak fails to overcome his masculine rigidity. Thus, a strong but morally conflicted character of Senanayak is threatened by Dopadi's unconventional reaction to his patriarchal oppression.

The most ancient Indian model of the stigmatization of women's sexuality can be found in in the *Adi Mahakavya – The Ramayana* in which the character of Meenakshi is condemned as 'Surpanakha' or 'a sharp nailed monster' by her own brother Ravana. When Surpanakha expresses her desire to marry Vidyujiva, a supposed rival king, Ravana denies to consent her marriage in reaction to which she threatens him to unearth his true face to Mandoodari. Here, to suppress her very first voice of rebellion, Ravana reminds her of her subordinate stance in the masculine world by taking away her subject of desire. Furthermore, the character of Mandoodari is also a victim of such patriarchal sexual politics as her husband Ravana is free to exercise polygamy; but as an ideal sister or a *Pativrata,* woman is expected to mold herself for masculine socio-cultural comforts and needs.

Later, she is accused as '*Rakshasi*' by the *Mariyada Purushottama* Ram, symbolizing the power structure and the male dominance, giving him the agency to marginalize the challengingly powerful woman. In the both the cases, her fault is to voice her feminine desire publicly. Ram's instruction to Laxman "Maim her… she will remember her dishonourable crime and not attack a helpless woman again"; here, Kane questions the motive behind this penalty as she writes;

> Maim her, what weird barbarity was this and for what…for displaying desire for these two handsome men...what were they furious about me attacking Sita or me assaulting their chastity, their moral righteousness? Was it their apprehension for my uninhibited behavior, assuming it to be an overt vulgarity, an open display of unleashed carnal anarchy? Was that they had laughed at me, reticulating me in their contempt and amazement, their arrogant condescendence condemning me for my feminine profanities? (Kané 2017 p.202).

Thus, by breaking the pre-established notions of patriarchal mythology, Kavita Kane recreates a feminine narrative highlighting a woman's censored consciousness, as she unveils women's quandaries and their struggles to break free from the stigmatization of sexuality as well as womanhood.

Lacan's phallic womanhood and Cixous' Jouissance

Jacques Lacan in his essay *The Signification of the Phallus* (1958) delineates the formulae of sexuation in the symbolic phallus which according to him is not just the signifier of the desire but it is the signified function itself. His formulaic distinction of the 'gendered roles' foregrounded in the 'phallic function' reveals the unconscious mechanization of gendered sexuality. Here, while talking about the masculine behavioural traits of a woman, he talks about the power of the imaginary phallus. So, Lacan's psychoanalytical conception of a phallic woman narrates the non-conventional masculine characteristics of a woman such as aggression, self-assertion, resistance, vengeance and others.

In Mahasweta Devi's *Draupadi,* the character of Dopadi is a personification of Lacan's idea of phallic femininity; when she was gang-raped, "Active pistons of flesh rise and fall, rise and fall over it " (Devi – 467) in order to "Make her" and to subvert her to the power of the phallus, she emerged as a new woman. In the morning, when the guards give Dopadi water to wash and clothes to cover her mangled naked body to answer Senanayak's call:

> Draupadi stands up. She pours the water down on the ground. Tears her piece of cloth with her teeth. Seeing such strange behavior, the guard says, she's gone crazy, and runs for orders. He can lead the prisoner out but doesn't know what to do if the prisoner behaves incomprehensibly. So, he goes to ask his superior. (p.402)

When Senanayak asks her to clothe herself, she mocks him by saying:

> The object of your search, Dopdi Mejhen. You asked them to make me up, don't you want to see how they made me?... What's the use of clothes? You can strip me, but how can you clothe me again? Are you a man? (p.402)

Dopdi's body serves an anecdote for the dictum: "your sex is a terrible wound". As her body is shown as a weapon for resistance which voices her identity and epitomizes as a synecdoche for survival. Through the characterization of Dopdi, Mahasweta Devi investigates the conflicts between the underline colonial morality and subalternity. As Spivak says, Dopadi's action strongly asserts, "My honour does not lie in between my legs." (p.109). According to Sunder Rajan:

> It is simultaneously a deliberate refulsa of a shared sign-system of pertaining to nakedness and rape and an ironic deployment of the same semiotics to create the disconcerting counter effects of shame, confusion and terror in the enemy."

Thus, the patriarchal power play is defeated by the demystification of gender performity roles by Dopdi who turns out as "terrifying super object – an unarmed target."

The French Feminist, Helene Cixous, in her magnum opus of *Ecriture feminine, The Laugh of the Medusa* (1975) writes about her feminist perception of the 'pleasure principle' or 'jouissance' as a woman's creative power to express herself through the gyno-phonocentric language of her body. On this, Sandra Gilbert comments:

> ...to escape hierarchical bonds and thereby come closer to what Cixous calls *jouissance*, which can be defined as a virtually metaphysical fulfillment of desire that goes far beyond [mere] satisfaction... [It is a] fusion of the erotic, the mystical, and the political.

But from the post-structuralist and psychoanalytical point of view, after Jacques Lacan, the concept of 'jouissance' is beyond the pleasure principle, often leading the subject towards transgressions and sufferings. As from Lacan's phallocentric perspective, 'jouissance' was related to castrastion complex, phallic aggression and death drive. Thus, suggesting the feminine jouissance to be the source of their deviant behaviour and suffering.

Kane's Surpanakha is a very expressive woman who speaks through her body; her father named her as Meenakshi because even as an infant, she had curious eyes. Her mother called her *Chandranakha* as her crescent nails representing her mood swings. Her dark but graceful physique, quite expressive of her 'desire' in front of Ram and Laxman and her loud expression of her inner most feelings in front of all masculine characters outline the discourse of her feminine resistance and defiance against the oppressive patriarchal forces. Through her character, Kane explores the forbidden arena of a woman's unconscious sexual desires and her need for love and 'completeness'. Out of Electra complex, she urged for the fatherly love but couldn't get it due to her gender performity; out of four brothers, three never treated her as equal created an emotional vacuum; only Kumbhkarna was the one who understood her but soon their compliance was broken up due to the *Nindrasana* curse. And as a victim of familial power play for the thrown of Lanka, she was untimely widowed. In a state of self-exclusion, she lost her young in *Dandaka* forest. To fill this emotional void she longed for connection.

> She wanted those two men just as she had wanted Vdyujiva. She wanted to share something, to blot out this awful lonliness…that was the kind of help she wanted, and yet how few could or would give her that?" (Kane 2017 p.195)

The way Helene Cixous sees feminine jouissance as a kind of body language through which a woman expresses her unconscious, Lacan, on the other hand, as a phallocentric psychoanalyst analyses the same jouissance as a cause of deviant behaviour and women suffering. This phenomenon of contrast between the masculine and feminine perspective can be seen in the novel as well when the character of Taraka and Mandoodari seem to understand Surpanakha's gyno-phonocentric narrative, the masculine phallocentric characters like her father, brothers and Ram-Laxman fail to recognize her. Ironically, Ravana as his brother and Ram as a noble gentleman destroys her inner sanctum by mutilating her inner as well as outer worlds.

Conclusion

Mahasweta Devi and Kavita Kane, belonging to two different socio-political backgrounds, through their feminist re-telling of mythology, acquire a new self-definition and become the active maker of a new and rogenous woman. Their female protagonists refuse to remain the objects of a male narrative, proclaim themselves as 'subject' and accentuate on the truth of their own presence; they construct a meaning which "Senanayak simply cannot understand", thus they are an allegory of the woman's battle against patriarchy in present-day times.

Works Cited

Butler, Judith. *Gender Trouble: Feminism and the Subversion of Identity*, Routledge, USA, 1990.

Cixous, Helene. *The Laugh of the Medusa,* Grin Verlag, India, 2013.

De alba, A. G. [Un]framing the "Bad Woman": *Sor Juana, Malinche, Coyolxauhqui, and Other Rebels with a Cause*, University of Texas Press, Austin, 2014.

Devi, Mahasweta. *Breast Stories,* Translated by Gayatri Chakravorty Spivak, Seagull Books, USA, 1997.

Devi, Mahasweta. *Untapped Resources Seminar: Literature and Society*. 359 (July 1989): 15-19 Print.

Dutta, Bhaskor Chandra. "Questioning Subalternity: Re-reading Mahasweta Devi's 'Draup'di'", *Journal of Research in Humanities and Social Science*, vol. 7, no. 2, 2019.

Gilbert, Sasndra M. Introduction. *The Newly Born Woman* by Helene Cixous and Catherine Clement, 1975 Translated by Betsy Wing, Minneapolise: University of Minnesota Press, 1986.

Kane, Kavita. *The Lanka's Princess,* Rupa Publications, New Delhi, India, 2014.

Kane, Kavita. "Through the Mythical Lens." Interview by R. Krithika. The Hindu 5th March 2020.

CHAPTER 31

Social Stigmatization and Victimization of Women: A Feminist Study of Vijay Tendulkar's *Silence! The Court is in Session*

Miraclin J.

Abstract

Pregnancy out of wedlock is generally considered taboo and the discourses surrounding premarital pregnancy describe the woman involved in the issue as a sinner and the one who deserves punishment, whereas the male involved in the act is ignored out of the discourse. Society's attitude towards such a woman is the focus of this study. Tendulkar's play depicts the plight of a woman who is pregnant without wedlock and the treatment of society. The paper aims to read the play *Silence! The Court is in Session* written by Vijay Tendulkar with the lens of Feminism. Drawing theoretical insights from Judith Butler, Emile Durkheim, Giorgio Agamben, and others, the paper analyses the way the play epitomizes the victimization of women in contemporary society and the social stigma that functions around the discourse of out-of-wedlock pregnancy. The act of female characters turning against the protagonist is interpreted using Stanley Cohen's idea of 'Moral Panic'. Moreover, the paper also attempts to examine in what way the humiliation psychologically affects the protagonist subsequently.

Keywords: Social Stigma, Victimization, Homo Sacer, Moral Panic, and Performativity.

Tony Lawson and Joan Garrod delineate the act of stigmatization in the following manner: "the process whereby individuals are labelled with some marginalizing characteristic, such as "deviant," "crazy," etc. Causes of stigma may vary from negative signs or names to some physical attribute, such as "staring eyes." The result of stigmatization is usually the prevention of full acceptance by the rest of society" (393). John Scott explains two patterns of deviants: "The first refers to deviance as a pattern of norm violation.. . A second property highlights deviance as a stigma construct, a label bestowed upon certain classes of behaviour at certain times, which then become devalued, discredited, and often excluded" (291).Todd D. Kendall and Robert Tamura, in their article, "Unmarried Fertility, Crime, and Social Stigma" have done a study in which they look at how reducing social stigma of unmarried fertility may decrease crime in the society. Erving Goffman in his book, *Stigma* (1986), delineates three types of stigmas thus:

> First there are abominations of the body – the various physical deformities. Next there are blemishes of individual character perceived as weak will, domineering or unnatural passions, treacherous and rigid beliefs, and dishonesty, these being inferred from a known record of, for example, mental disorder, imprisonment, addiction, alcoholism, homosexuality, unemployment, suicidal attempts, and radical political behaviour. Finally there are the tribal stigma of race, nation, and religion, these being stigma that can be transmitted through lineages and equally contaminate all members of a family (13).

The stigma that surrounds the protagonist is of second type. The society stigmatizes the girl because of a blemish in her behaviour. Leela is seen, throughout the novel, by other characters as a symbol of sin. Thus, they stigmatize her based on her behaviour. The act of deviance from the social facts leads to the de-normalisation of the subject. Labelling is another form of stigmatization. Naming the person, at first, disintegrates her/his identity. As S. Cohen in his work *Folk Devils and Moral Panics* (1972) argues labelling can increase the effect of deviance (5). Cohen, further argues that the unmarried mothers are often labelled as 'Moral Panics' to the society.

The act of victimization, in the play, happens through social exclusion. Victimization through social exclusion is done to people who infringe the social facts by adhering to the individual facts. Emile Durkheim, in his work contrasts social facts from individual facts thus: "social facts are more liable to be objectively represented the more completely they are detached from the individual facts by which they are manifested" (82). The stigmatized victim is excluded from the other group and becomes the target of the majority. Monica J. Harris articulates the effects of social exclusion as follows:

> If social exclusion produces an immediate defensive response designed to attenuate emotional distress, then it is possible that social exclusion impairs the capacity for people to experience emotions in a normal manner. This defensive response might have consequences not only for the ability for socially excluded people to experience their own emotions,

> but it may also impair excluded people's ability to respond emotionally to others. (205)

The protagonist Miss Leela Benare has a lively and cheerful personality who never hesitates to talk and befriend men she meets. In the mock trial Miss Leela Benare is forced to reveal her personal life by her colleagues who want to humiliate her as they consider her life immoral and sinful. She is made the accused on purpose to bring out her affair with a married man and is charged with infanticide. Although she is abandoned with child in her womb Ms Leela is blamed for her affair and the faults of Prof. Damle is left unspoken. It is believed that letting her teach the students is immoral and thus she is fired from her job as well. Although Miss Leela wants to bring up her child, the final judgement is made to destroy the child in her womb. Initially she is charged with infanticide which is regarded as a dreadly sin, but later judgement is made to destroy the child as it is considered to be a result of an immoral relationship. Thus by not following social facts Leela becomes deviant. She is victimized and stigmatized by the society for unmarried fertility.

The characters portrayed by Vijay Tendulkar in the play depict the male dominated society that constantly finds fault with women based on the way women behave. There has been a stereotype in the society that it is inappropriate for a woman to talk loudly and crack jokes in the presence of men. A woman is expected to abide by all the rules laid by the patriarchal society. Likewise, Miss Leela Benare's colleagues represent the gender stereotypes which paves way to criticize a woman on the basis of her behaviour. This notion of censuring women based on gender role is closely akin to Judith Butler's concept of 'Gender Performativity'. According to Butler, gender role is a construction of the society. Through assigning the gender role the female body is expected to behave in a certain way. The deviance from this role is seen as abnormal. Butler defines gender performativity in the following way:

> In the first instance, then, the performativity of gender revolves around this metalepsis, the way in which the anticipation of a gendered essence produces that which it posits as outside itself. Secondly, performativity is not a singular act, but a repetition and a ritual, which achieves its effects through its naturalization in the context of a body, understood, in part, as a culturally sustained temporal duration. (15)

Initially Miss Leela Benare can be viewed as an optimistic person. She confidently declares "My life is my own – I haven't sold it to anyone for a job" (5). She has a great confidence in her actions and is interested in living her life to the fullest. Ms Benare says "we should laugh, we should play, we should sing! If we can and if they'll let us, we should dance too" (8). After being unable to stand the filthy remarks of her colleagues she attempts to commit suicide. The crowd tends to humiliate and mock her for her misconduct with Prof Damle. When the mock trial is over, Sukhatme, after enquiring Miss Leela Benare says "we had some good fun" (77) revealing the private life of her.

Sukhatme is portrayed as a sly person who implicitly mocks Miss Leela Benare by calling her 'Leela Damle'. As Miss Leela Benare is charged with infanticide Sukhatme states that "there could be no baser or more devilish thing on earth" (31). The character Sukhatme is deeply rooted in gender bias as he claims that "woman is not fit for independence" (71). He seems to have a strong bond with culture and tradition as he states "the accused has plotted to dynamite the very roots of our tradition, our pride in ourselves, our culture and our religion"(71). He fears that a woman like Miss Leela Benare would influence other women in the society and he condemns Miss Leela Benare by stating that "her conduct has blackened all social and moral values. The accused is public enemy number one" (71). He considers that the existence of women like Leela benare is dangerous to the society and is persistent in his mindset against such women as he claims "if such socially destructive tendencies are encouraged to flourish, this country and its culture will be totally destroyed"(71). When Samant refers to the word 'hypnotism', Sukhatme misinterprets and tries to misguide the case, requesting the judge to pen it in evidence. Sukhatme constantly intends to find fault with Miss Leela Benare and aims at winning the case by arguing against the accused and bringing her 'severe punishment'

Vijay Tendulkar, through the character Mrs Kashikar, apparently proves that some women themselves are against women who break the traditions and rules formulated by the male chauvinistic society. When Mrs Kashikar is asked for a proof to prove that Ms Leela Benare is unjust, she says that her behaviour itself is a proof and says "Look how loudly she laughs! How she sings, dances, cracks jokes! And wandering alone with how many men, day in and day out" (55). She doesn't seem to accept women earning money as she states "It's the sly new fashion of women earning that makes everything go wrong" (54). According to Mrs Kashikar the women gain courage and liberty to lead a life on their own as they earn money and she also calls it "the sly new fashion". Apparently, Mrs Kashikar, being a woman is against women who earn money on their own. When Miss Leela Benare is made the prisoner, she refuses to get into the witness box and it was Mrs Kashikar who pulls her forcibly and puts Benare into the witness box"(50) as she intends to know the secret about Miss Leela Benare.

In the absence of Ms Leela Benare, Rokde exchanges the information with karnik about her misbehaviour and karnik, right away, intimates Ponkshe to inform what he heard about Miss Leela Benare. Rokde informs his colleagues that her behaviour is suspicious as he saw Ms Leela Benare with Prof Damle. He could not tolerate Ms Leela Benare being alone in Prof Damle's room and he says "I got such a shock! Sitting there in Damle's room-the night falling" (39). Sukhatme and the judge, Mr. Kashikar enjoy speaking of the divinity and sacredness of motherhood. Kashikar, while defending Sukhatme's argument about motherhood, quotes a proverb: "Mother and the Motherland both are even higher than heaven" (30).

But when it comes to the case of Ms Leela Benare, he denies her wish of bringing up her child. Initially Kashikar declares that he charges Ms Benare with infanticide because it's important from the social point of view. He states "Infanticide is one of great social significance. That's why I deliberately picked it. We consider society's best interests in all we do"(26). However, in contrast to his own statement, Kashikar makes the judgement that the child should be destroyed.

The life of the child can be defined in the words of Giorgio Agamben as *Homo Sacer*. The child is marked as an outcome of sin, which serves as a symbol of stigma. Therefore, the child is seen as a weed in the society which ought to be cleared. Thus the child becomes an object of moral panic in the society. Agamban explains the life *Homo Sacer* in the following manner: "his entire existence is reduced to a bare life stripped of every right by virtue of the fact that anyone can kill him without committing homicide" (183). Leela can also be considered as a *Homo Sacer* because of her social exclusion.

When Ponkshe is asked to describe the immoral conduct of the accused, he says "she runs after men too much" (33). He judges her on the basis of his meeting with Miss Leela Benare. The society believes that a woman should act according to the wishes of men and is supposed to follow and obey the rules laid down by her traditions and culture and would never let a woman like Miss Leela Benare live up a life as she desires.

Through the character Mrs Kashikar, Vijay Tendulkar reveals that some women themselves could not tolerate women who live without men's support and they always find themselves inferior to men because that is how they believe a woman should act, to be recognised as 'good women' in the society. Whenever Mrs Kashikar tries to speak she is silenced by Mr Kashikar. He constantly ignores and tries to shut her down irrespective of what she desires to speak.

Mr Kashikar never lets his wife speak up her opinions on the case and he enjoys belittling and humiliating her, "you've grown old, but you haven't grown any wiser" (54). Through the relationship between Mr and Mrs Kashikar, Vijay Tendulkar shows that men tend to dominate and tyrannize women and possess the tendency to disparage women, considering women as inferior creatures when compared to them. Throughout the play, Mr Kashikar despises and yells at her wife "Hold your tongue. Can't say a word!. Mrs Kashikar is silenced" (21).

In the trial Sukhatme says "women bears the grave responsibility of building up the high values of society" (71). Sukhatme stresses only upon women but never discusses the obligation and responsibility of men in building up a better society. Rokde represents the view of society on an unmarried woman with a child in her womb and is afraid of the ill speaking of the people around. He says "And if I marry you when you're in this condition, the whole world'll sling mud at me. No one in my family's done a thing like that" (65). Learning Ms Leela Benare's affair with her own maternal uncle, her colleagues make disdainful comments on her, "the present conduct of the accused is totally licentious. We know that. But it now seems that her past, too, is smeared in sin" (67).

Mr Kashikar who initially acted as a judge, joins the witnesses in order to reveal the misconduct of her and humiliate her. When he is asked if he knows the accused he interprets her as "a sinful canker on the body of society" (67) and says "that's my honest opinion of these grown up unmarried girls" (68). He declares that he wouldn't have mercy on her because of her behaviour. He is not ready to accept her behaviour and says "the arrogance with which you conducted yourself in society, having done all these things, that arrogance is the most unforgivable thing of all" (76). He is concerned about the future generation and the welfare of the society and fears that the very presence of a woman like Ms Leela Benare would be dangerous to mankind. He says "not only today's, but tomorrow's society would have been endangered by your misconduct" (76). He makes a judgement to destroy the child and adds a statement "neither you nor anyone else should ever do anything like this" (76). Thus Leela is seen as a 'moral panic' to the welfare of the society.

Ms Leela Benare, who was once contented and interested in her life, now begins to lament that "life is not worthy of life. Hold an enquiry against life" (73). It is clear that her colleagues, absolutely, are responsible for Ms Leela Benare's attempt to end her life by drinking the bottle of TIK 20. Her colleagues represent the society that tends to peek into the private life of women and possess the judgemental tendency toward the women who live on their own legs. Ms Leela Benare argues "my private life is my own business I'll decide what to do with myself" (73). She begs to have some mercy and wants to live a life for the sake of her son's welfare. She asserts, "I want my body now for him – for him alone" (75). She speaks up about the selfishness of men who consider women as an object of desire. She states "I offered up my body on the altar of my worship. And my intellectual god took the offering – and went his way" (75).

Throughout the play, Vijay Tendulkar explores the denial of a woman's desires to lead a life as she wishes and the victimization of women, whereas, men remain in the unquestionable state in society. Thus, the paper illustrates the way in which unmarried fertility is stigmatized and how victimization through social exclusion occurs in the society.

Works Cited

Agamben, Giorgio. *Homo Sacer*. Seuil, 1997.

Butler, Judith. *Gender Trouble*. Taylor and Francis, 2006.

Cohen, Stanley. *Folk Devils and Moral Panics: The Creation of the Mods and Rockers*. New York: St. Martin's Press, 1980.

Durkheim Émile, et al. *The Rules of Sociological Method: And Selected Texts on Sociology and Its Method*. Free Press, 2014.

Goffman, Erving. *Stigma: Notes on the Management of Spoiled Identity*. Penguin, 1963.

Harris, Monica J. Bullying, *Rejection, and Peer Victimization: A Social Cognitive Neuroscience Perspective*. Springer, 2009.

Kendall, Todd D., and Robert Tamura. "Unmarried Fertility, Crime, and Social Stigma." *The Journal of Law and Economics*, vol. 53, no. 1, 2010, pp. 185-221. https://doi.org/10.1086/596116.

Lawson, Tony, et al. *Dictionary of Sociology*. Fitzroy Dearborn, 2001.

Tendulkar, Vijay. *Silence! the Court Is in Session*. Oxford University Press, 1982.

Scott, John, and Gordon Marshall. *Oxford Dictionary of Sociology*. Oxford University Press, 2009.

CHAPTER 32

A Crochet of Matrimony and Expatriate Sensibilities in Manju Kapur's *The Immigrants*

Hitesh D. Raviya and Parul Malviya

Abstract

Marriage itself is an enormous step and a huge commitment in lives of both men and women. And by the same token comes additional precepts of it. Marriage brings question for equality, freedom, identity, ego, respect, trust, and sexual relationship etc. Yet, it does bring all of those unequivocally for a woman. And if that same woman must move to different land, she feels an expatriate. On the top of that, if her only support is insufficiently supportive, then it is a roller-coaster ride, and there is no anticipating to whether it will stop at a high or a low. *The Immigrant*, authored by Manju Kapur, delineates this trauma. She has been classified amongst the celebrated women writers of Indian English Literature. Her novels have depiction of marriage and its issues in the light of feminism. The present research paper envisages to study how Kapur has braided marriage and alienation in her novel *The Immigrant.* It will investigate how Kapur, a woman in literature, has frescoed women in true state, her condition when she is in marriage and her condition when she is in a distant land as she tussles for her identity.

Keywords: Women, feminism, matrimony, expatriate sensibilities, individuality

Women in literature have come all the way long. Starting from Sappho and Mirabai, Mary Wollstonecraft and Jane Austen to Sarojini Naidu and Mahashweta Devi, and from Butler and Morrison to Arundhati Roy and Manju Kapur today. Nevertheless, plenty of established names are absent here, but women have competed for their hold in literature. They have brought into being their voices from the time they have realized that they have one. Women in literature have written on several themes but the constant central theme of their writing remains fighting for their rights by delineating the discrimination faced by them. In the patriarchal arrangement, female writers have adopted a feministic writing style to address numerous concerns. India has seen women writers even from the ancient ages, such as Gargi, Maitreyi, Lopamudra, Ghosha, Avvaiyar and many more. Today, women writers in Indian English Literature, have unearthed Indian society at the fundamental level. And hence, they have been bearing transformations and development through subject of their writing. Presently, female writers in India including, Amrita Pritam, Nayantara Sehgal, Kamala Markandaya, Arundhati Roy, Anuja Chauhan, Jhumpa Lahiri, Sudha Murty, Anita Desai, Chitra Banerjee Divakaruni, Kavita Kane, and Manju Kapur have given us different windows to look at the world. They propel us to look around, ask questions and ponder over the differences that the world has for men and women.

As one of the distinguished and famed women in Indian English Literature, Manju Kapur is a feminist writer who focuses on man-woman relationship. A lot of contemporary women writers deal with the theme of feminism and portrayal of women in fictions, but Manju Kapur predominantly has different ways of treating this subject. Born in Amritsar in 1948, a town in north-eastern state of Punjab in India, Kapur has studied in Miranda House University College, Delhi for her graduation, and for her post-graduation she pursued M.A. in Dalhousie University, Halifax, Nova Scotia. She received her M.Phil. degree from Delhi University, India. Kapur is a professor of English in her own phrontistery, Miranda House College in New Delhi. She has seven works in total to her claim and many of which are adopted for television broadcasts in the form of daily soaps.

Her debut novel *Difficult Daughters* was published in 1998 which brought her acclaim and recognition in the writing world. In 1999, her debut work also got her Commonwealth Writers Prize for that year. Pinpointed in the span of 1940s, the novel has a setting of Indian Independence, and the author has delineated the free-will and courageous woman of that period. Virmati, the protagonist of the novel is a dauntless woman, and story of her audacities is recollected by her daughter, Ida. Virmati's affair with Harish, who was her neighbor and married, is the essence of breaking the patriarchal threshold in the male dominated society. Her affair is also a symbolistic of her own independence which is parallel to Indian Independence movement. Ida's grandmother Kasturi is the third woman in the novel who finds it hard to make her daughter understand the ways of the world. Through character of Virmati, Kapur has given an understanding of woman who are difficult to handle by the society. Woman who are bold, outright courageous, adamant and looks for themselves and decide for their relationship and marriages. Where society decides the paths for women and wants them to walk on it, Virmati paves her own path. Published in 2002, *A Married Woman* is Manju Kapur's second novel. The novel centers a female protagonist who protests the patriarchal set of the society. Astha, the main figure of the story, struggles to find her identity. Her quest to show her individuality continues from the time when she stays in her maternal house to even after she gets married. She fights with mindset and concepts of her parents who keep on focusing on Astha's marriage. Every action and decision of Astha's life is taken considering she must marry. When Astha actually gets married, then decisions for her life are taken by Hemant, her husband. But as a woman of today, Astha finds her liberation in art. She paints and writes and in both she uses her brush and pen to outbreak the limits set by patriarchy for woman. One important aspect of this novel is that it also discusses the event of dispute for Babri Masjid and Ramjanmabhumi. As Kapur describes situation of woman in marriage but through character of Astha in this novel, Kapur also shows that some women are moulded in a way that they cannot escape the aviary of patriarchy. Even after tasting the fruits of liberation, they return back to trees of boundaries.

Published in 2006, *Home* is Kapur's third novel. Also got shortlisted for Hutch Crossword Book Award in 2006, Kapur in *Home* shows the Indian family and its setup. Banwari Lal who runs a cloth business in a shop in Delhi has two sons and their wives. His own daughter is married to Murli, who is unemployed and due to his craving for money and greed he has for dowry, he has burnt Sunita alive at the age of 32. The sons are ready to take up the business, but their wives don't agree. There are disputes, urges for freedom, needs for space. This novel shows the ground realities of an Indian family, of an Indian home. Kapur's *Custody* was published in 2008, in which she brought novelty through her stylistic craft. As *Custody* is also a feminist piece of work, but it is somewhat different from other previous works written by Kapur. In the novel, chaos, tension and disruption occurs due to infidelity and infertility. *Custody* characterizes Shagun and Raman who have a daughter together as Roohi. Another woman Ishita, who cannot bear a child is the central figure of the novel. After Shagun and Raman gets divorced, Ishita and Raman fall in love together. The story revolves around the custody of the child and other dimensions of it. Through the novel, Kapur has shown how women have to struggle in all aspects of their lives. Although the constitution gives them equal rights but are they equally treated? The society has still got a hold on setting the limits for women. This novel is also adopted by famous Bollywood director Ekta Kapur as a daily-soap *Yeh Hain Mohabbatein*. Manju Kapur's latest novel is *Brothers* which was published in 2016. Looking at the title of the book we may assume it to be different from other works of Kapur, but there is hardly any truth in that. The novel has same themes as are in other novels. It is based on a conflict between two brothers and women who become part of this conflict. The novel is about different generations of brothers where there is politics, caste, freedom struggle and women suppression. Kapur has exposed a lot of realities and men to men relationship in the novel.

The researcher aims to understand writing style that the author has adopted for her fourth novel *The Immigrant*. The research paper will study two major highlights of the novel and observe the journey of a woman. How a woman would transform from following rules and regulations to breaking them free. Whether we can take the delineation of woman in *The Immigrants* as suitable for studying the condition of woman and their transformation after they cross the patriarchal threshold.

As the fourth novel authored by Manju Kapur, *The Immigrant* was published in 2008. The novel is set up in India and Canada. Centralizing the character of Nina, who is an English professor and also in her thirties. Set up in 1970s, the novel revolves around Nina and her husband Ananda. Ananda is a Dentist who lives in Halifax, Nova Scotia, Canada. Nina is married to Ananda and flies to Canada to live with him. The novel narrates the story of the couple but especially Nina as she first suffers from the patriarchal domination, then alienation in the remote land and finally struggles to find her true identity. In the novel, Kapur shows the realities of Indian marriages set up in a distant land, away from Indian society. Kapur has told the story of two women as she deals with the subject of feminism. The two women are Nina and her mother, and in this this context. Anagha states in her research paper, "*Immigrant* tells us about another highly educated girl Nina, she had no father; all she was able to look upon was her mother who looked after her needs made her grow to a position as a professor of English. The novel is about two women Nina and her mother, after the death of Nina's father her mother was left alone. Nina's grandparents never supported the two ladies. After completion of Nina's education both the ladies shift to Delhi. There too her mother never spent a carefree life" (Gawande, 15) Hence, we see how these two women build their life without a man in Delhi, but they are constantly reminded about how unfulfilled their lives are. There are several other themes that the novel deals with. Ideas such as infidelity, sexual relationship, cultural conflict, caste, familial relationships etc. are sketched in *The Immigrant* by Kapur.

Kapur has narrated the story in three parts where she pictures the three stages of Nina's life. In Part I of the novel, we see Nina's life before she leaves for Canada. It talks about Nina's home, where she lived with her mother only. Her father has died long back leaving both of them with nothing. Nina is a professor of English and she is the only source of income in the house yet Nina's mother is desperate to find a suitable boy for her only daughter. She wants to see her daughter married and happy. Nina is educated, and a working woman who strives to stay with her mother. Marriage is nowhere in her sight as of now but her mother's continuous tensions and thrust is now unbearable for her. In the same part, we are introduced to Ananda, "Far away, on the eastern seaboard of Canada, in Halifax, Nova Scotia, a young man stood at the window of his clinic and gazed at the trees lining the sidewalk. It was summer; the air was mild, the sun shining for a change." (Kapur, 11), who is a dentist in Halifax, Nova Scotia, Canada. The change here is symbolic of Ananda's marriage as he strives for a family and a companionship in the alien land. The same part of the novel also introduces us to Ananda's one of the major concerns of premature ejaculation while he would be in bed with any girl. As it was no big deal for the young people to talk about it there, Ananda was always hesitant and was not able to accept it himself. Alka, Ananda's sister, introduces Nina to him and asks him to marry her. Talking about feminism, Kapur does not bash men in the novel. She has aptly shown the Ananda as a man of modern generation who understands women and their thought process. We see Ananda respecting Nina's choices and decision all the while in the first part of the novel. He marries Nina and applies for a visa for her asking her to come with him to Canada. In a nutshell, this part gives an introduction and leads us to the next part that is the married life of Nina and Ananda in Halifax.

The second part of the novel begins with Nina's journey towards a new part of her life in Halifax with her husband Ananda. Kapur has clearly depicted the cultural conflict in the mind of an immigrant and here in this novel it is Nina. She struggles to adapt to a new place, new views, new habits and new culture. Everything is so different and alien to her here and she misses the touch of familiarity in Halifax. She misses a sense of belonging, she also longs for her own kinds, people from her own culture. She looks for it in uncle and aunt of Ananda, or we call him Andy when it comes to them. When Nina actually meets them, she realises why Andy left their house in the first place. As they have adopted to new place and culture, she could not find a string of familial feel in them. It was nothing that she has expected from visiting the relatives. She longs for home, she longs for her place, her country, the air of her place, although foul but it was 'her place'. In the same part Nina and Ananda also struggles with the problem of conceiving a child. Nina's concerns grow day by day. She wants to be a mother. Second part ends with Ananda finding a solution to his problem but he tries to hide it from Nina. Nina finds a job at the library which she's been visiting from her initial days in Halifax. And Nina facing the snow of Canada leads us to the third part of the novel.

Part III is the final part of the novel where differences between the couple grow stronger due to the one problem in their married life – sexual inadequacy. One problem brings in lots of lies, misunderstanding, stress, overreacting and ego in life of Nina and Ananda. By this time Nina has found her way to keep herself occupied, that is through her books and The La Leche League which was all ordinary woman sharing their situations and problems and finds it therapeutic by listening and understanding each other. Nina was introduced to it by Bethe to whom she met in her library. Kapur in this part explains how women help women despite of belonging to different culture. The beauty of sisterhood is nicely delineated by the novelist. We come across Nina as more ambitious woman, who wants to become much more than just Andy's wife. She applies for a scholarship and gets one for a course of librarian. While Nina finds her distraction in making her career and identity, Ananda finds it in infidelity. His affair with his office receptionist is unveiled in this part of the novel. Kapur here has managed to show us things on equal grounds. When we see Ananda committing infidelity, she also tells us about Nina's affair with Anton, who was her batchmate in librarian course. Kapur did not simply point a finger on man. She showed how need of man and woman must be fulfilled and here both of them did it outside of their marriage. The novel ends with two of them separating. Nina leaves Ananda's house as she gets a job in New York. She finds out about Ananda's affair and realises that they are two different being who cannot live together. She wanted to build her identity and she did through her education, her knowledge and her skills. It ends with the end of their marriage.

The Immigrant is a striking narration of marriage and despite of many references that ponder us to think otherwise, the ground realities remain same. The actuality and truth of marriage is that two lives come together to live together with their bodies and their souls. So, in order for a marriage to work, it needs both balance between the ideals of the two and satisfying the bodily needs of the two. Hence a good symmetry between both is essential for stability. Does it happen in the novel? The answer to this question is a 'no'.

The idea of marriage is craftly handled by Manju Kapur. She has brought to us the simpler aspects and facets of marriage that we don't usually talk about but is common to almost every marriage. Marriage is an important aspect significantly in a woman's life, as Beauvoir states, "Marriage is the destiny offered to woman by society. It is still true that most women are married or have been, or plan to be, or suffer for not being." (Beauvoir, 445). In the novel, Kapur has, time and again, showed the how 'coming of the age' for marriage is decided by the society. As Nina is in her thirties, every passing minute, every other person around her reminds of how her life is lonely without a husband. The society has led woman to think in a way that marriage is the ultimate goal of her life. In the starting of the novel itself Kapur shows Nina's condition,

> And her womb, her ovaries, her uterus, the unfertilised eggs that were expelled every month, what about them? They were busy marking every passing second of her life. Had she been married, thirty would have been heralded as a time of youthful maturity, her birthday celebrated in the midst of doting husband and children. (Kapur, 1)

And so was it for Ananda. Where in Nina's home her mother kept on worrying about her marriage, showing her suitable guys, even going to the astrologer, Ananda's sister Alka did the same to him. She too went to the astrologer and that is how she found Nina for his brother. Yet, it was not just their wish but on the part of Ananda's he was a lonely man in an alien land, he wanted to marry, to start a new life, to start a family. He would see other families around him, especially Gary and Sue's and feel all alone in Halifax. In the Indian set up of society, a woman single for a long time starts losing respect, there are questions and objections from people all around. When Nina gets married to Ananda, she returns to her workplace as a married woman and hence she feels, "She never anticipated though the respect that came with marriage, a tiny shift in focus and there it was; Nina Sharma, an accepted member of society, married, bound for the Western big time." (Kapur, 88) Ananda was a good man and so was Nina, a good woman, both of them open and understanding. Love and compassion between them start when they exchange letters with each other from Halifax in Canada to Delhi in India. After getting married, Nina has to leave her place and move to Canada with high hopes of a happy, loving and adventurous married life. Though she always has the fear of going to an alien land and leaving her mother behind, but she loved Ananda. During the novel these hopes of not only Nina but also of Ananda's gets crushed. Alienation and Nina's strive to find her identity in Halifax plays a major role in disrupting the smooth flow of their marriage. But then there is a main reason behind this disturbance, which was sexual inadequacy, and with which came ego of Ananda to not admit to his inadequacy.

> Sexuality was beginning to be studied scientifically, he had heard Masters and Johnson claimed a high rate of cure for premature ejaculation, but thank God, he would not have to go through the humiliation of medical investigation that his desperation had forced him to consider. He recognised this attitude as inimical to perfect health, but he would feel great shame if he had to submit his orgasms to the scrutiny of a doctor. And with the help of his dental anaesthetic spray, he had consummated his marriage. (Kapur, 121)

That is the point in the novel where distance between the couple starts growing. Both of them try hard to keep their marriage but unsatisfied needs lead them to have extra marital affairs. After her marriage Nina for the first time feels good and different while she gives up herself in bed to Anton, "For the first time she had a sense of her own self, entirely separate from other people, autonomous, independent. So strange that the sex did not make her feel guilty, not beyond the initial shock." (Kapur, 231) And so was the case with Ananda, "Mandy encouraged him to be wild, free, uninhibited, playful. With Nina he was his mother's son, his sister's brother, the good husband, playing out a role he had been trained for since childhood. Nine years in Canada had not dimmed the need to be this person." (Kapur, 211) This disharmony grows between the couple and eventually Nina finds out about her husband's affair with a white girl. Lack of communication, growing uninterest, longing for starting a family but not being able to do so, leads the couple to take the steps that ruin their marriage. Reading the novel, this concept of marriage and adjustments looks nothing new to us. It is something that has always been passed from generations that 'marriage equal to adjustments plus sacrifices.' When two individuals come together to spend their life with each other, adjustments are obvious, but should we make adjustments to the cost of losing our happiness or keeping quiet for our needs for the rest of our lives? Answers can be many, but in this context as they are in foreign culture, getting separate was an easy task and Kapur has showed us that in *The Immigrant.*

Another major theme that Kapur has depicted in the novel is alienation. Nina lived all her life in India until she gets married to Ananda. Leaving her people, her home, her homeland just for one person was difficult for her, "The tears Nina hadn't shed before, during or after her wedding, all came pouring out days before she was to leave. They came unsought, at all hours, trickling down her cheeks, hidden from her mother, mopped furtively only to come again. This was her true vida to her home, her friend, her job, her mother, everything." (Kapur, 91). At this time, she only felt the pain of separation but the feeling of being new to a land was yet to knock her door. It knocks when Nina is flying to Canada, she's been asked questions, judged, doubted at by the woman who was checking her visa. After she finally gets over with it, Nina feels humiliated and deceived and she says,

> "Dear Ananda This is not your country. You are deceived, and you have deceived me. You made it out to be a liberal haven where everybody loved you. This woman is looking for a reason to get rid of me. I am the wrong colour, I come from the wrong place. See me in this airport, of all the passengers the only one not allowed to sail through immigration, made to feel like an illegal alien. See, see, see. Love Nina." (Kapur, 105)

As she reaches Canada, her expatriate sensibilities start growing day by day. She is new to almost everything. Food, place, atmosphere, climate, people, their dress up and their ways of living everything was new to her. She felt alone and monotonous in this land where they treated her different. More she missed her homeland, more she wanted it and more Canadian her husband was. Ananda has adopted all the ways of this foreign land as after all he was a citizen of Canada. But it was difficult for Nina as the thinks, "Certain Indians become immigrants slowly. They are not among those who have fled persecution, destitution, famine, slavery and death threats, nor among those for whom the doors of their country slam shut the minute they leave its borders." (Kapur, 107). Their struggle with changing their land also results in their struggle with their identity which can be seen in the novel throughout. In this context Suresh states, "The immigrant's psyche undergoes a constant interaction with the traditional culture of the native home and the adopted culture of an alien land. It ushers a reconstruction in the inherited custom and culture of 'the immigrant'. Cultural diversity which the immigrants are concerned with is primarily taken as the setting of this novel." (53) Till the end of the novel, we see Nina struggling to find her own identity in a country across the ocean and she longs for home as her heart says, "Home. That was what she wanted. The Park, the trees, the harbour, the view, everything was so pretty, but it failed to satisfy her heart." (Kapur, 157) But she knew that there was no going back, she struggles with continuous feeling of expatriation, but her knowledge helps her find a job for herself and she manages to live without Ananda. In the end we see acceptance in her character, acceptance of reality by Nina and her confidence in herself. She understands that she cannot always feel this, she has to give up considering herself alien to the land and start a new life without her husband and with a new job. She says, "When one was reinventing oneself, anywhere could be home. Pull up your shallow roots and move. Find a new place, new friends, a new family. It had been possible once; it would be possible again." (Kapur, 194).

The two themes are dominant in the novel. They cannot be seen as separate from each other, but Manju Kapur has interwoven them so that the novel comes out as a whole. Marriage and alienation have been simplistically narrated in *The Immigrant* by Kapur, but it surely pushes us to ponder over these issues. In novel, the couple struggles to save their marriage which started with great anticipation and higher expectations yet ended in separation. The novel leads us from conventional dealing of the subject to novelty. What started in a very conventional way as in an arranged marriage through an astrologer but ended in separation which was not much hard for the couple as it could have been if they were in India. Modernity is also seen through change in Nina's character. Initially she longs for a child from Ananda and a complete family but later understands that life is much more than that. At the end of the novel, she is a different woman, and she welcomes reality with open arms. Kapur has successfully done her job of dealing with the themes of marriage and expatriate sensibility through the characters of Nina and Ananda.

Works Cited

Beauvoir, Simone-de. *The Second Sex*. Translated by Constance Borde and Sheila Malovany-Chevallier. Vintage Books, 2010. uberty.org/wp-content/ uploads/ 2015/09/1949_simone-de-beauvoir the-second-sex.pdf.

D.N.P, Prema Ponmani. "Trauma of Displacement and Quest for Identity in Manju Kapur's The Immigrant." *Journal of Advanced Research in Dynamical and Control Systems*, vol. 12, no. SP7, 2020, pp. 2683-87. *Crossref*, doi:10.5373/jardcs/v12sp7/20202405.

Gawande, Anagha A. "Woman and Marginality in the Novels of Manju Kapur." *Language In India*, vol. 19:9 September 2019, no. 1930-2940, 2019, pp. 12-17, anguageinindia.com/sep2019/mkuliterature2019/anagha.pdf.

Kapur, Manju. *The Immigrant.* New Delhi: Random House India, 2008.

Krishnaveni, V. "A Psychological Study of Alienation and Quest for Identity in Manju Kapur's The Immigrant." *International Journal of Research Culture Society*, vol. 2, no. 5, 2018, pp. 54-56. *academia*, ijrcs.org/wp-content/uploads/201805013.pdf.

Kundal, Shivali, and Ranbir KAur. "Investigation and Analysis of Contemporary Nuptial in 'The Immigrant.'" *International Journal of Pure and Applied Mathematics*, vol. 119 No. 14, no. 469-478, 2018, pp. 469-77, acadpubl.eu/hub/2018-119-14/articles/1/52.pdf.

Lal Gupta, Dr. Bajrangi. "Manju Kapur's The Immigrant: A Saga of Marital Disharmony." *Smart Moves Journal Ijellh*, Vol. 8, no. 9, 2020, pp. 30–38. *Crossref*, doi:10.24113/ijellh.v8i9.10751.

Suresh, Dr. M. "Alienation and Displacement in Manju Kapur's The Immigrant." *Pramana Research Journal A Peer Reviewed/Referred Journal*, vol. 9, no. 4, ser. 2017, pp. 51–55. *2017*, https://doi.org/10.32968 / 2249-2976.

Vansia, Kavita Surendrasinh and Hitesh D. Raviya. *Crossing the Patriarchal Threshold: Portrayal of the Incipient Indian Middle Class Women in Manju Kapur's Novels*. 2012. Department of English, Krantiguru Shyamji Krishna Verma Kachchh University. PhD. http://hdl.handle.net/10603/173742

CHAPTER 33

Interrogating Memory and Identity in Jean Rhys' *Wide Sargasso Sea*: A Post-Colonial Feminist Approach

Bidya Singh and Jayaprakash Paramaguru

Abstract

Identity is a complex term when it is related to human beings. The identification of the self is one of the key elements in human nature. The self and degradation of woman's identity help a person to prevail itself from being self-esteem, self-confident and self-control. Identity is an essential theme in Jean Rhys' *Wide Sargasso Sea* (1939). It deals with the post-colonial feminist aspects which discusses the racial conflicts, gender biased and migratory issues. The post-colonial and feminist study helps to understand the memory related to nostalgia and melancholy that helps to identify the self and its identity in compassionate mode of identification.

Keywords: Identity, post-colonial, self, memory, serenity, depiction of Women.

The question of 'I' has always created a chaotic situation in man's life. The day on which a man is born till the day he dies runs after an abstract concept *identity*. Every man has his own version of identity. The self is classified in terms of money, fame and name but the basic concept of identity still lingers around mystery. The mystery of identifying one's own self lies within the inner-self. In true sense, a person can be discovered or recognized by the self only when they sense alienation. The alienation may lead to dreadful consequences but the reward after that horrifying journey will always be a fruitful one. Sometimes, the realization of self is so dragged out that the awful tastes last throughout the life. The other way that degrades the identity is the biased society which discriminates the individualism to their end. The variance of the redundancy of the society may differ from one another but one of the major issues that the patriarchal society imposes is its dominance over the woman. Sociologist *Sylvia*

Walby describes patriarchy as, "a system of social structures and practices in which men dominate, oppress, and exploit women" (Giddens. *Sociology*, 473-4).

The awful taste of identity can be recognized through Jean Rhys' *Wide Sargasso Sea* which can also be read as a prequel to Charlotte Bronte's *Jane Eyre. Wide Sargasso Sea* is a psychological and mysterious artifact. The character of Antoinette Cosway in *Wide Sargasso Sea* is portrayed as a beautiful white girl who grows up in Caribbean land and gets into a disastrous marriage which finally ends up with her madness and imprisonment. The degraded relationship and madness is the superficial nature of the character and the loss of identity is the origin of all these fallacies. The analysis of the terms can be interpreted through feminism, post-structuralism, modernism and colonial theorist readings. The loss of identity is due to the negligence of self but to recognize it is a laborious task. To identify the self from being lost is the primary objective to seek the inner peace and satisfaction.

The loss of self and its identity may lead to different structural changes and beliefs. Humanism in the global scenario is questionable. It successfully secures and binds the individuals and connects the national and transitional borders in one's persona. It also helps to find the self which gets lost in the struggle and chaos of everyday life. It also presents a canvas of the socio-behavioral life of the people in the chaotic atmosphere. Moreover, it depicts the socio-economic and political struggle of everyday's life. The self helps to find its originality and helps in the development of a character. The study of self also helps to search the ambiguous identity which got lost in the medieval period. It also discusses the gap between the modern and the medieval ages. The search of one's self is prominent in every part of life. It is very important to break the existing gap and search for the self and establish one's self-identity. The search of self is beyond the concept of caste, creed, colour and sex but in the terms inducted themselves as an integral part. The concepts of racial, sexual and socio-political discrimination are the sub-themes which the reader comes across while studying an artifact that deals with the search of self and its identity.

Wide Sargasso Sea is a celebrated novel which deals with the complex issues. John Hearne described Rhys with comparison to Wilson Harris in 1947 as 'guerrillas, not outsiders', in his essay '*The Wide Sargasso Sea: A West Indian Reflection*' (Hearne, *The Wide Sargasso*

Sea,). The context is referred to the loss of identity in the post-colonial era. This is correctly pointed out in *Orientalism* by Edward Said where he posts the issues of how the European imperial power has put down the colonial subjects and the representation of the fear that is found in the period and which particularly discusses "the dark, the irrational, the other" (Said. *Orientalism*, 1979). The novel also examine the post-Emancipation period where the loss of self and its identity was a major issue. The prime problem that was faced in the era of post-colonial and post-emancipation was the marginalized group the passive female victims. Helen Carr correctly puts 'anger against injustice and hypocrisy behind Rhys' "terrific – almost lurid! – passion for stating the case of the underdog" disappears from view' (Carr. *Jean Rhys*, 7).

Jean Rhys's *Wide Sargasso Sea* is a prequel to Charlotte Brontë's *Jane Eyre* in 1847. *Wide Sargasso Sea* also sets some answers to the questions, "the mad woman in the attic", the very first question that why the protagonist of the novel goes mad in the first place. In a letter Jean Rhys calls the book, 'The first Mrs Rochester', and 'profound apologies to Charlotte Brontë and a deep curtsey too' (Rhys. Letters, 1931-1966, 64). Rhys apologies are in favour because she felt that the story is somewhere incomplete though the liked and respected both Charlotte Brontë and the novel *Jane Eyre*. So, *Wide Sargasso Sea* is a rewriting and retelling the story of Brontë's *Jane Eyre* from a point of view where the most marginalized character Bertha Mason was subjected imprisonment and rejection. The view point of the story changes as Antoinette narrates the story which also concerns the topics not only of the mad and female buts also the dejection of the self and its identity.

The novel also discusses the after effects of slave trading. The kowtow example is that of Antoinette who was stuck in between the two identities of her mother who was never approved by the Jamaican ladies as because she was 'a Martinique girl'. And she was objected to racist comments of a little girl who followed her singing, "'Go away white cockroach, go away, go away.' I walked fast, but she walked faster. 'White cockroach, go away, go away. Nobody wants you. Go away'" (*Jane Eyre*, 7). The racial comments from the very ground level shows that neither Annette, Antoinette's mother nor she was not accepted in the society. In the novel the splash of colours are very prominent like, 'We can colour the roses as we choose and mine are green, blue and purple' (29) the comparison of colour shows the colours of womanhood and as well as the Caribbean landscape. But the very next line in the novel shows the complexities in the female and the colonial interference, 'Underneath, I will write my name in fire red, Antoinette Mason, nèe Cosway, Mount Calvary Convent, Spanish Town, Jamaica, 1839' (29). In one hand it shows the beauty of the orients and on the other hand it shows the element of fire. Fire is considered one of the purifying agents or a plethora of things.

The novel also deals with different elements like the mad female, madness and the female. The three are different categories or the phases that is experienced by the female through the ideologies and sexism. The mad female is a deconstructed identity which is the result of the mad and the female. The madness shows the dejection of the society which made the self-alienated and the isolation which haunt the character like she always had dreams 'I was going to sleep. Then I imagined that I heard a footstep and I thought what will they say, what will they do if they find me here?' (*Jane Eyre*, 122). And the concept of female is also a very interlude point where the lost identity begins and the sense of isolation engulfs. One of the examples is that when Mr. Rochester mentioned Antoinette as 'Infamous daughter of an infamous mother' (120).

The concept of mad female made the prime character of *Wide Sargasso Sea* that questioned that Antoinette is mad and sexually incontinent, which was a serious accusation. The question of self is being questioned which her parrot Coco always talked "Qui estlà? And answer himself Chè Coco, Chè Coco" (*Jane Eyre*, 21). But Coco was clipped by Mr Mason, Antoinette's stepbrother. He was a white Nigger who restricted the freedom of Coco and it ended up growing bad temper. Same as in case of Antoinette, she was imprisoned in inhumane conditions that made her a rebel which leads to her outrageous attitude. The book *The Mad-Woman in the Attic: The Women Writer and the Nineteenth Century Literary Imagination* also takes the example of the protagonists of *Jane Eyre* and *Wide Sargasso Sea* as the central confrontation which shows 'an encounter… with her own imprisoned "hunger, rebellion and rage", a secret dialogue of self and soul on whose outcome… the novel's plot, Rochester's fate, and Jane's coming-of-age all depend' (Gubar. *The Mad-Woman in the Attic*, 339) is expressed by Sandra M. Gilbert and Susan Gubar which defines the link between women and madness.

Even though Annette treated the locals as equals but still they watched every movement of theirs and put poison in their food

"They invent stories about you, and lies about me. They try to find out what we eat everyday" (*Jane Eyre*, 14), which was a part of obeah otherwise known to be vodou a practice of black magic where as Mr. Mason who is an outsider never understands the situation and treated them as children who even though them to be dangerous but behaves like a white pappy to them, " 'They're too dam lazy to be dangerous', said Mr. Mason" (14) but Annette who on the other hand respected them and thought them equal, they tried to kill them by burning their house down and treated them as 'white cockroaches', which is associated with dirt that usually refers to black or brown. On the other hand Antoinette and Annette behave very kindly towards the parentless children because Antoinette's father had many affairs and it resulted in mixed-race children, "And all those women! She never did anything to stop him – she encouraged him. Presents and smiles for the bastards every Christmas" (12). But the freedom is restricted which happens in the case of Coco. It shows that man who crippled the woman "He made an effort to fly down but his clipped wings failed him and he fell screeching. He was all in fire" (22). So, the society did not accept the fact that Antoinette belongs to the same group due to the loss of identity "Soon the black people said it was haunted, they wouldn't go near it. and no one came near us" (3) because they were poor, they were abandoned by the other white people but the action of dislocation of identity also lead to the alienation of self, "I got used to a solitary life" (3) The question of 'I' is very prominent in this because the novel puts a very mysterious question why Annette marries? But the answer is within it as it says "Some of the big estates are going cheap, and one unfortunate's loss is always a clever man's gain" (12). It clarifies the idea behind the marriage of the Carole women whether it is Annette or Antoinette because marriage will give status to the Carole women and Englishmen come to Jamaica to marry rich heirs as Annette and Antoinette so that they can enjoy the money. And the experience of the mother and daughter are same.

Antoinette name means grace but that grace gets out casted when she is denoted as Bertha that is the dislocation of identity. Which resulted in fading out her grace and she was also drifted out of the looking glass. Looking glass is a very powerful imagery in the novel which shows that the identity of one own self is only reflected within a mirror. The self and identity of Antoinette is more questionable because her identity is lost when Rochester named her Bertha

"Goodnight, Bertha" here she can also be identified as the mad woman Bertha in *Jane Eyre.* Calling her by another name shows the denial of the identity: "He never calls me Antoinette now" (*Jane Eyre*, 70) which shows the concept of the invisible women it is also showcases the psychological condition of woman, which is described in *The Invisible Women* by Rosemarie Krausz that "It was inspired in the course of Psychotherapy with a woman who felt invisible in her feminine identity and who hid her feminine desire within an imaginary paper bag" (Krausz. *The Invisible Women*, 59-72). We can also find another example in one of the contemporary essay *To Name is to Possess* by Jamaica Kincaid searches the 'theme of naming' which is very crucial to possess because it gives an originality and identity to the self. Similarly, in case of Antoinette her chastity is being questioned even though she is betrayed by her husband, who had an affair with Christophine, "Christophine is a bad woman and she will lie to you worse than your wife" (78). The ideas in a woman are an outcome of her passion but still she was being abused in her madness, "Then she seemed to grow tired and sat down in her rocking-chair. I saw the man lift her up out of the chair and kiss her" (111) the interpretation of her is the undue passion that evokes inside her. But the minds are misread by the other sex which resulted both in the case of mother as well as daughter. And at last it leads to the outbreak of sanity like that of Antoinette, "Don't laugh like that, Bertha. My Name is not Bertha; why do you call me Bertha?" (86). So, it finally leads to the transformation of a sound persona into a mad woman. The transformation killed the self and its identity, when she refers to madness she says that, "Because they told me to say so and because it is true. She did when I was a child. There are always two deaths, the real one and the one people know about" (124). One is the death of the relationship between the self and its identity being talked about.

The result of insanity is due to the bridge between the native and the colonizers which will never reconnect to each other to bridge the distance. It is very difficult. But the sufferer is the more marginalized category that is of the women who are treated like slaves. Antoinette suffers more than a slave, "One morning when I woke I ached all over. Not the cold, another sort of ache. I saw that my wrists were red and swollen" (*Jane Eyre*, 181). A slit was made so, that some blood will move down so that the passion will go out and her madness can be controlled.

The image of fire has been a prominent image in the *Wide Sargasso Sea* as Antoinette dreams every time but in the last she had completed it before she dreams, "That was the third time I had my dream, and it ended" (121) which shows that there was something tempting her and that was her passion. The passion is being represented as the red dress, "I let the dress fall on the floor, and looked from the fire to the dress and from the dress to the fire" (121) which at last answers all the questions that Antoinette says, "I often wonder who I am and where is my country and where do I belong and why was I ever born at all" (63) and after fire engulfs everything as she set the house on fire, she simply says, "Now at last I know why I was brought here and what I have to do" (123).

Thus, the novel frameworks the ideas and describes the condition of women in the male – dominated society. It also explores the inter-textual concepts of gender, identity and post-colonialism. The novel rejects the concept of happy ending where everything goes well but it gives the ideas liberation, the search of self and its identity. It correctly deals with the binaries like England-West Indies, man-woman, reason-emotion, sanity-insanity, hope-despair and self-other. And at last, all ended in fire, "it was red and all my life was in it" (*Jane Eyre*, 123) which helps to understand the memory related to nostalgia and melancholy that helps to identify the self and its identity in compassionate mode of identification.

Works Cited

Brontë, Charlotte. *Jane Eyre.* Oxford: Oxford World's Classics, 2008.

Carr, Helen. *Jean Rhys.* Northcote House, 1966.

Christina-Georgiana Voicu, *Exploring Cultural Identities in Jean Rhys' Fiction,* Ed. Katarzyna Grzegorek, Warschau: De Gruyter, 2014.

Ed. Catherine Soanes and Angus Stevenson. *Concise Oxford English Dictionary.* 11th ed.Oxford: Oxford University Press, 2004.

Erik Williams, *From Columbus to Castro. The History of the Caribbean 1492-1969,* London: André Deutsch, 1970: 400.

Giddens, Anthony; Griffiths, Simon. *Sociology* (5th Ed.). Polity, 2006.

Gubar, Susan & Sandra M Gilbert. *The Mad-Woman in the Attic: The Women Writer and the Nineteenth Century Literary Imagination.* Yale University Press, 1979. 339.

Hearne. John, '*The Wide Sargasso Sea*: A West Indian Reflection' 1080. *Cornhill Magazine.* Summer, 1947.

Krausz, R. "The Invisible Women." *International Journal of Psycho-Analysis 75,* 1994: 59-72.

Rhys, Jean. *Wide Sargasso Sea.* Penguin Classics, 2000.

Said, Edward. *Orientalism.* Vintage, 1979.

Stuart Hall, "Who needs 'identity'?" In Paul Du Gay, Jessica Evans and Peter Redman, eds. *Identity: A Reader*, Thousand Oaks, Calif.: Sage, 2000.

Veronika Dibelková, *Multiple Identities in* Wide Sargasso Sea *by Jean Rhys*, University of Pardubice, 2013.

Wyndham, Francis and Melly, Diana. *Jean Rhys: Letters 1931-1966.* Ed. Francis Wyndham and Diana Melly. Penguin, 1985.

CHAPTER 34

Female Identity Crisis in the Novels of Arundhati Roy

Amar Singh

Abstract

Identity crisis is one of the most prominent themes in Arundhati Roy's novels. The characters described by her fight to build their personal identity and originality as they are sucked into a turbulence of ascribed and attained identities. On his blog, Roy has focused on the concept of identity. A variety of platforms, whether on the web or on stage. She has a thorough awareness of both individual and group dynamics and identities. The paper critically analyses the identity crisis experienced by the female protagonists in Roy's *The God of Small Things* and *The Ministry of Utmost Happiness*. MLA eighth edition has been used for documentation and referencing.

Keywords: Social isolation, stagnation, physical attributes, ego, identity, despair

Introduction

Psychology, philosophy, history, political science, sociology, science, geography, and economics have all looked into the concept of identity. In 1950, Erik H. Erikson, a well-known psychologist, invented the term 'identity crisis' in his book *Childhood and Society*. He describes eight stages of psychosocial growth in which an individual's identity is formed, changed, or lost. *The Eight Ages of Man'* listed in Erikson's book are Basic Trust vs. Basic Mistrust, Autonomy vs. Shame and Doubt, Initiative vs. Guilt, Industry vs. Inferiority, Identity vs. Role Confusion, Intimacy vs. Isolation, Generativists vs. Stagnation, and Ego Integrity vs. Despair. Wifehood, in general, is a special kind of womanhood.

The Marcian theory of identity, developed by James Marcia, explains four different types of identity statuses. The first is identity foreclosure, which occurs when someone makes a commitment without first considering other options. Ideas are unquestionably accepted here. The second condition that leads to social isolation is identity dispersal. It's a commitment-free, self-destructive identity role. Identity moratorium is the third type, which implies active study of alternatives.

It elucidates an individual's open-mindedness and thoughtfulness. One is willing to consider various options, but no final decision has been made. Identity attainment is the fourth status, and it is a good way to deal with various identity crises. It demonstrates a person's unwavering commitment. The research paper examines the subject of identity in the novels under consideration in light of Erikson and Marcia's psychosocial theories.

Most women writers inevitably lean towards female characters when speak about the issue of identity crisis. Roy and Desai have also portrayed their women characters in a highly noteworthy manner. Roy has depicted significant women characters, such as Ammu, Rahel, Baby Kochamma, Mammachi and Kalyani in *The God of Small Things* published in 1997 and Tilottama, Maryam Ipe, Jahanara Begum, Zainab, Loveleen Kaur, Sangeeta Madam and Revathy in *The Ministry of Utmost Happiness* published in 2017 who suffer from the malady of identity crisis.

In India and in the novel *The God of Small Things*, women's lifestyles are hampered by familial and domestic responsibilities, as depicted in Roy's novel. She backs up her claim with references from Hindu mythology. *The Pandavas* risked their wife, Draupadi, in a dice game in the *Mahabharata.* Draupadi's identity is utterly altered when Yudhishthira imposes his own idea of propriety on her. This tragic situation is given a thought-provoking twist by Roy: "Draupadi strangely angry only with the men that won her, not the ones that staked her". (Roy, *GST,* 234)

The novelist propagates that the life of almost all Indian wives is no better than that of Draupadi in a way or the other. There are a few who resist like Ammu, but the rest of them suffer silently like Mammachi. Moreover, Roy highlights the rampant atrocities against women in Indian society by discussing the physical and psychological strains on wives through not only prominent female characters but also minor ones like Kalyani, wife of K. N. M. Pillai. Kalyani is described by the novelist as a gorgeous woman with attractive physical attributes. Kalyani's position as a wife is not equal:

> She referred to her husband as *addeham* which was the respectful form of 'he', whereas 'he' called her 'edi' which was, approximately, 'Hey, you!'
>
> (Roy, *GST,* 270)

Chacko pays a visit to Comrade Pillai's house, but Kalyani urges him to wait because her husband is due back any minute. Latha, Kalyani's niece, is asked to deliver a poem for the guests. Meanwhile, Comrade Pillai, the master of the home, comes. The novelist demonstrates a man's dominance over all the women in the house:

> He had the easy authority of the Man of the House. He smiled and nodded a greeting to Chacko, but did not acknowledge the presence of his wife or his mother. Latha's eyes flicked towards him for permission to continue with the poem. It was granted. (Roy, *GST,* 272)

Comrade Pillai's subsequent gesture signals the supremacy of husbands as well as the degradation of wives:

> Comrade Pillai took off his shirt, rolled it into a ball and wiped his armpits with it.
>
> When he finished, Kalyani took it from him and held it as though it was a gift. A bouquet of flowers. (Roy, *GST,* 272)

In the conventional societal framework of India, Roy illustrates how gender roles are established and strict. More events are recounted by the novelist, in which the women suffer silently and humbly. Due to the diverse tones of her female characters, Roy discusses the problem of identity crisis in depth in her second novel, *The Ministry of Utmost Happiness*. Throughout the narrative, Tilo, her mother Maryam Ipe, Jahanara Begum, and Revathy play important roles. The patriarchal system is blindly followed in Indian society, and mothers are idolised, but they are also the ones who suffer the most:

> The suppression of women starts in their own house and is a consequence of a family and social mechanism that has evolved over centuries in traditional Indian society. (Neelima, 38)

The novel's three women, Jahanara, Maryam, and Revathy, face physical and mental challenges as a result of their daughters. They jeopardise their own identities in order to support their daughters' personal and societal identities. Maryam's daughter, Tilo, is born out of wedlock; Revathy's daughter, Miss UdayaJebeen, is the result of a horrific rape by six cops. The mothers are compassionate, although the conventional culture is hostile to them. Jahanara, like her daughter Anjum, is frightened. Maryam disowns her illegitimate daughter, Tilo, and suffers physical and mental suffering throughout her life. Throughout the narrative, Tilo also has to deal with the difficulties of life. Finally, Revathy tolerates the terrible rape, and her young daughter, Miss UdayaJebeen, suffers from an identity conflict. Roy portrays her female characters as victims of patriarchal Indian society.

Conclusion

Thus, Arundhati Roy shows considerable similarities while dealing with the theme of identity crisis, but at the same time, there are notable differences given in the portrayal of internal and external struggle in the lives of their women characters. A critical analysis of the novels of Roy reveal the different dimensions of womanhood in general and wifehood in particular. Roy portrays proactive wives in the form of Ammu, Rahel and Tilo who stress on their individuality by seeking separation from their husbands. Ammu is quite rebellious and Rahel has a tendency to break social taboos. Tilo, on the other hand, is least bothered when she violates social and sexual taboos imposed by the patriarchal society.

In a nutshell, in both the novels selected for the analysis, Roy contemplates the role of women in society and in households. Their inevitable significance is undeniable, but their status is a hostile one. She writes freely about women's worries in The God of Small Things, and the issue of identity crisis takes centre stage in, *The Ministry of Utmost Happiness,* thanks to the all polyphonic voices of her female characters.

Works Cited

Erikson, Erik H. *Childhood and Society*. W. W. Norton Company, 1950.

Erikson, Erik H. *Identity: Youth and Crisis*. W. W. Norton Company, 1968.

Neelima, C. "Women's Place in a Patriarchal Society: A Critical Analysis of Arundhati Roy's *The God of Small Things*." *European Journal of English Language and Literature Studies,* 4(1), 2016, 37-41.http://www.eajournals.org/wp-content/uploads/Women---s-Place-in-a-Patriarchal-Society. Accessed 30 Nov, 2021.

Roy, Arundhati. *The God of Small Things*. Penguin Random House India, 1997.

Roy, Arundhati. *The Ministry of Utmost Happiness*. Penguin Random House India, 2017.

CHAPTER 35

Crusade to Emancipation: Women in Contemporary Indian English Novel

Manisha B. Kale

Abstract

Greek philosopher Cynics said that 'mystery and enigma-thy name is woman.' Manu, the Indian law-giver denied the freedom and liberty for women. There is always a controversial view's about women in western and Indian society also. The woman held in high esteem as Adhishakti or energy in ancient India, she represents the Chaitanya or consciousness and not the weakness and role of Indian woman is that of different than western woman. In later years woman consider as a commodity and since that time the women's rebel for emancipation was begun. In modern era India followed the western model of feminism which separates man from woman it results in estrangement and growth of psychological diseases. Feminist have realized that the subject of women's emancipation in India should not be reduced to the contradictions between man and woman Feminism, a part of humanism should be studied and cultivated as a way of living and thinking. Uma Narayan rightly puts it, "Third World feminism is not a mindless mimicking of 'western agendas' in one clear and simple sense-Indian feminism is clearly a response to the issues specifically confronting many Indian women." Indian women's struggle for emancipation could not mimic its western counterpart for obvious reasons. The present paper focuses on the voyage of Indian women from crusade to emancipation with reference of women represented in major Indian novels, which shows emancipation does not mean liberty to do whatever, but it is movement to acquire self-respect.

Keywords: Culture, Traditions, Myth, Crusade, Emancipation.

Introduction

This article discusses the levels of autonomy and self-definition of the 'new Indian woman' and their emancipation in contemporary literature written in English by Indian women writers. The paper divides into two parts; the first section focuses on the history of the women's depiction in literature, the second part seeks to analyze women in post-modern literature after independence and highlights on the novels of Anita Desai, Shashi Deshpande and Arundahti Roy especially. Ample of times we are discussing about the predicaments of women, yes I agree the educated woman is also not free even in the twenty first century but there are a lot of positive changes occurred in the lives of women in India and this article aims to highlights on that.

The online dictionary defines the word crusade as "a holy war undertaken with papal sanction" "a campaign in support of a good cause", and "a vigorous concerted movement for a cause or against an abuse". The word emancipation means, "free from traditional social restraints bondage, oppression, or restraint" 'liberate'. Here the word Emancipation is used as the women's freedom from the oppressive conventions and customs of the society. Women's crusade against a male dominated society is of special importance in the Indian context. In Indian culture the words like self-denial, sacrifice, patience, devotion, and silent suffering are always consider with the ideal concept of woman. Women's crusade in India was against gender, empire, orthodox norms of culture and patriarchy and with sexual and textual politics.

The literature of any culture and society represents its cultural, sociological, political, and religious aspects. The literary artists directly, indirectly represent the society and its fruits and diseases, and suggest the ways to enjoy the fruits and also precautions and the ways to cure diseases. When we talk about the women's literature and especially about Indian women our mind capture the general picture of Indian women and I dare to say that it not pleases us. The portrayal of women since from the ancient ages in classical literary and religious texts represents the derogatory and secondary image of women and this is the factual portrayal of society. We heard tales from epics like 'Ramayana' and 'Mahabharata' that a woman is always the cause of destruction. Gandhari lives a life of blind for the sake of her husband, Draupadi being humiliated in the Kaurava's court, Sita entering in the fire to prove her loyalty and chastity, Ahalya hardened into stone, Shakuntala neglected and labeled as the liar in the court of her husband. And these women are the models and idols for Indian woman and they follow their footsteps and surrender all their desires. To understand women's literature it's crucial to know social, historical, and ideological context in which literary production and consumption took place. "The striking coherence we noticed in literature by women could be explained by a common female impulse to struggle free from social and literary confinement through strategic redefinitions of the self, art, and society". (Tharu and Lalita: 1991, 26). The emancipation of Indian women from oppressive conventions and customs of the society and religion is the output of reform movements and women's continuous rebel against culture and patriarchy. Indian women not only enslaved by patriarchy but also from religion.

Once upon a time India was ruled by matrilineal society in Harappa and Mohenjodaro civilization. Tharu and Lalita stated that the opportunity offered by Buddhism was a major factor in the rise of Indian women's literature in the early 6th century BC. One of Buddha's contemporary Mutta writes that, "So free am I, so gloriously free, free from three petty things – from mortar, from pestle and from my twisted lord" (Tharu and Lalita:1991,68). To know the history means we know the facts, and the history of women is always providing a gender dimension of any period. The facts about women are always rested on patriarchal assumption and it is invented and compiled by men. The nineteenth century witnessed a redefinition of women's place in Indian society. The perception about women, formed out of the intimate interaction with the colonial state in the eighteenth century, assumed a clearer shape in the early years of nineteenth century and manifested through a number of reform movements. The women's question started gaining ground in India during the nineteenth century. The campaign organized against 'sati', a custom of self-immolation of women in the funeral pyre of their husbands was the first notable move towards their emancipation. The women's participated in National freedom movement like Vina Mazumdar, Madhu Kishwar, and Devaki Jain consider that Gandhian movement was the true beginning of women's emancipation and modernization. National freedom movement was not in a sense the movement of women's liberation, after freedom women in India fight for freedom. Reform movements brought revolutionary changes in the life of Indian women that ultimately produced the modern Indian women who trying to understand herself and to preserve her identity as a wife, mother and above all as a human being. Indian women began writing in English towards the middle of the nineteenth century. Social movements gave women's writing clear vision and purpose. After independence the men writers especially focus on the freedom struggle and the social, economical and political disasters.

The emergence of a number of women writers in post-independence period dare to agitate against the stereotypical representation of women in creative writing. Toru Dutt, Amrita Pritam, Vijayalakshmi Pandit, Ramabai Ranade, Shudha Muzumdar, Urmila Haksar, Sharanjeet Shan and Pandita Ramabai are eminent among them. What Virginia Woolf stated about women's position is the fact about Indian woman. She writes, "Imaginatively she is of the highest importance; practically she is completely insignificant, she is all but absent from history. She dominates the lives of kings and conquerors in faction: in fact she was the slave of any boy whose parents forced a ring upon her finger. Some of the most inspired words, some of the most profound thoughts in literature fall from her lips; in real life she could scarcely spell and was the property of her husband"(Woolf,1929:66). The woman's crusade is against such brute condition in society. The literary works about women in this era cannot destroy the repressive social structure but raises the question about women's lives and suggesting solutions. Women's literature has evolved to show common experiences, a sense of sisterhood and a range of female experiences that question the recurring face of patriarchy.

The women represented in literature after independence is from different strata of society and their quest is for the autonomy for the self. These women are confronted with several obstacles emerging mainly from the irregularities in the social system. Their desire is to acquire self leads to disillusionment at every stage, but they firmly refuse to lose their hope and courage and they are always in search of something positive. Women are ready to meet the challenges of life arises due to changes in social, economic, political and patriarchal spheres of their life. Freedom does not come without responsibilities and women are not diverting from this. She prefers individual freedom no doubt, but she considers family bonds and personal relationships to be prime importance.

Kamala Markandaya, Anita Desai, Ruth Prawar Jhabvala, Nayantara Saghal, Bharati Mukherjee, Shashi Deshpande, Dina Mehta, Bapsy Sidhwa, Namita Gokhale, Arundhati Roy, and Shobha De are leading post modern novelist have written about women in a varied perspective. They have probed the psyche of their creations and thereby analyzed their relationship with society and culture at large. Their feminism is peculiarly Indian in the sense that it is born out of the predicament of Indian women placed between contradictory identities: tradition and modernity, family and profession, culture and nature. Their art is intensely personal, not political. It rooted in the native environment tends to be humanistic and optimistic in its outlook.

Anita Desai portrayed two kinds of women those who are symbol of growth and change and those who are powerful means of withdrawal, regression, decay, death, and destruction. Desai depicting the inner furies of women and their rising tone for emancipation and empowerment. She has rendered a new dimension to fiction by handling the pitiable and awful plight of the alienated self. She has often tried to explore a woman's world, most often, through the conventional stereotypes predominant in her times, of women pitted against patriarchy. The male characters – Nirode, Arun, Raman, Gautum are individuals who have taken a step forward in creating space for their female counterparts and re – establishing balance and preventing a virtual break down of the family. Sita in *Where Shall we go this Summer?* Is a woman who has set her own terms and conditions of living and throughout the novel the patriarch seems to be invisible. But even then the problems seem to exist and persist throughout the narrative. All these are indicative of a re-establishment of gender roles within the family. A mother in the postmodern is not just a caretaker of her family but is also a bread winner. Her roles gave shifted from the conventional home maker to a care taker. Sita decides to leave her children and her husband and wants to escape to Manori Island where she wants to be all alone, away from the busy, chaotic world that surrounds her and also from domesticity. Desai writes, "Everything stirred, tumbled, move around her. Strange, she thought – the man so passive, so grey, how could the very mention of him arouse such a tumult of life and welcome. She felt it herself – unwillingly, unexpectedly, but she felt it" (Desai, 1975: 94). The insecurities of Sita, her confusions and her anxieties are all resulting in incompatibility and Raman has come out from the constrains of a stereotyped male family head and has helped his wife to introspect and re-establish herself by shedding away her escapist attitude and finally reuniting and becoming a better individual, a better householder. After her reconciliation with Raman, she realizes that "her time on the island had been very much of an episode on a stage" (Desai, 1975:152). This novel is Desai's portrait of an Indian woman who rebels against the tradition – bound old mode of life in the life of the western liberty. Her character suffers from various complexes and mental diseases, which obstruct the healthy growth of their personality. In dealing with the psyche of the characters and their motivations she moves deeply and dwells in the inner reality of her characters like Maya in *Cry, the Peacock*, Sita in *Where shall we go this Summer?* and Nanda in *Fire on the Mountain.*

Women in Shashi Deshpande's writings evince sufficient vigour and courage to question the oppressive role of society, religion and culture. The woman is bolder, more self-reliant and rebellious. In treating woman as an individual, she highlights subtleties of human behaviour based on the subconscious and conscious mind rather than on high fluted resolutions to National problems. She cannot conform to the Sita's version of womanhood. It is towards the end of the novels, that her female protagonist realizes herself and learns to live up to the challenge. Searching for a solution to their private problems, the female protagonists in her novels shift from their personal pains to the sufferings of the other women around. Jaya the educated and sensitive protagonist of *That long Silence* (1983) has not experienced the tyranny of a patriarchal social order. She is more enlightened and more advanced feels too suffocated in her relationship with Mohan, her husband. She feels angry when she knows about Mohan's decision to stay at Dadar flat; he has just taken her acquiescence for granted. Her anger turns into frustration when she fails to bloom in her career as a writer due to the restrictive dictates of her husband. She irritates when she heard Vanita Mami, "remember, Jaya, a husband is like a sheltering tree, and without the tree, you're dangerously uprooted and vulnerable..." (Deshpande, 1983:32). She is torn from within. At the end of the novel there is a strong desire and an attempt to break the silence which could be well interpreted as a revolt against the tradition of suppression, a sort of frantic attempt to achieve one's true self. Jaya interprets that, "the truth is simpler. Two bullocks yoked together... it is more comfortable for them to move in the same direction. To go in different direction would be painful, and why animal would voluntarily choose pain?" (Deshpande, 1983:12). Jaya was succeeding to break this silence and emerge as an emancipated strong woman.

Arundhati Roy in her a very debut novel *The God of Small Thing* portrayed a rebel of woman against orthodox patriarchal norms. Ammu the protagonist break her marriage due to the authoritative and dissipated ways of her husband and living with her parents. Roy writes, "in her growing years, Ammu had a watched her father weave his hideous web… he worked hard on his public profile as a sophisticated, generous, moral man. But alone with his wife and children he turned into a monstrous, suspicious bully, with a streak of vicious cunning. They were beaten, humiliated and then made to suffer the envy of friends and relations" (Roy, 1997: 180). The desire of a son of family is considered as the "men's need" and that of daughter decrees the torture. Ammu not accept her condition as a fate but she tried to find out ways of her emancipation to acquire her 'self'.

The novelist's has shown the Indian woman as being something other than that of Sati-Savitri tradition, steeped in orthodoxy, hemmed in by taboos and leading a life of subordination. They depict the modern Indian woman as someone who can overcome handicaps, can live with the pain and come out of it, and can live as a twenty first century woman, modern in outlook, Indian in origin and with a mooring in traditional values. The act of confrontation gives them the courage to decide things for themselves and increasingly leads them to a positivistic detachment from life. Women characters questioning and answering with their own self and tried to find out what's wrong with them. Novelist not only represented women with their predicament but suggest the ways to come out from that. The women represented in Indian English literature in recent era emancipated from cultural norms but still psychologically she faces crisis.

The degree of attention, which women received, was unprecedented, as they had remained so long in obscurity as the second sex. Women's status in relation to men in society was redefined and the discrimination of being women gave way to a better definition of womanhood. They were no longer treated as inferior to men on account of their sex. However marriage proves to be no escape. The husbands accept their wives as working women but at the same time do not recognize or encourage the 'feminist self' in them. Their determination to face the situation and their dependence only on the self-show them the way to confront the crises in their lives.

The goals of Western Feminism are not the goals of Indian feminism. Feminism played a great role in India also, Indian woman struggling for emancipation and tried to make the bridge between her 'self' and family happiness. Feminism, the organized movement promotes equality for men and women in political, economic, and social spheres and not for to create the new system of domination and increasing divorce rates and mental disorders will not be the output of this freedom. The woman in India in order to liberate herself needs to empower herself to confront different institutional structures and cultural practices that subject her to patriarchal domination and control represented in recent literature. Women in India are not to follow the path suggested by western feminism but seek to find their own path. Culture is very complex phenomenon in Indian context especially because culture states different views about women that one is good and the other is worst, and the controversy still continued. The colonial legacy and the identification of women with national culture have made for a selective identification of feminism in India with an inauthentic westernization.

Crusade to emancipation, women emerge out of the darkness, bravely throwing off their legacy of humiliation, dependence and resignation seeking equality with their male counterparts. All of them are not succeeded but they have successfully come out from the barriers of orthodox social systems and emerging as a new social force. The contemporary women novelists are closer to the earthy reality, to the subtle nuances of social behaviour, to the complex structures of lives of woman in Indian society. Women not surrender her life for the sake of happiness of their counterparts; self-pity is not the answer for them. It is only through courage and resilience that one can change one's situation from despair to hope. Women are totally emancipated only when the women's rights will not separate from the rights of human beings.

Works Cited

Desai, Anita. *Where Shall we go this Summmer?.* Orient Paperbacks: New Delhi, 1982.

Deshpande, Shashi. *That Long Silence.* London: Virago Press, 1983.

Mores, Ellen. *Literary Women: The Great Writers.* Doubleday: New York, 1976.

Roy, Arundhati. *The God of Small Things.* India Ink: New Delhi, 1997.

Surendra, K.V. (Eds.) *Women's writing in India: New Perspectives.* Sarup and Sons: New Delhi, 2002.

Tharu, Susie and Lalita, K. (Eds). *Women Writing in India Volume 1, 600 BC to the Early Twentieth Century.* Oxford University Press: New Delhi, 1991.

Tharu, Susie and Lalita, K. (Eds). *Women Writing in India Volume II*: the 20th century. The Feminist Press: New York, 1993.

Woolf, Virginia. *A Room of One's Own.* Hogarth Press: London, 1929.

Web Bibliography

www.dictionary.reference.com/browse/crusade

www.dictionary.reference.com/browse/emancipation

www.boloji.com/bahinabai/articles10936

The Contributors

1. **Ayesha Khatun**, PhD. Research Fellow, International Islamic University Malaysia.
2. **Dr. Clara Ijeoma Osuji**, Department of English, Augustine University, Ilara-Epe, Lagos, Nigeria.
3. **Dr. A. Geetha**, Assistant Professor, Sri Sairam Engineering College, Chennai, Tamil Nadu.
4. **Dr. Abdul Anees Abdul Rasheed**, Associate Professor and Head, Dept. of English, Milliya Arts, Sci. & Management Sci. College, Beed. Maharashtra, India.
5. **Dr. Amar Singh**, Motivational Speaker, Professor and Head of the Department of English, Govt. Autonomous Post Graduate Lead College Chhindwara, MP.
6. **Dr. Anupriya Roy Srivastava**, Assistant Professor, Department of English and MEL, Banasthali Vidyapith, Rajasthan.
7. **Dr. Arvind M. Nawale**, Associate Professor & Head, Department of English, Shivaji Mahavidyalaya, Udgir, District: Latur (Maharastra) India.
8. **Dr. B. Kathiresan**, Professor and Head, Dept. of English, Thiruvalluvar University, Vellore.TN.
9. **Dr. Divya Das S P**, Asst. Professor, Dept. of English, Govt. Arts College, Autonomous, Chitradurga 577501. Karnataka.
10. **Dr. Elham Hossain**, Professor, Dhaka City College, Dhaka, Bangladesh.
11. **Dr. Eunice Fonyuy Fondze-Fombele**, Associate Professor of African Literature and Cultural Studies, University of Buea, Cameroon.
12. **Dr. Hitesh D. Raviya,** Professor and Head, Department of English, Vice Dean, Faculty of Arts, the Maharaja Sayajirao University of Baroda Vadodara, Gujarat.

13. **Dr. Jayaprakash Paramaguru**, Associate Professor, VSSUT, Burla, Sambalpur, Odisha.
14. **Dr. Kamlakar Gavane,** Associate Professor, Dept. of English, M.U.College, Udgir, Dist. Latur (Maharastra) India.
15. **Dr. M. Premavathy**, Associate Professor of English & Head Government Arts & Science College (Women), Orathanad, Tamilnadu, India.
16. **Dr. M. Shanmugathai**, Professor, Sri Sairam Engineering College, Chennai, Tamil Nadu.
17. **Dr. Mamta Garg**, Prof. in English, Govt. Narmada P.G. College, Hoshangabad (M.P.).
18. **Dr. Manisha B. Kale**, Assistant Professor, Dept of English, Pratishthan Mahavidyalaya, Paithan, Dist. Aurangabad, (MS).
19. **Dr. N. Poonkodi Shrri**, Assistant Professor of English, PG & Research Department of English, Government Arts College, Coimbatore.
20. **Dr. Prashant Raosaheb Shinde**, Assistant Professor and HoD, Department of English, Shivneri Mahavidyalaya, Shirur Anantpal, Dist. Latur, MS.
21. **Dr. Rajiv Kumar**, Associate Professor, Postgraduate Department of English, Sido Kanhu Murmu University, Dumka, Jharkhand.
22. **Dr. Rima Chakraborty**, Assistant Professor of English, Surendranath College, Kolkata, WB.
23. **Dr. Rima Namhata**, Assistant Professor, Department of Language and Literature, Faculty of Humanities, Liberal Arts and Social Sciences, Alliance University, Bangalore.
24. **Dr. Sandeep Kumar Nandlalji Saraiya**, Assistant Professor of English, Samarth Mahavidyalaya Lakhani Dist. Bhandara (M.S).
25. **Dr. Shitalbabu Ambadas Tayade**, HoD, Department of English, Ramkrushna Mahavidyalaya, Darapur (MS).
26. **Dr. Sindhu V. Jose**, Assistant Professor of English, Sona College of Arts and Science, Salem District, Tamilnadu.
27. **Dr. T. Manason**, Asso. Prof & Head, Department of English, Chikkaiah Naicker College, Veerappan Chatram, Erode, TN.
28. **Dr. V. G. Sadh**, Associate Professor, IPS Academy, Institute of Engineering and Science, Indore, MP.

29. **Dr. Varsha Vaidya**, Professor, Taywade College, Koradi, Maharashtra.
30. **Gopinath Khutia**, State Aided College Teacher-I, Department of English, Deshapran Mahavidyalaya, Durmuth, Purba Medinipur, West Bengal.
31. **Himadri Shekhar Dutta**, Research Scholar, Postgraduate Department of English, Sido Kanhu Murmu University, Dumka, Jharkhand.
32. **May Toudic**, Research Scholar, King's College, Aberdeen, The University of Aberdeen, Scotland, United Kingdom.
33. **Miraclin J.**, Department of English, Nazareth Margoschis College at Pillaiyanmanai.
34. **Mrs. S. Rajeswari**, Asst. Prof and Head, Department of English, Navarasam Arts and Science College for Women, Arachalur, TN.
35. **Ms Nandini Anand Vyas**, MA English, St. Xavier's College (Autonomous), Ahmadabad, Gujrat.
36. **Ms. Ayushi Zina**, Assistant Professor, Amity University Jharkhand.
37. **Ms. Bidya Singh**, Research Scholar in English, VSSUT, Burla, Sambalpur, Odisha.
38. **Ms. Parul Malviya**, PhD Scholar, Department of English, Faculty of Arts, The Maharaja Sayajirao University of Baroda, Vadodara, Gujarat.
39. **Ms. Rashmi Varma**, Professor, Dept. Of English, C.U. Shah Arts College, Ahmedabad.
40. **P-Ibrahim Firdaws Oyebisi**, Department of English, Faculty of Arts, University of Ilorin, Ilorin, Nigeria.
41. **Prachi Bhongale**, Research Scholar R.T.M. Nagpur University, Nagpur, Maharashtra.
42. **R. Devendiran,** Ph.D Research Scholar, Thiruvalluvar UniversityVellore.TN.
43. **S. Preethi**, Research scholar, Department of English, Government Arts & Science College (Women), Orathanad, Tamilnadu, India.

Index